Varieties of Jesus Mythicism: Did He Even Exist?

Edited by John W. Loftus and Robert M. Price

HYPATIA PRESS

© Copyright Hypatia Press 2021

All rights reserved. No part of this publication may be reproduced, stored in or introduced into a retrieval system, or transmitted, in any form, or by any means (electronic, mechanical, photocopying, recording or otherwise) without the prior written permission of the publisher.

Published in the United States of America by Hypatia Press in 2021

ISBN: 978-1-83919-380-4

www.hypatiapress.org

Praise for *Varieties of Jesus Mythicism*

"The essays contained within this anthology draw their readers out on a provocative adventure, a quest certain to yield many treasures. Yet, this quest is altogether different than that described by Albert Schweitzer in his landmark work *The Quest of the Historical Jesus* over a century ago. Despite the seeming nobility, such an academic pilgrimage to uncover the originary kernel of the Gospels, now having played out for decades in the halls of academia, has proven little more than a fool's errand. We now face the obvious: these cultic tales are not and were never given as historiographical "footage" of live first-century events in time and space." — Richard C. Miller, PhD, author of *Resurrection and Reception in Early Christianity*, 2014.

"For a long time, mainstream Bible scholars have known that the gospels are not, in fact, reliable histories of Jesus. Even so, there is consensus that Jesus existed, and doubting that he was a real person is seen as eccentric or fringe. But respected secular scholars—not beholden to what Hector Avalos has called the ecclesial-academic complex—have questioned that consensus. This new anthology is a welcome addition to the growing library of works that invite close inspection of the issue. These essays explore the diverse amalgam of theologies and superstitions in the ancient world, showing that the origins of Jesus-belief are far more complex than devout scholars have been willing to grant. The previous Loftus anthologies have thoroughly documented the falsification of Christianity—and this one adds dramatically to the case against it." — David Madison, PhD Biblical Studies, author, *Ten Tough Problems in Christian Thought and Belief*, 2016.

"The expert arguments in this book seek to understand how Christianity could have begun without a historical Jesus. All these Mythicist authorities make very compelling arguments for their respective theories. Which one is correct? Can all of them be correct? Let us think of each contribution as being a description of an evolving thread of religious traditions. If each thread intertwined—at various times and in various places—with all the other threads of tradition described in this book, it should be possible to produce a "grand unifying theory" of how the various forms of earliest Christianity began. Reading this book will be *sine qua non* for any scholar seeking to trigger a paradigm shift by showing how all these threads braided together to create a Christianity that did not begin at any single point in space or time." — Frank R. Zindler, author of *The Jesus the Jews Never Knew*, 2003.

"Mainstream experts mostly already agree the miraculous Jesus didn't exist, but what about a merely human Jesus? This anthology usefully exhibits the full gamut of doubting even that, from the absurd to the sound. Some contributions are not credible, but some are worth considering, and several are brilliant, indeed required reading for anyone exploring the subject." — Richard Carrier, Ph.D., author of *On the Historicity of Jesus*, 2014.

"The New Testament Jesus did not exist, but was there a historical figure on whom the legend was based? This anthology will adjust your assessment of the probability. It's a rollicking ride through a biblical battlefield." — Dan Barker, co-president of *Freedom from Religion Foundation* and author of *Godless: How an Evangelical Preacher Became One of America's Leading Atheists*, 2008.

"This is an important and intellectually adventuresome collection of articles, well worth considering, reflecting the wide spectrum of views of those challenging the traditional conservative paradigm on the historicity of

Jesus." — Russell Gmirkin, author of *Plato and the Creation of the Hebrew Bible*, 2017.

Dedicated to Jesus mythicist Frank Zindler:
blog.edsuom.com/2014/04/a-life-celebration-frank-zindler.html

Foreword

I come to this pleasure, honored to compose here a foreword for a book that raises many radical and disruptive questions for our conception of Western sacred history. For, curated within this tidy volume, one encounters a most unsettling miscellany of essays, each challenging the mainstream historical objectivity presumed to underpin the cultic iconography and tall tales we find within the pages of the New Testament Gospels. In this sense, each chapter stands as a tacit act of heroic sacrilege, a myth-critical lens by which to deconstruct earliest Christian proclamation and by which better to understand the designs and literary strategies of the original crafters of the religion. While myth-criticism of the Bible may not be new in Western thought, we find ourselves in this century at a fulcrum, an axial point in history wherein our sacred narratives no longer travel quite so unquestioned; that which was once held all-but-universally sacrosanct, namely, the Christian Bible, no longer obtains a normative credibility. While we may accurately attribute much of this decline to the baseless certitude and farcical historical claims of Christian clerics, apologists, and theologians, much of this trend arises through the daring free-criticism by modern thought leaders, Loftus and Price being two of our most dauntless and formidable.

In my own research and writing on such topics, I have taken inspiration from these two vanguard figures. We three arrive at an insolent "unbelief" by way of sincerest fidelity to the very virtues of the religion itself, that is, by a sheer tenacious commitment to truth and love. What irony that these two most central precepts of the religion should spell its very demise, certainly in traditional form. Christian devotees, you see, call their holy book the "Truth." Yet, unauthenticated implausibility constitutes the one common thread-line binding the entire odd collection of sacralized texts. And I am not the first to raise fundamental ethical questions concerning the tribalism, apathy, pettiness, and inhumanity of the varied depictions of the deity on offer in the pages of the Christian Bible. Loftus and Price, we observe, share a marvelous uncommon virtue: They both raise with unwavering honesty and vigor such culturally unsettling questions, questions that threaten the very legitimacy of modern Christianity.

The essays contained within this anthology draw their readers out on a provocative adventure, a quest certain to yield many treasures. Yet, this quest is altogether different than that described by Albert Schweitzer in his landmark work *The Quest of the Historical Jesus* over a century ago. Despite the seeming nobility, such an academic pilgrimage to uncover the originary kernel of the Gospels, now having played out for decades in the halls of academia, has proven little more than a fool's errand. We now face the obvious: these cultic tales are not and were never given as historiographical "footage" of live first-century events in time and space. The omission of any policy of authentication, the unapologetic literary showcase of the naturally impossible, and the replete application of language structures permuting the folklore, legends, and mytho-systems of the classical Mediterranean world, must point us in an altogether different direction.

Similar to contrived faith-based efforts to class the Gospels within the genre of historiography, despite close familiarity with the genre, early Christians likewise avoided applying biographical labels to the Gospels. Such labels now become perhaps most problematic regarding the matter of literary object, since most assume that a history aims to depict ontological reality and biography an ontological person, whereas such presumptions break down as one further critically contemplates the Gospels. Most all referential objectivity in effect became crushed, buried beneath a dense bricolage of cultural literary models governing the narrative construction. If ever an ontological Jesus did exist, that person was lost to us, indeed made irrelevant behind many layers of charged early Christian literary figmentation. In my own book *Resurrection and Reception in Early*

Christianity (Routledge, 2014), the analysis reveals a quite different modality and textual performance, that visible in the early Christian reception of the Gospels. Justin Martyr, the earliest and perhaps most vigorous of the earliest Christian apologists, c. 150 CE, confessed that these depictions of the Christian iconographic founding figure were "nothing new" with respect to other garden-variety myth-based patterns and tales commonly circulating in classical society (*1 Apology* 21). Divine birth, body-translation, and ascension provided the customary decorative frames embellishing the storied lives of those figures enlisted in the classical Mediterranean Hall of Fame, as it were. Unlike the Caesars, Hellenistic kings, philosophers, and other famed historical figures granted divine honors, Jesus instead appears to join the other group, that is, those of questionable or nonhistorical existence; the page-by-page unauthenticated showcase of the naturally impossible precludes any rational historicist modal reading. As Burton Mack pointed out a generation ago, the Gospels are data for a different kind of quest, not for a historical figure, but for reconstructing the social identities and ideological designs of the ancient cultic communities that crafted, recited, and sacralized these and so many other inventive texts.

Despite its range of at times rather creative hypotheses, one may appreciate the humanistic virtue of myth-criticism in the method's honest endeavor *to explain*, in culturological, sociological, ideological, psychological, and anthropological terms, the proliferation of early Christian literary products and the societies that produced them. As Robert M. Price has shown, Christ-Myth Theory, applied as a *methodology* in subset to secular myth theory (à la Frazier, Propp, Frye, Levi-Strauss, Segal, Bascom, Dundes, and a host of talented successors), provides guard-rails for a vital heuristic exercise that has yielded a number of powerful insights: As sacralized literature, to what extent might one explain the Gospels, when constrained by the supposition that these textual representations did not derive, be that primarily or at all, from any authentic historical figure Jesus? The present volume invites us to take up the call to explain, to theorize, and finally to recognize that Western sacred history's principal emblem has only and always ever been a cultural-literary phantasm.

Dr. Richard C. Miller, PhD, is a humanistic scholar of Christian origins in the ancient Hellenistic and Roman world.

Contents

Preface: The Jesus We Find in the Gospels Never Existed!   1

    By John W. Loftus

Introduction: New Testament Minimalism   4

    By Robert M. Price

Chapter 1: Why Mythicism Matters, or: How I Learned to Stop Worrying and Love Jesus (Myth Theory)   9

    By David Fitzgerald

Chapter 2: *Jesus Christ*   33

    by Barbara G. Walker

Chapter 3: Dying and Rising Gods   46

    By Derreck Bennett

Chapter 4: Christianity is a Western Branch of Buddhism   66

    By Michael Lockwood

Chapter 5: The Roman Provenance of Christianity   88

    By Joseph Atwill

Chapter 6: Pauline Origin of the Gospels in the Wake of the First Jewish-Roman War   110

    By R. G. Price

Chapter 7: Under the Mushroom Tree   131

R. Gordon Wasson versus John M. Allegro

    By Michael Hoffman

Chapter 8: Star-Lore in the Gospels   154

    By Bill Darlison

Chapter 9: The Mythic Power of the Atonement   207
By Robert M. Price

Chapter 10: A Sacrifice in Heaven The Son in the Epistle to the Hebrews   239
By Earl Doherty

Chapter 11: The Jewish Myth of Jesus   273
By Stephan Huller

Chapter 12: Jesus: Pre-Existent and Non-Existent   295
By Robert M. Price

Chapter 13: Mark's Gospel: A Performed Play in Rome   306
by Danila Oder

Chapter 14: Is There a Man Behind the Curtain? A Response to Bart Ehrman.   324
By Robert M. Price

Chapter 15: A Rejoinder to James McGrath's Case for Jesus   341
By Neil Godfrey

Chapter 16: "Everything Is Wrong with This" The Legacy of Maurice Casey   364
By Timothy A. Widowfield

Biographies A to Z   395

Preface: The Jesus We Find in the Gospels Never Existed!

By John W. Loftus

In 1929, E. C. Segar introduced his cartoon character, Popeye, in a comic strip based on a one-eyed, pipe-smoking sailor named Frank 'Rocky' Fiegel.[1]

So there was an actual person behind the Popeye cartoons.

Sir Arthur Conan Doyle's fictional detective Sherlock Holmes, with the knack for solving crimes through observation and reason, was modeled after Dr. Joseph Bell. Bell was one of Conan Doyle's medical school professors.[2]

So there was an actual person behind the Sherlock Holmes novels.

Santa Claus, who supposedly brings presents to good boys and girls on Christmas Eve, is based on a fourth-century Greek bishop named Saint Nicholas.

So there was an actual person behind the Santa Claus myth.

So what? Popeye the cartoon character never walked the earth. Neither did Sherlock Holmes. Neither does Saint Nicholas do a fly-by over it. At their absolute best, these characters are composite ones, with elements drawn from several sources, along with the mythical creative imaginations of human beings. But by speaking about composite persons, we're not speaking about *particular* persons, people who actually walked the earth, much less any literary/cartoonish or magical/mythical characters.

---

[1] Evon, D. 2019. "Was Frank 'Rocky' Fiegel the Inspiration for 'Popeye'?". *Snopes.com*: https://www.snopes.com/fact-check/frank-rocky-fiegel-popeye/.
[2] History.com, 2014. "Was Sherlock Holmes based on a real person?" Available at: https://www.history.com/news/was-sherlock-holmes-based-on-a-real-person.

The parallels are obvious. It's how Biblicists argue with regard to Jesus. They do it along these same lines:

> Since there was an actual person behind the Popeye traditions, Popeye existed according to mainstream Biblical historians. No one could reasonably doubt that Popeye was based on a real sailor who liked to get into fights, if they studied history properly. Since there was an actual person behind Sir Arthur Conan Doyle's stories, Sherlock Holmes really solved crimes in his day. So too Santa Claus really exists. Who else brings the presents on December 25th, and who else eats the cookies and drinks the milk left for him?
>
> All biblicists need for someone to exist is for a literary figure to be based on a real historical person. So Jesus existed too!

It doesn't really matter if Olive Oyl, or Dr. Watson existed, or Rudolph the red-nosed reindeer. These additional literary characters are not relevant to the "historically certain" fact that Popeye, Sherlock Holmes, and Santa Claus were based on historically attested figures. So likewise, it doesn't really matter if Lazarus or Judas Iscariot or Joseph of Arimathea existed. These additional literary characters are not relevant to the "historically certain" fact that Jesus existed.

But to say that since the gospel 'Jesus' was based on a real person he therefore existed, is no different than saying that since Popeye, Sherlock Holmes, and Santa Claus were based on real people, they existed.[3]

Let's say there is a human person behind the myths about the Jesus in the Gospels. So what? There are many non-historical myths about such a person to be found, significant ones. Examples of these include that he existed before creation, he was one with a father god, fulfilled prophecy with his life, born of a virgin in Bethlehem, had the authority to speak for a god, did miracles, atoned for our sins on the cross, bodily arose from the dead, and that he'd return soon. With so many non-historical myths as

---

[3] The above thoughts are adaptations from a comment by Steven Carr, available at: http://www.debunking-christianity.com/2010/08/jesus-in-gospels-never-existed.html.

these, it doesn't make a difference if the person pictured in the Gospels is a completely made up, mythical person.

He might as well be.

The Jesus pictured in the Gospels is a myth. If we must take the mythical tales at face value, then such a person found in the gospels never existed. So, the Jesus depicted in the Gospels never existed. If there was a real human being who was the basis for the Jesus character in the New Testament, he is dead now.

But what if it's worse than that? What if there was no actual person behind the Jesus found in the Gospels, at all? What can account for Gospel origins?

That's the focus of this present book.

Prepare to enter into the ancient mythical mind. In that world, anything can happen.

Introduction: New Testament Minimalism
By Robert M. Price

If there is no God, there may yet have been a historical Jesus. If Jesus never existed, there might still be a God. The two questions are quite different, I would say unrelated. You will certainly find many atheists who believe there was a historical Jesus and even admire him in the same way they regard, say, Confucius. They are rarer, but you can even find Christians (like Roman Catholic monk and New Testament scholar Thomas L. Brodie) who do not believe there was a man named Jesus of Nazareth who walked the earth in ancient times. This book does not consider theism and atheism, being instead devoted to the question of the Christ Myth in its many versions.

The opinion that Jesus never existed is a very old one. The pseudonymous author of 2 Peter found himself in a defensive posture when he wrote, "We did not follow cleverly devised myths when we made known to you the power and coming of our Lord, Jesus Christ, but we were eyewitnesses of his majesty" (2 Peter 1:16). He was fibbing, but that's not my point here. Rather, it shows that at least as early as the middle of the second century CE when this pious forgery was composed, some critics of Christianity were denying the Christian savior had ever lived. Strangely, you will find that mainstream biblical scholars mount a similar argument to 2 Peter's. That ancient author was appealing to the past to defend a historical Christ, claiming to have seen Jesus in person. In a mirror-image version, today's scholars also appeal to ancient history in order to discredit Mythicism by claiming there were no ancient Jesus Mythicists. How odd to hear them echoing the maxim of Medieval Catholics:

"If it's new it's not true. If it's true it's not new." Such opponents of Mythicism seem to believe that, without an ancient pedigree, a theory need not be taken seriously, never mind that their own rational-critical approach to Jesus studies is a historically recent invention.

Yes, mainstream academics laugh off Jesus Mythicism, consigning it (and those who espouse it) to the same "weirdo file" as moon landing deniers. Why? Because Mythicism is indefensible nonsense? That might be so, but I cannot help understanding the situation along the lines of Peter Berger's theory of "plausibility structures," according to which the plausibility of any notion is proportional to the number of one's peers who believe it. The result is "consensus scholarship," a box outside of which nothing can be taken seriously. Minority ideas will automatically appear bizarre and heretical. It is not that consensus scholars are afraid to dissent from the party line, lest they lose their jobs. No, it is more a matter of social psychology. But I am no mind reader, so I never dare try to explain away someone's rejection of my opinion on this basis.

In fact, as Thomas S. Kuhn explains in his great book *The Structure of Scientific Revolutions*, advances in science proceed at least as much by new paradigms for construing data as by the discovery of new data. New models, theories, and paradigms are suggestions for making new and better sense of the data we already had. These new notions must prove themselves by running the gauntlet of collegial criticism. That's the way it has to be; you don't want your colleagues to just accept your theory by faith. You want it to win out, so you welcome the initial skepticism. And eventually, despite their investment in traditional consensus viewpoints, your peers may be convinced, and your once-eccentric theory may become the consensus position—until some other upstart supplants it.

This is what happened with Continental Drift: once scientists dismissed it like Flat Earthism, but eventually, with the rise of Plate Tectonics, the wind shifted, and scientists reluctantly admitted that the fact that the outlines of the continents fit together like puzzle pieces was no mere coincidence. Heresy has morphed into Orthodoxy. It has also happened (many times) in the field of biblical studies. The most drastic recent instance is that of so-called "Old Testament Minimalism," the theory that Hebrew scriptural characters were almost all mythical: not just Adam and Eve, not only Cain and Abel, Enoch and Noah, but even Father Abraham, Moses, David and Solomon. The pioneer theorist of Minimalism, Thomas L. Thompson, was forced out of a promising academic career and had to take up house painting to make a living—until the tide finally turned. Now everybody's a Minimalist, everybody but fundamentalists, that is. And now Professor Thompson has received the recognition he deserved all along.

It turns out that the factors that led to Old Testament Minimalism (archaeological reevaluation, tradition criticism, etc.) are also operative in Jesus Mythicism, which ought, in fact, to be called "New Testament Minimalism." I expect, or suspect, that the wheel will keep turning and that Jesus Mythicism will sooner or later gain similar acceptance—not that I'll ever live to see it. I'm not even rooting for it. To me, it's just a fascinating subject. And I'm far from alone in this. The contributors to the present collection are creatures, eccentrics, like me. And, though we are few (at least at present), there is a surprising range of theories among us. And I think it will always be this way, because that's the way it is in scholarship.

As you are probably aware, today's mainstream Jesus scholarship is quite diverse. Many theories have attracted dedicated partisans, people who conclude that the historical Jesus was a revolutionist (Robert Eisenman, Peter Cresswell), a feminist (Elisabeth Schüssler Fiorenza, Luise Schottroff), a Cynic sage (John Dominic Crossan, F. Gerald Downing; Burton L. Mack, David Seeley), a Pharisee (Harvey Falk, Hyam Maccoby), a Hasidic master (Geza Vermes), a shaman (Stevan L. Davies, Gaetano Salomone), a magician (Morton Smith), a community organizer (Richard A. Horsley), an apocalyptic prophet (Bart D. Ehrman, Richard Arthur), and so on. It would be easy and tempting for an external observer to shake his head and to judge that all these Jesus reconstructions, though a pretty good case can be made for most of them, cancel each other out. If this one is as likely as the others, why choose any one of them? Well, of course, you have to look into them all (if you want to have the right to an informed opinion) and then make your own decision. But most likely it will be a tentative one—as it must be if you want to be intellectually honest. Your conviction should not be stronger than the (fragmentary and ambiguous) evidence allows.

If someday Jesus Mythicism should dominate the field, I'm afraid this predicament would not change. As this book will make absolutely clear, there are just as many Mythicist theories. Some believe that Jesus was a fiction devised by the Flavian regime in order to pacify Jews who had the nasty habit of violently rebelling against Rome. Others argue that Jesus was a Jewish/Essene version of the equally mythical Gautama Buddha. Another option is that Jesus was, like the Vedic Soma, a mythical personification of the sacred mushroom, Amanita Muscaria. Or perhaps Jesus was a historicization of the Gnostic Man of Light. Was Jesus a Philonic heavenly high priest figure? And there are more. I believe you will find yourself surprised and impressed by the cogency of these hypotheses. Once you probably regarded all these theories (if you ever even heard of them!) as equally fantastic. After you've finished *Varieties of Jesus Mythicism: Did He Even Exist?*, you may very well find them equally plausible. And who says you have to settle on any one of them? It's worth the mental effort to grasp and weigh each one. I say, let a hundred flowers bloom!

Robert M. Price
December 4, 2019

Chapter 1: Why Mythicism Matters, or: How I Learned to Stop Worrying and Love Jesus (Myth Theory)

By David Fitzgerald

The Christians won't like it, but here's a new and improved Gospel of Jesus I think the rest of us can all agree on:

About 2,000 years ago, more or less, a simple Galilean preacher gained a following with his radical teachings, until he so angered the Jewish authorities that they convinced the Romans to crucify him. After his death, his disciples and flock began to preach that he had appeared to them alive again before returning to Heaven. They wrote about him, spread legends about him, and over time, this small cult grew into the major world religion we know as Christianity.

I'm kidding, of course—we atheists can't agree on anything. I'm also kidding that this gospel makes any sense. Certainly, it used to be a valid hypothesis, but we are way past that point now.

Don't get me wrong; there's nothing intrinsically implausible about the idea that Jesus was merely one more failed apocalyptic prophet of the time, or even a composite of several of them. Lord knows there were plenty of them to go around. And we can all see a wealth of wildly contradictory, wildly exaggerated legends and myths surrounds him, but that doesn't prove there was no real figure at the core. After all, all legends have a kernel of truth at their center… don't they? Besides, the historical evidence for him is overwhelming, as all historians agree. Only a tiny lunatic fringe of crackpots says otherwise, and besides, all they have to go on are flawed arguments from silence. Right?

For argument's sake, let's just assume for a moment that the above paragraph is 100% true. It isn't, but it certainly encapsulates my attitude twenty years ago, when I was a young atheist activist perfectly fine with the idea Jesus was an actual historical figure. It had never crossed my mind to think otherwise. Ironically enough, it wasn't until I became curious about what we *could* know about the "real Jesus" that I first began to suspect there never was one—and realized I was not the only investigator to think so…

In my 2010 book, *Nailed*,[1] I discussed the top ten ways the official story of Christianity simply falls apart on close inspection—whether there was a real Jesus or not. In the penultimate chapter, entitled, "Can Jesus be Saved?" I pointed out the many ways the history of the church and the New Testament would look different if there had been a single human founder behind all the various competing early Christian movements.[2] Among several other reasons, we have this thorny paradox if Jesus had been an actual historical figure:

Either this Jesus was a remarkable individual who did (or at least, taught) a host of amazing, revolutionary things—but no one outside his fringe cult noticed for over a century. Or, he didn't… and yet shortly after his death, this otherwise unremarkable figure inspired tiny communities of worshipers to spring up everywhere, scattered all across the empire; small house cults that oddly couldn't agree about the most basic facts of his life—or if he had ever had a life on Earth at all.

Ten years ago, I was struck by the public response to the book, but also surprised by the intensity of its detractors—not from the Christian detractors (let's face it, what else are they going to say?), but from our fellow atheists. It turned out Jesus Myth theory set off all the red flags they get from conspiracy theories: In their minds, Jesus denial felt too much like Holocaust/Moon Landing/Climate Change denial. In an age

---

[1] Full title: Nailed: Ten Christian Myths that Show Jesus Never Existed at All (2010).
[2] And what questions would need to be better answered before I could ever become a Jesus Historicist again…

when Flat-Earthers are making a comeback, please believe me when I say I have sympathy for those who are extra-skeptical of the fringe and the woo. But there are serious differences between calling NASA a Jesuit-run Illuminati hoax and pointing out the myriad historical difficulties of a beloved religious figure's problematic backstory.

So, what sort of historical difficulties are we talking about?

Why Mythicism Matters, Reason #1: Too Many Jesuses

As it turns out, parsing any actual facts about Jesus from our sources is deeply problematic, as generations of biblical scholars have been discovering for over two hundred years. The prevailing attitude (among both secular scholars and laymen alike, it seems) is that once we sift out the obviously mythological elements from the gospels, we're left with reliable biographical information. And yet, using this dubious approach, secular scholars have managed to tease out a bewildering variety of contradictory Jesus figures.

"*Who do men say that I am?*" asks Jesus in Mark's gospel. It remains an open question. Christians love to crow that virtually all historians believe Jesus existed; they conveniently ignore the fact that no non-Christian historians believe *their* Jesus existed. In fact, the level of disagreement among Jesus scholars over the most basic facts concerning him is astounding. Of course, first comes the divide between "the Jesus of Faith" and "the Historical Jesus"—and both are simply placeholders for entire family trees of hypothetical, reconstructed Jesuses. Even if we ignore the plethora of faith-based Jesus figures, there are still a multitude of competing secular options to consider: Was he a Zealot rebel, or nonviolent peacemaker? Radical social reformer or royal pretender? Cynic philosopher, or Essene heretic? Pagan-style magician or exorcist/faith healer? Cult guru? Liberal Pharisee? Charismatic Hasid? Conservative rabbi? All these and still more have been put forward as the "Real Jesus."

However, it remains to be seen if *any* of these scholarly reconstructions reflect a genuine historical figure. As Robert M. Price and others have commented, all—well, almost all—of these proposed Jesuses are plausible enough. As far as it goes, none are hopelessly far-fetched. All tend to focus on particular constellations of Gospel elements, interpret them in certain ways, and reject other data as inauthentic. Each appeals to solid historical analogies for their new take on Jesus.

Still, all of them *do* suffer from two serious deficiencies. First, Bart Ehrman has observed that most, if not all, fail to make sense of Jesus' death—albeit, neither do the gospels. Ironically, Ehrman's own favored "Jesus as failed apocalyptic prophet" theory also fails to account for why the Romans would kill Jesus; it was not against Roman or Jewish law to be an apocalyptic prophet—or to declare oneself to be the messiah, for that matter.

Secondly, as Price notes in his 2000 book *Deconstructing Jesus*, this multiplicity of convincing possibilities is precisely the problem. All of them sound persuasive until you hear the next one. They cancel each other out.

> Jesus simply wears too many hats in the Gospels—exorcist, healer, king, prophet, sage, rabbi, demigod, and so on—(He) is a composite figure... The historical Jesus (if there was one) might well have been a messianic king, or a progressive Pharisee, or a Galilean shaman, or a magus, or a Hellenistic sage. *But he cannot very well have been all of them at the same time.*[3]

Could Jesus have been a stealth messiah? It's not uncommon to hear atheists muse that perhaps the real Jesus was none of these things, just one more itinerant Jewish preacher wandering the Galilee. But again, how does just another failed apocalyptic prophet go on to suddenly become deified all across the ancient world?

Besides, there comes a point when it no longer makes sense to give Jesus the benefit of the doubt. Even if we make allowances for legendary accretion, pious fraud, the criterion of embarrassment, doctrinal disputes, scribal errors and faults in translation, there are simply too many

---

[3] For even more options, see Price, *Deconstructing Jesus*, pp. 13-15.

irresolvable problems with the default position that assumes there simply *had* to be a single historical individual (or even a composite of several itinerant preachers) at the center of Christianity.

There's also a less-obvious problem with supposing Jesus was a fairly unknown figure in reality. What about all the *other* messianic figures we know about in this period, a surprising number of wanna-be Judaean messiahs from around the time of the early first century: John the Baptist, Apollonius of Tyana, Jonathan the Weaver, Athronges the Shepherd, Simon of Peraea, 'the *Taheb*' (the Samaritans' messiah) and more; over a dozen in all?[4]

If Jesus' fame was anywhere near the levels depicted in the Gospels—multitudes following him, fame spreading throughout Judea, to Syria, Egypt, the ten cities of the Decapolis league, etc.—his achievements were easily on par with even the best of these. But every one of these was able to accomplish something Jesus couldn't. How did also-ran messianic figures like 'the *Taheb*', Jonathan the Weaver, and all the rest manage to leave a historical footprint—but not Jesus? How could everyone outside his own cult fail to notice him, or even his new religion, for nearly a century? Conversely, if Jesus was so forgettable that he wasn't even as interesting as any of these others, then how could he inspire a fringe religion of tiny feuding house churches to pop up all across the far-flung corners of the Roman empire?

And there's still another consideration: what about all the *other* Jesuses and Christs of the first and second century that we find in the Gospels, Paul's letters, and other early Christian writings? As I mention in *Nailed* (pp. 151–52):

> Paul himself complains about the diversity among early believers, who incredibly treat Christ as just one more factional totem figure, some saying they belong to Paul, or Apollos, or Cephas—or to Christ. Paul

---

[4] For a complete list and details of all of them, see *Jesus: Mything in Action*, vol. 1, pp. 111-116.

asks, "Has Christ been divided?" (1 Cor. 1:10-13). Paul also repeatedly rails against his many rival apostles, who "preach another Jesus."

In his letters, Paul often rages and fumes that his rivals are evil deceivers, with false Christs and false gospels so different from his own true Christ and true Gospel, that he accuses them of being agents of Satan and even lays curses and threats upon them![5]

Other early Christians were just as concerned as Paul. The *Didakhê*, an early manual of Christian church practice and teachings, spends two chapters talking about wandering preachers and warning against the many false preachers who are mere "traffickers in Christs," or "Christmongers."[6]

The evidence is clear; there were many different gospels, Jesuses, and Christs being preached by different groups in the first century (and even into the early second century, when the *Didakhê* was likely written). No single individual Jesus made an impact on history, but many different ones made an impact on theology—at least on the cultic fringe. The 'stealth messiah' approach to the problem simply fails to make any sense of the evidence.

In reality, the more we uncover about Christian origins, the more we see that early Christianity dissolves into an exuberant diversity of competing Christ movements with little in common. All our secular reconstructions of the "real Jesus" (like the one I offered at the beginning of this chapter) turn out to be two orders of wrong, no more than myths based on myths.

Why Mythicism Matters, Reason #2: A Source of a Different Color

Increasingly, it's become obvious that all our so-called "biographical" information sources for Jesus boil down to Christian writings fully dependent upon our four canonical gospels—and in turn, these four have shown

---

[5] 2 Corinthians 11:4, 13–15,19–20, 22–23; Galatians 1:6-9; 2:4.
[6] Didakhê 12:5.

they are not based on any oral traditions or eyewitness reports, but are entirely literary constructions,[7] and all appear to ultimately derive from a single text,[8] the allegorical[9] writing we call Mark's Gospel. Before that pivotal work, the various strands of early Christianity and their competing "apostles"[10] worship Christ figures very different from the later varieties

---

[7] As many historians have demonstrated, throughout all four gospels there are many different indications of both literary borrowing (literary seams, intercalation, deliberate rearrangements, ongoing evolution and embellishment of the storyline, etc.) as well as sophisticated literary structure; including impossible miracles and improbable events, literary devices and artistry (e.g., puns, extremely apt names of characters and places, etc.), symbolic narratives, artificial plot structures, chiasmus ring composition, revamped vignettes from the Old Testament and other ancient writings, new takes on classic mythemes, and still more. (For more discussion, see "Constructing (and Deconstructing) the Gospels" in *Jesus: Mything in Action*, vol. 2, pp. 21-60).

[8] This interdependency has long been recognized by biblical historians as "the Synoptic Problem"—but of course it's only a problem to those that wish the gospels were independent of one another. See *Jesus: Mything in Action*, vol. 1, p. 209 for more details.

[9] From "Jesus Gets a Life" (in *Jesus: Mything in Action*, vol. 1, p. 227): Mark tells us what he is doing right from the outset: he is writing a gospel, not a history or a biography (Mark 1:1). Numerous historians across the theological spectrum, both Historicists and mythicists alike, have confirmed this; including Thomas L. Brodie, Calum Carmichael, Richard Carrier, John Dominic Crossan, Tom Dykstra, Arnold Ehrhardt, Randel Helms, Ernst Käsemann, Dennis R. MacDonald, Jennifer Maclean, Norman Perrin, Robert M. Price, Paul Nadim Tarazi, Thomas L. Thompson and many others. All have detailed the ways that Mark's entire Gospel is a treasure trove of symbolic, rather than historical, meaning, with parts created by borrowing from the Old Testament, the Homeric epics, and the letters of Paul. None of his gospel was meant to be taken literally. From start to finish, this is allegory, not history. Mark wasn't writing a biography of Jesus any more than C.S. Lewis was writing a biography of Aslan.

[10] It's important to note that for Paul, an "apostle" is *not* one of Jesus' group of twelve disciples—Paul not only never mentions that Jesus ever had any disciples, he never uses the word "disciple" in *any* context, ever. According to Paul and the early Christians, an "apostle" was someone like himself, who received divine revelations (1 Cor. 9:1; Gal. 1:1; etc.) and confirmed their status by proving that God had granted them miraculous powers (2 Cor. 12:12). Paul puts himself and his fellow apostles at the top of the hierarchy of believers. Then come prophets, teachers, those with "powers" (most likely exorcists), faith healers, aides, administrators, and finally, those who speak in tongues (1 Cor. 12:28). Notice who doesn't

of Jesus that arrive only post-gospels.

Some critics say it is a *non sequitur* to conclude from confusing and contradictory evidence that their subject didn't exist at all. I agree. The fact is, it's only the evidence for a *historical* Jesus that remains confused and contradictory. The evidence for an allegorical, "celestial" Jesus is compelling and found in both Christian and non-Christian sources,[11] an evolutionary process that can be seen across the centuries in extant texts, from before the rise of Christian movements to after the gospels.

On the other hand, as Raphael Lataster points out in his incisive 2015 book, *Jesus Did Not Exist*, Historicists like Ehrman are forced to rely on purely hypothetical source materials, although they have no guarantee these documents say what Historicists assume they say[12]—or, more to the point, even whether these postulated "source" texts ever really existed at all in the first place...

In fact, in recent years, *all* the criteria for Jesus' historicity have been weighed and found wanting. It's not only secular critics who have rejected them; even devout scholars on a first name basis with Jesus have bowed to decades of withering criticism to admit that all our tools to verify his existence have proven fatally flawed. Christian historians Chris Keith and Anthony Le Donne's 2012 book *Jesus, Criteria, and the Demise of Authenticity* (T & T Clark Int'l) ably documents this unexpected development, as well as Richard Carrier's *Proving History* (Prometheus, 2012), which exposes the failure of all the would-be criteria brought forth in attempts to solidify the shifting sands beneath the slippery, elusive figure of the historical Jesus.

---

make the list. Disciples don't. Relatives of Jesus don't. These categories simply don't exist for Paul. (See *Jesus: Mything in Action*, vol. 2, pp. 153-54 for more discussion.)

[11] Besides *Jesus: Mything in Action*, see also Carrier's *On the Historicity of Jesus Christ*, esp. elements 6, 8, 10, 14, and 37-42.

[12] Or, in the case of Christian apologists, what they desperately want them to say.

Why Mythicism Matters, Reason #3: But the Evidence…

One constant refrain from laypeople who haven't been following the current state of Jesus Studies is: "How do Mythicists explain away all the evidence for Jesus?" Their assumption is that there must be far too much contrary evidence to explain away in the case of Jesus…

Too much evidence? The dearth of evidence for Jesus—and the shoddy state of what little we do have—are two of the factors that should compel any Historicist toward a healthy agnosticism on the Jesus question at the very least.

Consider this: we have nothing written by Jesus, and we do not know who really wrote any of the Gospels. Of the four evangelists, only "Luke" even *claims* to be writing history, but neither he nor any of the others ever cite their sources, or give a sign that they critically examined any, or justify why we should trust their particular version of many conflicting gospel claims.

All these gospel authors are anonymous, writing at least a generation or more after the fact. None claim to be eyewitnesses; on the contrary, "Luke" explicitly tells us he is investigating the story inherited by his generation of believers,[13] and the gospel we attribute to "John" purports to be handed down from an unnamed "beloved disciple." However, this clearly fictitious "beloved disciple" character doesn't exist in any of the earlier gospels—and has been gratuitously inserted into their rebooted plotlines. For example, in Luke, Peter runs to go see the empty tomb (24:12). In John, both Peter and the beloved disciple run to the tomb—and the beloved disciple conspicuously outruns Peter there (20:3-4).[14]

---

[13] Luke 1:1-2.
[14] Who is this mystery disciple? A good argument can be made that we *do* know who this was meant to be—and it wasn't John, or any of the twelve disciples… (See *Jesus: Mything in Action*, vol. 1, p. 206).

As their actual identities are completely unknown,[15] we have no other literature or scholarship to their credit that we can test for their skill and accuracy. Far from being objective, dispassionate historians, all freely declare their bias toward persuading new converts. What's more, all derived their accounts from Mark's gospel, even the multitude of non-canonical gospels that didn't make the cut to be accepted as Scripture. And then there's the unpleasant matters of Christian forgeries in our gospels and New Testament epistles, their deliberate alterations in theological edit wars, and the honest scribal mistakes that were never caught and now can't be rectified.[16]

What's more, we have no original New Testament texts. As Bart Ehrman and numerous other historians have long made very clear, we don't have the original of *any* book of the New Testament. What we have are copies of copies of copies of copies… It's not until the late second/early third century that we begin to get the complete texts of some of the individual books of the New Testament,[17] and not until the early-to-mid fourth century that we have our first two complete New Testaments, the *Codex Vaticanus* and the *Codex Siniaticus*. Even that is a bit misleading since both codices have different books from each other—and, for that matter, from our own Bibles. They have books we don't have. We have books they don't have.[18] This means for the first 150 to 200 years of

---

[15] Nor do we know how many editors were involved, what redactions were made, or how many more interpolations remain to be discovered. We only know that so many have already been found, statistically others must remain that we have no way of detecting at present.

[16] Bart Ehrman's The Orthodox Corruption of Scripture and Forgery and Counter-forgery: The Use of Literary Deceit in Early Christian Polemics are must-reads on the topic; though his Forged is an excellent and accessible resource as well.

[17] Our dating methods are not precise enough to be more specific. Despite persistent Christian attempts to deny it, the earliest complete text of any epistle is from 200 CE +/-30 years. No complete gospel text is even that old.

[18] For exact contents of *Vaticanus* and *Siniaticus*, see *Jesus: Mything in Action*, vol. 1, p. 181.

Christianity, we have a complete textual black-out period, where we simply cannot know what was originally written about Jesus at all.[19]

We all know there is no physical evidence of any kind in the case of Jesus, apart from countless medieval forgeries and hoaxes like the Shroud of Turin[20] or the eight or more competing foreskins of Jesus.[21] Nor is there any contemporary historical corroboration for any of the Gospels' depictions of Jesus' life. This should not surprise either side of the historicity debate, but the puzzling "silence of Paul" concerning Jesus' life is less explicable.[22] That lacuna has troubled scholars for centuries, but to make matters worse, it isn't just Paul. *Every* Christian writing before the Gospels exhibits the same bewildering ignorance about Jesus' life and teachings, and even our familiar New Testament books have passage after passage that make no sense if Jesus was the figure from the gospels.[23]

Christian apologists have always upheld Jesus' historicity with absurdly exaggerated claims, such as when Douglas Geivett put the resurrection on the same level of certainty as Julius Caesar crossing the

---

[19] And yes, I'm afraid it's even (far) worse than all this. See "Curiouser and Curiouser" in *Jesus: Mything in Action*, vol. 1, p. 186-190 for more of the ugly truth behind all our Bible translations.
[20] See the Skeptic's Dictionary entry on the "Shroud of Turin" (http://www.skepdic.com/shroud.html) for a nice summary of the many proofs of its forgery.
[21] You read that right. "Depending on what you read, there were eight, twelve, fourteen, or even 18 different holy foreskins in various European towns during the Middle Ages." See David Farley's *An Irreverent Curiosity: In Search of the Church's Strangest Relic in Italy's Oddest Town* (Penguin, 2009) for more details.
[22] It's not just Paul's *silence*, either. Paul—and all our other early Christian writers—say many bizarre things about their Jesus. Even the few snippets that are often held up as proof that Paul believed Jesus was a real person on earth, knew the disciples, etc., don't hold up to examination. See the full discussion in "Paul's Jesus," Ch. 15 of *Jesus: Mything in Action*, vol. 2.
[23] For just one of several examples, Jesus' jaw-dropping revelation in Mark 4:10-13 makes no sense at all if his Jesus came to earth to save the world—but makes perfect sense if Mark's Jesus was a typical mystery faith savior deity. See "The Mystery of the Kingdom of God" in *Jesus: Mything in Action*, vol. 1, pp. 231-32.

Rubicon.[24] Richard Carrier pointed out that in this case, for four of the five proofs cited in support of the Rubicon crossing's historicity, the resurrection has no evidence at all—and the single "proof" that it *does* have is not the best, but the very *worst* kind of evidence: a handful of biased, uncritical, unscholarly, unknown, second-hand witnesses (falsely passed off as personal eyewitnesses), writing expressly to sell a new religion. As Richard Carrier wrote, "Indeed, you really have to look hard to find another event that is in a worse condition than this as far as evidence goes."[25]

We can (and should) laugh at this, but the truth is, even the mundane and non-miraculous "facts" of Jesus' biography are no better attested. Jesus' arrest, his trial, his execution, the last supper and his cleansing of the temple are just a few examples of events that we know simply could not have happened as presented in the gospel stories.[26]

The standard approach of Jesus scholars has been to cull all these elements of the gospels that are obvious impossibilities and reject them as theological fictions. Having winnowed out the chaff, they assemble their version of "the Real Jesus" from whatever is left. But the result, as Albert Schweitzer recognized more than a century ago,[27] is that the new Jesus becomes a Rorschach test for the searcher; their version of who Jesus "really" was turns out to be their own mirror image.

What we *should* be doing before we claim any fact of Jesus' life has been established with an acceptable level of certainty is to begin with two simple questions: What is our source for any claim about Jesus, and how

---

[24] And to be fair, even quite respected historians have made some incredible howlers about the state of evidence for Jesus, such as when E.P. Sanders, in *The Historical Figure of Jesus* (Penguin Press, 1993, p. 3) boldly asserted that "the sources for Jesus are better... than those that deal with Alexander the Great"—when nothing could be further from the truth.

[25] Carrier, Sense and Goodness Without God, pp. 242-244.

[26] Besides *Jesus: Mything in Action*, vol.1 & 2, Randel Helms' 1989 book *Gospel Fictions* and Carrier's *On the Historicity of Jesus* contain plentiful demonstrations of obvious ahistorical events from the Gospels (and also the Book of Acts).

[27] Schweitzer, *The Quest of the Historical Jesus*, (English trans. 1910).

reliable is that source?[28] Otherwise, which camp is operating under dogma and wishful thinking: the mythicists, or the Historicists?

After all, it has become undeniably apparent to everyone but the most hidebound believers that—historical Jesus or no—our gospels are myths about Jesus. The question remains: are they myth all the way down?

Why Mythicism Matters, Reason #4: But the Consensus...

So what about the supposed overwhelming consensus among historians? Consensus? *What* consensus? We've seen that Jesus Studies is already split into two camps, and neither half believes the other half's Jesus ever existed. But if you (like me) tend to gravitate to the work of the secular scholars,[29] there is scarcely any consensus on who the "real Jesus" was. Besides, for the most part, mythicists are in agreement with the same arguments the majority of secular scholars are making.[30] In fact, the most credible segments of the mythicist camp aren't out on a limb or bucking *any* scholarly consensus; they are merely following the same lines of evidence to a conclusion just a little past most biblical scholars' comfort zone.

Indeed, the evidence for a historical Jesus is so problematic, several scholars, including Brandon University's Kurt Noll, Princeton sociologist Rodney Stark, and others already argue that the question is moot.[31]

---

[28] And not to crucify a dead horse, but again—whether Jesus was a real person or not, all our allegedly biographical sources for him are *completely* dodgy...

[29] Not to say there are no religious historians doing fine work in Jesus Studies (and truly, I do cite their work, often—as often as I can, in fact) but the thing is—and maybe it's just me, but often I get the feeling their side seems more concerned with circling the wagons against new findings than in considering their merits...

[30] For instance, when it comes to Markan Priority, the Synoptic Problem, commonly recognized interpolations, rejection of Gospel elements as unhistorical (and still more issues), mythicists and secular Historicists are in total agreement.

[31] Kurt Noll. "Investigating Earliest Christianity without Jesus," in Thompson and Verenna, ed., 'Is This Not the Carpenter?' The Question of the Historicity of the Figure of Jesus, pp. 233-66; Rodney Stark, The Rise of Christianity: A Sociologist

Knowing what we know now, any contributions that a historical founder may or may not have made are irrelevant—we can already completely account for the rise of the various strands of the Christian movement *whether there was a real Jesus or not*.

Myth theory is not creationism for atheists; it's a wake up call for a theory that has been in crisis for centuries. This isn't (or shouldn't be) seen as a squabble between heretical mythicists and orthodox Historicists. It is a fight between those who take Jesus Myth theory seriously—whether or not it ultimately prevails over Jesus Historicism—and those who simply dismiss it out of hand.[32]

Case in point is Bart Ehrman, who remains one of the most influential and important secular biblical scholars today, and for good reason. Perhaps no other historian has done as much to pull back the curtain on the subfield of biblical history, or shed as much light on the ways its foundation has been built upon sand.[33] So it is especially curious to see how he clings with such certainty to the questionable notion that "whether we like it or not," Jesus *definitely existed*.

Reading his 2012 book *Did Jesus Exist?* was an exercise in disappointment and lost opportunity. Mythicists didn't dislike the book because we had expected him to agree with us; we panned the book because we were anticipating it would be both the best defense of what facts do hold up in Jesus Historicism theory, and a vigorous critique of Mythicism that would at least help clear some of the dead wood from the field.

Reconsiders History, (Princeton University Press, 1996); James G. Crossley, Why Christianity Happened: a Sociohistorical Account of Christian Origins (26-50 CE), (Louisville: Westminster John Knox, 2006); Davies cites Michael F. Bird and James G. Crossley in How Did Christianity Begin?: A Believer and Non-Believer Examine the Evidence, (Grand Rapids: Baker Academic, 2008) as a pleasant surprise: a largely noncombative conversation between secular and non-secular approaches.

[32] Because Historicists aren't the enemy. Even Christians aren't the enemy. Bullshit is the enemy.

[33] Especially in his books like Misquoting Jesus, Jesus Interrupted, Forged, The Orthodox Corruption of Scripture, Lost Christianities, Lost Scriptures, and Forgery and Counter-forgery: The Use of Literary Deceit in Early Christian Polemics, just to name a few.

But as his fellow Historicist, University of Sheffield's Emeritus Professor Philip R. Davies pointed out, Ehrman's smug dismissal of the questions raised by mythicists is part of the problem in biblical studies, just as serious as the ones Ehrman himself has so ably spotlighted.[34] The late Davies chided Bart Ehrman and his 2012 book *Did Jesus Exist?* for this very attitude, and his perspective was a refreshing change:

> ...surely the rather fragile historical evidence for Jesus of Nazareth should be tested to see what weight it can bear, or even to work out what kind of historical research might be appropriate.
>
> Such a normal exercise should hardly generate controversy in most fields of ancient history, but of course New Testament studies is not a normal case and the highly emotive and dismissive language of, say, Bart Ehrman's response to Thompson's *The Mythic Past* shows (if it needed to be shown), not that the matter is beyond dispute, but that the whole idea of raising this question needs to be attacked, ad hominem, as something outrageous.
>
> This is precisely the tactic anti-minimalists tried twenty years ago: their targets were 'amateurs', 'incompetent', and could be ignored. The 'amateurs' are now all retired professors, while virtually everyone else in the field has become minimalist (if in most cases grudgingly and tacitly). So, as the saying goes, déjà vu all over again.
>
> I don't think, however, that in another 20 years there will be a consensus that Jesus did not exist, or even possibly didn't exist, but a recognition that his existence is not entirely certain would nudge Jesus scholarship towards academic respectability. In the first place, what does it mean to affirm that 'Jesus existed', anyway, when so many different Jesuses are displayed for us by the ancient sources and modern NT scholars?

---

[34] What's more, Ehrman shows some painful blind spots in his defense of historicity, such as his over-reliance upon hypothetical sources, his acceptance of highly questionable evangelical assertions as established facts, and ironically, that his own scholarship inadvertently makes him one of the finest mythicist historians around.

In fact, as things stand, what is being affirmed as the Jesus of history is a cipher, not a rounded personality (the same is true of the King David of the Hebrew Bible, as a number of recent 'biographies' show)...Does this matter very much? After all, the rise and growth of Christianity can be examined and explained without the need to reconstruct a particular historical Jesus.[35]

Why Mythicism Matters, Reason #5: That One Slight Problem with Biblical Studies

Davies brings up an important point here, one also raised by biblical historian Hector Avalos in his devastating critique of his own field, *The End of Biblical Studies* (Prometheus, 2007).[36] Avalos notes that in the uniquely insular world of biblical studies, theological concerns have always dominated. There is a bizarre Russian-doll nature to biblical studies; it's what I call *the Belfast Analogy*:

Northern Ireland during the Troubles of the 1960s to the 1990s saw a minority, the Ulster Protestants, surrounded by the majority Catholic Ireland. Meanwhile, nested within Ulster was its own Catholic minority. Feeling under siege, Ulster Protestants in turn made life intolerable for their captive minority-within-a-minority.

Likewise, Christians feel surrounded by the secular world, and this is no less true in academia. But while believers may feel under siege in all other fields of history, in the rarified world of biblical studies, Christian presuppositions, biases and above all, theological (and their accompanying financial) interests still hold sway, making life very hard for any scholars whose findings threaten Christian doctrine.

---

[35] For the complete article (a must-read), see Davies' review of Ehrman's *Did Jesus Exist?* on *The Bible and Interpretation* website at: https://www.bibleinterp.com/opeds/dav368029.shtml.
[36] Another must-read. Avalos argues convincingly why the Bible is irrelevant, if not downright dangerous, to contemporary needs and concerns, and that the field is far more concerned with self-preservation than about giving an honest account of its own findings to the general public.

Am I saying this is a conspiracy theory? Of course not.

Am I saying Christian biases and presuppositions pervade the entire field? Of course I am—*and how could it be otherwise?*

When I was researching for my book *Jesus: Mything in Action*, I was surprised that no one had ever verified the seemingly intuitive observation that the overwhelming majority of biblical scholars have a religious affiliation. It seemed fairly problematic to survey every biblical scholar's religious position(s), but it occurred to me that it was quite possible to not just survey, but in fact to conduct a complete census of every single American learning institution that offers Biblical/Jesus/New Testament Studies and/or degrees.

Which is precisely what the book's research team did. For "U.S. Biblical Studies Depts. Census (2015)," the team, spearheaded by Susi Bocks, investigated all 4,726 degree-granting institutions of higher education in the United States, and conducted a full survey of the 1,417 that offered any kind of relevant Biblical/Jesus/New Testament Studies. Nearly 60% of these proved to be religiously affiliated.[37] The real surprise came when we looked into their scholarly restrictions. A full third of these religiously affiliated schools frankly confirmed that they required a statement of faith or similar religious commitment from their staff. That was not the surprising part.

What was shocking was the number of schools that refused to admit this, or indeed, the number that explicitly *lied* about requiring a statement of faith. When the team dug deeper, they soon discovered that in fact, actually at least two-thirds of all religiously affiliated schools required their teachers to tow a strict theological line—and the actual number is almost certainly even higher, and may well be as high as 100%.[38] So perhaps the question shouldn't be, "How many biblical scholars reject myth theory?" but, "How many biblical scholars are *contractually obligated* to reject myth theory?" As Upton Sinclair noted long ago: "It is difficult to get a man to

---

[37] To be exact, 814 out of 1,417; 57%.
[38] And I would welcome anyone who would like to do a follow-up investigation to pin down the exact number.

understand something, when his salary depends on his not understanding it."

Wait, I hear you ask. Could a *whole field* of professionals be wrong? Why not ask your pastor and see what he says? The truth is, the majority of biblical historians are just as wrong about there being a Jesus as they are about there being a god. And for the same reason.

We should not forget that the field of Jesus Studies is in crisis because Christianity is in crisis. Both are under tremendous pressure to show that all is well and under control, even while their evidentiary foundations are crumbling. The subject of biblical studies is also dying out in secular academia, which first of all means there are fewer and fewer jobs for current and future biblical historians, period.

What's worse for us, it also means that increasingly, the *only* institutions offering positions in biblical studies are the religious institutions—which makes it that much more difficult for any would-be secular biblical historians to espouse blasphemous theories…

And speaking of blasphemy, we should also note that even in such a thoroughly Christian-dominated subfield, yesterday's blasphemy is tomorrow's consensus.

Did eyewitnesses write the Gospels? Did their authors copy from each other? Do their Gospels contradict one another? Are any of Paul's letters forgeries? Are any of the other epistles in the New Testament really by the authors whose names they bear, or even written during their lifetime? Was forgery rampant in Christian scriptures? Was John the Baptist's sect part of Christianity, or was it a rival cult? Is our New Testament the same as that of the early Christians? Were our scriptures tampered with? Do we have any way to determine which, if any, of our extant scriptural texts reflect the reading of the original text?

The real answers to all these and still other questions greatly displeased—and were dismissed and ridiculed by—the majority of biblical scholars, which is to say, those with a religious affiliation. But the truth eventually prevailed. The history of biblical studies is littered with such overturned verdicts.[39]

Why Mythicism Matters, Reason #6: It's Not Just Jesus...

By the way, Christianity is not alone in wrestling with uncomfortable questions and troublesome facts about its own origins. One unexpected side effect of studying the historicity of Jesus was discovering that he's *not* the only religious founder who has been put under the microscope in recent years. Both Buddhists and ex-Muslims have contacted me to let me know they are having the same debates in their respective circles over whether the Buddha or Muhammad were actual historical figures.

Like Jesus, whose name works well as an allegory (in Hebrew, *Y'shua*, "to deliver/to rescue,") the name "Muhammad" can also mean "the chosen/praised one." Muhammad purportedly lived in the late sixth to early seventh century (570-632 CE), but none of our contemporary non-Muslim sources of the seventh century corroborate the canonical story, and it's not until over a hundred years later, towards the middle of the eighth century, that we get any clear epigraphic Arabic evidence for him. For example, an inscription from 677 or 678 CE, attributed to Muawiya, the first Umayyad caliph, makes reference to belief in God—but has no indication of belief in Muhammad as his messenger, or in the Qur'an as revealed Scripture.

Also like Jesus, the biographical data for Muhammad—the *ahadith* (plural of *hadith*) and *sira*—appear generations after the fact, and their reliability has come into severe question.[40] At the same time, there are

---

[39] For just one example, in the 1970s, biblical historian Thomas L. Thompson's career was nearly derailed when he concluded that the Old Testament patriarchs were not historical figures. Today, it is more or less the mainstream opinion, even in many evangelical institutions. (See *Jesus: Mything in Action*, pp. 71-75.)

[40] As early as the 8th century, Muslim scholar Shu'bah ibn Al-Hajjaj, known as the 'King of *Hadith*' for his investigation into the subject, declared that roughly two-thirds of them were fabrications. Modern researchers are even more skeptical (See *Jesus: Mything in Action*, vol. 1, pp. 80-81 for more details and citations).

good grounds to hypothesize that the Qur'an itself is not the work of a single writer, but developed from different texts over the seventh and eighth centuries. Unbelievable as it seems, Islam appears to be a result—not a cause—of the religious and cultural milieu of the Arab conquests.[41]

Perhaps unsurprisingly, the Eastern traditions have tended to a more detached stance on the historicity of founder figures like Prince Siddhārtha Gautama, the Buddha. In the influential Mahayana scripture the *Lotus Sutra*, the Buddha himself calls his own historical authenticity into question.[42]

Buddha has come down through the ages with a dutifully miracle-laden biography, including a divine conception and birth and the usual attendant miracles and extraordinary events throughout his divine career. But as Columbia University Professor Bernard Faure points out, the fact that similar events are also said to have occurred during the life of the founder of Jainism, Mahavira—another allegedly historical figure—indicates that a degree of caution must be exercised in accepting their factual basis.[43]

The line-up of semi-legendary religious founder figures continues in both the eastern and western spiritual traditions: Zoroaster, Moses, Abraham, the traditional founder of Taoism Laozi (or Lao Tzu), Confucius, and the list goes on.

Even some figures whose writings have come down to us have fallen into question: Isaiah, Homer and Aesop, to name just a few. For well over two centuries, the Old Testament book of Isaiah has been recognized as the work of multiple authors from at least three different time periods. The question of Homeric authorship is still debated, but increasingly the epics are seen as the result of a process of working and reworking by many

---

[41] For a thorough discussion of these issues, see for instance: *Did Muhammad Exist? An Inquiry into Islam's Obscure Origins* by Robert Spencer (ISI Books, 2012), and *The Quest for the Historical Muhammad*, edited by Ibn Warraq (Prometheus Books, 2000).
[42] For more, see Bernard Faure's "The Myth of the Historical Buddha," in *Tricycle: The Buddhist Review*, (Spring, 2016).
[43] Ibid.

contributors, and "Homer" a label for an entire tradition. Aesop's biographical data is a chimera that has appeared to marinate for centuries before coalescing into written form.[44]

So the idea that Christianity, or indeed, any and all of the other major world religions, may have begun with a purely mythical founder, is far from ridiculous. Indeed, it appears to be the norm.[45]

Conclusion

"Facts are sometimes the most radical critics of all," theologian William Wrede commented about his own field of study back in the day. The Historical Jesus question has the potential to be the biggest paradigm shift in the study of Christian origins. And the importance of Jesus Mythicism goes far beyond the Historical Jesus question itself. For instance, it highlights all the uniquely problematic elements plaguing biblical studies historically and currently, such as the pervasive bias affecting biblical studies—a remarkable condition different from any other field of history.

At the very least, this debate will point out that strong agnosticism is warranted towards everything that we think we know about who and what Jesus said, did, and was. And at best, it will utterly change the way we look at the founding figures of virtually all major religions, not only the Abrahamic, but from the Eastern traditions as well.

As James Burke noted long ago in his excellent show *The Day the Universe Changed*, what you *think* you know conditions what you actually *can* know. If you "know" that the sun goes around the Earth, then you can never know the real reason Mars goes retrograde, or any number of other facts about how the solar system really works.

---

[44] See Neil Godfrey's recap of our evidence, "Did Aesop Exist?" in *Vridar* (August 8, 2017).
[45] This would make modern founders like Mary Baker Eddy, L. Ron Hubbard and Joseph Smith outliers—then again, the author of the *Book of Mormon* is supposedly an ancient American Nephite prophet-turned-angel Mormon, so we're back to yet another mythical founder figure again...

After two decades of investigating the matter, I am increasingly convinced that myth theory holds the answer to unravel Christianity's perplexing origins, and that we will never understand the rise of the various Christian movements until we recognize this fact: our Jesus is a Jewish version of the other rebooted mystery faith savior deities that dominated the ancient Hellenistic world, and our Gospels all derive from the original "Mark's," a blatantly allegorical story written far from and generations after the place and time it describes.

This is not from dogma or wishful thinking; if the evidence could be shown to warrant it, I'd be happy to change my mind back to Historicism,[46] and still be a perfectly contented atheist. After all, it's not like Christianity is suddenly going to start making sense if it turns out Jesus was real.[47]

But what's never going to change my mind—nor should it yours—are the kinds of critical responses we've seen to date: the same weak, special pleading, ostrich-headed, knee-jerk responses trotted out to resist every single theology-threatening advance in biblical studies, ever. Bad enough that the Christians stonewall and ridicule any scholarship that exposes the cracks in their party line; worse that secular skeptics have echoed their chorus.

I am far from the first or best qualified to point out that dogma and wishful thinking have long interfered with sound scholarship when it comes to the Historical Jesus question. In the case of religiously motivated scholars, we can at least appreciate how hard it is to overcome their Christian bias, and recognize how strained and self-serving their objections are.

---

[46] Or, for that matter, embrace some alternative form of Jesus Myth theory that I don't currently find convincing, such as Jesus-as-a-Roman-invention, Jesus-as-a-character-from-a-passion-play, etc. Not all myth theories are created equal (not even some of the ones presented in this book)—though it's worth pointing out that even the most hopelessly crank myth theory is more plausible than any of the mainstream Christian species of Jesus Historicism...

[47] For example, see any of John W. Loftus' earlier anthologies, or ex-minister David Madison's *Ten Tough Problems in Christian Thought and Belief*, (Tellectual Press, 2016)—And again, it's not just Christianity in this dilemma...

Sadly, too many of our fellow humanists are copying from the Christians' play book, aping the same smug defensive reaction, replacing analysis with hand-waving, and trotting out the same old tired dismissals, false analogies, and appeals to authority. And in the end, there's really no need for any such secular hostility towards myth theory at all.

Why Mythicism Matters, Reason #7: The Best Reason of All

Here's why you should love Jesus Myth theory, too: Critics fail to appreciate the simple value that comes from the mythicist/Historicist debate, *regardless of which side prevails.* For all the pious hysteria over evolutionary theory, Christians increasingly are finding that they can wiggle and reinterpret their faith to accommodate Darwin's unavoidable truth of natural selection, the delightfully oxymoronic "theistic evolution." However, Christians can't play that game with Mythicism.

Jesus Myth theory is kryptonite for Christianity. Unlike us, they can't even enjoy a relaxed agnosticism about the *mere possibility* of Mythicism being true. They *need* Jesus NOT to be a myth.

Unfortunately for them, Jesus *is* a myth.

And that remains true, no matter whether it's the mythicist camp or the Historicist camp that ultimately comes out on top. The believer's "Jesus of Faith" gets debunked either way. Atheists who roll their eyes and wonder why Mythicism doesn't seem to be going away might be relieved to realize that.

I find myself constantly quoting Price's apt observation that whether or not there ever had been a real Jesus, for all intents and purposes, *there isn't one anymore*—because everything we think we know about that elusive figure comes to us from a handful of much later, deeply problematic writings that have no connection to anyone who actually lived in the first century. And again, this is the case, whether a real Jesus ever existed or not, even whether Christianity is true or not.

What *is* important about this argument—and what makes it worthwhile for secular humanists of all stripes to argue about the details—is that when one actually takes the trouble to look into the matter, it's valuable (and fascinating) to see where Christianity really came from, and to discover just how remarkably shaky its foundations actually are. And if nothing else, the debate reveals the limits of just what we can and can't know about who or what—or if—Jesus really was... Everything we learn from the back-and-forth of this historical argument helps you call the bluff of anyone who tries to tell you they know how Jesus wants you to behave, or think, or vote.

And that by itself is a very good thing for all of us to know.

Chapter 2: *Jesus Christ*
by Barbara G. Walker

Excerpted from *The Woman's Encyclopedia of Myths and Secrets* by Barbara G. Walker, published by Harper, 1983:

The Jesus who was called Christos, "Anointed," took his title from Middle-Eastern savior-gods like Adonis and Tammuz, born of the Virgin Sea-goddess Aphrodite-Maria (Myrrha), or Ishtar-Mari (Hebrew Mari-amne). Earlier biblical versions of the same hero were Joshua son of Nun (Exodus 33:11), Jehu son of Nimshi, whom Elijah anointed as a sacred king (1 Kings 19:16), and Yeshua son of Marah. The Book of Enoch said in the second century BC that Yeshua or Jesus was the secret name given by God to the Son of Man (a Persian title), and that it meant, "Yahweh saves."[1]

In northern Israel, the name was written Ieu.[2] It was the same as Ieud or Jeud, the "only-begotten son" dressed in royal robes and sacrificed by the god-king Isra-El.[3] Greek versions of the name were Iasion, Jason, or Iasus, the name of one of Demeter's sacrificed consorts, killed by Father Zeus after the fertility rite that coupled him with his Mother.[4] Iasus signified a healer or Therapeuta, as the Greeks called the Essenes, whose cult groups always included a man with the title of Christos.[5] The literal

---

[1] Homer Smith, *Man and His Gods*. (Boston: Little, Brown & Co, 1952), p. 19.
[2] William Foxwell Albright, *Yahweh and the Gods of Canaan*. (New York: Doubleday, 1968), p. 262.
[3] James G. Frazer, *The Golden Bough*. (New York: Macmillan, 1922), p. 341.
[4] Robert Graves, *The Greek Myths*. (New York: Penguin Books, 1955), vol. 1, p. 89.
[5] H.J. Rose, *Religion in Greece and Rome*. (New York: Harper & Brothers, 1959), p. 111.

meaning of the name was "healing moon-man," fitting the Hebrew version of Jesus as a son of Mary, the almah or "moon-maiden."[6]

It seems Jesus was not one person but a composite of many.[7] He played the role of sacred king of the Jews who periodically died in an atonement ceremony as surrogate for the real king.[8] "The Semitic religions practiced human immolations longer than any other religion, sacrificing children and grown men in order to please sanguinary gods. In spite of Hadrian's prohibition of those murderous offerings, they were maintained in certain clandestine rites."[9] The priesthood of the Jewish God insisted that "one man should die for the people...than the whole nation perish not" (John 11:50). Yahweh forgave no sins without bloodshed: "without shedding blood is no remission" (Hebrews 9:22).

Middle-Eastern traditions presented a long line of slain and cannibalized Saviors extending back to prehistory. At first kings, they became king-surrogates or "sacred" kings as the power of real monarchies developed. The Gospels' Jesus was certainly not the first of them, though he may have been one of the last. One passage hints at a holy man's understandable fear of such brief, doomed eminence: "When Jesus therefore perceived that they would come and take him by force, to make him a king, he departed again into a mountain himself alone" (John 6:15).

This Jesus seems to have made little or no impression on his contemporaries. No literate person of his own time mentioned him in any known writing. The Gospels were not written in his own time, nor were they written by anyone who ever saw him in the flesh. The names of the apostles attached to these books were fraudulent. The books were composed after the establishment of the church, some as late as the second century CE or later, according to the church's requirements for a manufactured

---

[6] Graves, *Greek Myths*, vol. 2, p. 396.
[7] Albright, p. 262.
[8] Richard Payne Knight, *A Discourse on the Worship of Priapus*. (New York: University Books, 1974), p. 113.
[9] Franz Cumont, *Oriental Religions in Roman Paganism*. (New York: Dover Publications, 1956), p. 119.

tradition.[10] Most scholars believe the earliest book of the New Testament was 1 Thessalonians, written perhaps 51 CE by Paul, who never saw Jesus in person and knew no details of his life story.[11]

The details were accumulated through later adoption of the myths attached to every savior-god throughout the Roman Empire. Like Adonis, Jesus was born of a consecrated temple maiden in the sacred cave of Bethlehem, "The House of Bread."[12] He was eaten in the form of bread, as were Adonis, Osiris, Dionysus, and others; he called himself the bread of God (John 6:33). Like worshippers of Osiris, those of Jesus made him part of themselves by eating him, so as to participate in his resurrection: "He that eateh my flesh, and drinketh my blood, dwelleth in me, and I in him" (John 6:56).

Like Attis, Jesus was sacrificed at the spring equinox and rose again from the dead on the third day, when he became God and ascended to heaven. Like Orpheus and Heracles, he "harrowed hell" and brought a secret of eternal life, promising to draw all men with him up to glory (John 12:32). Like Mithra and all the other solar gods, he celebrated a birthday nine months later at the winter solstice, because the day of his death was also the day of his cyclic re-conception.

From the elder gods, Jesus acquired not only his title of Christos but all his other titles as well. Osiris and Tammuz were called Good Shepherd. Sarapis was Lord of Death and King of Glory. Mihra and Heracles were Light of the World, Sun of Righteousness, Helios the Rising Sun. Dionysus was King of Kings, God of Gods. Hermes was the Enlightened One and the Logos. Vishnu and Mithra were Son of Man and Messiah. Adonis was the Lord and the Bridegroom. Mot-Aleyin was the Lamb of God. "Savior" (Soter) was applied to all of them.

---

[10] H. Smith, *Man and His Gods*, pp. 179-180.
[11] Morton Scott Enslin, *The Literature of the Early Christian Movement*. (New York: Harper & Brothers, 1938), pp. 233-238.
[12] Frazer, *Golden Bough*, p. 402; Robert Briffault, *The Mothers*. (New York: Macmillan, 1927), vol. 3, p. 97.

Mystery cults everywhere taught that ordinary men could be possessed by the spirits of such gods, and identified with them as "sons" or alter egos, as Jesus was. It was the commonly accepted way to acquire supernatural powers, as shown by some of the charms used by magicians:

> Whatever I say must happen For I have taken to myself the power of Abraham, Isaac, and Jacob and of the great god-demon Iao Ablanathanalba...for I am the Son, I surpass the limit....I am he who is in the seven heavens, who standeth in the seven sanctuaries; for I am the son of the living God....I have been united with thy sacred form. I have been empowered by thy sacred name. I have received the effluence of goodness, Lord, God of gods, King, Demon....having attained that nature equal to the God's.[13]

The skeptical Celsus noted that beggars and vagabonds throughout the Empire were pretending to work miracles and become gods, throwing fits, prophesying the end of the world, and aspiring to the status of saviors:

Each has the convenient and customary spiel, "I am the god," or "a son of God," or "a divine spirit," and "I have come. For the world is about to be destroyed, and you, men, because of your injustice, will go (with it). But I wish to save, and you shall see me again coming back with heavenly power. Blessed is he who worships me now! On all others, both cities and countrysides, I shall cast eternal fire. And men who (now) ignore their punishments shall repent in vain and groan, but those who believed in me I shall preserve immortal."[14]

Of course this "conspicuously false" doctrine was the central message of the Gospels too. Persian eschatology passing through a Jewish-Essenic filter predicted "the Son of Man coming in a cloud with power and great glory" (Luke 9:27; 21:27). Jesus promised the end of the world in his own generation. The rest of the Gospel material was largely devoted to the miracles supposed to demonstrate his divine power, since religions

---

[13] Morton Smith, *Jesus the Magician*. (San Francisco: Harper & Row, 1978), pp. 102-104.
[14] Ibid. p. 117.

generally "adduce revelations, apparitions, prophecies, miracles, prodigies and sacred mysteries that they may get themselves valued and accepted."[15] Even these miracles were derivative. Turning water into wine at Cana was copied from a Dionysian ritual practiced at Sidon and other places.[16] In Alexandria the same Dionysian miracle was regularly shown before crowds of the faithful, assisted by an ingenious system of vessels and siphons, invented by a clever engineer named Heron.[17] Many centuries earlier, priestesses at Nineveh cured the blind with spittle, and the story was repeated of many different gods and their incarnations.[18] Demeter of Eleusis multiplied loaves and fishes in her role of Mistress of Earth and Sea. Healing the sick, raising the dead, casting out devils, handling poisonous serpents (Mark 16:18), etc., were so commonplace that Celsus scorned these "Christian" miracles as: "nothing more than the common works of those enchanters who, for a few *oboli*, will perform greater deeds in the midst of the Forum....The magicians of Egypt cast out evil spirits, cure diseases by a breath, and so influence some uncultured men, that they produce in them whatever sights and sounds they please. But because they do such things shall we consider them the sons of God?"[19]

Magicians often claimed that their prayers could bring flocks of supernatural beings to their assistance.[20] Thus Jesus declared that his prayer could summon twelve legions (72,000) of guardian angels (Matthew 26:53). Magicians also communed with their followers by the standard mystery-cult sacrament of bread-flesh and wine-blood. In texts on magic, "a magician-god gives his own body and blood to a recipient who, by eating it, will be united with him in love."[21] The ability to walk on water

---

[15] Charles Guignebert, *Ancient, Medieval and Modern Christianity*. (New York: University Books, 1961), p. 371.
[16] M. Smith, *Jesus the Magician*, pp. 25, 120.
[17] L. Sprague de Camp, *The Ancient Engineers*. (New York: Ballantine Books, 1960), p. 258.
[18] Edward S. Gifford, Jr., *The Evil Eye*. (New York: Macmillan, 1958), p. 63.
[19] T.W. Doane, *Bible Myths and their Parallels in Other Religions*. (New York: University Books, 1971), p. 272.
[20] M. Smith, *Jesus the Magician*, p. 109.
[21] Ibid. p. 123.

was claimed by Far-Eastern holy men ever since Buddhist monks praised it as the mark of the true ascetic.[22] The Magic Papyri said almost anyone could walk on water with the help of "a powerful demon."[23] Impossibilities have always been the props of religious credulity, as Tertullian admitted: "It is believable because it is absurd; it is certain because it is impossible."[24]

However, repetitive miracles were not so believable as original ones. Therefore early Christians insisted that all the older deities and their miracle-tales were invented by the devil, out of his foreknowledge of the true religion, so the faithful would be confused by past "imitations."[25] Pagan thinkers countered with the observation that "the Christian religion contains nothing but what Christians hold in common with heathens; nothing new, nor truly great." Even St. Augustine, finding the hypothesis of the devil's inventions hard to swallow, admitted that "the true religion" was known to the ancients, and had existed from the beginning of time, but it began to be called Christian after "Christ came in the flesh."[26]

Nevertheless, adherents of the true religion violently disagreed as to the circumstances of its foundation. In the first few centuries CE, there were many mutually hostile Christian sects, and many mutually contradictory Gospels. As late as 450, Bishop Theodore of Cyrrhus said there were at least 200 different Gospels revered by the churches of his own diocese, until he destroyed all but the canonical four.[27] The other Gospels were lost as stronger sects overwhelmed the weaker, wrecked their churches, and burned their books.[28]

---

[22] W.Y. Evans-Wentz, trans., *Bardo Thödol* [Tibetan Book of the Dead]. (New York: Oxford University Press, 1927), p. 158; Mark Tatz and Jody Kent, *Rebirth*. (New York: Doubleday Anchor Books, 1977), p. 167.
[23] M. Smith, *Jesus the Magician*, p. 120.
[24] Samuel Angus, *The Mystery Religions*. (New York: Dover Publications, 1975), p. 268.
[25] J.M. Robertson, *Pagan Christs*. (New York: University Books, 1967), p. 112.
[26] Doane, Bible Myths and their Parallels in Other Religions, pp. 409-411.
[27] M. Smith, *Jesus the Magician*, p. 2.
[28] H. Smith, *Man and His Gods*, p. 189.

One scripture, later thrown out of the canon, said Jesus was not crucified. Simon of Cyrene suffered on the cross in his place, while Jesus stood by laughing at the executioners, saying, "It was another...who drank the gall and vinegar; it was not I...it was another, Simon, who bore the cross on his shoulder. It was another upon whom they placed the crown of thorns. But I was rejoicing in the height....And I was laughing at their ignorance."[29] Believers in this scripture were persecuted and forced to sign an abjuration reading: "I anathematize those who say that Our Lord suffered only in appearance, and that there was a man on the cross and another at a distance who laughed."[30]

Some Christians interpreted Jesus's *noli me tangere* ("Touch me not") to mean he came back from death as an incorporeal spirit, after the manner of other apotheosized heroes, such as the Irish hero Laegaire, who also told his people not to touch him.[31] Later, an unknown Gospel writer inserted the story of doubting Thomas, who insisted on touching Jesus. This was to combat the heretical idea that there was no resurrection in the flesh, and also to subordinate Jerusalem's municipal god Tammuz (Thomas) to the new savior. Actually, the most likely source of primary Christian mythology was the Tammuz cult in Jerusalem. Like Tammuz, Jesus was the Bridegroom of the Daughter of Zion (John 12:15). Therefore his bride was Anath, "Virgin Wisdom Dwelling in Zion," who was also the Mother of God.[32] Her dove descended on him at his baptism, signifying (in the old religion) that she chose him for the love-death. Anath broke her bridegroom's reed scepter, scourged him, and pierced him for fructifying blood. She pronounced his death curse, Maranatha (1 Corinthians 16:22). As the Gospels said of Jesus, Anath's bridegroom was

---

[29] Elaine Pagels, *The Gnostic Gospels*. (New York: Random House, 1979), pp. 72-73.
[30] Salomon Reinach, *Orpheus*. (New York: Horace Liveright, 1930), p. 245.
[31] P.W. Joyce, *A Social History of Ancient Ireland*. (New York: Arno Press, 1980), vol. 1, p. 298.
[32] Geoffrey Ashe, *The Virgin*. (London: Routledge & Kegan Paul, 1976), p. 31.

"forsaken" by El, his heavenly father.[33] Jesus's cry to El, "My God, my God, why hast thou forsaken me?" seems to have been a line written for the second act of the sacred drama, the pathos or Passion (Mark 15:34).

Of course this Passion was originally a sexual one. Jesus' last words "It is consummated" (*consummatum est*) were interpreted as a sign that his work was finished, but could equally apply to his marriage (John 19:30). As a cross or pillar represented the divine phallus, so a temple represented the body of the Goddess, whose "veil" (hymen) was "rent in the midst" as Jesus passed into death (Luke 23:45). As usual when the god disappeared into the underworld, the sun was eclipsed (Luke 23:44). In their ignorance of astronomical phenomena, Christians claimed that the moon was full at the same time—Easter is still a full-moon festival, though an eclipse of the sun can only occur at the dark of the moon.[34] The full moon really meant impregnation of the Goddess.

The parting of Jesus' garment recalls the unwrapping of Osiris when he emerged from the tomb as the ithyphallic Min, "Husband of his Mother." If Jesus was one with his heavenly father, then he also married his mother and begot himself. A fourth century scripture said in the underworld he confronted his mother as Death, *Mu*.[35] She was also the Bride disguised as Venus, the evening star, presiding over the death of the sun. Jews still recall her in a ritual greeting to the evening star, "Come, O friend, let us welcome the Bride."[36]

Like pagans, early Christians identified the Bride with the Mother. They said Jesus "consummated on the cross" his union with Mary-Ecclesia, his bride the church. Augustine wrote: "Like a bridegroom Christ went forth from his chamber, he went out with a presage of his nuptials....He came to the marriage bed of the cross, and there, in mounting

---

[33] *Larousse Encyclopedia of Mythology*. (London: Hamlyn Publishing Group, 1968), p. 77.
[34] Henry Cornelius Agrippa, *The Philosophy of Natural Magic*. (Secaucus: University Books, 1974), p. 71.
[35] S.G.F. Brandon, *Religion in Ancient History*. (New York: Scribners, 1969), p. 45.
[36] Eithne Wilkins, *The Rose-Garden Game*. (London: Victor Gollancz, 1969), p. 143.

it, he consummated his marriage..., he lovingly gave himself up to the torment in place of his bride, and he joined himself to the woman for ever." John 19:41 says, "In the place where he was crucified there was a garden; and in the garden a new sepulchre, wherein was never man yet laid." A garden was the conventional symbol for the body of the mother/bride;[37] and a new tomb was the virgin womb, whence the god would be born again. On the third day, Jesus rose from the tomb/womb like Attis, whose resurrection was the Hilaria, Jesus Christ or Day of Joy.[38] Jesus' resurrection day was named after Eostre, the same Goddess as Astarte, whom the Syrians called Mother Mari.[39] Three incarnations of Mari, or Mary, stood at the foot of Jesus' cross, like the Moerae of Greece. One was his virgin mother. The second was his "dearly beloved" (see Mary Magdalene). The third Mary must have represented the Crone (the fatal Moera), so the tableau resembled that of the three Norns at the foot of Odin's sacrificial tree. The Fates were present at the sacrifices decreed by Heavenly Fathers, whose victims hung on trees or pillars "between heaven and earth." Up to Hadrian's time, victims offered to Zeus at Salamis were anointed with sacred ointments—thus becoming "Anointed Ones" or "Christs"—then hung up and stabbed through the side with a spear.[40] Nothing in Jesus' myth occurred at random; every detail was part of a formal sacrificial tradition, even to the "procession of palms" which glorified sacred kings in ancient Babylon.[41]

Far-Eastern traditions were utilized too. The Roman Empire was well aware of the teachings and myths of Buddhism. Buddha images in classic Greek style were made in Pakistan and Afghanistan in the first century

---

[37] Richard Cavendish, *The Powers of Evil*. (New York: Putnam's, 1975), p. 54; Cavendish, *The Tarot*. (New York: Harper & Row, 1975), p. 75.
[38] Frazer, *Golden Bough*, p. 407.
[39] H. Smith, *Man and His Gods*, p. 201.
[40] Ibid. p. 135.
[41] James B. Pritchard, ed., *The Ancient Near East: An Anthology of Texts and Pictures*. (Princeton: Princeton University Press, 1958), p. 204.

CE[42] Buddhist ideas like the "footprints of Buddha" appeared among Christians. Bishop Sulpicius of Jerusalem reported that, as in India, "In the dust where Christ trod the marks of His step can still be seen, and the earth still bears the print of His feet."[43] Buddhist metaphors and phrasing also appeared in the Gospels. Jesus' formula, "Dearly Beloved," was the conventional way for Tantric deities to address their teachings to Devi, their Goddess.[44]

Scholars' efforts to eliminate paganism from the Gospels in order to find a historical Jesus have proved as hopeless as searching for a core in an onion.[45] Like a mirage, the Jesus figure looks clear at a distance but lacks approachable solidity. "His" sayings and parables came from elsewhere; "his" miracles were old twice-told tales. Even the Lord's Prayer was a collection of sayings from the Talmud, many derived from earlier Egyptian prayers to Osiris.[46] The Sermon on the Mount, sometimes said to contain the essence of Christianity, had no original material; it was made up of fragments from Psalms, Ecclesiastes, Isaiah, Secrets of Enoch, and the Shemone Esreh.[47]

Moreover, it was unknown to the author of the oldest Gospel, pseudo-Mark.[48] The discovery that the Gospels were forged, centuries later than the events they described, is still not widely known even though the Catholic Encyclopedia admits, "The idea of a complete and clear-cut canon of the New Testament existing from the beginning…has no foundation in history." No extant manuscript can be dated earlier than the fourth

---

[42] Nancy Wilson Ross, *Three Ways of Asian Wisdom*. (New York: Simon & Schuster, 1966), p. 100.
[43] Jacobus de Voragine, *The Golden Legend*. (New York: Longmans, Green, 1941), p. 287.
[44] John Woodroffe, trans., *Mahanirvanatantra*. (New York: Dover Publications, 1972), p. 173.
[45] M. Smith, *Jesus the Magician*, p. 4
[46] E.M. Wallis Budge, *Egyptian Magic*. (New York: Dover Publications, 1971), vol.1, p. 16.
[47] H. Smith, *Man and His Gods*, p.186.
[48] Rudolf Augstein, *Jesus Son of Man*. (New York: Urizen Books, 1977), p. 260.

century CE; most were written even later.[49] The oldest manuscripts contradict one another, as also do even the present canon of synoptic Gospels.

The church owed its canon to the Gnostic teacher Marcion, who first collected Pauline epistles about the middle of the second century. Later he was excommunicated as a heretic because he denied that the scriptures were mystical allegories full of magic words of power. The epistles he collected were already over a century old, if indeed they were written by Paul; much of their material was made up of forged interpolations.[50]

The most "historical" figure in the Gospels was Pontius Pilate, to whom Jesus was presented as "king" of the Jews and simultaneously as a criminal deserving the death penalty for "blasphemy" because he called himself Christ, Son of the Blessed (Luke 23:3; Mark 14:61-64). This alleged crime was no real crime. Eastern provinces swarmed with self-styled Christs and Messiahs, calling themselves Sons of God and announcing the end of the world. None of them was executed for "blasphemy."[51] The beginning of the story probably lay in the tradition of sacred-king sacrifice in Jerusalem long before Pilate's administration, when Rome was trying to discourage such barbarisms.

From 103 to 76 BC, Jerusalem was governed by Alexander Janneaus, called the Aeon, who defended his throne by fighting challengers. One year, on the Day of Atonement, his people attacked him at the altar, waving palm branches to signify that he should die for the Earth's fertility. Alexander declined the honor and instituted a persecution of his own subjects. Another king of Jerusalem took the name of Menelaus, "Moon-king," and practiced the rite of sacred marriage in the temple.[52] Herod also made a sacred marriage, and had John the Baptist slain as a surrogate for himself.

---

[49] Charles F. Pfeifer, *The Dead Sea Scrolls and the Bible*. (New York: Weathervane Books, 1969), p. 103.
[50] Reinach, *Orpheus*, pp. 256, 277.
[51] Brandon, Religion in Ancient History, p. 248.
[52] Pfeifer, The Dead Sea Scrolls and the Bible, pp. 72-74, 120.

If there was a Jesus cult in Jerusalem after 30 CE, it completely disappeared forty years later when Titus conquered the city and outlawed many local customs, including human sacrifice. Jerusalem was wholly Romanized under Hadrian. It was newly named Aelia Capitolina and rededicated to the Goddess. The temple became a shrine of Venus.[53] Tacitus described the siege of Jerusalem, but his writing is abruptly cut off at the moment when Roman forces entered the city as if the final chapters were deliberately destroyed—so no one knows what the Romans found there. However, Romans did express disapproval of the Jews' or Christians' cannibalistic sacraments. Porphyry called it "absurd beyond all absurdity, and bestial beyond every sort of bestiality, that a man should taste human flesh and drink the blood of men of his own genus and species, and by doing should have eternal life."[54]

From the Christians' viewpoint, a real historical Jesus was essential to the basic premise of the faith: the possibility of immortality through identification with his own death and resurrection. Wellhausen rightly said Jesus would have no place in history unless he died and returned exactly as the Gospels said.[55] "If Christ hath not been raised, your faith is vain" (1 Corinthians 15:17). Still, despite centuries of research, no historical Jesus has come to light. It seems his story was not merely overlaid with myth; it was mythic to the core.

Like all myths, it revealed much about the collective psychology that created it. In earlier pagan religions, the Mother and Son periodically ousted the Father from his heavenly throne. The divine son Jesus Christ of Christianity no longer challenged the heavenly king, but tamely submitted to his fatal command: "Not my will, but thine, be done" (Luke 22:42). Some early sects said the Father who demanded his son's blood was cruel, even demonic.[56] These were suppressed, but scholars have

---

[53] "Jerusalem," *Encyclopaedia Britannica*. (Third Edition, 1970).
[54] M. Smith, *Jesus the Magician*, p. 66.
[55] Guignebert, Ancient, Medieval and Modern Christianity, p. 47.
[56] Francis Legge, *Forerunners and Rivals of Christianity*. (New York: University Books, 1964), vol. 2, p. 239.

discerned in Christianity "an original attitude of hostility toward the father figure, which was changed in the first two Christian centuries into an attitude of passive masochistic docility."[57]

If orthodox Christianity demanded subordination of the Son, it was even more determined to subordinate the Mother. The Gospels' Jesus showed little respect for his mother, which troubled the church in its Renaissance efforts to attract women to the cult of Mary. "Any hero who speaks to his mother only twice, and on both occasions addresses her as 'Woman,' is a difficult figure for the sentimental biographers."[58] Together with Jesus' avowed opposition to marriage and the family (Matthew 22:30; Luke 14:26), women's primary concerns, New Testament sexism tended to disgust educated women of the pagan world.

But the Jesus who emulated Buddha in advocating poverty and humility eventually became the mythic figurehead for one of the world's preeminent money-making organizations. The cynical Pope Leo X exclaimed, "What profit has not that fable of Christ brought us!"[59]

Modern theologians tend to sidestep the question of whether Jesus was in fact a fable or a real person. In view of the complete dearth of hard evidence, and the dubious nature of the soft evidence, it seems Christianity is based on the ubiquitous social phenomena of credulity:

> An idea is able to gain and retain the aura of essential truth through telling and retelling. This process endows a cherished notion with more veracity than a library of facts.... [D]ocumentation plays only a small role in contrast to the act of re-confirmation by each generation of scholars. In addition, the further removed one gets from the period in question, the greater is the strength of the conviction. Initial incredulousness is soon converted into belief in a probability and eventually smug assurance.[60]

---

[57] Augstein, *Jesus Son of Man*, p. 309.
[58] M. Smith, *Jesus the Magician*, p. 25.
[59] Sprague de Camp, *The Ancient Engineers*, p. 399.
[60] W. Arens, *The Man-Eating Myth*. (New York: Oxford University Press, 1979), p. 89.

Chapter 3: Dying and Rising Gods
By Derreck Bennett

Ever since Sir James Frazer published *The Golden Bough* in the late nineteenth century, there has been scholarly discussion and debate over the existence of a dying and rising god mythotype. Frazer proposed that various deities from antiquity were modeled after the yearly cycle of vegetation, undergoing death and resurrection in a symbolic portrayal of seasonal death and rebirth. The implications for Christianity were clear, thus the topic has never been without controversy. Religious and even secular scholars, including bestselling author Bart Ehrman, have challenged the concept on several grounds. Most notably among them:

1. The concept is wholly an invention of late nineteenth and early twentieth century scholars, attempting to undermine the resurrection of Jesus.
2. Among the gods who are said to have died and risen, none of them rise bodily or return to the world of the living. Thus, they are not actually resurrected.
3. Some of the gods in question do not truly die. Thus, they are not raised from the dead.
4. Christianity arose from a purely Jewish context, unsullied by pagan ideas from the surrounding Mediterranean world.

I shall examine each of these objections as they apply to some of our strongest examples of dying and rising gods from the ancient world. I will also discuss the various ties that these divinities have with the Judeo-Christian religion, demonstrating the plausibility for their having served as a prototype for Christ. But, first, let us begin with the notion that dying and rising gods are a fabrication of late nineteenth and early twentieth century scholars.

The Scholarly Tide

As early as the second century CE, the Greek philosopher Celsus charged that belief in the resurrection of Jesus was nothing new, that similar tales had been told of Zalmoxis among the Scythians, as well as Pythagoras, Orpheus, Heracles, and Theseus (*Contra Celsum* 2.55). The second century Christian apologist Justin Martyr defended Christianity against pagan critics by arguing that they, too, believed in the heavenly exaltations of Asclepius, Bacchus, and Hercules, following their deaths (*First Apology* 1.21). In asserting the truth of Christianity, however, he reasoned that wicked demons had imitated the prophecies of Christ in advance. In his commentary on Ezekiel, the church father Origen wrote in the third century CE of those who mourned the death of Adonis and rejoiced at his "having risen from the dead" (*Comments on Ezekiel* 8.14). And in the fourth century CE, Christian apologist Firmicus Maternus lamented the sacred rites of Osiris, detailing the burial and raising of an idol, followed by rejoicing (*The Error of the Pagan Religions* 22.1-3).[1] Firmicus derided the practice, emphasizing that, unlike Christ, this god's resurrection had neither been foretold by prophecy nor proven by postmortem appearances. Whether seeking to undermine or uphold the Christian faith, these ancient authors attest to a belief in resurrected gods (or divine men) long before the nineteenth century.

Historically, there doesn't appear to have been any more talk of dying and rising gods until Frazer's bold thesis in the nineteenth century. Though it's hardly difficult to imagine why. After the Emperor

---

[1] Firmicus does not explicitly identify the god in question, leading some scholars to attribute this to the cult of Attis. However, his description of symbolically reassembling the body of the cult-deity matches Osiris, not Attis. See Clarence A. Forbes, trans., Firmicus Maternus: *The Error of the Pagan Religions*. (New York: Newman Press, 1970), 207.

Theodosius banned all pagan practices in the fourth century, there were no competing cults or revivified gods to speak of. And nary would one speak of such a thing until after biblical criticism arose in the eighteenth century, in the wake of the Enlightenment. This, of course, was when the doors were thrown open to investigate the past and question long-held dogmas.

But Frazer's thesis would undergo criticism for many years to come, including a perceived oversimplification, i.e., that all such dying and rising gods could be subsumed under a single category. These deities cropped up in different locales, under disparate cultural contexts, and not all of them could be directly tied to the seasonal death and return of vegetation. The biggest blow to the Frazerian concept of dying and rising gods came in 1987, with Jonathan Z. Smith's deconstruction of the concept in an article that was published in Mircea Eliade's *Encyclopedia of Religion*.[2] Smith argued that a closer examination of the sources revealed two types of divinities among those in question: dying gods, who stayed dead, and gods who merely disappeared. Thus the Egyptian Osiris, whose revivification does not entail a return to this world, is essentially a dead god, while Baal, Tammuz, and Adonis only undergo a seasonal departure to the underworld—thus not a genuine death. Texts that do suggest a resurrection of Attis and Adonis appear in the early centuries of the Common Era, following the rise of Christianity, thus any borrowing may have been from the latter to the former. Scholars have generally followed Smith's lead, thus the long-held consensus in scholarship could well be encapsulated by biblical scholar Mark S. Smith's article: *The Death of 'Dying and Rising Gods' in the Biblical World*.[3]

In 2001, this consensus began to be challenged by Swedish scholar Tryggve Mettinger, in his comprehensive work, *The Riddle of Resurrection:*

---

[2] Jonathan Z. Smith, "Dying and Rising Gods," *The Encyclopedia of Religion*, Mircea Eliade, ed. (New York: Macmillan, 1987), vol. 4, pp. 521-27.
[3] Mark S. Smith, The Death of 'Dying and Rising Gods' in the *Biblical World: An Update with Special Reference to Baal in the Baal Cycle.* (SJOT, 1998), vol. 12, pp. 257-313.

"Dying and Rising Gods" in the Ancient Near East. According to Mettinger,[4] Baal, Melqart-Heracles, Adonis, and Eshmun-Asclepius qualified as having died in some manner and returned to life, though the latter two are still only attested in the Christian era. Osiris, though raised, remained king of the netherworld. Despite this apparent vindication of dying and rising gods, Mettinger cautioned against making any definitive connections with the death and resurrection of Christ.[5]

In 2014, M. David Litwa, a scholar of ancient Mediterranean religions, published *Iesus Deus: The Early Christian Depiction of Jesus as a Mediterranean God.*[6] There, he upholds Jonathan Z. Smith's critiques of dying and rising gods, but nevertheless argues that the corporeal immortalizations of, e.g., Asclepius, Heracles, and Romulus form the backdrop for understanding the earliest depictions of Christ's resurrection and apotheosis.[7] Litwa makes the case that, like Jesus, these figures were raised in a new and glorified body, by which they were deified and made immortal. Though, in the case of Heracles and Romulus, their immortalizations may be better understood as post-*mortal*, rather than post-*mortem*, since the narrative evidence for their deaths is ambiguous. Litwa's work represents an attempt to restore balance to comparative religion and Christian origins, seeking a middle ground between parallelomania (focusing on pure similarity) and apologetics (focusing on pure difference).[8]

Most recently, in 2018, New Testament scholar John Granger Cook affirmed the existence of dying and rising gods in his 717-page tome,

---

[4] Tryggve N.D. Mettinger, The Riddle of Resurrection: "Dying and Rising Gods" in *The Ancient Near East*, Coniectanea Biblica Old Testament Series 50. (Stockholm: Almqvist & Wiksell International, 2001).

[5] Mettinger, The Riddle of Resurrection: "Dying and Rising Gods", p. 221.

[6] M. David Litwa, Iesus Deus: The Early Christian Depiction of Jesus as a Mediterranean God. (Minneapolis: Fortress Press, 2014).

[7] Ibid. 141-79. Similar comparisons are made by Richard C. Miller, in *Resurrection and Reception in Early Christianity*. (New York: Routledge, 2015). See also Dag Øistein Endsjø, *Greek Resurrection Beliefs and the Success of Christianity*. (New York: Macmillan, 2009).

[8] Ibid. p. 33.

Empty Tomb, Resurrection, Apotheosis.[9] Cook's survey of the deities in question "indicates fairly clearly that the category of 'dying and rising gods' is still useful to describe the vicissitudes of a number of ancient divinities," and thus "the thesis that the concept is dead cannot be sustained."[10] Cook summarizes his findings thusly:

> The review in this chapter thoroughly justifies the continued use of the category of dying and rising gods. The resurrection of Osiris is the closest analogy to the resurrection of Jesus, although Osiris remains in the netherworld—wherever it is located. Horus's resurrection is a clear analogy. The rebirth or resurrection of Dionysus also provides a fairly close analogy to the resurrection of Jesus. The revival of Heracles and probably that of Melqart are also strong analogies. Dumuzi's, Baal's, and Adonis's returns from the netherworld are less useful as comparisons, but their power to overcome death is an important analogy to the NT. Lucian was willing to use the image of resurrection for Adonis's return from Hades. Traditions for a resurrection of Adonis and Attis are later than the Gospels, but are nevertheless in good continuity with those from earlier periods (e.g., that of Osiris). Just as the Greek of the LXX and NT has its place in the matrix of classical Greek, so the resurrection of Christ can be placed in the matrix of the bodily resurrections of cult figures from the Mediterranean world.[11]

Cook seeks only to establish analogical, rather than genealogical, similarities between the resurrection of Christ and other divinities from the ancient world. There is no attempt to demonstrate influence in one direction or the other—only an insistence that the category of dying and rising gods is viable and worthy of comparison with the New Testament imagery of resurrection. Thus, Mettinger and Cook, on the one hand, uphold the existence of a dying and rising god mythotype, but withhold from drawing any conclusions about their influence on nascent Christianity. Litwa,

---

[9] John Granger Cook, *Empty Tomb, Resurrection, Apotheosis.* (Tübingen: Mohr Siebeck, 2018).
[10] Cook, Empty Tomb, Resurrection, Apotheosis, p. 62.
[11] Ibid. p. 143.

on the other hand, dispenses with the category of dying and rising gods, but ventures to demonstrate the adoption and adaption of Hellenistic motifs in the early Christian depiction of Christ's resurrection. Whatever the case may be, the notion that dying and rising gods and pagan influences are a fossil of scholarly speculation from the nineteenth and twentieth centuries is demonstrably false. The discussion is alive and well.

Baal of the Canaanites

Steeped in the culture of their Canaanite ancestors, many Israelites continued to worship the mighty storm and fertility god, Baal. Despite the condemnation of such practices in 1 Kings 18 and Hosea 2, the Baal myth made its impression upon scripture. Yahweh's conquest over Leviathan in Job 41 and Psalm 74 is prefigured by Baal's battle with the serpent, Lotan, which features also in Revelation 20. Hosea 2:16-17 indicates that many identified Baal and Yahweh as one and the same, much to the chagrin of Yahweh: "No longer will you call me Baal" (v. 16). Psalm 104 describes Yahweh as riding on the wings of the wind, just as Baal was the "cloud-rider," and depicts Yahweh's power over the sea using the imagery of Baal's conquest over the sea god, Yam.[12] Likewise, Daniel 7 casts the "Ancient of Days" and the "Son of Man" in roles reminiscent of Baal and the supreme god, El. In Canaanite myth, Baal, the son of El, conquers Mot, the god of death, and is enthroned as king of gods and men.[13] It is no coincidence that Daniel's vision portrays the one like a son of man "coming with the clouds of heaven," a la the cloud-rider, "given authority, glory and sovereign power" (7:13-14).

The myth of Baal's death at the hands of Mot, and subsequent restoration to life, was almost certainly known to the Israelites. Old Testament scholar John Day states that "the imagery of death and resurrection in

---

[12] Walter C. Kaiser Jr. and Duane Garrett, "The Ugaritic Text of the Myth of Baal," *NIV Archaeological Study Bible*. (Grand Rapids: Zondervan, 2005), p. 905.
[13] John J. Collins and Peter W. Flint, ed., *The Book of Daniel: Composition and Reception*. (Leiden: Brill Academic Publishers, 2002), pp. 114-22.

Hosea," which informs subsequent passages in the Hebrew Bible, "is directly taken over by the prophet from the imagery of the dying and rising fertility god, Baal."[14] Texts from the Canaanite city of Ugarit (modern day Ras Shamra) depict the victorious fate of Baal Aleyan, as beheld in a dream by his father, El:

> How has Aleyan the lord died?
> How has perished Zebul, lord of the earth?...
> Like the longing of a young cow for her calf, Like the longing of a ewe for her lamb,
> So was the longing of Anath for the shrine of Baal...
> And he, (Aleyan the lord), lives,
> And he, Zebul, lord (of earth) exists,
> In a favorable dream El (heard);
> "Good tidings, O my son (whom) I have begotten,
> The heavens shall rain oil,
> The valleys shall flow with honey,
> And I know that Aleyan, the lord, lives..."[15]

According to Jonathan Z. Smith, the gaps within the discovered texts make an interpretation of resurrection speculative. Both he and Mark S. Smith deem this a mere descent into the underworld, rather than a genuine death and return to life. However, the texts in question repeatedly emphasize Baal's death: "You must be counted among those who go down into the earth...And the gods will know that you are dead."[16] The goddess Anath even weeps over his corpse and buries him. On this basis, John Day aptly refutes the objections raised by Smith:

> That Baal was regarded as a dying and rising god cannot seriously be disputed...There have been attempts to deny that Baal was a dying and rising god, but these have failed in my view. Mark Smith claims

---

[14] John Day, *Yahweh and the Gods and Goddesses of Canaan*. (New York: Sheffield Academic Press, 2002), pp. 116-17.
[15] George A. Barton, *Archaeology and the Bible*, 7th Edition. (Philadelphia: American Sunday-School Union, 1952), pp. 535-39.
[16] Mettinger, The Riddle of Resurrection: "Dying and Rising Gods", p. 61.

that Baal is a disappearing and returning god like the Hittite weather god Telepinus. However, the two myths use clearly distinct language: Telepinus vanishes, is sought for and eventually found, whereas, as noted above, in the Baal myth there are repeated references to his death, after which he is spoken of as alive. Both H.M. Barstad and Mark Smith claim that the words 'mightiest Baal is alive' do not have to imply resurrection. However, their context in the text, which has previously spoken of Baal's death, requires such an interpretation. I agree with T.N.D. Mettinger when he states that 'The contrast between life and death is basic to the myth.'[17]

Mettinger even includes an ancient immortality spell whereby the hero, Aqhat, is revived in the manner that Baal was:

Ask for life, O hero Aqhat,
Ask for life, and I shall give it to you, Immortality—I shall bestow it on you.
I shall let you count your years with Baal.
Count your months with the sons of El.
Like Baal, as he is revived,
One makes a banquet for the one that is being revived,
One makes a banquet and gives him to drink,
One chants and sings over him, One celebrates him with songs,
So I will make Aqhat the Hero live.[18]

The sources and scholarship firmly establish that Baal was a dying and rising god, the risen son of El, who conquered death and reigned henceforth upon his heavenly throne. Given Jewish familiarity with the Baal myth—the long constancy of his worship in Israel and the indelible mark his story made upon the scriptures—it should come as no surprise that Baal served as a prototype of Christ, the risen Son of God who vanquished death, was enthroned as Lord, and comes upon the clouds of heaven in power and glory.

---

[17] Day, *Yahweh*, p. 117.
[18] Mettinger, The Riddle of Resurrection: "Dying and Rising Gods", p. 69.

The Egyptian Osiris

The New Kingdom period of Egypt saw its empire stretch well into northern Palestine from about the sixteenth to eleventh centuries BCE. Archaeological excavations have unearthed numerous Egyptian artifacts throughout the Levant, including funerary stelae from a cemetery at Deir el-Balah in Gaza depicting the deceased worshiping Osiris, god of the afterlife.[19] As with Canaan, we see in scripture the vestiges of the once dominant culture and its myths. A stele from the Eighteenth Dynasty depicts Osiris' reign over Egypt, and the institution of pharaoh as his earthly representative, in striking analogy to Psalm 78's portrayal of God's reign over Israel, with David installed as his earthly regent.[20] The sibling rivalry between Osiris and his brother Set, who betrayed and murdered him, is reflected in the stories of Cain and Abel, Esau and Jacob, and Joseph and Judah.[21] The book of Revelation features eschatological imagery from ancient Egypt, including judgment of the dead before the throne of Osiris, damnation and torment by a lake of fire, the ominous second death, and the re-creation of the world.[22] The impact that Egyptian religion had upon Judeo-Christianity is unmistakable. And Osiris' place of

---

[19] Carolyn R. Higginbotham, *Egyptianization and Elite Emulation in Ramesside Palestine.* (Leiden: Brill Academic Publishers, 2000), p. 237.

[20] Kaiser and Garrett, "Power Over Egypt in the Hymn to Osiris," *Archaeological Study Bible*, p. 877.

[21] James H. Cumming, *Torah and Nondualism: Diversity, Conflict and Synthesis.* (Lake Worth: Ibis Press, 2019), pp. 57-63.

[22] For judgment of the dead, see Jon Davies, *Death, Burial, and Rebirth in the Religions of Antiquity.* (London: Routledge, 2002), vol. 7, p. 31. Also Jan Assmann, *Death and Salvation in Ancient Egypt.* (Ithaca: Cornell University Press, 2005), pp. 73-77. Job 31 features the confessions of innocence and weighing upon scales known to this Egyptian motif. For the lake of fire and second death, see Erik Hornung, *The Valley of the Kings: Horizon of Eternity.* (New York: Timken Publishers, 1990), pp. 155-56; and Andreas Schweizer, *The Sungod's Journey Through the Netherworld: Reading the Ancient Egyptian Amduat.* (Ithaca: Cornell University Press, 2010), p. 113. For the re-creation of the world, see Erik Hornung, *Conceptions of God in Ancient Egypt.* (Ithaca: Cornell University Press, 1982), pp. 163-64. Also James P. Allen, "The Human Sphere," *Ancient Egypt*, D.P. Silverman, ed. (New York: Oxford University Press, 2003), p. 131.

prominence in the Egyptian pantheon seems to have captured the imaginations of many throughout the Mediterranean world, even on up to the Greco-Roman period.[23]

That Osiris was believed to have been physically raised from the dead is undeniable, given the sheer abundance of texts emphasizing the corporeal reconstitution of the god following his death and dismemberment by Set. A few examples:

> Osiris awakes, the languid god wakes up, the god stands up, the god has power in his body. (Pyramid Texts, Utterance 690 § 2092)[24]
>
> Raise yourself, O King; receive your head, collect your bones, gather your limbs together, throw off the earth from your flesh...Rise up, O King, for you have not died! (Pyramid Texts, Utterance 373 § 654-57)[25]
>
> Osiris, collect thy bones; arrange thy limbs; shake off thy dust; untie thy bandages; the tomb is open for thee; the double doors of the coffin are undone for thee; the double doors of heaven are open for thee...thy soul is in thy body...raise thyself up! (Pyramid Texts, Utterance 676 § 207-209 and 2010-2011)[26]
>
> Raise yourself because of your strength, may you ascend to the sky...may you have power in your body. (Pyramid Texts, Utterance 690 § 2115)[27]

---

[23] Osiris was known to many throughout the Greco-Roman world, including the 1st century Jewish historian Josephus. See *Against Apion* 1.250, translation by W.G. Waddell in Manetho. (Cambridge: Harvard University Press, 1964), p. 131.
[24] Raymond O. Faulkner, *The Ancient Egyptian Pyramid Texts*. (Oxford University Press, 1969), p. 298.
[25] Ibid. pp. 123-24. Invocations such as these are directed at the deceased king, the earthly representative of Osiris, who undergoes the same process of death and resurrection as the god via imitative magic. See S.G.F. Brandon, "The Ritual Technique of Salvation in the Ancient Near East," *The Saviour God: Comparative Studies in the Concept of Salvation*, E.O. James, ed. (Manchester University Press, 1963), p. 17-33.
[26] Samuel Mercer, *The Pyramid Texts*. (London: Longmans, Green, 1952).
[27] Faulkner, The Ancient Egyptian Pyramid Texts, p. 299.

As renowned Egyptologist Erik Hornung states, "The belief that the body lives on after death is one of the most salient features of Egyptian conceptions of the hereafter."[28] This is evident from the references to standing up, shaking off the dust, untying the bandages, being bodily empowered, etc. However, Osiris does not resume his earthly life; rather, he journeys onward, variously to the underworld realm of the Duat or the heavens above, where he rules henceforth from beyond.[29] For this reason, Jonathan Z. Smith and countless Christian apologists dismiss any comparison with the resurrection of Christ. But how sensible is this objection? As comparative religions scholar S.G.F. Brandon noted:

> A crucial factor in the comparison here is that, despite the vivid Gospel accounts of the appearances of the Resurrected Jesus, he is not related to have resumed his life on earth in contemporary Judea, but to have ascended to heaven, where he was believed to live a supernatural existence. There is, therefore, justification for a phenomenological comparison between the deaths and resurrections of Osiris and Christ. Each is raised to life again, by supernatural means, after an unjust death; but each is transformed into a new mode of being, i.e. neither Osiris nor Christ resume their earthly lives but pass on to another world, where they acquire a new status and office, which in each case is that of saviour and judge of the dead.[30]

---

[28] Erik Hornung, *Idea into Image: Essays on Ancient Egyptian Thought*. (New York: Timken Publishers, 1992), p. 103.

[29] Oft-repeated references to the underworld as the "realm of the dead" are misleading. The Egyptian Duat is not equivalent to the Greek Hades. As James P. Allen, Curator at the Department of Egyptian Art, states, the related texts "are not about death but about life: specifically, eternal life which every Egyptian hoped to attain after death" (*Ancient Egyptian Book of the Dead*, Raymond O. Faulkner, trans. [New York: Barnes & Noble Publishing, 2005], p. 11.) Thus was Osiris known, among his many epithets, as "king of the living" (Erik Hornung, *Conceptions of God in Ancient Egypt: The One and the Many*, John Baines, trans. [Cornell University Press, 1996], 233.)

[30] S.G.F. Brandon, "Redemption in Ancient Egypt and Early Christianity," *Types of Redemption: Contributions to the Theme of the Study-Conference Held at Jerusalem*, J. Zwi Werblowsky and C. Jouco Bleeker, ed. (Leiden: E.J. Brill, 1970), pp. 38-39.

This point can be pressed even further when considering the earliest New Testament accounts of Christ's resurrection in the Pauline corpus. There, we read of "the mighty strength [God] exerted when he raised Christ from the dead and seated him at his right hand in the heavenly realms" (Ephesians 1:19-20). Likewise, Hebrews 10:12, Philippians 2:8-9 and 1 Peter 3:21-22 have Christ exalted to heaven upon his resurrection, with no indication of an earthly sojourn beforehand. According to the seminal study by A.W. Zwiep in *The Ascension of the Messiah*, "the general conviction in the earliest Christian preaching is that as of the day of his resurrection Jesus was in heaven, seated at the right hand of God. Resurrection and exaltation were regarded as two sides of one coin; resurrection meant 'resurrection to heaven' or 'resurrection from grave to glory'."[31] Thus, the distinction between the resurrection of Osiris and Christ is not as great as Smith and the apologists would have us believe. Christ's return to a temporal, earthly existence is only emphasized in the later Gospels, and even there it is only temporary. Ultimately, both he and Osiris venture to the world beyond, where they are nonetheless raised to new life.

The comparison is especially profound when we consider the salvific significance attached to these divinities and their conquest of death. In each case, the resurrection of the godman serves as the hope and guarantee of resurrection to eternal life for their devotees.[32] Just as Christians mystically participate in the death and resurrection of Christ via the ritual of

---

[31] A.W. Zwiep, *The Ascension of the Messiah in Lukan Christology*. (Leiden: Brill Academic Publishers, 1997), p. 130. Even the appearances of the risen Christ in 1 Cor. 15:3-8 entail this view, according to Zwiep. They are appearances of the exalted Lord from heaven, just as Paul had claimed for himself (Gal 1:16), and by which he defended his apostleship (1 Cor. 9:1). Paul places his vision of the risen Christ on the same footing as Peter, James, and the other apostles (1 Cor. 15:8), strongly suggesting that they are all of the same nature. See p. 129-31 for elaboration. Resurrection to heaven for those saved is implied in 1 Thess. 4:16-17.

[32] S.G.F. Brandon, "Osiris," Man, Myth, and Magic: Beliefs, Rituals, and Symbols of Ancient Egypt, Mesopotamia, and the Fertile Crescent. (New York: Cavendish Square, 2014), p. 96.

baptism, the Egyptians were ritually identified with the death and resurrection of Osiris via embalmment.[33]

As Christians are justified by the resurrection of Christ, so the Egyptians hoped to be justified in the image of the risen Osiris.[34] And as both divinities were considered saviors, they likewise both presided as judge, determining the final fate of those passing from this world to the next. S.G.F. Brandon said it best: "Phenomenologically, if not historically, Osiris was thus a prototype of Christ."[35]

Greco-Roman Resurrection and Apotheosis

In the fourth century BCE, Alexander the Great conquered half the known world, extending his empire as far east as India and including such territories as Asia Minor, Egypt, Persia, Babylonia, and the Levant. He inaugurated what is known as the Hellenistic Age, a time of unprecedented sharing of ideas between formerly disparate cultures, resulting in rampant religious syncretism. Alexander himself became known as the son of Zeus-Ammon, a fusion of the supreme gods of Greece and Egypt. Under the Ptolemies, Greek rulers of Alexandria, the god Serapis was introduced, a composite of Osiris and the Apis bull of Egypt with major Greek divinities including Zeus, Helios, Dionysus, Hades, and Asclepius. No less affected by these cultural mergings were the Jews of the Second Temple period. Despite zealous opposition against such cultural appropriation by more conservative Jews, 2 Maccabees informs us of "an extreme of Hellenization and increase in the adoption of foreign ways" (4:13). Thus the discovery of Hellenistic astrology in the Dead Sea Scrolls, the

---

[33] Brandon, *Redemption*, pp. 39-41. See also Mark J. Smith, "Resurrection and the Body in Graeco-Roman Egypt," The Human Body in Death and Resurrection, T. Nicklas, ed., *Deuterocanonical and Cognate Literature Yearbook*. (Berlin: 2009), p. 35.
[34] Ibid. pp. 42-43. Cf. Mark J. Smith, "Osiris and the Deceased," *UCLA Encyclopedia of Egyptology*, W. Wendrich, ed. (Los Angeles: 2008), pp. 1-2.
[35] Brandon, Man, Myth, and Magic, p. 96.

adoption of Greek ideas like the Logos and immortality of the soul in Jewish literature, and the use of mystery religion concepts and terminology by Paul of Tarsus, arguably a Hellenized Jew like his contemporary, Philo of Alexandria.[36] As M. David Litwa observes:

> Christianity was born from a Jewish mother who was already hellenized...In the time of Jesus himself, Palestinian Jews had thoroughly adopted and adapted Greek ideas (including theological ones) to such an extent that in many cases what appears to be a distinctly "Jewish" notion is in fact a "Greco-Jewish" cultural hybrid.[37]

Among the Greeks, Dionysus was the god of theater, fertility, and wine, and was believed to be the son of Zeus and a mortal woman, Semele. The infant Dionysus was torn apart by the evil Titans (giants), but restored to life, variously by Rhea or Demeter. The Epicurean, Philodemus, records that "after his dismemberment by the Titans, Rhea gathered together his limbs and he came to life again" (*On Piety* 44). Similarly, Diodorus of Sicily relates, "his members were brought together again by Demeter and he experienced a new birth as if for the first time" (*Library of History* 3.62.6). Plutarch explicitly identifies Dionysus with Osiris, stating, "the tales regarding the Titans and the rites celebrated by night agree with the accounts of the dismemberment of Osiris and his revivification

---

[36] For Hellenistic astrology in the Dead Sea Scrolls, see Matthias Albani, "Horoscopes," *Encyclopedia of the Dead Sea Scrolls*, Lawrence H. Schiffman and James C. Vanderkam, ed. (New York, Oxford: Oxford University Press, 2000), vol. 1, p. 370. Also Helen R. Jacobus, "4Q318: A Jewish Zodiac Calendar at Qumran?" *The Dead Sea Scrolls: Texts and Context*, Charlotte Hempel, ed. (Brill, 2010), pp. 365-95. For immortality of the soul in Jewish literature, see Geza Vermes, *The Resurrection: History and Myth*. (New York: Doubleday, 2008), pp. 35-45, 124. For adoption of the Greek Logos, see Samuel Sandmel, *A Jewish Understanding of the New Testament*, 3rd Edition. (Woodstock: Jewish Lights Publishing, 2005), pp. 48-51, including discussion of Paul and Philo as Hellenized Jews. For the most recent exposition of mystery religion concepts and terminology in the Pauline corpus, see Richard Carrier, *On the Historicity of Jesus: Why We Might Have Reason for Doubt*. (Sheffield Phoenix Press, 2014), pp. 96-124. Also noteworthy is Marvin Meyer, *The Ancient Mysteries: A Sourcebook of Sacred Texts*. (Philadelphia: University of Pennsylvania Press, 1987), pp. 225-27, 252-54.
[37] Litwa, *Iesus Deus*, pp. 15-16.

and regenesis" (*Isis and Osiris* 35.364). Clearly, there had been syncretism with the Egyptian myth of Osiris, given the imagery of bodily dismemberment, reassembly, and resurrection.

Origen's description of rejoicing for the risen Adonis is entirely consistent with that of the second century author Lucian:

> They say, at any rate, that the deed that was done to Adonis by the boar (the death of the god) occurred in their land, and in memory of that misfortune every year they beat their breasts and mourn and perform the ceremonies, making solemn lamentations throughout the country. And when the breast-beating and weeping is at end, first they make offerings to Adonis as if to a dead person; and then, on the next day, they proclaim that he is alive and fetch him forth into the air (*On the Syrian Goddess* 6-8).

Jonathan Z. Smith infers from the fetching forth into the air of Adonis that a statue or replica of the god was in use, thus proclamations of being "alive" are not indicative of resurrection but are "the common presupposition of any cultic activity in the Mediterranean world that uses images."[38] But, once again, Smith seems to overlook the contrast between life and death, as in the Baal myth. And the use of statues or idols does not preclude a belief in resurrection for Adonis any more than it did for Osiris, whose resurrection was celebrated in much the same manner.[39] John Granger Cook remarks that Smith "probably does not succeed in showing there is no proof of belief in resurrection" for Adonis.[40] But if Adonis was believed to have risen from the dead, was he so conceived prior to Christianity? The answer must come in the affirmative on the basis of a poem by Theocritus of the third century BCE, wherein Adonis dies and returns annually from the underworld (*Idylls* 3, 15). As classical

---

[38] J.Z. Smith, Dying and Rising Gods.
[39] Firmicus Maternus, *Error of the Pagan Religions*, 22. 1-3. Cf. Jan Assmann, Death and Salvation in Ancient Egypt, pp. 227-29 concerning the use of a statue or idol of "the vindicated and resurrected Osiris" in the festival procession of Ikhernofret, according to a well-known stela of the Middle Kingdom era.
[40] Cook, *Empty Tomb*, p. 99.

historian Robin L. Fox states, "Lucian is not innovating when he reports the worshippers' claim that Adonis had 'come alive.'"[41]

The seventh century BCE poet and wonder-worker Aristeas was said to have died in a fuller's shop, after which he appeared alive again. Herodotus tells us that, following his death, his relatives came to the shop prepared to bury him, but he was no longer there. Meanwhile, a man had reported meeting him on the road to Cyzicus (*Histories* 4.14; cf. Plutarch, *Life of Romulus* 28.4). Likewise, Apollonius reports that "at the very time of his death in a fuller's shop in Proconnesus, many saw him in Sicily teaching" (*Mirabilia* 2.1-2). His continued appearances in Sicily afforded him recognition and honors as an immortal god.

The Greek physician Asclepius was struck dead by Zeus after raising too many from the dead, though Zeus later relented and raised Asclepius to godhood (Ovid, *Metamorphoses* 2.647-48). Thus, the second century Christian apologist Theophilus of Antioch declares to the pagan, "You believe that Heracles, who burned himself up, is alive and that Asclepius, struck by lightning, was raised" (*Autolycus* 1.13). Asclepius thereafter appeared in dream visions, healing the lame, the blind, and the paralytic (*First Apology* 22:6). Though, as Celsus states, Greeks and barbarians alike saw "no mere phantom, but Asclepius himself, healing, doing good and predicting the future" (*Contra Celsum* 3.24). Maximus of Tyre likewise claims to have seen Asclepius, "and that not in a dream" (*Orations* 9.7). Philostratus reports that Antiochus of Aegae conversed with Asclepius while fully awake (*Lives of the Sophists* 2.568). As classical scholar Emma Edelstein writes, "if Asclepius the god had died, he had to come to life again, he had to become immortal, for he was ever-present in his temples."[42]

---

[41] Robin L. Fox, *Travelling Heroes in the Epic Age of Homer*. (New York: Alfred A. Knopf, 2009), p. 234.
[42] Emma J. Edelstein and Ludwig Edelstein, *Asclepius: Collection and Interpretation of the Testimonies*. (Baltimore: Johns Hopkins Press, 1945), vol. 2. p. 75. In some versions of the myth, Asclepius is raised and placed among the stars as a constellation in the night sky (Ovid, Fasti 6.735; cf. Daniel 12:2-3). Variation on

"Not even the mighty Heracles escaped death," Homer tells us in the *Iliad* (18.117). Though Hesiod informs us that, after he died and went to Hades, he became a god upon Mt. Olympus, "immortal and ageless" (*Catalogue of Women*, frag. 25.25-28). According to Diodorus of Sicily, Heracles was dying from poison when he mounted a funeral pyre which was set ablaze.

And immediately lightning fell from the heavens and the pyre was wholly consumed. After this, when the companions of Iolaüs came to gather up the bones of Heracles and found not a single bone anywhere, they assumed that, in accordance with the words of the oracle, he had passed from among men into the company of the gods (*Library of History* 4.38.3-5).

The missing body of Heracles is comparable to Jesus' empty tomb. Even more striking is the portrayal of Hercules' death and resurrection in the first century play, *Hercules Oetaeus*. There, he appears to his grieving mother Alcmene and implores her to refrain from mourning, that he has been "granted [his] place in heaven" among the gods.[43] Afterwards, he ascends to the realm above.[44] One is instantly reminded of Jesus' appearance to Mary Magdalene in the gospel of John, where he is in the process of ascending to the Father.[45]

Romulus, first king of Rome, was taking stock of his army when "a violent thunder storm suddenly arose and enveloped [him in] a cloud," after which he "was no longer seen on earth."[46] The prevailing belief was that "he had been snatched away to heaven," and he was thereafter hailed "the son of a god."[47] But it was rumored by some that the senators had torn him

---

the idea of resurrection existed within early Christianity and Judaism as well. See C.D. Elledge, *Resurrection of the Dead in Early Judaism: 200 BCE-CE 200*. (Oxford University Press, 2017). Also Bart Ehrman, *How Jesus Became God: The Exaltation of a Jewish Preacher from Galilee*. (New York: HarperCollins, 2014), pp. 205-208 concerning divergent views of Jesus' resurrection in the New Testament.

[43] Felice Le Monnier, *Hercules Oetaeus*, pp. 1940-43.
[44] Ibid. p. 1975.
[45] John 20:11-18.
[46] Livy, *History of Rome*, 1.16.1.
[47] Ibid. 1.16.3; cf. Rom. 1:4.

limb from limb.[48] The grief caused by Romulus' disappearance was lifted by a report from a most trusted witness, Proculus Julius:

> At break of dawn, today, the Father of this City suddenly descended from heaven and appeared to me. Whilst, thrilled with awe, I stood rapt before him in deepest reverence, praying that I might be pardoned for gazing upon him, 'Go,' he said, 'tell the Romans that it is the will of heaven that my Rome should be the head of all the world.'[49]

Much the same story is relayed by Ovid:

> The sun vanished, and rising clouds obscured the sky, and a heavy shower of torrential rain fell. Then it thundered. Then the sky was split by lightning: All fled, and the king rose to the stars behind his father's horses. There was mourning, senators were falsely charged with murder, and perhaps that belief might have stuck in people's minds. But Julius Proculus was travelling from Alba Longa, with the moon shining, and having no need of a torch. When suddenly the hedge to his left moved and shook: So that he drew back a step, his hair bristling. It seemed to him that Romulus, handsome, more than human, and finely dressed, stood there, in the centre of the road, saying: 'Prevent the [Romans] from mourning me, and profaning my divinity by their tears: Let the pious crowds bring incense and propitiate the new god Quirinus, and cultivate their father's art of war.' So he commanded and vanished into the upper world from before Julius' eyes.[50]

These stories share in common the belief that Romulus was translated to heaven while still alive, though such elements as grief and mourning, as well as suspicions of murder by the senate, still accompany them. M. David Litwa's suggestion that this constitutes a post-*mortal* rather than post-*mortem* account is instructive. Ovid relates that Romulus' "mortal body dissolved in the clear atmosphere, like the lead bullet, that often melts in

---

[48] Livy, *History of Rome*, 1.16.4
[49] Ibid. 1.16.6-7
[50] *Fasti* 2.475-511; cf. Plutarch, *Life of Romulus*, pp. 27-28.

mid-air."[51] Granting this distinction, it would appear to be a minor variant on the overarching theme of death, resurrection, and exaltation witnessed in the tales of Baal, Osiris, Aristeas, Asclepius, and Heracles. Most illuminating are the vivid parallels to the darkness that befell Christ's crucifixion, appearances to witnesses, declaration of divine sonship, and great commission before ascending on high.

Conclusion

Upon closer examination, the apologetics concerning dying and rising gods simply do not hold up. The divinities in question rose bodily: Osiris is physically reconstituted, shaking the earth from his flesh, untying his bandages, and ascending bodily to the heavens; Dionysus is likewise physically restored to life; Asclepius appears in full bodily presence to others after his death, as do Aristeas and Heracles, whose bodies go missing after they've been raised to immortality. The relocation of Osiris, Asclepius, Heracles, et al., to a realm beyond this world makes them no less resurrected than Christ, who is seated at the right hand of God upon his resurrection in the New Testament epistles. All of these divinities suffer death before they are raised to life again, with the exception of Romulus—though, even there, an intimation of death remains. It may be a matter of semantics as to whether the term 'dying and rising gods' is appropriate, since figures like Aristeas and Asclepius were mortal prior to deification. One could just as easily quibble over the differences in the manner in which these ancient figures died and rose. But the overriding themes of death, resurrection, and exaltation make dubious any attempts to undermine the core concept, or "ideal type," as Robert M. Price aptly describes it.

Of course, acknowledging analogues to the death and resurrection of Christ is one thing. By itself, it's enough to cast doubt on the resurrection of Jesus. (Do these all not alike look like ancient myths?) But is there good

---

[51] Ovid, *Metamorphoses*, vol. 14, pp. 805-28.

reason to think that the resurrection of Jesus is inspired by these earlier tales? That the stories are not merely analogical (similar) but genealogical (related)? There is simply no way to prove the latter, though reasonable inference can be made. As noted earlier, Christ as the risen Son of God who vanquishes death and is enthroned Lord sounds like a direct survival of ancient Israelite devotion to Baal. Jesus as the resurrected god-king who ascends to heaven and presides as judge of the dead, whose resurrection secures a similar fate for devotees, is strikingly reminiscent of Osirian myth and soteriology. And the accretion of motifs such as missing bodies, celestial signs and portents, heavenly exaltation, and post-mortem appearances bespeak a shared cultural understanding of divinity and resurrection in the Hellenistic-Roman world. There are differences between the various myths, to be sure, but this is precisely what we'd expect given the nature of religious syncretism. The similarities, meanwhile, are too numerous and extensive to be mere coincidence.

In all of this, we need not ignore the obvious and considerable contribution of Judaism to nascent Christianity. Indeed, expectation of a mass resurrection of the dead was a staple of Second Temple Judaism, particularly among the Pharisees. But the bald assertion by Christian apologists that the resurrection of Jesus stems from apocalyptic Judaism, not paganism, is an either-or proposition that runs afoul of the old bifurcation fallacy. Judaism itself was a synthesis of Ancient Near Eastern beliefs and traditions, including Mesopotamian, Canaanite, Egyptian, and Persian ideas. And any notion of a monolithic Judaism to which all first century Jews conformed is an absolute distortion of history, especially in light of Hellenization, which infiltrated all aspects of cultural life, including, as we have seen, religious ones. Christ as the dying and rising messiah, the first fruits of those who sleep in the dust, who conquers death, ascends to heaven, sits enthroned as judge of the living and the dead, confers eternal life by the power of his own resurrection, and appears to followers with signs and portents and heavenly mandates, must be understood as a composite figure, the culmination of a long, winding, and rich tradition of religious ideas from around the Mediterranean world.

Chapter 4: Christianity is a Western Branch of Buddhism

By Michael Lockwood

"The idea of a Buddhistic origin of Christianity has been suggested more than once; but it is incumbent upon us to state that some of the men who must be regarded as the most competent to judge this matter are either extremely reticent or scorn the suggestion as quite impossible. While it is true that Arthur Lillie and Rudolf Seydel, who have done most to make the theory popular, introduce many vague speculations, we cannot regard a refutation of some of their vagaries as sufficient to settle the subject. No argument has as yet been offered to dispose of the hypothesis, which possesses, to say the least, a great probability in its favor."

—Paul Carus, "Buddhism and Christianity," *The Monist*, vol. 5 (1895), p. 66.

I may be the only contributor of this volume who will be writing about Buddhism and Christianity, but if there is any truth in what I have to say, it may alter the perspective on much of what other contributors have presented—excepting, of course, our general agreement that Jesus of the gospels and his disciples just didn't exist historically.

Summary of Twenty Years of Research Behind this Chapter

This is written after the final volume of my trilogy of books dedicated to clarifying the historical relation of Buddhism to Christianity has recently been published in print. The titles of the three volumes, in order, are:

Buddhism's Relation to Christianity (2010), *Mythicism: A Seven-Fold Revelation of the Buddhist 'Branch' Grafted onto Jesse's 'Lineage Tree'* (2013), and *The Unknown Buddha of Christianity: The Crypto-Buddhism of the Essenes (Therapeutæ and Qumranites)* (2019).

All three volumes are, in large part, anthological—though such reproduced matter forms an integral part of what is a *tripartite monograph* dedicated to vigorously clarifying the historical relation of Buddhism to Christianity. All three books, with other books and papers of mine, are freely accessible at Academia.edu.

Volume I—Buddhism's Relation to Christianity (BRC)

This volume is intended as a reference work collating many sources with bearing on the topic, aimed at surveying within categories the many, many remarkable parallelisms between the messages and the lives of the Buddha and Jesus.

The **First Section** of this volume presents a select annotated bibliography highlighting fourteen authors who have noticed and discussed these parallelisms. These entries span the nineteenth century and several decades into the twentieth.

The **Second Section** deals with Buddhist narrative sculptures in India—some created in centuries BCE—which were paralleled later by similar narrative episodes in Christian scriptures.

The **Third Section** considers several mid-third century BCE 'Rock Edicts' of the Buddhist emperor, Aśoka, ruler over most of India. The 13th Major Rock Edict, in particular, reveals his intense pride in spreading abroad the Buddha's "Good News" (his doctrine of 'Dharma') as far west as Egypt and other kingdoms around the Mediterranean. This "Good News" of Buddhism has numerous parallels with the "Good News" of the Christian gospels.

The **Fourth Section** examines the most widespread legend of sainthood during medieval times, in which the Buddha was cast as a *Christian* saint, credulously believed by members of the Catholic Church to be historical, and who was, by 1583, listed in the *Roman Martyrology*, which provided an extensive list of saints officially recognized by the Church.

The **Fifth Section** discusses several instances of parallel parables. To my knowledge, only Buddhism and Christianity have made such extensive use of parables.

The **Sixth Section** lists various parallels in the sayings of the Buddha and Jesus.

The **Seventh Section** emphasizes certain pioneering developments achieved by Buddhism, as a missionary religion, prior to similar developments in Christianity.

The **Eighth Section** takes up the contentious debate about the historicity of Jesus. Various arguments for, and a few against, his being historical are considered.

And, finally, the **Ninth Section** deals with two examples of extreme revisionism. Both of these theories argue that Jesus was not a historical person. And, further, they both hold that the evangelists who wrote the gospels of the New Testament were actually Buddhists. The pioneer of this extreme revisionism is the Danish Sanskrit scholar, Christian Lindtner.

Volume II—Mythicism: A Seven-Fold Revelation

This second volume of my trilogy presents the negative side of the debate whether 'Jesus of Nazareth' was or was not a historical person. It examines five major distinct *meta-layers* of narrative hypotexts upon which the narrative hypertexts of the New Testament (gospels, epistles, *Revelation*) have a historical-fictive dependency—thus continually and gravely undermining Jesus' historicity.

In the **First Section**, Robert M. Price's masterpiece article, "New Testament Narrative as Old Testament Midrash," and Thomas L. Brodie's epochal book, *Beyond the Quest for the Historical Jesus*, reviewed by René Salm, discuss the concept of mimesis in ancient literature. In this concept, the hypertext (what is actually written) imitates or varies in some pertinent way from the hypotext (the document alluded to), gaining significance from it. Price and Brodie, thus, reveal a massive layer of mimetic dependence of many works of the New Testament on passages in the Old Testament.

In the **Second Section**, Dennis R. MacDonald's book, *The Homeric Epics and the Gospel of Mark* (reviewed by Richard Carrier), reveals an astonishing second layer of fictional mimetic dependence of Mark's gospel on Homer's *Iliad* and *Odyssey*. As Mark's is the earliest of the four Gospels, this dependence must also extend to the other three gospels. This is fictional mimesis as the *Iliad* and *Odyssey* are considered fictional stories.

In the **Third Section**, an examination of a book by John H. C. Pippy (*Egyptian Origin of the Book of Revelation*) and of another, by D. M. Murdock (*Christ in Egypt*), reveals a third layer of fictional mimetic dependence of the New Testament on ancient Egyptian religious writings.

In the **Fourth Section**, ten very short reports by Christian Lindtner reveal an astounding fourth layer of fictional mimetic dependence of the canonical Gospels on Buddhist scriptures. These reports are worth reading in their entirety, as the mimetic index (the degree to which a mimetic heritage could be considered as real, rather than just a possible coincidence) is extraordinarily high.

In the **Fifth Section**, Robert Eisenman's book, *The New Testament Code*, reviewed by Robert Price, reveals a fifth layer of fictionalized mimetic dependence of the New Testament on a coded transformation of historical material from the writings of Philo of Alexandria, Flavius Josephus, and others.

In addition to the five major literary sources of the New Testament discussed in *Mythicism*, there are a number of other notable sources which are included, such as, for example, the zodiacal (astrological) material embedded in New Testament works. This area of interest has been researched by authors including Count M. Volney,[1] David Fideler,[2] D. M. Murdock,[3] and Bill Darlison.[4] It is unfortunate that many Christian theologians and historians of primitive Christianity have not explored such research.

A major thesis of *Mythicism*, therefore, was to argue that New Testament narratives (hypertexts) constantly allude mimetically to a surprising number of non-Christian hypotexts simultaneously. The evangelists created the New Testament gospels involving exceedingly complex multi-layered meta-narratives, and this degree of complexity is to be found elsewhere *only* in the literary works that have come down to us from India.

As an example, the great South Indian poet Daṇḍin, is credited with having composed a Sanskrit work in the genre called *dvisañzdhana-kavya* in the seventh century CE. This type of poem can be read from beginning to end in two completely different ways. In the case of Daṇḍin's work, it could be read either as an account of the epic *Ramayana* or, alternately, as an account of the epic *Mahabharata*. One particular manner of arbitrarily (vocally/mentally) dividing the long compound Sanskrit passages would result in the whole poem recounting the epic of the *Ramayana*. But if the compound expressions were divided differently, it was instead an account of the epic of the *Mahabharata*. Which epic did Daṇḍin's *dvisañzdhana-kavya* really relate? The answer is: *both*. Unfortunately, this work of Daṇḍin's has been lost. We only have admiring reports of it.

In the same century as Daṇḍin's, the great playwright, King Mahēndra-I, wrote one of the earliest extant Indian farces, *Bhagavadajjukam* (*The Saint-Courtesan*). My late colleague Prof. Vishnu Bhat and I published an edition and translation of this Sanskrit farce as far back as 1978,

---

[1] Count M. Volney, *The Ruins: Or a Survey of the Revolutions of Empires*. (New York, NY: E. Duyschink & Co., 1796).
[2] David Fideler, Jesus Christ, Sun of God: Ancient Cosmology and Early Christian Symbolism. (Wheaton, IL: Quest Books, 1993).
[3] Acharya S. (D. M. Murdock), *Suns of God: Krishna, Buddha and Christ Unveiled*. (Kempton, IL: Adventures Unlimited Press, 2007).
[4] Bill Darlison, The Gospel and the Zodiac: The Secret Truth About Jesus. (London: Duckworth Overlook, 2007).

and continued to study it over the next 27 years, issuing three more, revised editions of the play, with the last two editions, under the title *Metatheater and Sanskrit Drama*.[5]

What the poet Daṇḍin accomplished with his *dvisaṁdhāna-kāvya*, King Mahēndra-I equaled in his own way with multiple suggested layers of drama sustained throughout the play, from beginning to end. In nearly thirty years of our research on the metadramatic structure of Sanskrit drama, it never entered my mind that such a study would eventually result in gaining insight into the meta-narrative structures of passages in the New Testament. When I read such works as those of Lindtner and Murdock, the multi-layered domains of reference of passages in the gospels became apparent. As Lindtner has remarked, the result is not only multi-layered but is also a 'literary mosaic' assembled from multiple sources; or to use another metaphor, an impressive multi-layered literary patchwork quilt.

An analogy used in *Mythicism* to characterize these multi-layered domains of reference in the New Testament was from music. The words written in the New Testament passages represent one "voice" in harmony or dissonance with other "voices" (of passages from other literary works alluded to).

In the anthological survey, five different major sources were evident, illustrating *mimetic* allusions made by the New Testament hypertext "voice" to: 1) the *Septuagint*; 2) the Homeric Epics; 3) Egyptian scriptures; 4) Buddhist scriptures; and 5) the historical works of Philo, Josephus, and others. Often, several of these different allusions are made simultaneously.

As an example of the intentional use of many "voices" of allusion, consider the passages in the gospels and epistles of the New Testament which

---

[5] *Metatheater and Sanskrit Drama*. (Madras: Tambaram Research Associates, 1994/Munshiram Manoharlal Publishers, 1995); *Metatheater and Sanskrit Drama: Second, Revised and Enlarged Edition*. (Madras: Tambaram Research Associates, 2005).

recount the events around the 'Last Supper' hypertexts, which also simultaneously allude to at least three different hypotexts:

The 'Last Supper' of the Buddha in Buddhist scriptures;
The Jewish 'Last Supper' (in the Septuagint's *Exodus*);
Osiris's 'Last Supper' (in the Egyptian Annual Passion Plays).

There are detailed arguments in *Mythicism* (pp. 203-204) supporting such simultaneous multi-level allusions.

Volume III—The Unknown Buddha of Christianity (UBC)

This final volume presents arguments supporting the theory that Christianity is in actuality a branch of a hidden, 'crypto-Buddhism,' apparently rising from nowhere, but with many indications that its generation was closely aligned with the teachings and the accounts of the life of the Buddha.

This theory must of necessity be superficially unverifiable by direct historical report. The clues that support this theory are scattered widely, yet become compelling when considered en masse. The following epigraph, attributed to the poet Ralph Waldo Emerson, puts it this way:

> *'If the right theory should ever be discovered, we shall know it by this token:*
> *that it will solve many riddles.'*

Following Charles Sanders Peirce's abductive reasoning, the hypothesis that 'Christianity is a branch of Buddhism' may be tested and found to be of worth if it can be shown that it provides sensible, unremarkable solutions for riddles that otherwise seem inexplicable.

First Riddle

As one example from many, consider the *riddle* that Chris Keith wrestles with in his article, "The Oddity of the Reference to Jesus in Acts 4:13b," as expressed in his opening Abstract (p. 791):

> This essay argues that Luke's strong association of Jesus with the manual-labor class in Acts 4:13b, and specifically with the disciples'

"illiteracy" and "unlearnedness," is out of step with a sustained redactional strategy in his Gospel, whereby he consistently removed the Gospel of Mark's associations of Jesus with the manual-labor class and offered an alternative image of Jesus as a scribal-literate teacher. This redactional strategy is particularly clear in Mark's and Luke's differing portrayals of Jesus as a synagogue teacher.... Acts 4:13b presents a moment of discontinuity between Luke's Gospel and Acts that has been overlooked. The primary purpose of the article is to articulate the oddity of Luke's interpretive choice in Acts 4:13b in light of his other images of Jesus and his portrayal of the Spirit in Luke-Acts. The essay closes with a possible solution: Luke has, in his Gospel, portrayed Jesus in *imago Pauli*.[6]

Keith continues, on the same page:

Previous scholarship on Acts 4:13 has focused primarily on the Sanhedrin's references to Peter and John as "illiterate" (agrammatoi) and "untrained" (idiōtai) men. In this essay, I shift the focus of critical interpretation to the neglected second half of Acts 4:13, where Luke notes that, on the basis of Peter's speech and the disciples' illiteracy, the Jewish leadership recognized them as companions of Jesus. Scholars almost universally have taken this statement concerning Jesus and his disciples as a straightforward and obvious deduction by the Jewish leaders in the narrative world of Luke-Acts and by the audience of Acts engaging that world as readers. In contrast, I argue that the Lukan comment that the Sanhedrin recognizes Peter and John as companions of Jesus on the basis of their illiteracy, unlearnedness, and rhetorical performance is far from straightforward and is, in fact, contrary to at least one interpretive agenda that Luke has worked carefully to forward in his Gospel.

There is an alternate, crypto-Buddhist solution to Keith's 'riddle' (the 'oddity') he finds in *Acts 4:13b*, which appears to be casting aspersions on

---

[6] Keith, C., The Oddity of the Reference to Jesus in Acts 4:13b. *Journal of Biblical Literature*. (2015), 134, no. 4. pp. 791-811.

the two great disciples of Jesus (Peter and John) by claiming that they were "illiterate" and "untrained."

When Indian scholars were invited by King Ptolemy-I (Soter) to come to the Royal Library of Alexandria, in the third century BCE, to learn the Greek language and to translate their religious and secular works into Greek for the Library's collection, they did so under very strange circumstances. These Buddhist scholars were scholars, but incredibly (by Western standards) they had no knowledge of any Indian system of writing. They were literally *illiterate* in the language of their learning. However, no country has ever approached the supreme level of oral mastery of learning which was attained in India. Students learned from their gurus through speech alone. Never in writing. There has been no convincing evidence found of any Indian writing system/alphabet for over a thousand years prior to the third century BCE—in spite of some recent challenges based on arguable grounds.

The problem of Jesus' disciples, Peter and John, being called "illiterate" and "untrained" will forever remain a problem for those who believe that Jesus and his disciples were historical persons. In contrast, those who understand that the gospels (canonical and apocryphal) are extended parables about the imaginary characters of Jesus and his disciples, become free to perceive the multiple levels of allusion in the gospels.

The extensive research of Christian Lindtner has made it abundantly clear that the imaginary characters of Jesus and his disciples, Peter and John, are stand-ins for the Buddha and his disciples, Sariputra and Ananda. According to Lindtner, the Buddha and his disciples are *also* mythical. But according to me, inscribed relic caskets retrieved from stupas in India indicate the historicity of the Buddha and his disciples. Therefore, Jesus, Peter, and John are euhemeristic (semi-mythical) characters. 'Euhemerism,' is the actual meaning underlying the misleading term, 'Docetism.'

Keith's riddle is solved by elimination. The disciples were indeed illiterate and untrained in the *written* languages—if they were Buddhist monks.

As an aside, this also means that the Buddhist legendary work, the *Lalitavistara*, is anachronistic when it describes Prince Siddhartha's (the future Buddha's) first day of school, where he is to begin learning the Brahma alphabet, but amazes his teacher by his preternatural knowledge of not only the Brahma alphabet, but of sixty-three other alphabets! The Buddha certainly never learned the Brahma alphabet, as that alphabet was only invented in the third century BCE. In fact, there was no Indian alphabet at all during the life of the Buddha.

Where would the author of the *Lalitavistara* have had the idea of multiple ancient alphabets/scripts being the object of study? One good answer might be the Royal Library of Alexandria, probably the only library in the world, during the early Common Era, which had documents written in so many different alphabets.

Alphabetical Evidence that Links Christianity to Buddhism

Further evidence for the link between the two religions, Buddhism and Christianity, is found in two little fanciful stories, one of which is the short, *erudite* mythical episode presented in the tenth chapter of the *Lalitavistara*. The second episode, this one lacking erudition, is repeated in three different versions, in chapters six through seven, fourteen, and fifteen of the Christian apocryphal *Infancy Gospel of Thomas*.

Over one hundred years ago, Albert J. Edmunds wrote in his authoritative book, *Buddhist and Christian Gospels*,[7] about the parallelism between various Buddhist accounts of the first day of school for the young prince, Siddhartha (the future Buddha), and several Christian versions of Jesus' first day of school. In both these cases, their schooling is to begin with learning the letters of the alphabets (the Brāhmī letters, for Siddhārtha; the *Greek* [!] letters, for Jesus). In order to elucidate the great significance of this parallelism, the major part of the Buddhist *sūtra*'s tenth

---

[7] Albert J. Edmunds, *Buddhist and Christian Gospel of Thomas*. (1909). pp. 241-25

chapter, dedicated to Siddhārtha's 'Alphabet-Episode,'[8] is reproduced here:

CHAPTER 10

'The Demonstration at the Writing School'

As soon as the Bodhisattva [the future Buddha] arrived in school, the schoolmaster, who was called Viśvāmitra, was unable to withstand the Bodhisattva's splendor and radiance, and prostrated to him facedown on the ground.

[After the schoolmaster had recovered,] the Bodhisattva [Prince Siddhārtha] took up a writing board made of sandalwood. It was decorated with flecks of divine gold of prime quality and studded with precious gems on all sides. He then addressed the master Viśvāmitra:

"Which script, O master, will you be teaching me? Will it be the Brāhmī script, the Kharoṣṭhī script, or the Puṣkarasāri script? Will it be the Aṅga script, the Vaṅga script, the Magadha script, the Maṅgalya script, the Aṅgulīya script, the Śakāri script, the Brahmavali script, the Pāruṣya script, the Drāviḍa script, the Kirāta script, the Dākṣiṇya script, the Ugra script, the Saṁkhyā script, the Anuloma script, the Avamūrdha script, the Darada script, the Khāṣya script, the Cīna script, the Lūna script, the Hūṇa script, the Madhyākṣaravistara script, the Puṣpa script, the Deva script, the Nāga script, the Yakṣa script, the Gandharva script, the Kiṃnara script, the Mahoraga script, the Asura script, the Garuḍa script, the Mṛgacakra script, the Vāyasaruta script, the Bhaumadeva script, the Antarīkṣadeva script, the Uttarakurudvīpa script, the Aparagodānī script, the Pūrvavideha script, the Utkṣepa script, the Nikṣepa script, the Vikṣepa script, the Prakṣepa script, the Sāgara script, the Vajra script, the

---

[8] *Lalitavistara*/The Play in Full (Arya-lalitavistara-nama-mahayana-satra), Toh 95, Degé Kangyur, vol. 46 (mdo sde, kha), folios 1b-216b, trans. by the Dharmachakra Translation Committee (version 2.22: published by 84000, 2013), pp. 1-345; chapter 10, 'The Demonstration at the Writing School,' pp. 90-94.

Lekhapratilekha script, the Anudruta script, the Śāstrāvarta script, the Gaṇanāvarta script, the Utkṣepāvarta script, the Nikṣepāvarta script, the Pādalikhita script, the Dviruttarapadasaṁdhi script, the Yāvaddaśottarapadasaṁdhi script, the Madhyāhāriṇī script, the Sarvarutasaṁgrahaṇī script, the Vidyānulomāvimiśrita script, the Ṛṣitapastapa script, the Rocamāna script, the Dharaṇīprekṣiṇī script, the Gaganaprekṣiṇī script, the Sarvauṣadhiniṣyanda script, the Sarvasārasaṁgrahaṇī script, or the Sarvabhūtarutagrahaṇī script? Master, which of those sixty-four scripts will you teach me?"

The schoolmaster Viśvāmitra was amazed, and he smiled. Setting aside pride, conceit, and arrogance, he replied with the following verses:
"How wonderful! Even though the Pure Being [*i.e.*, Prince Siddhārtha] Is learned in all topics in the world,
He follows the conventions of the world.
Thus he has come to school.
He has learned scripts Even the names of which I have not heard,
Yet he has come to school.
I see his face,
But the crown of his head is invisible.
If he has mastered the knowledge of scripts, How can I teach him?
This god, great god of gods,
Supreme divine scholar among all gods,
Is superior and without equal.
No person in the world is comparable to him.
Only because of his unparalleled expertise
In applying knowledge and means, Will I teach this learned being—The final refuge of all beings."

Then the schoolmaster taught writing to the Bodhisattva, along with ten-thousand other children. However, through the power of the Bodhisattva, as the schoolmaster was saying the alphabet to the children, he did it in the following manner:

When he said the letter *a*, out came the statement: "Every composite phenomenon is impermanent (*anityaḥ sarvasaṁskārāḥ*)."

When he said the letter *ā*, out came the statement: "Beneficial to self and others (*ātmaparahita*)."

When he said the letter *i*, out came the statement: "The vast development of the senses (*indriyavaipulya*)."

When he said the letter *ī*, out came the statement: "The world is riddled with plague (*ītibahulaṁ jagat*)."

When he said the letter *u*, out came the statement: "The world is rife with misfortune (*upadravabahulaṁ jagat*)."

When he said the letter *ū*, out came the statement: "The world is of little substance (*ūnasattvaṁ jagat*)." When he said the letter *e*, out came the statement: "Faults come from desire (*eṣaṇāsamutthānadoṣa*)."

When he said the letter *ai*, out came the statement: "The noble path is virtuous //93// (*airyāpathaḥ śreyāniti*)."

When he said the letter *o*, out came the statement: "The stream has been forded (*oghottara*)."

When he said the letter *au*, out came the statement: "Spontaneously generated (*aupapāduka*)."

When he said the letter *aṁ*, out came the statement: "The emergence of what is efficacious (*amoghotpatti*)."

When he said the letter *aḥ*, out came the statement: "Reaching an end (*astaṁgamana*)."

When he said the letter *ka*, out came the statement: "Immersion in the full ripening of actions (*karmavipākāvatāra*)."

When he said the letter *kha*, out came the statement: "All phenomena are like space (*khasamasarvadharma*)."

When he said the letter *ga*, out came the statement: "Immersion in the profound Dharma of dependent origination (*gambhīradharmapratītyasamutpādāvatāra*)."

When he said the letter *gha*, out came the statement: "Eradicating the darkness of delusion and the thick veils of ignorance (*ghanapaṭalāvidyāmohāndhakāravidhamana*)."

When he said the letter *ṅ*, out came the statement: "The complete purification of factors (*aṅgaviśuddhi*)."

When he said the letter *ca*, out came the statement: "The path of the four noble truths (*caturāryasatyapatha*)."

When he said the letter *cha*, out came the statement: "Abandoning the passion of lust (*chandarāgaprahāṇa*)."

When he said the letter *ja*, out came the statement: "Transcending old age and death (*jarāmaraṇasamatikramaṇa*)."

When he said the letter *jha*, out came the statement: "Vanquishing the forces of the god of love (*jhaṣadhvajabalanigrahaṇa*)."

When he said the letter *ña*, out came the statement: "Making known (*jñāpana*)."

When he said the letter *ṭa*, out came the statement: "Severing the round of rebirths (*vaṭṭopacchedana*)."

When he said the letter *ṭha*, out came the statement: "A question rejected out of hand (*ṭhapanīyapraśna*)."

When he said the letter *ḍa*, out came the statement: "Vanquishing the evil one and those who cause discord (*ḍamaramāranigrahaṇa*)."

When he said the letter *ḍha*, out came the statement: "The impure regions (*mīḍhaviṣayāḥ*)."

When he said the letter *ṇa*, out came the statement: "Afflictions are subtle (*reṇukleśāḥ*)."

When he said the letter *ta*, out came the statement: "Suchness is undifferentiated (*tathatāsaṁbheda*)."

When he said the letter *tha*, out came the statement: "Strength, power, force, and self-confidence (*thāmabalavegavaiśāradya*)."

When he said the letter *da*, out came the statement: "Generosity, discipline, restraint, and gentleness (*dānadamasaṁyamasaurabhya*)."

When he said the letter *dha*, out came the statement: "The wealth of the noble ones is sevenfold (*dhanamāryāṇāṁ saptavidham*)."

When he said the letter *na*, out came the statement: "Full knowledge of name and form (*nāmarūpaparijñā*)."

When he said the letter *pa*, out came the statement: "The absolute (*paramārtha*)."

When he said the letter *pha*, out came the statement: "The actualization of the attainment of the fruition (*phalaprāptisākṣātkriyā*)."

When he said the letter *ba*, out came the statement: "Liberation from bondage (*bandhanamokṣa*)." When he said the letter *bha*, out came the statement: "The destruction of existence (*bhavavibhava*)."

When he said the letter *ma*, out came the statement: "The cessation of arrogance and pride (*madamānopaśamana*)."

When he said the letter *ya*, out came the statement: "Understanding phenomena exactly as they are (*yathāvaddharmaprativedha*)."

When he said the letter *ra*, out came the statement: "Dissatisfaction with pleasure is delighting in the absolute (*ratyaratiparamārtharati*)."

When he said the letter *la*, out came the phrase: "Severing the vine (*latāchedana*)."

When he said the letter *va*, out came the statement: "The best vehicle (*varayāna*)."

When he said the letter *śa*, out came the statement: "Calm abiding and insight (*śamathavipaśyanā*)."

When he said the letter *ṣa*, out came the statement: "Destroying the six sense bases and obtaining the super-knowledges and wisdoms (*ṣaḍāyatananigrahaṇābhijñajñānāvāpti*)."

When he said the letter *sa*, out came the statement: "Attaining the perfect awakening to omniscient wisdom (*sarvajñajñānābhisaṁbodhana*)."

When he said the letter *ha*, out came the statement: "Destroying the afflictions and parting from desire (*hatakleśavirāga*)."

When he said the letter *kṣa*, out came the statement: "Reaching the end of letters, all phenomena are ineffable (*kṣaraparyantābhilāpya sarvadharma*)."

Thus, while the schoolmaster taught the children the alphabet, there emerged innumerable hundreds of thousands of excellent Dharma teachings due to the Bodhisattva's power.

First, at its beginning, this little story might appear to be a childish fable, with its description of thousands of children attending the school along with the young prince, Siddhārtha, who is portrayed as preternaturally omniscient, and blessed with supernatural powers. Nevertheless, this alphasyllabary is certainly not suitable for children learning their first alphabet! Rather, this story is a fanciful, but highly sophisticated exercise for teaching illiterate adult Buddhist scholars their first Indian alphabet, the newly invented Brāhmī alphabet, along with a good dose of advanced Buddhist doctrine.

Note that something is still missing when the schoolmaster proceeds to teach the alphabet. He does so purely orally, never once mentioning anything to do with the shape of the letters of the alphabet! On the surface this is the old illiterate way of phonetically teaching the phonemic elements of a language. But add the shapes of the letters assumed to be on the children's 'writing boards' and on the schoolmaster's exemplary 'writing board,' and then there will be literacy.

Also note that after the teacher pronounces the letters of the Brāhmī, it is only through the miraculous influence of Siddhārtha, that the schoolmaster is empowered to come out with all those profound philosophical statements in Sanskrit.

Finally, note that, in this Buddhist tale, the prince never misuses his miraculous powers, nor does he ever fail to be kind and compassionate.

Child Jesus' Encounter with the Alphabet

The Jesus 'Alphabet-Episode' is repeated in three versions in the *Infancy Gospel of Thomas*, ably edited, translated, and commented on by Bart D. Ehrman and Zlatko Pleše in their book, *The Other Gospels: Accounts of Jesus from Outside the New Testament*.[9] The three versions[10] have been rather crudely redacted by their author, "Thomas," so as to appear sequential.

For the record, Ehrman and Pleše make no mention of the Buddhist version which parallels—and surely pre-dates—the 'Alphabet Episode' of the *Infancy Gospel*. But Ehrman and Pleše present much interesting information about the significant impact that the Jesus 'Alphabet Episode,' in the *Infancy Gospel*, had on early Christianity:

> What ever its oldest form, there can be no doubt that this Gospel was one of the most popular of the early Christian apocrypha down through the ages. We have copies of it in an astonishing number of late antique and medieval languages—thirteen altogether.[11]...In part the the early dating is based on the circumstance that one of the most familiar stories—where the young Jesus confronts and confounds a potential teacher by explaining to him the mysteries of the alphabet (see ch. 14)—is attested already in the writings of Iraeneus from around 180 CE (*Against Heresies*, 1. 20. 1) and in the book known as the *Epistle of the Apostles* (the *Epistula Apostolorum*) (ch. 4), which dates possibly several decades earlier....Irenaeus does intimate that he found it in a "heretical" book (rather than having simply heard it from an oral source).[12]

---

[9] Erhman, B. & Pleše, Z., *The Other Gospels: Accounts of Jesus from Outside the New Testament*. (Oxford: Oxford University Press, 2014), pp. 3-14.
[10] Chapters 6-7, 14, and 15 of *The Infancy Gospel*.
[11] Ehrman & Pleše, *The Infancy Gospel*, p. 1.
[12] Ibid. p. 5.

From Ehrman and Pleše's translation of the *Infancy Gospel of Thomas*, short excerpts are given below of the three versions of a teacher's harrowing effort to teach the child Jesus the alphabet:

First Version of the Jesus 'Alphabet Episode' (Chapters 6-7)

In the first version, a teacher named Zachaeus had observed the child Jesus reprimanding with wise words his 'father' Joseph who had been a little severe in disciplining his son. A few days later Zachaeus approached Joseph and said:

> "You have a bright child with a good mind. Come hand him over to me that he may learn his letters, and along with the letters I will teach him all knowledge...." And [Zachaeus] told [Jesus] all the letters from Alpha to Omega, clearly and with great precision.[13]
>
> **Note**: Jesus was being taught the Greek alphabet!
>
> But Jesus looked at the instructor Zachaeus and said to him, "Since you do not know the true nature of the Alpha, how can you teach anyone the Beta? You hypocrite! If you know it, first teach the Alpha, and then we will believe you about the Beta." Then he began to interrogate the teacher about the first letter, and he was not able to give him the answers.[14]
>
> And so Zachaeus was duly humiliated.
>
> **Note**: In adapting the Indian 'Alphabet Episode,' in which the young Prince Siddhārtha has of *sixty-four* alphabets (the first two being Brāhmī and Kharoṣṭhī, the actual alphabets developed by Indian scholars at the Royal Library of Alexandria), the Christian 'Alphabet Episode' has Jesus demonstrating his knowledge in just *one* alphabet, the Greek—not Hebrew. The writer of this tale was evidently presenting it to persons who were conversant with Greek but not Hebrew.

---

[13] Ehrman & Pleše, *The Infancy Gospel*, p. 9.
[14] Ibid. pp. 9-10.

Second Version of the Jesus 'Alphabet Episode' (Chapter 14)

In Jesus' so-called *'second encounter* with a teacher,' we seem to be back at square one:

> When Joseph observed the mind of the child and his age, and saw that he was starting to mature, he again resolved that he should not be unable to read, and so took him out and gave him over to another teacher.
> The teacher said to Joseph, "First I will teach him to read Greek, and then Hebrew."[15]

The teacher went through the whole Greek alphabet attempting to explain it to Jesus. But the young Jesus was not satisfied:

> Then Jesus said to him, "If you are really a teacher and know the letters well, tell me the power of the Alpha, and I will tell you the power of the Beta." The teacher was aggravated and struck him on the head. The child was hurt and cursed him, and immediately he fainted and fell to the ground on his face.[16]

Whether the Greek word translates to 'fainted' or 'died' doesn't really matter because Jesus later brings him back to good health.

Third Version of the Jesus 'Alphabet Episode' (Chapter 15)

In the so-called *'third encounter* with a teacher,' we find a version which comes much closer to the spirit of the tenth chapter of the *Lalitavistara*:

> Sometime later there was another instructor, a close friend of Joseph, who said to him, "Bring the child to me at the school. Maybe I can use flattery to teach him his letters." Joseph said to him, "If you are courageous, brother, take him along with you." He took him with

---

[15] Ehrman & Pleše, *The Infancy Gospel*, p. 12.
[16] Ibid. p. 12.

great fear and much anxiety, but the child went along gladly. He entered the school with confidence and found a book lying on the reading desk. He picked it up, but instead of reading the words in it, he opened his mouth and began to speak in the Holy Spirit, teaching the Law [the Dharma] to those who were standing there. A great crowd gathered and stood there listening to him; they were amazed at the beauty of his teaching and his carefully crafted words—amazed that he could speak such things though still an infant.[17]

These stories of the alphabet contain parallelisms, divergences, and anachronisms. The similarities are obvious, yet they are not clone copies. We have the *Lalitavistara* with Prince Siddhārtha, who knows many scripts, even though this is anachronistic; and a polite and respectful attitude toward his teacher (who is instantly overwhelmed by his divine nature and respects it). We have the *Infancy Gospel of Thomas* with three versions of the same tale, where a young Jesus is taught in Greek rather than his national language. One of the Thomasine versions approaches the *Lalitavistara* style with minimal confrontation between Jesus and his teacher, and has Jesus delivering new teachings rather than recounting 'the Law and the Prophets.'

Second Riddle

Another riddle is the puzzling evidence of literary parallelisms between Mahāyāna's preëminent *Perfection of Wisdom* series of scriptures and the New Testament's *Book of Revelation*—a riddle which was highlighted by Edward Conze in a passage of an article of his in the *Encyclopedia of the World's Religions*:[18]

> Occasionally we find close verbal coincidences between the Christian and the Mahāyāna scriptures. Just one instance must suffice. At the time when the *Revelation of St John* was written down in Greek in the Eastern Mediterranean, the Mahāyānists produced in the South of India one of their most revered books, *The Perfection of Wisdom in 8,000*

---

[17] Ehrman & Pleše, *The Infancy Gospel*, p. 13.
[18] Conze, E., *Encyclopedia of the World's Religions*. (1959), pp. 293-294.

Lines. *Revelation* [5:1] refers to a book 'closely sealed' with seven seals, and likewise *The Perfection of Wisdom* is called a book 'sealed with seven seals'. It is shown to a Bodhisattva by the name of 'Everweeping' (*Sadāprarudita*), and St John 'weeps bitterly' ([*Rev.* 5:4]) because he sees no one worthy to open the book and to break its seals. This can be done by the Lamb alone, slaughtered in sacrifice ([*Rev.* 5:9]). In the same way, chapters 30 and 31 of the Mahāyāna book describe in detail how Everweeping slaughtered himself in sacrifice, and how he thereby became worthy of the 'Perfection of Wisdom' (see pp. 302-303 [of the *Encyclopedia*]). This parallel is remarkable not only for the similarities of the religious logic, but also for the fact that both the number seven and the whole notion of a 'book with seven seals' point to the Judaeo-Mediterranean rather than to the Indian tradition. Here is a fruitful field for further study. At present we cannot account for the parallels between the Mediterranean and Indian developments which occur at the beginning of the Christian era. For the interpretation of the Mahāyāna they are significant and should not be ignored.

In *Mythicism*, there is a possible solution to Conze's puzzlement over these strange parallelisms between the Buddhist scripture and the Christian scripture: the *sources* of these *two scriptures* were not separated by the great geographical distance assumed by Conze—one in India and the other near the Mediterranean—but, rather, there was only one geographical location for both sources: Alexandria, Egypt. Following Christian Lindtner, *Mythicism* proposed that the author of *The Perfection of Wisdom in 8,000 Lines* and the author of *Revelation* were both Buddhist scholars working in the environs of the *Royal Library of Alexandria*, where there would have been access to Greek translations of composed works from all over the world—including the purely orally memorized works of some societies, such as the Indian—these latter being committed to writing for the first time (which was in *Greek*). The *Book* of *Revelation* along with the other twenty-six books of the New Testament were authored in the second century CE by crypto-Buddhists, who three centuries earlier, in the early third century BCE, had become the first-ever "God-Fearers" (Semi-

Proselytes) of their fellow Jewish scholars at the *Royal Library*. These "seventy" Jewish scholar (à la Russell E. Gmirkin's research)[19] had composed the Hebrew Pentateuch around 270 BCE, and soon afterward also translated it into Greek, for the *Royal Library*.

Third and Fourth Riddles

Albert J. Edmunds, in his book, *Buddhist Texts Quoted as Scripture by the Gospel of John* (1906), argues that the following two passages from the Fourth Gospel have quoted Buddhist Scriptures:

> *John 7:38:* "He that believeth on me, as the Scripture hath said, out of his belly shall flow rivers of living water."—*American Standard Version*
>
> *John 12:34:* The multitude therefore answered him, "We have heard out of the Law, that the Christ abideth for the æon" [*eis ton aiCna*, 'for the age'].

The Unknown Buddha of Christianity, provides support for Edmunds' insight by providing the Zoroastrian background of the *Buddhist scripture* which is quoted by Jesus, in *John 7:38*.[20]

In *The Unknown Buddha of Christianity* I go beyond Edmunds and trace the real significance of the passage in *John 12:34* to a particular Buddhist source which no one else has ever noted—an ultra Mahāyāna source![21]

For the explanation of these last riddles, the interested reader is directed to *The Unknown Buddha of Christianity*, which is freely available for reading online or downloading from my site at Academia.edu.

---

[19] In Gmirkin's two books, *Berossus* and *Genesis, Manetho and Exodus: Hellenistic Histories and the Date of the Pentateuch*. (New York/London: T. & T. Clark, 2006); and Plato and the Creation of the Hebrew Bible. (London: Routledge, 2016).

[20] Michael Lockwood, *The Unknown Buddha of Christianity*. (Memoir Bank, 2019), pp. 24-66.

[21] Ibid. pp 393-394.

Chapter 5: The Roman Provenance of Christianity
By Joseph Atwill

Perhaps the often most asked questions by New Testament scholars are who wrote the Gospels and what was the basis for their story of Jesus Christ? One strand of modern NT scholarship—Mythicism—has attempted to answer these questions by positing that the story of Jesus was a myth that somehow developed into a history. While this theory can point to other myths that became history, absent an archeological miracle, it can never rise above logic and speculation because there is no physical evidence of either the proto-Christian religious communities or of the literature that evolved into the Gospels.

Moreover, Mythicism has no advantage over historicism in its explanatory power. If Jesus was a myth that became historical, this would not help answer the Synoptic problem or explain the anti-Semitic flavor of literature written to worship a Jew. Neither would a mythical origin for Jesus present an explanation for why the Gospels authors were so focused upon the 66-73 CE war between the Romans and the Jews.

In *Caesar's Messiah*, I presented the theory that while Jesus was fictional, he was not mythical. In other words, the Flavians, the family of Caesar's that had conquered Judea in the first century, had created the Gospels for two purposes. The first was straightforward: simply to promote a more pro-Roman version of messianic Judaism. The second, amazingly, was to create a messianic legacy for themselves.

Though these ideas may seem far-fetched to readers not familiar with *Caesar's Messiah*, the Flavian court, at the very least, should have received more scrutiny from scholars as the creators of the Gospels as it had both the capacity and the motivation to have produced them. The capacity to have produced them came from the intellectual circle around the Flavians. Titus' mistress Bernice and his primary general during the Jewish war, Tiberius Alexander, the nephew of Philo, were both from Jewish families that were financially dependent upon Rome. Moreover, Josephus, the Jewish historian, became an adopted member of the Flavian family. Having just waged a costly war with a militaristic sect of messianic Judaism, the motivation for their creation of Jesus is self-evident.

Unlike Mythicism, the theory of a Roman provenance of Christianity has great explanatory power. For example, the seemingly unsolvable Synoptic problem becomes nonexistent within a Roman provenance. When a single editorial board controls the literature, the verbatim passages do not need to be explained by some impossible-to-define sharing process between three different authors. They are simply first-century word processing.

However, the most important explanatory power of the theory of Roman provenance occurs when comparing the sequence of events in Josephus' history of the Roman/Jewish war with the storyline in the Gospels. As I showed in *Caesar's Messiah*, when viewed carefully, the entire ministry of Jesus was based upon the Flavians' campaign through Judea.

The parallel sequence between Jesus' ministry and Titus' military campaign was obviously deliberately created and done for a purpose. It created a typological linkage between the two, which produced the typological meaning that Jesus' life had foreseen Titus'. It is not difficult for a reader to verify this once he or she understands the system used in the Gospels to create typological linkage.

The authors of the Gospels created their typology as a mockery of the "divine" typology in the Hebrew Scripture which was used as a way of transferring meaning from one story to another. In general, such parallels were created to show that the "hand of God" was at work in the history of the Jews. For example, the Book of Esther used type scenes from the story of Joseph in the Book of Genesis to inform the alert reader that Esther and Mordecai were repeating the role of Joseph as an agent of God.

Joseph	Esther/Mordecai
Rises to high position in the Egyptian government through his beauty and wisdom	Esther rises to high position in the Persian government through her beauty and wisdom
Joseph's good deed (interpreting the butler's dream) is forgotten for a long time	Mordecai's good deed (saving the king's life) is forgotten for a long time
A character refuses to listen—"she spoke to Joseph every day but he refused to listen" (Gen. 39:10)	Character refuses to listen—"they told him every day but he refused to listen" (Est. 3:4)
Pharaoh's chief servant is hanged	The king's chief servant is hanged
Joseph reveals his identity to Pharaoh after a feast	Esther reveals her identity to the king after a feast

As is well known, the authors of the Gospels used typology overtly to create the impression that events from the lives of prior Hebrew prophets were types for events from Jesus' life. In doing so, they were trying to convince their readers that Jesus was another Jewish prophet with a divine relationship to God.

At the very beginning of the Gospels, the authors created a typological relationship between Jesus and Moses. The sequence begins in Matthew 2:13, where Joseph is described as bringing Jesus, who represents the "new Israel," down to Egypt. This event parallels Genesis 45–50, where a previous Joseph brought the "old Israel" down to Egypt. The authors of the Gospels associated their Joseph with the prior one by means of more than just a shared name and a journey to Egypt. The New Testament Joseph is described, like his counterpart in the Hebrew Bible, as a dreamer of dreams and as having encounters with a star and wise men.

Both stories regarding the journey of a Joseph to Egypt are immediately followed by a description of a massacre of innocents. The stories concerning the massacre of innocents are not exactly parallel. Jesus is not, for example, saved by being put in a boat on the river Jordan and then by being adopted by Herod's daughter. The typology used within Judaic literature does not require verbatim quotations or descriptions; rather, the author takes only enough information from the event that is being used as the type to allow the reader to recognize that the prior event relates to the one being described. In this case, each massacre-of-the-innocents story depicts young children being slaughtered by a fearful tyrant, but the future savior of Israel being saved.

The authors of the New Testament then continue mirroring Exodus by having an angel tell Joseph, "They are dead which sought the young child's life" (Matthew 2:20). This statement is a clear parallel to the statement made to Moses, the first savior of Israel, in Exodus 4:19: "All the men are dead which sought thy life." The parallels then continue with a harder-to-recognize parallel of Jesus receiving a baptism (Matthew 3:13), which uses as its type the passing through water described in Exodus 14. Next, Jesus spends forty days in the desert, which parallels the forty years the Israelites spend in the wilderness. Both sojourns in the desert involve three sets of temptations. In Exodus it is God who is tempted; in the Gospels it is Jesus, the son of God.

In Exodus it is the Israelites who tempt God. They first tempt him by asking for bread, at which time they learn that "man does not live by bread alone" (Exodus 16). The second time is at Massah, where they are told to not "tempt the Lord" (Exodus 17). On the third occasion, when they make the golden calf at Mount Sinai, they learn to "fear the Lord thy God and serve only him" (Exodus 32). Jesus' three temptations are by the devil and are a mirror of God's temptations by the Israelites, as his responses show. To his first temptation, he replies, "Man shall not live by bread alone" (Matthew 4:4). To the second, he replies, "Thou shalt not tempt the Lord thy God" (Matthew 4:7). And to the third, he replies, "Thou shalt worship the Lord thy God, and only him shalt thou serve" (Matthew 4:10).

OLD TESTAMENT	MATTHEW
Gen. 45-50 Joseph goes to Egypt	2:13 Joseph goes to Egypt
Ex. 1 Pharaoh massacres boys	2:16 Herod massacres boys
Ex. 4 "All the men are dead which sought thy life"	2:20 "They are dead which sought the young child's life"
Ex. 12 From Egypt to Israel	2:21 From Egypt to Israel
Ex. 14 Passing through water (baptism)	3:13 Baptism
Ex. 16 In the wilderness "Tempted by bread"	4:4 In the wilderness "Tempted by bread"
Ex. 17 "Do not tempt God"	4:7 "Do not tempt God"
Ex. 32 "Worship only God"	4:10 "Worship only God"

Thus, the Moses/Jesus typology in Matthew was constructed with four elements: names, locations, concepts and sequence. Of these elements, the relationship of sequence to Gospel typology has been by far the least investigated within NT studies. This seems an analytic oversight as, of all the elements, sequence is the one most liable to make occulted parallels coherent, as the is the case with the "baptism" parallel above.

In the Flavian Signature edition of *Caesar's Messiah*, I compared a block of text from the Gospel of Luke to a section of Josephus' description of the military campaign of Titus. I showed that there are over forty recognizable parallels between the texts and that the parallels occurred in the same sequence. Within this chapter, I will present several of them to show how obvious parallels between Jesus' ministry and Titus' military campaign were used to create a sequence and how the sequence permits the more occulted parallels to become visible.

GALILEE

1) On to Jerusalem – The Messengers are Sent Ahead

At the end of his Galilean campaign, Luke recorded that Jesus marched out of Galilee towards Jerusalem:

> Now it came to pass, when the time had come for Him to be received up, that He steadfastly set His face to go to Jerusalem, and sent messengers before His face.[1]

Josephus, keeping in sequence, recorded that, following his Galilean campaign, Titus marched on to Jerusalem and, like his typological forerunner, he sent out "messengers"—part of his army—before him. It is important to note that the typological system between Jesus and Titus is the same one that linked Jesus to the first savior of Israel, Moses. In other words, parallel names, concepts, and locations occur in the same sequence. Thus Jesus' ministry follows the sequence of locations of Titus' military campaign.

> Titus, when he had gotten together part of his forces about him and had ordered the rest to meet him at Jerusalem, marched out of Caesarea.[2]

---

[1] Luke 9:51
[2] Flavius Josephus, *The Wars of the Jews*, translation by William Whiston. (Worcester, 1794), 5.1.40. [Available at https://lexundria.com/j_bj/0/wst].

2) The Good Samaritan

Luke 10:25-37 tells the story of the Good Samaritan. It is an example of a parallel to Titus' campaign that can be recognized only when reading with the understanding of the parallel sequences.

In the story, the man who had been attacked by bandits symbolizes the Twelfth Legion, that had been left "half dead" by the Jewish "bandits" on the road from Jerusalem to Jericho at the start of the Roman/Jewish war. In Josephus' description of the battle, he used the same word Luke used to describe the "robbers," to depict the rebels that stole the Legions' belongings: "*lestes*."[3] The Gospel story of the Good Samaritan typologically parallels Titus marching in from Samaria and refurbishing the legion that had been "stripped" by the "robbers," or "*lestes*."

> Now Titus, according to the Roman usage, went in the front of the army after a decent manner, and marched (with the Twelfth Legion) through Samaria to Gophna, a city that had been formerly taken by his father, and was then garrisoned by Roman soldiers; and when he had lodged there one night, he marched on in the morning...[4]

Josephus' passage also notes how well provisioned the Legion was, "the servants of every Legion came after these, and before these last their baggage." Thus, Luke's parable envisions Titus restoring the Legion that had been left "half dead" and "stripped" of its belongings on the road from Jerusalem to Jericho, its mules and provisions.

> But he, wanting to justify himself, said to Jesus, "And who is my neighbor?"
>
> Then Jesus answered and said: "A certain [man] went down from Jerusalem to Jericho, and fell among thieves, who stripped him of his clothing, wounded [him], and departed, leaving [him] half dead. Now by chance a certain priest came down that road. And when he saw him, he passed by on the other side. Likewise a Levite, when he arrived at the place, came and looked, and passed by on the other side. But a

---

[3] Josephus, *The Wars of the Jews*, 2.19.554.
[4] Ibid. 5.2.50-51.

certain Samaritan, as he journeyed, came where he was. And when he saw him, he had compassion. So he went to [him] and bandaged his wounds, pouring on oil and wine; and he set him on his own animal, brought him to an inn, and took care of him. On the next day, when he departed, he took out two denarii, gave [them] to the innkeeper, and said to him, 'Take care of him; and whatever more you spend, when I come again, I will repay you.' So which of these three do you think was neighbor to him who fell among the thieves?"

And he said, "He who showed mercy on him."

Then Jesus said to him, "Go and do likewise."[5]

OUTSIDE OF JERUSALEM

The Gospels record a series of stories on the outskirts of Jerusalem. These stories are full of conflict between Jesus and the Jews—and of martial imagery. The stories parallel the battles between Titus and the Jewish rebels before his "triumphant entrance" into the city.

3) The House of Satan Divided Against Itself

Josephus then describes a "house of Satan" that is divided against itself. In other words, the different groups of Jewish rebels realized when the Romans showed up, that they must join together or their house would "fall."

> Now when hitherto the several parties in the city had been dashing one against another perpetually, this foreign war, now suddenly come upon them after a violent manner, put the first stop to their contentions one against another; and as the seditious now saw with astonishment the Romans pitching three several camps, they began to think of an awkward sort of concord, and said one to another, "What do we here, and what do we mean, when we suffer three fortified walls to be built to coop us in, that we shall not be able to breathe freely?"[6]

---

[5] Luke 10:29-37
[6] Josephus, *The Wars of the Jews*, 5.2.71-73.

Luke describes a parallel to the rebels' plight—the house of Satan divided against itself that will fall, which, like the "Good Samaritan" above, is visible only when read in the context of the sequence.

> But He, knowing their thoughts, said to them: "Every kingdom divided against itself is brought to desolation, and a house [divided] against a house falls. If Satan also is divided against himself, how will his kingdom stand? Because you say I cast out demons by Beelzebub. "And if I cast out demons by Beelzebub, by whom do your sons cast [them] out? Therefore they will be your judges. "But if I cast out demons with the finger of God, surely the kingdom of God has come upon you."[7]

The next six parallels are obvious, but when seen as a group they create a solid sequence that makes the more occulted ones visible.

4) The Crowds Increase

Josephus and Luke each record the Jews' massing around a "son of god" (Luke 11:29).

> As the crowds were increasing...[8]

> The Jews became still more and more in number...[9]

5) Lying in Wait

Luke then describes Jesus being assailed by Jews "lying in wait" for him and seeking to "catch him" before his triumphant entrance into Jerusalem. These expressions in Luke symbolize the battle Titus experienced with the Jews before his "triumphal entrance" into Jerusalem.

> And as He said these things to them, the scribes and the Pharisees began to assail [Him] vehemently, and to cross-examine Him about many things, lying in wait for Him, and seeking to catch Him in something He might say, that they might accuse Him.[10]

---

[7] Luke 11:17-20
[8] Luke 11:29.
[9] Josephus, *The Wars of the Jews*, 5.2.78.
[10] Luke 11:53-54.

...Caesar himself: [who spake to them thus] "These Jews, who are only conducted by their madness, do every thing with care, and circumspection: they contrive stratagems, and lay ambushes..."[11]

6) Divide the Group Three for Two

The next parallel is important in that not only is it obvious but created by a unique concept. The parallel would be unlikely to be accidental under any circumstances but could not be so within a sequence. Luke underscores the linked concept, the "division by reducing from 3 to 2," by repeating it:

> "Do [you] suppose that I came to give peace on earth? I tell you, not at all, but rather division. For from now on five in one house will be divided: three against two, and two against three."[12]

> These followers of John also did now seize upon this inner temple, and upon all the warlike engines therein; and then ventured to oppose Simon. And thus that sedition, which had been divided into three factions, was now reduced to two.[13]

7) Cut Down the Fruit Tree

Again, the next parallel is obvious. Jesus "envisions" that a fruit tree outside of Jerusalem would be cut down, which Titus then made to "come to pass."

> He also spoke this parable: "A certain [man] had a fig tree planted in his vineyard, and he came seeking fruit on it and found none. Then he said to the keeper of his vineyard, 'Look, for three years I have come seeking fruit on this fig tree and find none. Cut it down; why does it use up the ground?' But he answered and said to him, 'Sir, let it alone this year also, until I dig around it and fertilize [it]. And if it bears fruit, [well]. But if not, after that you can cut it down.'"[14]

---

[11] Josephus, *The Wars of the Jews*, 5.3.121.
[12] Luke 12:51-53.
[13] Josephus, *The Wars of the Jews*, 5.3.104-105.
[14] Luke 13:6-9.

But Titus, intending to pitch his camp nearer to the city than Scopus, placed as many of his choice horsemen and footmen as he thought sufficient opposite to the Jews, to prevent their sallying out upon them, while he gave orders for the whole army to level the distance, as far as the wall of the city. So they threw down all the hedges and walls which the inhabitants had made about their gardens and groves of trees, and cut down all the fruit trees that lay between them and the wall of the city…[15]

8) How to Build a Tower

"For which of you, intending to build a tower, does not sit down first and count the cost, whether he has [enough] to finish [it—] lest, after he has laid the foundation, and is not able to finish, all who see [it] begin to mock him, saying, 'This man began to build and was not able to finish.'"[16]

Titus went round the wall looking for the best place to build a tower.[17]

9) Send a Delegation

"Or what king, going to make war against another king, does not sit down first and consider whether he is able with ten thousand to meet him who comes against him with twenty thousand? Or else, while the other is still a great way off, he sends a delegation and asks conditions of peace."[18]

…Josephus…attempted to discourse to those that were upon the wall, about terms of peace…[19]

INSIDE THE CITY

10) The Triumphal Entrance and the Stones that Cried Out

---

[15] Josephus, *The Wars of the Jews*, 5.3.106-107.
[16] Luke 14:28-30.
[17] Josephus, *The Wars of the Jews*, 5.6.258.
[18] Luke 14:31-32.
[19] Josephus, *The Wars of the Jews*, 5.6.261.

Luke then describes Jesus beginning his triumphant entrance into Jerusalem. In the passage, Luke describes "stones" that "cry out," and then that which was "hidden from the eyes."

> And they threw their own clothes on the colt, and they set Jesus on him. And as He went, [many] spread their clothes on the road. Then, as He was now drawing near the descent of the Mount of Olives, the whole multitude of the disciples began to rejoice and praise God with a loud voice for all the mighty works they had seen, saying: "Blessed [is] the King who comes in the name of the LORD! Peace in heaven and glory in the highest!" And some of the Pharisees called to Him from the crowd, "Teacher, rebuke Your disciples." But He answered and said to them, "I tell you that if these should keep silent, the stones would immediately cry out."[20]
>
> Now as He drew near, He saw the city and wept over it, saying, "If you had known, even you, especially in this your day, the things [that make] for your peace! But now they are hidden from your eyes."[21]

Josephus then describes Titus' "triumphant entrance" into Jerusalem. In other words, Josephus describes Titus' "entrance" into the city, i.e., the stones hurled by his catapults. In the passage, Josephus made an apparent mistake, writing the "son cometh" rather than the "stone cometh." Though the apparent error has puzzled scholars, recognizing the sequence within which the two events occur makes the satirical and typological meaning of Josephus' "error" clear. Notice that Josephus first describes "the coming of the stone," then a stone that "cries out," and finally he says that the "son/stone" was "hidden from your (the Jews') eyes." It is amusing that in Whiston's translation below he inadvertently, but correctly, captures the real meaning of Josephus' wordplay concerning "stones crying out" with his phrase, "and the stone came from it, and cried out aloud." In other words, the Greek statement can be logically read in two ways. One way is just as Jesus predicted: the stones cried out. Notice

---

[20] Luke 19:35-40
[21] Luke 19:41-42

also that what the stones would "cry out" in the Gospels: the true identity of the son of God. This is exactly what Josephus says the "stone" did in the passage below.

> The engines, that all the legions had ready prepared for them, were admirably contrived; but still more extraordinary ones belonged to the tenth legion: those that threw darts and those that threw stones were more forcible and larger than the rest, by which they not only repelled the excursions of the Jews, but drove those away that were upon the walls also. Now the stones that were cast were of the weight of a talent, and were carried two furlongs and further. The blow they gave was no way to be sustained, not only by those that stood first in the way, but by those that were beyond them for a great space. As for the Jews, they at first watched the coming of the stone, for it was of a white color, and could therefore not only be perceived by the great noise it made, but could be seen also before it came by its brightness; accordingly the watchmen that sat upon the towers gave them notice when the engine was let go, **and the stone came from it, and cried out aloud,** in their own country language, **"The son cometh:"** so those that were in its way stood off, and threw themselves down upon the ground; by which means, and by their thus guarding themselves, the stone fell down and did them no harm. But the Romans contrived how to prevent that by blacking the stone, who then could aim at them with success, when the stone was not discerned beforehand, as it had been till then; and so they destroyed many of them at one blow.[22]

Note that, in Hebrew, "son" is "*ben*" and stone is "*eben*." Josephus' pun on these words in the passage above was established earlier in the Gospels:

> "…and do not think to say to yourselves, 'We have Abraham as [our] father.' For I say to you that God is able to raise up sons to Abraham from these stones."[23]

---

[22] Josephus, *The Wars of the Jews*, 5.6.269-273.
[23] Matthew 3:9

11) Jerusalem Encircled with a Wall

Luke then describes Jesus "envisioning" the encircling of Jerusalem with a wall. Thus the overall pattern connects to a parallel that cannot be disputed. Scholars have always recognized that Luke 19:43 was dependent upon Josephus' description of Jerusalem encircled with a wall, but heretofore have not seen the parallel within an overall pattern.

> "For days will come upon you when your enemies will build an embankment around you, surround you and close you in on every side, and level you, and your children within you, to the ground; and they will not leave in you one stone upon another, because you did not know the time of your visitation."[24]

Josephus then describes Titus' encircling of Jerusalem with a wall. Scholars have always understood this event as the basis for Jesus' prophecy above.

> ...they must build a wall round about the whole city; which was, he thought, the only way to prevent the Jews from coming out any way, and that then they would either entirely despair of saving the city, and so would surrender it up to him, or be still the more easily conquered when the famine had further weakened them; for that besides this wall, he would not lie entirely at rest afterward, but would take care then to have banks raised again, when those that would oppose them were become weaker. But that if anyone should think such a work to be too great, and not to be finished without much difficulty, he ought to consider, that it is not fit for Romans to undertake any small work, and that none but God himself could with ease accomplish any great thing whatsoever.[25]

12) The Abomination of Desolation

Jesus predicted the Abomination of Desolation would occur during the coming war and though Daniel's prophecy is noted, it is not technically referred to in Luke. This parallel perhaps sheds light on why different

---

[24] Luke 19:43-44
[25] Josephus, *The Wars of the Jews*, 5.12.499-501.

Gospels were written, as it enables the authors to make the relationship between Jesus and Titus more difficult to see. The specific reference to the Abomination of Desolation was placed into Matthew, and the authors required that a reader remember that fact in order to "understand" that the passage in Luke is placed in the correct spot in the sequence.

Notice the witticism whereby the author of Matthew notes that the "reader" needs to "understand" something about the "Abomination of Desolation." What he needs to understand is that, if it had been included in the same passage in Luke, with its numerous typological parallels occurring in the same sequence, the Jesus/Titus typology would be too obvious. Instead, Matthew felt it sufficient to drop a hint, which he would not have done had his intention been simply to hide the truth.

> Then He said to them, "Nation will rise against nation, and kingdom against kingdom. And there will be great earthquakes in various places, and famines and pestilences; and there will be fearful sights and great signs from heaven. But before all these things, they will lay their hands on you and persecute [you,] delivering [you] up to the synagogues and prisons. You will be brought before kings and rulers for My name's sake. But it will turn out for you as an occasion for testimony. Therefore settle [it] in your hearts not to meditate beforehand on what you will answer; for I will give you a mouth and wisdom which all your adversaries will not be able to contradict or resist. You will be betrayed even by parents and brothers, relatives and friends; and they will put [some] of you to death. And you will be hated by all for My name's sake. But not a hair of your head shall be lost. By your patience possess your souls.
> "But when you see Jerusalem surrounded by armies, then know that its desolation is near."[26]
> "For nation will rise against nation, and kingdom against kingdom. And there will be famines, pestilences, and earthquakes in various places. All these [are] the beginning of sorrows.

---

[26] Luke 21:10-20

"Then they will deliver you up to tribulation and kill you, and you will be hated by all nations for My name's sake. And then many will be offended, will betray one another, and will hate one another. Then many false prophets will rise up and deceive many. And because lawlessness will abound, the love of many will grow cold. But he who endures to the end shall be saved. And this gospel of the kingdom will be preached in all the world as a witness to all the nations, and then the end will come.

"Therefore when you see the 'abomination of desolation,' spoken of by Daniel the prophet, standing in the holy place (whoever reads, let him understand)..."[27]

Josephus recorded that Daniel's prophecy came to pass at the correct place within the sequence.

And now Titus gave orders to his soldiers that were with him to dig up the foundations of the tower of Antonia, and make him a ready passage for his army to come up; while he himself had Josephus brought to him (for he had been informed that on that very day, which was the seventeenth day of Panemus, [Tamuz,] the sacrifice called "the Daily Sacrifice" had failed, and had not been offered to God, for want of men to offer it, and that the people were grievously troubled at it,)...And who is there that does not know what the writings of the ancient prophets contain in them,–and particularly that oracle which is just now going to be fulfilled upon this miserable city? For they foretold that this city should be then taken when somebody shall begin the slaughter of his own countrymen. And are not both the city and the entire temple now full of the dead bodies of your countrymen? It is God, therefore, it is God himself who is bringing on this fire, to purge that city and temple by means of the Romans, and is going to pluck up this city, which is full of your pollutions."[28]

---

[27] Matthew 24:7-15
[28] Josephus, *The Wars of the Jews*, 6.2.93-110.

Whiston recorded the "miraculous" date of the Abomination of Desolation in a footnote: "This was a remarkable day indeed, the seventeenth of Panemus, [Tamuz,] AD 70, when, according to Daniel's prediction, six hundred and six years before, the Romans 'in half a week caused the sacrifice and oblation to cease,' (Daniel 9:27). For from the month of February, AD 66, about which time Vespasian entered on this war, to this very time, was just three years and a half." Daniel, it must be remembered, predicted that the "abomination of desolation" would occur in the middle of a week to seven years.

> From the time that the daily sacrifice is abolished and the abomination that causes desolation is set up, there will be 1,290 days.[29]

13) The Son of Mary who was a Human Passover Lamb

Though it is too complex a parallel to analyze in this short paper, Josephus does present a deliberate parallel to the son of Mary who was a human Passover lamb in the Gospels at the correct point in his narration. This is the famous "Cannibal Mary" story found at *Wars* 6, iii,191-212.

OUTSIDE JERUSALEM

14) Three Crucified, One Survives

When doing the original analysis that led to *Caesar's Messiah*, one thing seemed strange to me. Why had Josephus not recorded a parallel to the most central event in the ministry of Jesus—his crucifixion? There seemed to be no parallel to the event in *Wars of the Jews*. Armed with the understanding that the campaigns of Jesus and Titus occurred in the same sequence, however, I began to analyze Josephus' other works to see if any of them contained a parallel to the Gospels' crucifixion story.

I discovered the parallel to Jesus' crucifixion in Josephus' biography, *The Life of Flavius Josephus*. The author of the works of Josephus understood that if the crucifixion parallel had been placed next to the story of

---

[29] Daniel 12:11

the human Passover lamb, the combination would have made their relationship to the Gospels' story too transparent. He therefore placed it in another section of the work. To establish its place in the overall sequence, however, the author provided the necessary details to place the event between the "human Passover lamb" and the condemnation of "Simon" and the sparing of "John," shown below, which occurs at the conclusion of the Gospels.

Below is the parallel, which, when seen within the sequence, becomes too vivid to dispute and in my opinion can be seen as a concrete demonstration of a typological linkage between the two "saviors" of Israel, Jesus and Titus.

> Moreover, when the city Jerusalem was taken by force...I was sent by Titus Caesar...to a certain village called Thecoa, in order to know whether it were a place fit for a camp; as I came back, I saw many captives crucified, and remembered three of them as my former acquaintances. I was very sorry at this in my mind, and went with tears in my eyes to Titus, and told him of them; so he immediately commanded them to be taken down, and to have the greatest care taken of them, in order to their recovery; yet two of them died under the physician's hands, while the third recovered.[30]

Not only does Josephus' passage mirror the Gospels by depicting three men being crucified and one who "miraculously" survives, but the name of the "good counselor" who begs the Roman commander to take the survivor down from the cross is *Joseph*. In fact, the name of the Gospels' "good counselor"—Joseph of "Arimathea" is obviously a play on the full name of Titus' "good counselor," Joseph bar Matthias.

15) Simon Condemned and John Spared

The Gospels conclude with a discussion between Simon (Peter) and Jesus. Jesus foresees that Simon will be bound and carried "where you do not wish to go." Jesus also tells Simon that he will have a martyr's death,

---

[30] Flavius Josephus, *The Life of Flavius Josephus*, translated by William Whiston. (1737), 75, 417-421. [Available at: https://lexundria.com/j_vit/0/wst].

"to glorify God." In the midst of this discussion, "the disciple that Jesus loved," clearly meaning the Apostle John, appears. Simon asks Jesus what the fate of John is to be. Jesus replies, "It is my will that he remain." The passage then points out that John "is the disciple who is bearing witness to these things, and who has written these things" referring to the Gospel of John itself.

Below is the entire passage. Notice how the author goes to great lengths to avoid calling the Apostles by their real names, Simon and John.

> "Truly, truly, I say to you, when you were young, you girded yourself and walked where you would; but when you are old, you will stretch out your hands, and another will gird you and carry you where you do not wish to go." (This he said to show by what death he was to glorify God.) And after this he said to him, "Follow me."
> Peter turned and saw following them the disciple whom Jesus loved, who had lain close to his breast at the supper and had said, "Lord, who is it that is going to betray you?" When Peter saw him, he said to Jesus, "Lord, what about this man?" Jesus said to him, "If it is my will that he remain until I come, what is that to you? Follow me!" The saying spread abroad among the brethren that this disciple was not to die; yet Jesus did not say to him that he was not to die, but, "If it is my will that he remain until I come, what is that to you?"
> This is the disciple who is bearing witness to these things, and who has written these things; and we know that his testimony is true.[31]

This passage, which is the conclusion to Jesus' ministry, is exactly parallel to Titus' judgments concerning the rebel leaders Simon bar Gioras and John of Gischala at the conclusion of his campaign through Judea. Thus, at the conclusion of the Gospel above, Jesus tells Simon, "when you are old, you will stretch out your hands, and another will gird you and carry you where you do not wish to go." Jesus tells Simon to "follow me"

---

[31] John 21:18-24

and that his death will "glorify God." However, Jesus also states that it is his will that John is to "remain."[32]

At the conclusion of his campaign through Judea, Titus, after capturing "Simon," girds him in "bonds" and sends him "where you do not wish to go," this being Rome. During the parade of conquest at Rome, Simon follows, that is, is "led" to a "death, to glorify God," the god "glorified" being Titus' father, the *diuus* Vespasian. However, it is Titus' will to spare the other leader of the rebellion, John.

Notice that in the following passage, Josephus records Simon's fate before John's, just as it occurs in John 21. A seemingly innocuous detail, but one that I will show has great significance.

> Simon...was forced to surrender himself, as we shall relate hereafter; so he was reserved for the triumph, and to be then slain; as was John condemned to perpetual imprisonment.[33]

Josephus also records that Jesus' vision of Simon "following" also comes to pass for the rebel leader Simon.

> Simon...had then been led in this triumph among the captives; a rope had also been put upon his head, and he had been drawn into a proper place in the forum.[34]

In the passage from the Gospel of John above, notice that the author does not call the Apostle John by his name but rather as "the disciple whom Jesus loved" and as the individual who had said at the Last Supper, "Lord, who is it that is going to betray you?" Later in the chapter the

---

[32] But isn't Jesus only speaking hypothetically, not actually revealing the fate of the Beloved Disciple? Scholars have long recognized that the original point of the saying *was* a prediction, like Mark 9:1, "There are some standing here who will not taste death before they see the kingdom of God come with power." When the author of John 21 says "the brethren" have misinterpreted the saying as a real prediction, it is rather *he* who has *re*interpreted it as a hypothetical, in light of the delay of the expected Parousia of Jesus (which itself would have been a misunderstanding of the original denotation of the Parousia, i.e., that of Titus in 70 AD).

[33] Josephus, *Wars of the Jews*, 6.9.433-434.

[34] Ibid. 7.5.154

author identifies this disciple with yet another epithet when he states, "This is the disciple who testifies of these things, and wrote these things"—even here not referring to John by name but requiring the reader to determine it by knowing the name of the author of the Gospel. The author's use of epithets here, instead of simply referring to the disciple as "John," seems clearly an attempt to keep the parallel conclusion of Jesus' and Titus' "ministries" from being too easily seen. The author also has Jesus call Simon by his nickname, "Peter," for the same reason.

The same technique is used throughout the New Testament and *Wars of the Jews*. To learn the name of an unnamed character, the reader must be able to recall details from another, related passage. In effect, the New Testament is designed as a sort of intelligence test, whose true meaning can be understood only by those possessing sufficient memory, logic, and irreverent humor.[35]

For clarification, I present the following list showing the parallels between the ends of Jesus' ministry and Titus' campaigns:

1. Characters are named Simon and John.
2. Both sets of characters are judged.
3. Both sides of the parallel occur at the conclusion of a "campaign."
4. Jesus predicts and Titus fulfills Simon going to a martyr's death after being placed in bonds and taken someplace he does not wish to go.
5. In each, John is spared.
6. In each, Simon "follows."

Like the Arch of Titus, the typological system in the Gospels seems to have been created to assuage the vanity of the Flavian Caesars. If this was the case, the typology performs the same function as the Moses/Jesus

---

[35] This is no foreign or anachronistic notion, as witness passages like Mark 4:9-12, 23, and Revelation 13:18 (which also seems to hint at the identity of a Flavian Emperor, Domitian as Nero Redivivus, predicted to destroy Rome as Titus destroyed Jerusalem).

typology given at the beginning of the Gospels and "reveals" an identity. The typology indicates that the "Son of Man" who Jesus predicted would bring destruction to Jerusalem was Titus Flavius, and Christians have been unwittingly worshipping Caesar for 2,000 years.

Chapter 6: Pauline Origin of the Gospels in the Wake of the First Jewish-Roman War

By R. G. Price

I understand the initial reaction that many people have to the proposition that Jesus wasn't a real person. I had that reaction too. The proposition may seem absurd. Claims made by some advocates of the proposition are absurd.

I was already an atheist when I began addressing the issue of mythicism around the year 2000. I believed that it was important to refute the claims of mythicists because taking unsupportable and anti-academic positions on matters of religion could be damaging to the already challenged position that atheists are in in our society. I felt that as atheists it was important to stick to the facts and stick to what is provable, certainly not to get wrapped up in so-called conspiracy theories. Thus, rebutting mythicism was about protecting the already suspect and fragile reputation of atheists like myself.

Yet, the more I studied the subject the more I started to see that underneath the overzealous claims of pagan influences and pious frauds, there actually was biblical analysis put forward by some so-called mythicists that seemed to make sense. After having read several books and websites on the subject, largely for the purpose of debunking them, I read Robert M. Price's book, *The Incredible Shrinking Son of Man*, which was the first scholarship on the subject that I personally had read that actually seemed to have merit. After finishing Dr. Price's book, I thought, "Okay, maybe there is something to this idea."

Price's work led me to Earl Doherty's work and Arthur Drews, among others. But my approach to any subject that I want to deeply understand is to study the subject first-hand myself, not to rely on the interpretations of others. So once I had grasped the concept behind the analysis put forward by Price, Doherty, and others, I decided to study the Bible and early Christian literature myself to see if their claims held up under broader scrutiny, and to develop my own understanding of the material.

I easily understood that there was an important relationship between the Christian idea that Jesus had fulfilled prophecies and the manner in which the Gospels had likely been constructed. So, after having read the Gospels, the first thing I did was simply research the lists of prophecies that Christians claimed Jesus had fulfilled. It didn't take long to see that what Christians were calling examples of "prophecy fulfillment" were in fact examples of literary construction. These weren't examples of recorded events that corresponded to passages from the Jewish scriptures; these were clearly instances where the writers of the Gospels had fabricated scenes based on the scriptures. Many of these scenes were in fact foundational to the biography of Jesus.

As I first learned from Dr. Price in *The Incredible Shrinking Son of Man*, even the Crucifixion itself was one of these scenes clearly derived from scriptures. Every aspect of the Crucifixion scene, in every single Gospel, indicates that the scene is fully fabricated and not in any way based on eyewitness testimony or even merely on oral accounts. The scene is clearly meticulously crafted from scriptural references, a product of literary development, not secondhand accounts or even urban legends.

So at this point, around 2006, I had gone from thinking that mythicism was utter nonsense, to starting to develop my own theory of Christian origins in the absence of a human Jesus. For me, it all came down to understanding what was now widely agreed to be the earliest account of the life of Jesus: the Gospel of Mark. I focused my attention on the Gospel of Mark and sought to understand the purpose and inspiration behind every sentence and detail in the work. I identified dozens of literary relationships between Mark and the Jewish scriptures. I then went on to look for sources of Jesus' teachings and found that virtually all of them in the Gospel of Mark could be traced back to the letters of Paul. After having catalogued and analyzed this information, and after having read through the story multiple times, it finally started to dawn on me what this story actually was. This was an allegorical story written in reaction to the First Jewish-Roman War and the destruction of the Temple, written by a follower of Paul the apostle, in which Paul himself was the inspiration for the Jesus character.

At this point you may think that seems speculative and that, even if it is true, it doesn't prove that Jesus didn't exist. Let's now fast-forward to today to look at some of the relevant scholarship surrounding this issue and the larger case that presents itself.

In 1988, Wolfgang Roth had published a little-known book that laid out the relationship between the Gospel of Mark and the story of Elijah and Elisha from the books of Kings in the Jewish scriptures, called *Hebrew Gospel: Cracking the Code of Mark*. This work was followed up in 2010 by Adam Winn with another book on this topic, called *Mark and the Elijah-Elisha Narrative*. These works show how the writer of Mark constructed his narrative from one of the most popular and well-known narratives in the Jewish scriptures.

In 2011, David Oliver Smith published *Matthew, Mark, Luke, and Paul: The Influence of the Epistles on the Synoptic Gospels*. Smith's work expertly and convincingly laid out a multitude of relationships between the Synoptic Gospels, particularly the Gospel of Mark, and the letters of Paul. Smith also highlighted Michael Turton's work on the use of chiasmus by the writer of Mark, further showing the literary complexity of the narrative.

In 2012, Tom Dykstra published *Mark, Canonizer of Paul: A New Look at Intertextuality in Mark's Gospel*. Dykstra's analysis and conclusions regarding the relationship between the Gospel of Mark and the letters of Paul were remarkably similar to my own, and Dykstra provided essential background into the subject of the relationship between Mark and the Pauline letters. Dykstra showed that the proposition that the Gospel of

Mark was dependent upon the letters of Paul had been put forward as far back as 1857 by the German biblical scholar Gustav Volkmar, at which time it was harshly criticized by establishment scholars and generally disregarded for over a century.

In addition to these works, there has been a growing realization that the Gospels, particularly the Gospel of Mark, are not historical in any sense. Works such as Mary Ann Tolbert's *Sowing the Gospel: Mark's World in Literary-Historical Perspective*, John Shelby Spong's *Liberating the Gospels: Reading the Bible with Jewish Eyes*, and many others, have made the case that the Gospels are literary constructs, filled with allegory and symbolism, not historical accounts of real events.

On top of all this, we have the growing case against the so-called two-source hypothesis of Q. The most prominent work on this matter is Mark Goodacre's 2002 publication, *The Case Against Q: Studies in Markan Priority and the Synoptic Problem*. In this work, Goodacre lays out the evidence showing that the Q hypothesis does not hold up and that the proposition that Luke had simply used both Mark and Matthew as his sources, instead of Mark and a theoretical independent source known as "Q," far better explains the evidence we find in the Synoptics. This case is further bolstered by David Oliver Smith's previously mentioned work, which shows that Paul's epistles are at the heart of much of the supposed Q material.

So what does all of this amount to? How does any of this support the idea that "Jesus never existed"?

My 2018 book, *Deciphering the Gospels Proves Jesus Never Existed*, shows that once we establish that the Gospel of Mark is a literary invention, created by the author himself, constructed from references to the Jewish scriptures and the letters of Paul, not based on "oral traditions" or other such sources, the conclusion that every account of the life of Jesus can be traced back to the Gospel of Mark becomes inescapable. If indeed every account of the life of Jesus can be traced back to a single fictional allegory, the implications here are obvious.

What, then, is the proposed model for Christian origins under this scenario? First let's get an overview of the general model put forward by so-called mainstream biblical scholars. I must note, of course, that there is no singularly agreed upon model, but I will summarize here the model put forward in the highly influential work put out by the Jesus Seminar, *The Five Gospels, What Did Jesus Really Say?*

The model put forward by the Jesus Seminar, and I believe widely accepted by many biblical scholars, proposes three main sources of traditions, all of which trace back to the life of Jesus the man. Those three main sources are teachings of Jesus contained in the Gospel of Thomas and Q, stories about Jesus conveyed by oral traditions, and a primitive narrative gospel represented by the "miraculous signs" narrative in the Gospel of John. As the Jesus Seminar itself endorsed, Paul is not a part of the sources at all. Indeed, Paul is seen in the mainstream view as completely orthogonal to the development of the Gospels. For mainstream biblical scholars, Paul is an "independent witness" to the Gospel teachings of Jesus. But beyond that, it is acknowledged that Paul himself really provides no account of Jesus the man—Paul shows no interest in a human Jesus.

> Accordingly, the gospels may be understood as corrections of this creedal imbalance, which was undoubtedly derived from the view espoused by the apostle Paul, who did not know the historical Jesus. For Paul, the Christ was to be understood as a dying/rising lord, symbolized in baptism (buried with him, raised with him), of the type he knew from the Hellenistic mystery religions. In Paul's theological scheme, Jesus the man played no essential role.[1]

So in this view, a view widely held by mainstream biblical scholars, the first person to write about Jesus really tells us nothing about him, is not concerned with a human Jesus, and is in some sense a misguided advocate

---

[1] R. W. Funk, & R. W. Hoover, The Five Gospels: What Did Jesus Really Say? The Search for the Authentic Words of Jesus. (New York and Toronto: Macmillan, 1993), p. 7.

expounding proto-gnostic mystery religion. The Gospels, then, are a correction to Paul's misguided views. Even though we now recognize that Paul's letters were written before the Gospels, the widely held view is that the Gospels actually trace back to older sources that pre-date Paul. Those older sources are, at the very least, the hypothetical document "Q," "oral traditions," and a hypothetical primitive "miraculous signs" gospel. Even though the Gospels were penned after the works of Paul, they actually present to us older sources of information about Jesus. The letters of Paul are seen as a separate independent witness to the oral traditions and teachings that underly the Gospels. Thus, similarities between teachings found in the letters of Paul and teachings attributed to Jesus in the Gospels are seen as evidence of broadly disseminated knowledge of the teachings of Jesus within an early community, despite the fact that Paul does not attribute his teachings to Jesus.

The following is one simple example of how the relationship between the letters of Paul and the Gospel sayings of Jesus are understood by mainstream scholars:

> There is a reference to moving mountains in 1 Cor 13:2, although it is not attributed to Jesus. Paul's knowledge of the saying indicates that the connection between faith and moving mountains was widespread in the early tradition.[2]

So, in this model we have a person Jesus who comes from a remote village and becomes a travelling preacher who garners a following of students and worshipers. This Jesus comes into conflict with Jewish authorities in Jerusalem and is ultimately executed for his transgressions. A community of people who worship this Jesus maintain accounts and develop narratives about his teachings and the events that led to his execution. For unknown reasons these accounts are either not written down or are later lost. Someone named Paul, who was not an original member of this community, is the first major advocate of the cult to produce a volume of

---

[2] Funk & Hoover, The Five Gospels: What Did Jesus Really Say? The Search for the Authentic Words of Jesus. (New York and Toronto: Macmillan, 1993), p. 99.

preserved writings, yet this Paul gives no account of Jesus himself, instead claiming that his knowledge of Jesus comes from revelation. This Paul focused on revelations and mysteries about the coming of a new age in which the souls of the righteous would enter the Kingdom of God in heaven. Paul claims not to have learned about Jesus from others and Paul makes no claim that his teachings come from Jesus (with rare exception—and then via revelation). Time passed. Shortly after Paul's death, a major conflict broke out between the Jews and Romans now known as the First Jewish-Roman War, during which the Romans sacked Jerusalem, destroyed the Temple, and enacted harsh repressions against the Jews. Unrelated to these events, accounts of the life of Jesus started to be produced. Many accounts of the life of Jesus were produced in the late first century and early second century, including the four canonical Gospels. These accounts, however, are based on sources from prior to the war and primarily reflect a pre-Pauline understanding of Jesus. Their primary concern is with conveying information about the life and teachings of Jesus. It is these later accounts that tell us how people thought about Jesus before Paul had come onto the scene. Where exactly the Gospels came from, who wrote them, why they wrote them, when they wrote them, etc., are all essentially unknown and perhaps unknowable. Knowledge of Jesus the man emanates from a multitude of sources, including community traditions and various independent writings. Other heretical sects who worshiped a purely spiritual Jesus were a product of later confusion and superstition.

What I've just laid out above is the basic mainstream model for Christian origins. We can see that this model leaves many open questions. Why were the Gospels not written until after Paul's death and the sack of Jerusalem? Why didn't Paul attribute his teachings to Jesus if they came from Jesus? Why are the Gospels anonymously written? Why were so many Gospels written so quickly following the production of the first Gospel? How did this presumably illiterate country teacher inspire such fervent worship in a culture with no history of worshiping people as gods? Why was this simple man worshiped as "the Lord" so quickly following his death? Why did Paul claim that the reason he and others worshiped "the Lord Jesus" was because he had overcome death and risen from the grave? Why does the first Gospel portray the followers of Jesus as fools who cannot understand him, indeed calling Peter Satan? The questions go on from here.

All of these questions, and many more, are answered when we recognize that the Gospel of Mark was written by a Pauline follower in the wake of Paul's death and the destruction of the Temple, and that every account of the life of Jesus flows from the Gospel of Mark.

The implications here are profound. Indeed, in my book *Deciphering the Gospels* I propose merely that the Gospel of Mark was written by a "follower" of Paul, yet I now believe that such an assessment is insufficient. The Gospel of Mark must have been written by much more than simply a Pauline "follower." The Gospel of Mark must have been written by someone within the inner Pauline circle. This must be the case because the Gospel of Mark is actually our earliest witness to the collected letters of Paul. All in all, there are thirteen letters attributed to Paul in the New Testament. Of those thirteen, between six and eight are now widely believed to be authentic, with the others now being regarded as later forgeries. Intertextual analysis identifies relationships between seven of the letters of Paul and the Gospel of Mark. Those seven letters are among those deemed most likely to be authentic, and we can use those relations to indeed confirm that these seven letters are part of the original collection.

The fact that the author of Mark has a collection of all seven letters, and is the first person we can identify to possess them, potentially some forty to eighty years before Marcion, tells us that this person must have been a part of the community that produced the letters of Paul to begin with. That the writer of Mark had possession of the collection of Paul's letters tells us that, when the letters were produced, copies must have been made. If the letters were indeed actually sent to the groups they were addressed to at all, what would had to have happened is that one copy was sent while the other copy was retained. The collection of letters comes from the community that preserved the retained copies. That community would have been the intimate associates of Paul. This means that the person who wrote the Gospel of Mark almost certainly personally knew Paul. This was not a mere "follower" of Paul; this was an intimate associate of Paul.

We now go back to what the Jesus Seminar has said about Paul, which is widely acknowledged by biblical scholars. Paul was engaged in the promotion of a mystery religion in which, "Jesus the man played no essential role." If the first Gospel is written by an associate of Paul, casting Paul himself in the role of Jesus, and all of the other Gospels flow from the first, then of course the very idea that the Gospels can be viewed as corrections to the "creedal imbalance" of Pauline teachings falls apart entirely. But beyond that, it also gives us a much better understanding of why the first Gospel was written, how it was written, and the genre of its form. The first Gospel is not historical in any sense. The first Gospel, written by an intimate insider of Paul's mystery cult, is itself a mystical allegory, written in the form of Orphic theogonies. This is a work that is consciously filled with mysteries, riddles, and enigmas, intended to be fully understood only by initiates. These types of writings were heavily associated with mystery religions and had been for centuries. Indeed, the fourth century BCE Derveni Papyrus provides a concise description of how such mystery writings were understood by initiates.

> <I shall also prove that Orpheus composed a> hymn that tells of wholesome and permissible things. For he was speaking allegorically with his poetic composition, and it was impossible to state the application of his words and what was meant. His composition is prophetic and riddling for people. But Orpheus himself did not wish to utter disputable riddles, but important things in riddles. In fact he is speaking allegorically from his very first word right through to his last, as he reveals even in his easily-explained verse: for the one who bids them 'shut the doors' on their ears is saying that he is certainly not making laws for the many, but instructing those who are pure in hearing...
> - Derveni Papyrus col. VII (translation by Richard Janko, PhD.)

Mystery religions were filled with allegories that contained hidden meaning that could only be fully understood by initiates and those who deeply studied them. That is exactly what we find in the Gospel of Mark.

In addition, we can see that the Gospel of Mark is in fact a polemic attack against Paul's opponents, Peter, James, and John, those "reputed to be pillars," but whom Paul opposed. And why did Paul oppose them? Paul opposed them because Paul was advocating Jesus as a universal savior, while Peter, James, and John advocated the Jewishness of Jesus. Paul said that you didn't have to become a Jew to be saved by Jesus, while Peter, James, and John denied that. So, Paul's message was one of universality and reconciliation between Jews and Gentiles, while the other leaders of the movement opposed such a universal view. The war between the Jews and the Romans that resulted in the destruction of the Temple was then viewed by the writer of Mark through this lens. The Jews had brought destruction upon themselves because they had failed to heed the message of the prophet Paul. Peter, James, and John, the reputed pillars of the Jesus movement, were a party to this failure. This is what the allegory of Mark is all about.

This is why Peter, James, John, and the other disciples in the story cannot understand Jesus' parables. This is why the disciples fail to recognize who Jesus is. Aside from demons, Peter is the one who finally recognizes him, but Jesus then calls him Satan and Peter goes on to deny and abandon Jesus, just as Paul describes in his letter to the Galatians. The story itself is an allegorical mystery that presents Paul's apostolic opponents as individuals who themselves fail to grasp the mysteries of Christ. We also know that, during this time, pseudonymous works attributed to Paul were being produced as well. These works, such as Ephesians, Colossians, 2 Thessalonians, and the Pastorals, often advocated non-Pauline theology in Paul's name. They show that there was a struggle going on to define the theology of Christ worship, in which one of the best tools available was to forge letters in the name of Paul himself. Among the half dozen or more writers of the early forgeries, it was always Paul or other leaders such as James, whose authority was appealed to, not Jesus'. The way to resolve theological disputes was not to refer to "teachings of Jesus," but rather to claim that your teachings came from Paul or James. It is within this context that the author of Mark put Paul's teachings directly into the mouth of Jesus himself, thereby establishing the authority of "true" Pauline theology.

This also explains why the Gospel of Mark is written anonymously. Firstly, these types of prophetic writings were often written either anonymously or pseudonymously, i.e. falsely attributed to a reputable name. Most pseudonymous works of this nature were written in the name of ancient authorities, like Isaiah, Enoch, Moses, Orpheus, Musaeus, etc. This story was not set in the ancient past, however, so none of those names could apply. In addition, the story is a polemic attack not just on Peter, James, and John, but on the Jewish people as a whole. The story was dangerous. These types of attacks were often produced anonymously because the author did not want to be exposed to reprisals. And lastly, the entire story itself a mystery. The story is supposed to be enigmatic. That the story is about Paul is part of the enigma. If a name like Barnabas or Timothy were associated with the story, it would give too much of the mystery way, and as well could expose the Pauline community to reprisals. So that a story like this would have been produced anonymously makes sense. However, there is no good reason why a genuine history—a sincere attempt to document established teachings of a community—would be produced anonymously. Those types of works were virtually always signed by their writers. This work was not signed because it was not an attempt at recording history; it is a polemic allegory in the genre of mystery theogony.

So, this understanding of the Gospel of Mark has tremendous explanatory power. It explains why the letters of Paul share dozens of teachings with the Gospels, yet Paul attributes none of them to Jesus. It is because those are Paul's teachings, not Jesus' teachings. The writer of Mark used Paul's teachings for his Jesus character, which were then copied into the other Gospels. In addition, David Oliver Smith's work shows that much of the so-called Q material can be traced back to the Pauline letters as well. Thus, the similarities between Paul's teachings and the words of Jesus in the Gospels are not evidence that such sayings were, "widespread in the early tradition," indeed quite the opposite. The similarities between Paul's teachings and those of Jesus in the Gospels indicate that all of these teachings come from a single late source who had no direct knowledge of any real Jesus at all, and indeed who showed no interest even in the concept of such a Jesus. The fact that even the later Gospel writers had only Paul's writings to fall back on indicates that there were no other sources for "sayings of Jesus" to be found when they set out to produce their versions of the Markan story.

And as I discuss in *Deciphering the Gospels*, the fact that the Gospels are ahistorical and provide no actual information about a real Jesus, does not mean that the Gospels can merely be set aside and discounted as evidence either for or against the existence of Jesus, as some may claim. If the first account of the life of Jesus is a fictional allegory and all other accounts copy from and build on that story, it tells us that there was no other biographical material about Jesus to go on. Surely later Gospel writers like Luke sought-out additional information about Jesus. The fact that Luke obviously came up empty handed in his first century search for real sayings of Jesus and real anecdotes about Jesus tells us that there were no existing communities that possessed or even purported to possess knowledge of "Jesus the man."

So, what then is the ultimate model that emerges from this case? I will put forward here what I believe is an account of Christian origins that is supported by the evidence. Certainly, there will be details here that merit debate, but I believe this outline is one that deserves serious consideration.

In the early first century, there were widespread beliefs among Greeks, Romans, and Jews that a "new age" was dawning in which the so-called Roman age would come to an end and a new race of man would rule the world. We see speculation about this new age in the writings at Qumran, in which the Qumranic writers put forward prophecies about how Jews would become the new dominant race of man, aided by both a priestly messiah and a military messiah, who would call down the armies of heaven to aid them in a final battle to overthrow Roman rule as described in the famous Qumranic War Scroll. We see that the teachings of these Qumranic writers relied heavily on scriptural divination—the supposed finding of hidden prophecies in the Jewish scriptures, and the reinterpretation of ancient Jewish texts to find new meaning in them and to "discover" the "true nature" of various figures from the Jewish scriptures.

It is from these types of practices that many of the apocalyptic works of the second century BCE through first century CE are derived. We find stories from figures such as Enoch, an obscure individual from Genesis, who was reinterpreted in this period as a semi-godly figure who travelled up to the heavens and recorded the mysteries of the heavenly powers. Enoch was eventually revealed as the savior himself—the "Son of Man." We find at Qumran a description of Melchizedek, another person from the Jewish scriptures, who was now being interpreted as an eternal heavenly high priest, whose real identity had been kept hidden and secret, only now to be revealed by the prophets.[3] Melchizedek is called *Elohim*—God. It is said that he would judge the world, atone for the sins of the world, and that he would bring about the final defeat of Belial—Satan. Melchizedek combines the features of God, the priestly messiah and the war messiah all into one.

It is from these types of practices and scriptural interpretations that a cult worshiping a Melchizedek-like interpretation of Joshua emerged. Joshua—the one who led the Jews into the promised land. *Yehoshu'a*, the one whose name means "YAHWEH is salvation." It was this new *Yehoshu'a*, revealed by prophets through the scriptures, who was going to be the heavenly messiah who would bring about salvation for the Jewish people at the end of their present age, according to this small millenarian cult.

Paul became a part of this cult, but Paul was a Hellenized Jew. Paul's vision was not one of a new Jewish dominance, but rather of a new savior who would bring about salvation for all people, not just Jews. Paul developed his particular theology. We do not know how much of Paul's

---

[3] 11Q13.

theology was unique to him and how much came from the pre-existing cult of *Yehoshu'a*, but certainly some aspects of Paul's teaching were unique to him. Paul taught that *Yehoshu'a*, now *Iesous* in Greek, delivered himself as the ultimate final sacrifice, thereby overcoming death and leading the way into the new promised land of heaven itself. *Iesous* had set in motion the coming destruction of the corrupt material world and the raising of the souls of the dead. The souls of the righteous who had faith in him would then join *Iesous* in the new heavenly Jerusalem once the material world had been destroyed.

Paul promoted this cult through mystery practices that involved the use of images of the Crucifixion of *Iesous* and teachings about the death and resurrection of *Iesous* that were familiar to Greeks who had worshiped the mysteries of the death and rebirth of Dionysus. Paul presented sometimes strained interpretations of the supposedly prophetic Jewish scriptures to his Greek audience in support of his teachings.

During a time of growing tensions between Jews and Gentiles, Paul taught a message of reconciliation and peace. Paul promoted the Jewish messiah as a universal savior for all people. Paul presented Christ Jesus as a mystery—a mystery to be grasped only through faith. It was Paul who taught the primacy of faith over the law. It was Paul who was in conflict with the Jewish authorities. It was Paul who suffered arrest and abuse. It was Paul whose message was not understood by the pillars of the Jesus cult.

Paul died shortly before the outbreak of the First Jewish-Roman War, or perhaps even during the war. Paul's message of peace and reconciliation had not been heeded. The result was not a glorious new age for Jews—it was the decimation of the Jewish people and the destruction of the Temple.

In the wake of these events, one of Paul's companions produced the story that we now call the "Gospel of Mark." This story makes extensive use of the Jewish scriptures and letters of Paul to construct an allegorical narrative filled with hidden meaning. Virtually every scene is constructed from references to the Jewish scriptures. Virtually every teaching of Jesus comes from the letters of Paul. The Gospel of Mark is written by a master of both Jewish and Greek prophetic literature, following in the footsteps of the Jewish authors of pseudo-Orphic and pseudo-Sibylline works such as *Testament of Orpheus* and the *Sibylline Oracles*.

It is unknown how this story circulated or came into the hands of the writer called Matthew. But when the writer called Matthew read the story, he recognized some of "Mark's" references to the Jewish scriptures. Matthew, for unknown reasons, expanded the story and built upon the scriptural references used by Mark. When Matthew recognized Mark's references, he called them out, stating to his readers that such events, "fulfilled what the Lord had said through the prophets." Matthew also created his own new narratives using scriptural references like Mark had, but calling his references out again with the claim that such events "fulfilled" the words of the prophets. Matthew changed Mark's narrative to be less hostile to Peter, James, John, and the other disciples. Matthew's Jesus was no longer a mystery, but now a clear teacher. Matthew's narrative points out the relationship between Jesus and the Jewish scriptures, and in Matthew's narrative Jesus' teachings are expanded upon and explained. It is unclear whether the writer of Matthew thought that Jesus was a real person or not, but the writer of Matthew certainly knew that he was fabricating his own narrative.

It was Matthew's expanded and clearer narrative that gained prominence and broader circulation. It was Matthew's narrative that seemed far more realistic.

Some wealthy Greek named Theophilus heard some of the stories about Jesus and sought out further confirmation of the claims. This Theophilus consulted the person now known as Luke, likely sometime around the end of the first century. This "Luke" likely believed that Jesus was a real person. Luke worked from the Gospels of Mark and Matthew as well as the letters of Paul, and likely other historical sources such as the works of Josephus, to produce what he believed was a historically credible account. Luke understood that the writer of Matthew had used the account we now attribute to Mark and that Mark had used the writings of Paul.

Luke viewed the writings of Paul as more authoritative than the writings of Mark and the writings of Mark as more authoritative than the writings of Matthew. Thus, when the writer of Luke saw overlap between these sources, he often followed the source that he deemed most authoritative. Luke cut out some of the elements that seemed most unlikely, such as Jesus cursing the fig tree and walking on water. Because Luke viewed Matthew's work as the least credible, he was not compelled to closely follow the material unique to Matthew, but did structure it as best he could into a more believable narrative that more closely followed Mark's original flow. Luke then likely sold his story, along with Acts of the Apostles, to Theophilus, knowing that he was wealthy and would be able to pay for it. The type of work that Luke had done in producing his "well researched account" would have been laborious and certainly warranted payment. Works such as this could command around a year's income for an average Roman at this time. After having paid for these writings, Theophilus may well have sold copies of them in the Roman book market to offset his costs, thus bringing them into wider circulation.

At this point, the Gospel narratives had likely started to circulate in the Roman book market. Some opportunistic writer, now known as John, sought to render his version of the story, perhaps to turn a profit in the Roman market. When "John" wrote his story, he followed Matthew's cue of calling out cases of prophecy fulfillment. This writer also made the effort to convince his readers of the reliability of the narrative, repeatedly assuring his readers that his version of the story was supported by eyewitness testimony. This writer, knowing that multiple similar copies of the story were already in circulation, intentionally changed his up and invented the mysterious "beloved disciple" whose role was to vouch for the truth of his altered account. Unlike the Gospels of Mark, Matthew, and Luke, which he had likely all read, he decided not to copy everything word for word. He reordered events. He invented his own narrative elements to put his unique stamp on the account. John's story, now written during the height of Jewish pogroms in Rome, was, like many other Christian writings at this time, viscerally anti-Jewish. Thus, "John" eliminates the

Jewish leaders James and John from his story altogether and portrays Peter even more poorly than in Mark. The writer builds on the line from the Gospel of Mark about Jesus not giving Jews the "miraculous signs" they called for. The writer invents his own new "miraculous signs" narrative showing that Jesus did perform the "miraculous signs" Jews demanded of him, but yet, *"Even after Jesus had done all these miraculous signs in their presence, they still would not believe in him"* (John 12:37). Thus the Jews could not be absolved of blame for killing the Son of God. This "miraculous signs" narrative is clearly not an early narrative, as the primary function of the narrative is to implicate the Jews in a way that would have been entirely inappropriate to the origins of the original Jewish cult. The "miraculous signs" narrative only makes sense in light of the fate of the Jews after the First Jewish-Roman War, once the religion had become firmly Gentile in orientation.

The belief that Jesus was a real person stemmed entirely from the Gospel stories themselves. The original cult that worshiped the heavenly messiah Joshua was now long gone. That tiny cult was likely wiped from existence in the wake of the First Jewish-Roman War. By the time that the Gospel of Mark was written, Peter, James, and John, like Paul, were likely dead and gone. Vague ideas about the spiritual heavenly Jesus of the original cult persisted in various communities, known generally as Gnostics, but even these communities, likely primarily Pauline in orientation, had only fragmentary and confused knowledge about the mystical beliefs of the original cult. Once the Gospels came on the scene, their stories quickly took precedence over any vague remnants of the original cult. Roman readers of the Gospels took them literally and declared beliefs in a spiritual Jesus heresy. It is likely that, at the very least, the Gospels of Luke and John *were* intended to be taken literally. Though determining the intent of Matthew may be impossible, Matthew's account certainly lends itself to literal interpretation. In all of this, Mark's allegory received little attention. The complexity of Mark's writing, its brevity, its obviously enigmatic nature, its somewhat unpleasant Jesus, its poor portrayal of the disciples, all led to Mark being virtually ignored. Mark was clearly similar enough to the other accounts to be included among the canonical Gospels, but it wasn't considered worthy of serious study. It was widely believed that there was little to be learned from Mark that wasn't better and more clearly represented in the other Gospels. Thus, the allegorical nature of Mark was not recognized. Mark, when it was read, was read through the lens of the other more historicized Gospels.

What caught the attention of Roman scholars were all of the so-called instances of prophecy fulfillment laced throughout the Gospels. Matthew of course had led the way, pointing out Mark's literary references and describing them as instances of prophecy fulfillment. The Gospels, while all essentially being copies of Mark, were just different enough from one another that Roman scholars believed them to be independent accounts. Likewise, they were just similar enough to one another that they appeared to corroborate each other's narratives. Thus, for Roman scholars, these four separate works became powerful proof of prophecy fulfillment, the likes of which they had never seen before. Here they had what they believed to be four independent witnesses who had all recorded narratives that contained dozens, if not hundreds, of parallels between the events of Jesus' life and the Jewish scriptures. As the emperor Constantine's spiritual advisor Lactantius wrote of Jesus in *Divine Institutes*, "we believe Him to be God, not because He performed miracles, but because we have seen that He fulfilled all the things that were foretold to us by the preaching of the prophets."

So this, essentially, is how I believe Christianity originated and developed. The basic model here is one in which the worship of Jesus begins as a small Jewish cult worshiping a messianic heavenly Joshua that had been conceived of through prophetic interpretations of the Jewish scriptures. Paul then became a part of this cult, added his own twists to it, and promoted it to a Gentile audience through the context of a mystery religion. Paul's group likely produced a number of works such as the Letter to the Hebrews and other epistles. Paul and his associates were the major producers of early Christian literature. In the wake of Paul's death and the destruction of the Temple, a member of Paul's inner circle wrote an allegory in which they cast Paul himself as Jesus, put Paul's teachings in Jesus' mouth, and constructed an allegorical narrative through the use of hidden references to the Jewish scriptures. The fact that the Gospel of Mark was written in this way is what makes it possible to determine that the Markan narrative is purely fabricated. The other Gospels are all copied from Mark in one way or another. The new material that is unique to the other Gospels is largely invented by the writers themselves and serves their narrative purposes. What we end up with is a continuous chain of borrowing and building from a single source. The original source is the collected letters of Paul, and then the Gospel of Mark. Everything can be traced back to these sources, along with the Jewish scriptures themselves. The fact that so much of the material was from a few common sources is what made all of the material appear to be cohesive and corroborative. This model, I believe, does a far better job of explaining the data than the mainstream model does.

The case I've laid out may not be entirely correct in every detail, but what is important here is that nothing about this model is outlandish or even novel. In fact, it is the mainstream model that requires a novel view of Christian origins. The mainstream model actually requires miraculous events in order to explain why Jesus would have been worshiped. According to the mainstream model, the development of Christianity is unique and unprecedented. According to the mainstream model, some group of Jews inexplicably worshiped a mundane person as God, though there are no prior examples of this. According to the model I've laid out, the worship of Jesus begins in a way for which we have multiple other examples, such as the examples of Melchizedek and Enoch. The mainstream model requires the use of a multitude of hypothetical lost sources to explain the development of the Gospels. The model I've laid out accounts for the development of the Gospels using existing evidence that we have in-hand. The mainstream model brushes aside the peculiarities of the letters of Paul and the fact that Paul doesn't attribute his teachings to Jesus, while the model I've laid out here explains those features. The mainstream model fails to acknowledge the broader context of Pauline forgeries and the role of Paul as an authority in early Christian writings. The mainstream model ignores the impact of the First Jewish-Roman War and the destruction of the Temple in relation to Gospel narratives, while the model I've laid out specifically addresses the context in which the Gospels were produced. In fact, what the model I've laid out here does is present a more mundane and more typical explanation for the origins of Christianity than the mainstream model does. The mainstream model holds out a less typical, more novel—more miraculous—explanation for the development of Christianity.

The idea that mythicism rests on "conspiracy theories" or wildly unsupportable claims has always been false. It is true that there have been claims made by some so-called mythicists that are wildly unsupportable or that involve "conspiracy theories," but this is true of just about any field, including most certainly the field of Jesus historicity. In fact, it is the idea that Christianity originated with the worship of a real person that requires contortions of the data and wildly unsupportable claims.

I believe that mythicism today is at a place where the concept of biological evolution was prior to the acceptance of Darwin's theory. Prior to Darwin, the accepted view in the Western world was that the earth and all living things had been directly created by God. The suitability of living things to their environment was due to God's design. It was clear to many intellectuals, however, that this couldn't possibly be true, and thus, for centuries prior to Darwin, various alternative explanations to the mainstream answer were put forward. Some of these were more reasonable than others. Some were clearly outlandish. But people kept putting these proposals out there because it was obvious that the accepted view could not possibly be right because it didn't do a good job of accounting for all of the evidence.

As more and more refined proposals came forward, like those of Lamarck, they were ridiculed by defenders of the mainstream. Often the most outlandish evolutionary proposals were used to paint newer, more refined proposals as equally outlandish. When Charles Darwin finally published his *On the Origin of Species*, the same of course was done to him, putting him in the same boat with all of the other rejected proposals of the past. But eventually Darwin's view gained traction and won out, in no small part because it was necessary for science to advance.

I believe we are seeing the same thing today in regard to mythicism. The evidence is mounting. The proposals are getting more refined. And yet of course the new proposals are still painted with the same brush as the outlandish ones by defenders of the mainstream. I get it. I was once there myself. But I do believe that the case being put forward for a new explanation of Christian origins, in which no human Jesus played a role, will eventually win out based on the merits. How long that will take and what the implications will be when it happens, I cannot say, but I do believe it will happen.

I think that, ultimately, the evidence shows that belief in a human Jesus stems from the Gospel stories themselves. The evidence shows that all accounts of the life of Jesus stem from the Gospel of Mark, and that the Gospel of Mark is itself a fictional allegory that was written in the wake of the First Jewish-Roman War, in which the Jesus character is heavily based upon the apostle Paul. The evidence shows that the Jesus being worshiped by Paul was an imagined figure, revealed through the scriptures by Jewish prophets using practices like those we see evidence of at Qumran.

There is nothing outlandish, conspiratorial, or unlikely about this interpretation of the evidence. Indeed, this view of the evidence resolves many issues that are unaddressed by mainstream interpretations. At the same time, we know that the so-called mainstream consensus on Christian origins is built heavily on theology and faith, as opposed to science and objectivity. Understanding Christian origins is not a matter of faith and it is not a responsibility to be abdicated to Christian theologians. Understanding the origins of Christianity is one of the most important matters of history today—it is something that impacts everyone, not just Christians. Understanding the origins of Christianity is extremely important for understanding the development of Western Civilization. It is a matter too important to be left to faith.

Chapter 7: Under the Mushroom Tree
R. Gordon Wasson versus John M. Allegro
By Michael Hoffman

John Allegro's once-infamous book *The Sacred Mushroom and the Cross*[1] generated fierce controversy, at least among those willing to take it seriously enough to be affronted by it. Few take it seriously these days, rightly or wrongly, but it remains fascinating and well worth a new exploration,

---

[1] John M. Allegro, The Sacred Mushroom & the Cross: A study of the nature and origins of Christianity within the fertility cults of the ancient Near East. (New York: Bantam Books, 1971).

especially as a distinctive version of Jesus Mythicism. For Allegro argued that "Jesus" was a Jewish counterpart to the Vedic Soma, a mythic personification of the hallucinogenic mushroom Amanita muscaria, and that the myth presupposes an original ritual use of the sacred mushroom by the first Christians. This proposed parallel is important, showing that the very idea of a sacred mushroom cult is by no means absurd: we know of one that actually existed. But possibility does not equal probability, and with that in mind, let us examine Allegro's case, focusing on the Plaincourault fresco, which appears to show Adam, Eve, and the Serpent flanking the Tree of Knowledge pictured as a giant Amanita muscaria mushroom.

We will attempt to straighten out the citations, issues, and relationships between R. Gordon Wasson, Erwin Panofsky, and John M. Allegro, clearing up some inaccurate assessments and characterizations regarding these basic points. This chapter provides more precision in exactly which arguments or issues were mentioned by whom, and what the reasoning and argumentation were, specifically. The whole treatment of Allegro has always been too sloppy, too careless, too broad-brushed, imprecise—limited to a sound-bite level.

This should represent substantial progress in setting the record straight and integrating Allegro's work properly into the corpus so research can move forward through the Plaincourault Amanita Eden mushroom tree, affirming Allegro's reading rather than the Panofsky/Wasson reading.

Wasson asserted the Eden trees in the text of Genesis deliberately meant Amanita and its host tree, but that the painter of the Eden tree in the Plaincourault fresco was unaware of that meaning (even though the Plaincourault tree looks like Amanita mushrooms). Wasson appears to take it for granted, without even thinking to question, the assumption that no one after pre-history understood Amanita. Moreover, Wasson was likely insincere regarding his position on entheogens in Christianity.

Wasson's View on Mushrooms in the Bible: The Eden Trees Meant Amanita

In both *Soma: Divine Mushroom of Immortality*[2] and *Persephone's Quest: Entheogens and the Origins of Religion*,[3] R. Gordon Wasson asserts that the author of the Eden Tree story in Genesis intended to allude to the Amanita mushroom. When he says, "I once said that there was no mushroom in the Bible. I was wrong. It plays a...role...a major one, in...the Garden of Eden story" in *Persephone's Quest*,[4] he's not referring to some assertion in *Soma*, but rather a specific statement he made in a presentation or another publication, that there are no mushrooms in the Bible. I haven't found any clear and definitive statement, in *Soma* at least, along the lines of "There was no mushroom in the Bible."

Wasson says in both books that the Eden tree in Genesis was intended as Amanita, but he assumes that the Genesis text in itself has nothing to do with the specific image of a mushroom-shaped tree. It's a dogmatic assumption in *Soma* that only the original Genesis author—not the later Jews and Christians—was aware of the Amanita meaning of the two trees in Eden.

Between *Soma* and *Persephone's Quest* he changed—without mentioning it—from saying that the Amanita host tree was sacred because it provided fire-starting punk and Amanita (in *Soma*) to saying that the host tree was sacred "precisely because"[5] and "only because"[6] (*Persephone's Quest*) it provided Amanita. In his indirect, roundabout manner here, he doesn't say, "I was wrong about Birch, and I overemphasized the importance of punk"—he leaves us unsure of his updated position on those

---

[2] R. Gordon Wasson and Wendy Doniger O'Flaherty, *Soma: Divine Mushroom of Immortality*, Ethno-mycological Studies No. 1. (New York: Harcourt Brace Jovanovich, 1968), pp. 220-222.
[3] R. Gordon Wasson, *Persephone's Quest: Entheogens and the Origins of Religion*. (New Haven: Yale University Press, 1986), pp. 74-77.
[4] Wasson, *Persephone's Quest*, p. 74.
[5] Ibid. p. 76.
[6] Ibid. p. 77.

points. He changed from identifying the Eden Tree as a Birch to "a conifer."

Wasson's View on the Plaincourault Eden Tree

Wasson asserts it is an incorrect interpretation of the mycologists in thinking that the Plaincourault fresco artist deliberately intended to allude to mushrooms: he agrees with Erwin Panofsky's assertion that "the plant in this fresco has nothing whatever to do with mushrooms…and the similarity with Amanita muscaria is purely fortuitous."[7]

> The misinterpretation…of the Plaincourault fresco [as a deliberate and conscious reference to Amanita mushrooms]…must be traced to the recent dissemination in Europe of reports of the Siberian use of the fly-agaric…the commentators have made an error in timing: the span of the past is longer…and the events that they seek to confirm took place before recorded history began.[8]

Here, Wasson is asserting that the comprehension of the Eden trees in the text of Genesis as Amanita, and the deliberate use of the Eden trees to indicate Amanita mushrooms, only and exclusively occurred in pre-history; after recorded history began, people no longer recognized, understood, or utilized the Eden trees, in text or painting, to deliberately evoke Amanita mushrooms. He puts forth no evidence, no basis, for his fundamental, unquestioned assumption that no one recognized the Eden trees as Amanita except himself and the ancients of pre-history. Wasson fully retains this assumption in the later part of *Soma*, in the "no inkling" passage, and he did not retract this view in *Persephone's Quest*. In the later "no inkling" passage, Wasson asserts that the Plaincourault fresco does slightly connect with mushrooms, albeit unconsciously by portraying the serpent, which, in forgotten prehistory long before, used to be the caretaker of the mushroom.

---

[7] Panofsky in a 1952 letter to Wasson excerpted in *Soma*, p. 179.
[8] Wasson, *Soma*, p. 180.

In the quote from Wasson in Ramsbottom's book, *Mushrooms and Toadstools* (1953), Wasson asserts that "for almost a half-century mycologists have been under a misapprehension on this matter" of reading the tree in the Plaincourault fresco as deliberately intending Amanita.[9] In *Soma*, Wasson asserts that the painter of the tree in the Plaincourault fresco didn't intend to depict mushrooms, but accidentally did so in the figure of the serpent itself—not the mushroom-shaped tree. Wasson does not, in *Persephone's Quest*, retract the specific view he expressed in *Soma*, that the Plaincourault fresco's tree is just coincidentally mushroom-like.

Wasson[10] incorrectly agrees with Panofsky that the particular tree in the Plaincourault fresco has nothing to do with mushrooms, and that altogether, Jewish-Christian mushroom trees in art don't represent mushrooms. He doesn't appear to retract or revisit these particular views in *Persephone's Quest*.[11] What basis does he mention to support the view that the trees aren't allusions to mushrooms? Again, *no* basis—only a mention of the view of art historians (according to Panofsky) that mushroom trees don't allude to psychoactive mushrooms. That's not an argument, or evidence, just a mention of a supposedly established view.

Wasson in *Persephone's Quest* doesn't state whether he abandoned his idea that mushroom trees don't indicate psychoactive mushrooms, or that only the serpent in the Plaincourault fresco had a connection to mushrooms, and that connection was long forgotten. Did mushrooms only appear in the Eden Tree story in the Bible? Was the Eucharist dependent on visionary plants? He doesn't state his view on these obvious major questions in these book sections about the Plaincourault Eden tree and the Eden trees in the text of Genesis. He fell far short of the maximal entheogen theory of religion. He gives the subject of "mushrooms in the Bible"

---

[9] Probably of: John Ramsbottom, *Mushrooms and Toadstools: A Study of the Activities of Fungi*. (London: Collins, 1953), p. 48.
[10] Wasson, *Soma*, pp. 178-180.
[11] Wasson, *Persephone's Quest*, pp. 74-77.

surprisingly brief and narrow coverage, leaving Heinrich's chapters on the Bible[12] with plenty to cover.

The Panofsky Argument Is Merely Anti-Entheogen Apologetics

People for too long have attempted to refute Allegro's theory that Jesus was none other than the mushroom, or that Christianity is based on mushroom use, by the dull and undiscriminating shout of, "Panofsky disproved Allegro in the excerpt from the letter to Wasson!" But they brandish the Panofsky argument without actually reading and paying careful attention to the distinct issues, the caliber of reasoning about the single issue addressed in the excerpt, and Wasson's exact views on these issues.

The Panofsky excerpt is often treated as though it were forcefully compelling, but it actually amounts to no more than unconvincing apologetics for the anti-mushroom reading, apologetics that have no power to reassure anyone except those who are already *a priori* committed to rejecting the mushroom reading of mushroom trees.

> …the plant in this fresco has nothing whatever to do with mushrooms…and the similarity with Amanita muscaria is purely fortuitous. The Plaincourault fresco is only one example—and, since the style is provincial, a particularly deceptive one—of a conventionalized tree type, prevalent in Romanesque and early Gothic art, which art historians actually refer to as a 'mushroom tree'…It comes about by the gradual schematization of the impressionistically rendered Italian pine tree in Roman and early Christian painting, and there are hundreds of instances exemplifying this development…the medieval artists hardly ever worked from nature but from classical prototypes

---

[12] Carl A.P. Ruck, Clark Heinrich, and Blaise Daniel Staples, *The Apples of Apollo: Pagan and Christian Mysteries of the Eucharist*. (Oxford, North Carolina: Carolina Academic Press, 2000).

which in the course of repeated copying became quite unrecognizable.[13]

A hallmark of apologetics exemplified by this passage and the brandishing of this passage by entheogen diminishers is the failure to state what the opposing objections of the maximal entheogen theorists would be, and address those. If Wasson and Panofsky were not doing apologetics here, but were uncommitted critical thinkers genuinely following reason where it leads, they would have stated the obvious likely objections to this argument, and would have refuted those objections. But instead, Wasson and those who apply the Panofsky argument treat this passage as though it were simply final, unassailable, and beyond all possibility of objections—a telling sign that what we have here is one-sided apologetics, not the outcome of a back-and-forth reasoned argument.

The Pine Alternative Supports, Not Replaces, the Amanita Reading

If the artist had a species of pine, specifically, in mind, that would point right back again to an Amanita host tree, which supports the plausibility of reading the Plaincourault tree and all mushroom trees as intending the Amanita. Thus the argument that the painter intended a pine tree, not at all the Amanita, inherently backfires against Panofsky and Wasson.[14] Wasson probably overlooked this backfiring of Panofsky's alternative explanation in *Soma* because in that book he overemphasized the birch to the near-exclusion of considering the pine as a major host tree for Amanita.

In *Persephone's Quest*, Wasson switches to asserting that the trees in Genesis are "probably a conifer" and silently refrains from mentioning the clearly self-contradictory Panofsky argument that the Plaincourault tree could not have meant Amanita because mushroom trees instead intend

---

[13] Erwin Panofsky in a 1952 letter to Wasson excerpted in *Soma*, p. 179.
[14] Personal correspondence with Jan Irvin.

the Italian Pine: "the fruit of the Tree of Knowledge of Good and Evil was Soma,...was Amanita muscaria...The Tree was probably a conifer, in Mesopotamia.[15]

Panofsky Conflates Artistic Development with the Intent Behind It

Panofsky's argument is completely weak: he reasons that the art historians hold that these mushroom trees were developed by increasingly schematized copying, and therefore the mushroom trees didn't intend, could not have intended, mushrooms. But that particular jump, as it appears in the passage Wasson quotes from Panofsky's letter, is completely baseless; it has no compelling force whatsoever. There is not the slightest contradiction between the gradual development of a mushroom tree schematization and the intention to portray mushrooms. The hundreds of mushroom trees of course involved some type of gradual schematization, but that fact says nothing about the intention of the artists. It is completely likely, in fact highly likely and plausible, that the gradual schematization occurred because the artists did intend to portray mushrooms. So Panofsky's argument that mushroom trees developed schematically and "therefore" didn't intend mushrooms, is worthless, and tells us nothing one way or another about the intention of mushroom tree artists in general, nor the Plaincourault Eden mushroom tree in particular.

Wasson's Vague Argument from Authority and His Competence in Art-History

The art historians say it—we are to believe them—that settles it. A weird, telling bias is the way it never occurs to Wasson that the failure of communication between disciplines cuts both ways, with a subtle irony when

---

[15] Wasson, *Persephone's Quest*, p. 75.

he berates only the mycologists for the ignorance resulting from the failure of two-way communication:

> Professor Panofsky gave expression to what I have found is the unanimous view of those competent in Romanesque art. For more than half a century the mycologists have refrained from consulting the art world on a matter relating to art. Art historians of course do not read books about mushrooms. Here is a good example of the failure of communications between disciplines: the misinterpretation [by the mycologists] of the Plaincourault fresco [as Amanita].[16]

With the wave of a hand, Wasson excuses the ignorance on the part of the art historians with "of course," while chastising the mycologists, as though mutual non-communication is a fault solely on the side of the mycologists, and in any disagreement under these conditions, the art historians are immediately to be granted the victory. Wasson pits mycologists who are ignorant of the field of art history against art historians who are ignorant of the field of mycology, and automatically takes it for granted that the art historians win. It doesn't even occur to Wasson that the failure of communications between disciplines works against the credibility of the art historians as much as it may work against the mycologists. Why should we trust Wasson's judgment and credence in "those competent in Romanesque art," especially when he declares that they "of course do not read books about mushrooms"?

Wasson's Pseudo-Argument as a Smoke Screen to Protect the Status Quo

Wasson here presents no names of art historians, none of their arguments, no criteria for certainty about their competence, and all but calls these art historians incompetent to judge one way or the other on the mycologists' reading. Given such a travesty of persuasive argumentation, one is forced

---

[16] Wasson, *Soma*, p. 180.

to explain Wasson's strangely superficial, vague, and uncompelling presentation of the Panofsky position by speculating on Wasson's preventative purpose and objective in laying out such a presentation in such a manner. Such a self-confident and certain judgment, accompanied by the complete lack of any real argumentation from evidence, is reminiscent of deceitful and pretense-driven Christian apologetics, where the shallow posture of argumentation is considered suitable, with no need for actual point-by-point argumentation that cites specific scholars by name, with specific arguments as spelled out in specific pages of books and articles. Wasson's commentary on consulting art historians amounts to nothing but assertions from vague authority, right where the specific compelling arguments are most needed, given that this Eden tree looks like Amanita.

Wasson's treatment, this reassuring covering-over of the subject, looks more like a protective circling of the wagons in the wake of Huxley's mescaline writings and Zaehner's reaction to the looming entheogen theory.[17] This treatment, or rather a preventative anti-treatment of the subject, served as a way of avoiding argumentation by providing a smoke screen of pseudo-argumentation in its place, all to insulate Christianity and the bulk of its Jewish origins from the obvious implications were we to admit that the Plaincourault tree intended Amanita: to admit it would be to open the floodgates, so we must come up with pseudo-arguments to cover over the implications and head off a genuine argument on the subject.

Wasson Is Pulling Our Leg, to Toe the Party Line While Ridiculing It

We cannot assume that Wasson believes what he writes. An old trick to get past the censors in a religious State is to pretend to believe what the censors want people to believe, by pretending to vehemently and

---

[17] R.C. Zaehner, *Mysticism: Sacred and Profane*. (New York: Oxford University Press, 1967).

confidently defend it, while actually demonstrating how lame the arguments in support of the party line are. It's a form of sarcasm. Instead of saying that Wasson is stupid, gullible, and insane—that would miss the mark in an analysis of his inner motives and strategy—it's better to ask what Wasson's strategy and covert objective was. Wasson must be pulling our leg. It would be perspicacious to condemn or disparage him for not writing what he actually believed (unlike Allegro), but it's a misreading if we disparage Wasson for "believing" the Panofsky argument.

We don't know what Wasson believed; we only know what Wasson wrote, and we'd do well to try several modes of reading, under various assumptions about his intent. When one mode of reading and argument delivers results that couldn't even convince a gnat, and we know the author is smart, we must try a different mode of reading. For example, he's sending us a signal by writing that of course the art historians don't know squat about mushrooms, yet goes on to write that therefore the art historians—vaguely unspecified authorities—are right regarding mushrooms.

We need to use a different reading of Wasson regarding mushrooms in the Bible and Christianity after the Eden story was composed. He blatantly censored his speculations to avoid a confrontation with the Christian status quo, but Allegro didn't. Allegro went ahead with what Wasson backed away from: refuting the Christian status quo. We don't know anything about what the early Christians "believed," and those scholars who chatter on and on about how the Christians believed this, and the Christians believed that, as a rule don't have the first clue what they're presuming to pontificate on. We cannot talk about what the early Christians "believed;" we know only what they wrote. Whenever a scholar of early Christianity writes "believed," that's a sign that he is about to fall headlong into literalism. The word "believed" is tantamount to literalism on the part of scholars, a sort of synonym.

What *did* Wasson believe about the matter of mushroom trees? We cannot assume that he simply straightforwardly believed what he wrote—look at his silent omission of the "Italian pine" argument from *Persephone's Quest*, which appears to have been written shortly after he wrote

Soma (based on "a few months ago"). If the Panofsky Plaincourault argument is such a slam-dunk argument as the people who brandish it (and Wasson in *Soma*) act like it is, then why is it dropped silently in *Persephone's Quest*?

We can pick up signals that something is very, very fishy about Wasson's super-brief coverage of mushrooms in the Jewish-Christian religion after the very earliest writing of the Eden story. His approach toward treating mushrooms in Christianity is to retreat—to stay silent and to wave aside the issue with a blatantly unconvincing pseudo-argument from vague authority.

Hastening to Cordon off the Inrushing Entheogen Theory of "Our Own" Culture

Wasson's argument is incredibly tortuous, as if he's trying to tiptoe around a dragon's lair called Religion without breathing a word about Christianity for fear of waking the dragon.[18] For Wasson, mushrooms must not be admitted into "our own" European Middle Ages; they may only be permitted in the pre-historical ancient beginnings of "our" religion, or in the more recent religion of the primitive and alien Others—the shamans and foreign folk religion. This is why Wasson takes it as a fixed dogmatic fact, emphatically not to be even considered for discussion, that medieval Christians and their culture cannot have had any understanding of Amanita and its representation. He chose to propose alternative views that would only require revising long-ago religion; this felt radical enough for him, and he didn't want to additionally take on the task of calling for the wholesale revision of religious and cultural history that comes rushing through, as with Allegro, in a tidal wave crashing against the very shores of the modern era, per the maximal entheogen theory of religion. Wasson was dedicated to publicly expressing only a controlled, restrained, conservative entheogen theory of religion, that only the long-

---

[18] Personal correspondence with Jan Irvin.

ago origins or roots before "our own" culture's religion—"our own Holy Agape"—may be permitted to be read as entheogen-influenced, and even then, we must always frame it as a secret that only a small handful of inner circle mystery initiates knew of: "Let us...reconsider the archetype of our own Holy Agape. On what element did the original devotees commune, long before the Christian era?"[19] "The story [of Eden] carries the mystical resonance of the early days."[20]

> "...the Tree of Knowledge was the tree that has been revered by...Early Man in Eurasia...that supplies the entheogenic food to which Early Man attributed miraculous powers. He who composed the tale...in Genesis...refrained from identifying the 'fruit': he was writing for the initiates...Strangers and the unworthy would remain in the dark....the 'fruit'...the initiates call by...euphemisms."[21]

Note Wasson's choice to use the words "the unworthy" (instead of "noninitiates") and "euphemisms" (instead of the neutral "metaphors"), as reflecting Wasson's own value system and sets of assumptions and connotations. "Early Man has been discovered revering a 'Tree of Life.'"[22] For Wasson, "Early Man" emphatically does not mean, and must not be permitted to mean, Christians in 1200, 1500, or 1700.

Art Historians' Term "Mushroom Trees" Belies the Apologetics

Panofsky correctly reports that art historians found hundreds of what they call "mushroom trees." Art historians' choice to use the term "mushroom trees" instead of "mushroom pines" belies the apologetics behind the denial of the mushroom intent. The trees altogether clearly look like mushrooms (though a pairing of Psilocybe cubensis and Mandrake trees is

---

[19] Wasson, *Soma*, p. 220.
[20] *Persephone's Quest*, p. 76.
[21] Ibid. p. 76.
[22] Ibid. p. 77.

shown in the Abbey of Montecassino). If mushroom tree artists so definitely intended the Italian Pine, art historians should call them "mushroom pines" with confidence, but, tellingly, they continue to characterize them as "mushroom trees," because that—not the Italian Pine—is plainly and generally what these trees appear, visually, to be modeled on.

There's Not Just a Single, Deviant Instance of an Eden Mushroom Tree

Wasson in *Soma* apparently thinks there's only a single, deviant instance of a mushroom-shaped tree set in Eden: "The gentleman who presented the fresco to the Societe Mycologique made the sensational statement that, instead of the customary Tree, the artist had given us the fly-agaric. A serpent was entwined around a gigantic fly-agaric."[23]

In Wasson's "no inkling" passage, he's (incorrectly) saying that the tree itself in the Plaincourault fresco doesn't represent Amanita because (supposedly) as art historians know, mushroom trees don't represent psychoactive mushrooms, and that the serpent isn't offering a mushroom to Eve, but that rather the serpent itself, unbeknownst to the artist and mycologists, represents the psychoactive mushroom. "If these perceptions are right, then the mycologists were right also, in a transcendental sense of which neither they nor the artist had an inkling, when they saw a serpent offering a mushroom to Eve in the Fresco of Plaincourault."[24] In *Soma*, he maintains that only the original Genesis author comprehended that the Eden Tree meant Amanita, and he wrongly asserts that all later Jewish people and Christians forgot that, and the Plaincourault fresco artist

---

[23] *Soma*, p. 179. Against that assumption of this being such a deviant portrayal, connecting the Eden tree to a mushroom-shaped portrayal of a tree, see, as just one additional example, another mushroom-shaped Eden tree at Irvin's site (http://www.pharmacratic-inquisition.com/nontesters/pharmacratic/) – "Adam and Eve with serpent-entwined Psilocybe mushroom (caduceus). Italy [Abbey of Montecassino]; circa 1072 – British Library." (On the right, I've identified a Mandrake Eden tree; I don't presently know whether Irvin recognized or noted it.)
[24] Wasson, *Soma*, p. 221.

didn't intend to allude to mushrooms (but was instead blindly following an accidental convention of coincidentally mushroom-shaped trees), but accidentally alluded to mushrooms in that the serpent itself represented, in long-forgotten antiquity, the mushroom.

Wasson's Strangely Contorted "Coincidence without an Inkling" View

It's unbelievable, the contorted view Wasson has constructed. Bunk assumption-sets (systems) produce such bizarre, contorted, unwieldy results. Wasson was crazily coherent and brittle in his "no inkling" passage, relentlessly persistent in his assumption that the Middle Ages must have been ignorant of entheogen metaphors—no matter what the cost, no matter how implausible, cumbersome, and roundabout an interpretation thereby results. It's as though he finds a medieval painting of people taking mushrooms and declares that they had no idea what they were doing but instead thought they were eating tomatoes, because we all know that medievals were ignorant, unlike us moderns and the glorious ancients in pre-history.

Wasson simultaneously seems to ridicule mycologists who saw the tree in the Plaincourault fresco as a mushroom, and the snake as giving a mushroom, while also at the same time asserting that the mycologists were, by a huge unconscious coincidence, correct that the snake was giving a mushroom. Based on the authority of art historians as portrayed by Panofsky, Wasson dogmatically and absolutely takes it for granted as an unimpeachable and routine fact, that the painter only intended to portray a tree, not a mushroom—and only intended a regular tree, at that (not one associated with psychoactives).

For him, it's a dogmatic fact that the Christians were ignorant of the Amanita nature of the Eden trees. Then Wasson acts smugly surprised when it turns out, supposedly coincidentally, that the mycologists are correct in seeing the snake as guardian and provider of the mushroom. He acts like it's a brute, dumb coincidence that the mushroom-shaped tree is comparable to the birch in that the birch is host to a mushroom. Wasson's "no inkling" passage is a wondrous monstrosity of entrenched bunk assumptions. He presents it as an unassailable fact that mushroom trees don't at all intend to represent a mushroom, and then smugly smiles at the dumb luck of the brutes who draw a mushroom-shaped tree because they accidentally happen to be right, in that an accidentally mushroom-shaped tree has a snake on it, and unbeknownst to the painter and mycologists (ignorant misinterpreters), the snake actually was (in pre-history only) associated with the mushroom.

Thus Wasson presents for our critique an argument that by a complicated circuitous coincidence—if you are very in-the-know like no one has been during all of recorded history until Wasson himself—we may actually discern that the mushroom-shaped tree has echoes of mushrooms, unconsciously and accidentally. Sometimes labored scholarship announces with great fanfare and self-accolades, what is plainly obvious with humble common sense to the unlettered. Wasson's take on this—the "no inkling" passage—is weird, over-elaborated and contrived. He's here sticking steadfastly to his previously stated position, that it's a misinterpretation to read the Amanita-looking tree in the Plaincourault fresco as intending a mushroom.

The Acuity of the Unlettered versus Wasson's Blinding Assumption

Why not just accept the obvious image that is manifestly presented to us, that the artist knew everything about the Amanita host tree, and deliberately drew a mushroom-delivering snake in a deliberately and knowingly mushroom-shaped tree, to consciously and deliberately allude to the Amanita host tree and the Amanita it delivers? The complexity all immediately collapses; the supposed unconscious, highly coincidental, accidental portrayal of the serpent (spirit guardian of the mushroom) is replaced by the far simpler assumption of comprehension on the part of the artist. Instead of Wasson's, "Wow! He painted the right thing, even though he had no inkling what he was doing!" Such absurdity raises the question: why not settle for the more straightforward and plain, "He understood the Amanita nature of the Eden trees, so that's what he painted"? How do we explain Wasson's bizarre brittleness here? He's pulling our leg to toe the party line of the Christian status quo, while revealing how absurd the resulting argument is.

He appears as though he has no grasp of metaphorical art, but that can't be, given that the book is about mushroom metaphor recognition. He ends up demonstrating the absurdity and blindness that results from the dogmatic assumption that the later Christians and artists cannot possibly have comprehended the Amanita nature of the Eden trees, and cannot possibly have understood at that later date that the serpent is guardian/provider of the psychoactive mushroom.

What would induce Wasson to take up his bizarre set of dogmatic assumptions that leads to him being surprised by the mycologists' supposed "rightness in a transcendental sense of which they had no inkling?" Perhaps this move enables Wasson to look smarter than the clumsy half-conscious oaf who painted the fresco, and smarter than the other mycologists, by introducing complicating assumptions and then announcing that he, a brilliant man, has solved the complexity, while other mycologists (simpletons) are merely confused and are right only by dumb luck. Or perhaps Wasson is speaking to us, signaling to us, between the lines.

The "Entheogens Only in Pre-history" Fallacy

Wasson demonstrates a basic overarching fallacy similar to that of typical modern-era Bible scholars: he shows the result of assuming that the later religious practitioners and artists were muddle-headed and weren't masters of their metaphors and material. He demonstrates, perhaps ironically, the all-too-common, moderate-entheogen-theory fallacy of assuming that only the most ancient religionists understood the entheogenic nature of their religion (a fallacy related to the first, basic fallacy). A safer assumption is that until 1700, Christians generally recognized and understood the Eucharist and the Eden Trees to be visionary plants. Wasson assumes that the ancient Eden Tree story author, only way back then, understood the Eden tree as mushrooms—but that "quickly" that understanding was lost. When the story was composed, the authentic fly-agaric (or an alternative hallucinogen) must have been present, for the fable would not possess the sharp edge, the virulence, that it does if surrogates and placebos had already come into general use.[25]

The tepid moderate entheogen theory of religion readily accepts that way back in time at the very beginning of the Bible's writing, there were entheogen initiates, but God forbid we should even consider the possibility that there were still authentically entheogen-utilizing initiates in the Middle Ages—for that would ruin the story everyone desires to tell, that the big bad Church at its very beginning, and even in Second-Temple Jewish religion, had of course stamped out all knowledge of entheogens.

The Moderns, Not the Medievals, Are in the Dark

It's the moderns, not the ancients and pre-moderns, who were muddle-headed and confused about the nature of the Eucharist and fruit of the tree in Eden. Moderns such as Wasson and McKenna are committed to telling a sort of evolution-affirming story that, in pre-history, people understood the entheogenic nature of religion, but in pre-modern history, people were stupid and didn't understand it, but only now, wonderful modern scholars have brought the truth to light for the first time since pre-history. That particular cultural-evolution-affirming story won't fly. Here, modern-era scholars have been the odd man out (although there have always been a few scholars in modernity who have haltingly recognized the entheogenic wellspring of the religions). Constructive postmodern scholars will have recovered, and clarified more than ever before, the entheogenic wellspring of the religions. Pre-history and pre-modernity had a practical comprehension of the entheogenic nature of religion;

---

[25] Wasson, *Soma*, p. 221.

modernity almost completely forgot that; post-modernity will have formulated a better comprehension of the entheogenic nature of religion than ever before.

John Allegro and the Battle of the Careless Asides

Many people would be interested in a fresh take on Allegro. To most scholars, Allegro *is* the entheogen theory of Christianity. To utter "Allegro" is to raise the subject of the entheogen theory of Christianity, and vice versa. This problem of Allegro's abused reputation serves as a total block for most people—most religious scholars—whenever anyone puts forth any sort of entheogen theory of Christianity or of religion. Many people effectively consider the problem of Allegro as the most important issue possible regarding the entheogen theory of Christianity or religion; for them, the entheogen theory of Christianity or religion stands or falls with Allegro's reputation.

We've reached the point where we cannot move forward with research in the entheogen theory without going through Allegro's contributions. He cannot be ignored; he can be properly integrated into the corpus of new publications, only with, of course, the appropriate, normal scholarly fact-checking and corrections that Allegro himself wanted and invited. Scholars can choose to ineffectively and inadequately discuss him in asides in parentheses and footnotes, or speculate on his motives as a possible hoaxer and thus avoiding real engagement in honest intellectual debate with him, or, discuss his theses in a mature, honest, direct, straightforward way.[26] But it is becoming ever less possible for entheogen theorists to pretend he doesn't exist, and quietly tiptoe around him. Like the subject of entheogens is danced-around in mainstream religious studies, you can either diminish, disparage, misportray, and try to ignore the subject; or, you can work through the subject in an honest and direct, normal way.

---

[26] Cf. the critical treatment of Morton Smith and his Secret Gospel of Mark.

Allegro's Citation and Dismissal of the Panofsky/Wasson Reading

The argument that Christian mushroom trees were a developed schematization and "therefore" didn't intend mushrooms was not seen as compelling by Allegro, who cites Wasson's view in an endnote, in order to dismiss it. Allegro apparently didn't consider the Panofsky/Wasson argument or view it worthy enough to warrant an analysis and rebuttal.

> The prime example of the relation between the serpent and the mushroom is, of course, in the Garden of Eden story of the Old Testament. The cunning reptile prevails upon Eve and her husband to eat of the tree, whose fruit "made them as gods, knowing good and evil" (Gen 3:4). The whole Eden story is mushroom-based mythology, not least in the identity of the "tree" as the sacred fungus, as we shall see. Even as late as the thirteenth century, some recollection of the old tradition was known among Christians, to judge from a fresco painted on the wall of a ruined church in Plaincourault in France...There the Amanita muscaria is gloriously portrayed, entwined with a serpent, whilst Eve stands by holding her belly.[27]

Endnote 20 on page 253 comments tersely: "Despite rejection of the identity of the subject ('rightly or wrongly') as being a mushroom by R. G. Wasson: 'for almost a half-century mycologists have been under a misapprehension on this matter.'"[28] In *Sacred Mushroom*, Allegro acknowledges Wasson's dismissal of reading the Plaincourault tree as intending a mushroom, yet holds steadfastly to his judgment of the correct, plain reading the Amanita-looking tree as intending Amanita; Allegro refers to the quote of Wasson in the book by Ramsbottom.

---

[27] Allegro, *Sacred Mushroom*, p. 80. Plate 2 is placed on facing page 74 in some printings, on the back cover in other printings.
[28] Quoting Allegro, *Sacred Mushroom*, endnote 20, p. 253. The op. cit. appears to be John Ramsbottom, *Mushrooms and Toadstools: A Study of the Activities of Fungi*. (London: Collins, 1953), p. 48.

Allegro in *Sacred Mushroom* references Wasson, Andrija Puharich, Richard Evens Schultes, Albert Hofmann, John Ramsbottom, and Robert Graves. Allegro merely mentions and dismisses Panofsky, with a single word: "despite." He basically just says, "I'm against Panofsky's statement." Allegro treated Panofsky in a careless way, enabling confusion to spread, by relegating the mention of Panofsky's argument to a vague terse dismissal in a footnote. Allegro wrote only the word "despite," in a hard-to-find endnote, which did not amount to "addressing" Panofsky's argument. Allegro ought to have written a pointed refutation of Panofsky's argument, to prevent what happened: the popular rumor that "Panofsky disproved Allegro" by "disproving" the reading of the Plaincourault tree as Amanita. Allegro would've benefited from critiquing the Panofsky/Wasson argument against mushroom trees and the Plaincourault Eden tree meaning Amanita, in the body of the text of *Sacred Mushroom*. Allegro and misuse of endnotes and asides have gone together—the failure to enter into conversation on the issues.

The Too-Vague Rejection of Allegro's Theories

Allegro has been rejected without warrant, even though it's claimed that he based his work on Wasson. Jonathan Ott incorrectly makes a broad-brush, over-generalized dismissal of Allegro. Ott dismisses Allegro's theories in *Sacred Mushroom* without stating which theories are absurd, or supplying any evidence or argumentation of why he considers them absurd, or specifying to what extent Allegro's theories were "based on" Wasson's research: "Perhaps most unfortunate was the appearance of farceurs like Andrija Puharich and the late John Allegro, who spun absurd theories based on Wasson's research to make a fast buck."[29]

---

[29] Jonathan Ott, in Thomas J. Riedlinger, ed., *The Sacred Mushroom Seeker: Essays for R. Gordon Wasson*, Historical, Ethno- & Economic Botany Series. (Dioscorides Press, 1970), vol. 4, p. 190.

How much and in what sense is it true that Allegro's theories about Amanita were based on Wasson's research? Allegro seems more dismissive of Wasson than building on him (at least regarding mushrooms in the Bible). A master thesis of Wasson's is that only the pre-historical ancients (and himself) understood the Eden trees in the Genesis text as Amanita; Wasson takes it as unquestionable that the Christians cannot have known about mushrooms—specifically, that they cannot have known of the association of the serpent and mushrooms, or the Amanita nature of the Eden trees in the Genesis text.

Price's Attempted Dismissal of Acharya's Agreement with Allegro

In Robert M. Price's review of Acharya's *Christ Conspiracy*,[30] he points out that Acharya desires, with Allegro, to see psychoactives in Christianity. Price attempts to refute Acharya and Allegro's broad theory by invoking Wasson's view on one isolated aspect of the issue. Price points out that Wasson agreed with Panofsky's assertion that art historians don't believe mushroom tree artists intended mushrooms. Panofsky's quoted argument is completely weak, as explained above. Further, even if it could be proven that Christian mushroom trees in general never intended mushrooms, or that the Plaincourault Eden mushroom tree didn't intend mushrooms, that would hardly amount to a wholesale refutation of Acharya's and Allegro's view that Christians used visionary plants. It's not as though the entheogen theory of religion rests on a single painting, so that refuting the intention of that painting would deal a fatal blow to the entire entheogen theory of Christianity. Price's argument also misfires because Price omits the fact that Wasson positively asserted that the Eden trees do intend mushrooms. Price attempts to use Wasson/Panofsky in an over-general way against Acharya's and Allegro's reading of the Bible as attesting

---

[30] Acharya S., *The Christ Conspiracy: The Greatest Story Ever Sold*. (Kempton: Adventures Unlimited Press, 1999).

visionary plants. But, against Price, Wasson in fact asserts that the Bible does have entheogens, at least in the textual story of the Eden trees. Price generalizes his critique of Acharya as: she's unreliable, a grab bag, kettle logic, an indiscriminate shotgun approach. But Price's treatment of the entheogen issue in his review is itself imprecise, a blunt club, conflating the general issue of whether the Bible has entheogens with the particular issue of whether the Plaincourault artist intended mushrooms. Furthermore, Wasson asserted that the Plaincourault fresco does slightly connect with mushrooms, albeit unconsciously by portraying the serpent, which in forgotten pre-history long before, used to be the caretaker of the mushroom.

Price later stated that he's interested in hearing proposed alternatives to the Panofsky reading of the Plaincourault tree.[31]

---

[31] Note: Actually, I was very disappointed when I read that the fresco did not depict Amanita muscaria as the Tree of Knowledge! When I reviewed *The Christ Conspiracy*, I knew no better. Now I am delighted to learn that Allegro and Acharya were right about it.

Chapter 8: Star-Lore in the Gospels
By Bill Darlison

Part 1

The Gospels and the Constellations

I must expect to be condemned by the matter-of-fact people, who are persuaded that the Eastern prophets who wrote three or four thousand years ago, composed their works upon the same model, and with the same regard to facts, as may be always attended to in the praiseworthy pages of the Annual Register, and of the London Gazette.
—Sir William Drummond, 1811

Of all the controversies with which the Fathers of the early church entertained themselves, few seem as irrelevant to the contemporary mind as that which concerned the duration of Jesus' ministry. For about eighteen centuries, the common assumption throughout Christendom has been that, between Jesus' baptism and his crucifixion, three years elapsed. This is based on a legitimate inference from the number of Passover festivals mentioned in the Gospel of John, and it is difficult to see how anyone could, or would even want to challenge it. And yet it was a dispute over which a considerable amount of ink was expended towards the end of the second Christian century. Irenaeus, orthodoxy's first systematic apologist (writing about 185 CE), goes to great lengths to prove that Jesus exercised his ministry over many years in order to counter the contention of the followers of Valentinus that Jesus taught for one year only and, further, that "he suffered in the twelfth month."[1]

The controversy was not just over any arbitrary twelve-month period. It concerned the solar year, which begins at the spring equinox, and Valentinus's claim is absolutely startling: the career of Jesus is connected with the sun's annual journey through the heavens, and he implies that the various stages of it correspond with the signs of the zodiac.

> In Valentinus...the twelve months of preaching by Jesus from the Baptism to the Passion correspond to the twelve signs of the zodiac, which, we remember, were sometimes depicted on the synagogue floor as a visual Calendar.[2]

Zodiac in the Beth Alpha Synagogue (Wikipedia)

For Valentinus and his followers, the Gospel story is not a rudimentary biography of a single individual, pieced together from reminiscences of eye-witnesses or those who had known eye-witnesses, but an allegory, in which the sun's cycle, from its 'birth' in Aries when spring begins, to its 'death' in Pisces twelve months later, symbolically reflects the initiate's

---

[1] Irenaeus, p. 200.
[2] Carrington, p. 52.

journey towards spiritual liberation or enlightenment. Clement of Alexandria (c150-c215 CE) expresses a similar point of view when he writes: "The path for souls to ascension lies through the twelve signs of the zodiac."[3]

Valentinus and Clement were Gnostics and Gnosticism, despite the variety of ways in which it manifested, was concerned with the interior life of the spirit, with 'illumination.' God was to be experienced within the depths of the individual rather than demonstrated rationally or objectified historically. 'Gnosis,' which comes from the Greek word for knowledge, is not primarily rational knowledge, but 'insight.'

> "Gnosis involves an intuitive process of knowing oneself. And to know oneself...is to know human nature and human destiny...Yet to know oneself, at the deepest level, is simultaneously, to know God."[4]

Manuscripts which have surfaced relatively recently, particularly the Nag Hammadi documents, discovered in 1945, are demonstrating that the conventionally held view that Gnostic works are invariably later than the canonical Gospels and of inferior literary quality can no longer be sustained. What is emerging is a picture of early Christianity which is, in Elaine Pagels' words, "far more diverse than orthodox sources choose to indicate."[5] Out of this diversity sprang a variety of writings. In one of them, the Gospel of Thomas, the central figure is 'the living Jesus' who has a different relationship with his followers than does the traditional Jesus of Christendom. The latter is a uniquely divine figure whose sacrifice ensures the salvation of those who believe in him. The Jesus of Thomas' Gospel, however, "comes as a guide who opens access to spiritual understanding. But when the disciple attains enlightenment, Jesus no longer serves as his spiritual master: the two have become equal—even identical."[6]

---

[3] Clement of Alexandria, *Stromata*, Book V, Chapter 14.
[4] Pagels, p. xix.
[5] Ibid. p. xxxiii.
[6] Ibid, p. xx.

Such thinking has always been anathema to orthodoxy. What is interesting about it, from the point of view of the present study, is its antiquity. If, as Professor Koester of Harvard maintains, the Gospel of Thomas contains some traditions which belong to the "second half of the first century,"[7] then such ideas were not later perversions of the orthodox, history-based scheme; they were contemporary with it. Perhaps they even preceded it.

Indeed, it is no longer unthinkable for us to invert the customary view of the relationship between 'historic' and 'esoteric' Christianities. It seems increasingly likely that the former was a perversion of the latter, that the attempt to establish historical credentials for the Jesus story came sometime after the story itself originated in the fertile imagination of some esoteric group, whose poetic account of the spiritual journey was transformed into history by people who had either misunderstood the story, or who were motivated by more cynically pragmatic political or ecclesiastical considerations.

The gradual 'historicization' of imaginative religious stories is by no means restricted to Christianity. In *The Perennial Philosophy*, Aldous Huxley points out that the same process has occurred in Buddhism in which 'the Mahayana expresses the universal, whereas the Hinayana cannot set itself free from historical fact.'[8] He goes on to quote the orientalist, Ananda K. Coomaraswary:

> The Mahayanist believer is warned—precisely as the worshipper of Krishna is warned in the Vaishnaivite scriptures that the Krishna Lila is not history, but a process for ever unfolded in the heart of man—that matters of historical fact are without religious significance.[9]

Christianity has never been 'liberated from its servitude to historical fact' and has "remained a religion in which the pure Perennial Philosophy has been overlaid, now more, now less, by an idolatrous preoccupation

---

[7] Pagels, p. xvi.
[8] Aldous Huxley, *The Perennial Philosophy*, p. 62.
[9] Ibid.

with events and things in time—events and things regarded not merely as useful means, but as ends intrinsically sacred and indeed divine."[10]

The suggestion that the Gospel story is not history but 'a process for ever unfolded in the heart of man' no doubt seems pretty absurd to those of us who have been raised on a flesh and blood Jesus readily locatable in time and space. But, in fact, it is no more outrageous than the historical schema proposed to us by orthodoxy. Indeed, it is much less problematic, since it frees us from having to defend the historicity of incidents which are, to say the least, unlikely. Only familiarity with such incidents, and, perhaps, a sentimental attachment to them, prevent us from declaring them fanciful. Virgins do not give birth; people do not walk on water; storms cannot be calmed with a word; a few loaves and a couple of fish cannot feed thousands of people; and people, once dead, do not come back to life again.

Valentinus' contention that there is a connection between the constellational patterns and the Gospels seems to have been ignored by orthodoxy, which has forgotten that the Gospels come out of a culture that was *dominated* by astrological thinking. Mithraic scholar Franz Cumont, who considered astrology to be 'the most monstrous of all chimeras begotten of superstition,' nevertheless admits that it:

> …was indissolubly linked not only with astronomy and meteorology, but also with medicine, botany, ethnography, and physics…It left its mark on the religious life of past generations, dominating the religion of Babylon, informing the highest phases of ancient paganism and, by changing the character of ancient idolatry, it was to prepare in many respects for the coming of Christianity.[11]

It was also, as physicist and data-scientist, Henry Boxer Ph.D., has shown in his recent (2020) book *A Scheme of Heaven*, to prepare for the coming of modern science. We sceptical moderns associate astrology with

---

[10] Aldous Huxley, *The Perennial Philosophy*, p. 62.
[11] Franz Cumont, Astrology and Religion Among the Greeks and Romans, p. xxiv.

seaside fortune-tellers and glossy magazine 'horoscope' columns, completely unaware that:

> Astrology was the ancient world's most ambitious applied mathematics problem, a grand data-analysis enterprise sustained by centuries by some of history's most brilliant minds...Just consider that for much of the last two thousand years, the word 'mathematician' (*mathematicus*) simply meant an astrologer; there was no distinction.[12]

Boxer considers that the astrologer Claudius Ptolemy was the most famous scientist of the ancient world and, quoting historian of science Otto Neugebauer, declares Ptolemy's *Almagest* "one of the greatest masterpieces of scientific analysis ever written."[13] The astrological thinkers of the past were people of extraordinary intellectual gifts.

The Hebrew Scriptures with their sevens and twelves, their bulls, rams, twins, snakes, scorpions, bears, dragons, virgins, heavens, and heavenly hosts (stars!) are full of astronomical imagery. The British astronomer Edward Maunder (1851-1928) suggested that the first ten chapters of Genesis contain references to at least one third of the visible constellations of the sky as they appeared in the middle of the third millennium BCE.[14] The stories of Moses, Samson, Jephthah, Jael and Sisera, which make little sense when read as history, come alive when considered as astronomical allegories.[15]

The Hebrew prophets, who most certainly denounced divination by the stars, did not condemn the notion that there was an intimate connection between earth and sky; indeed, the Bible opens with a declaration that God had ordained it so: the Sun, Moon, and stars were created for

---

[12] Henry Boxer, *A Scheme of Heaven*. (2020), p. 2.
[13] Ibid. p. 106.
[14] Edward Maunder, p. 168.
[15] The name 'Samson' is derived from the Hebrew word שמש (shemesh), which means 'Sun'; Jephthah's daughter represents the constellation Virgo; and Jael hammers a tent-peg, (shaped, as every student of astronomy knows), like the constellation Capricorn, into the head of Sisera. See Darlison *Moses the Matador* for a full account of these stories.

'signs'[16] and for 'seasons' (Genesis 1:14), and Psalm 147 tells us that God calls 'each of the stars by name.' Apocalyptic literature throughout the Bible is full of references to this connection: disorder on earth would be presaged by and accompanied by disorder in the heavens. In the prophet, Joel, we read that "the great and dreadful day of the Lord" will be signaled by wonders in the heavens: "The Sun will be turned to darkness and the Moon to blood" (Joel 2:30-31). We find similar expressions in the Gospels. For example, in Luke, we read that, before 'the end,' "there will be signs in the Sun, Moon, and stars...for the heavenly bodies will be shaken" (Luke 21:25-26).

What is this but astrology?

Orthodox Christian scholars have followed Irenaeus in their obsession with history, and we moderns, 'matter-of-fact people,' who live with bowed heads under cloudy skies, probably conclude that any astronomical elements there may be in the Gospels are both infrequent and incidental.

Singular Images

However, to those who know what they are looking for, the astronomical elements are neither incidental nor infrequent. The 'Star' of Bethlehem, along with the astrologers (μάγοι) who observed it (Matthew 2), are prominent features of the Jesus story, and the man carrying a jar of water (Mark 14:13) looks very much like the pictogram of the zodiacal constellation Aquarius. Even the person with just a rudimentary knowledge of the sky would recognise these.

The more astronomically literate readers would perhaps perceive the constellation Aries in John the Baptist's description of Jesus as the Lamb of God (John 1:29), and references to a virgin (in Matthew and Luke) might remind them of Virgo, just as references to Didymus ('Twin') in John's Gospel (e.g. John 21:1) might suggest Gemini. Such a reader, who also has some knowledge of Greek mythology, would no doubt spot that

---

[16] לְאֹתֹת

Jesus's declaration that his followers will pick up snakes, lay their hands upon the sick and heal them (Mark 16:17-18), is a possible reference to the constellation Ophiuchus, *the Serpent Bearer*, who is associated with Asclepius, *the Healer*. They might also consider that Cepheus, *The Robed and Crowned King*, is alluded to in the story of the scourging of Jesus (Mark 15:16-20), and Peter's mother-in-law, said to be 'reclining with a fever' (Mark 1:29-31), is an ingenious reference to Cassiopeia, *The Reclining Woman*, a constellation which appears close by Aries.

These may be seen as serendipitous narrative commonplaces, but when Jesus says that he has often wanted to take Jerusalem into his care as a hen gathers her chickens (Matthew 23:37; Luke 13:34), the accomplished sky-watcher would notice that he is using a singular image which, throughout the ages and throughout the nations, has been used to describe the Pleiades, a beautiful asterism in the constellation Taurus. (See below, *Taurus*.) He or she might also notice that the Syrophoenician woman's statement that "even the dogs under the table eat the children's crumbs" (Mark 7:28) is an allusion to the stars below the constellation Gemini (symbolised, generally, by twin *children*) which seem to be falling like crumbs into the mouths of the two celestial dogs, Sirius (the *Dog Star*, in Canis Major) and Procyon (*Before the Dog*), in Canis Minor. (See below, *Cancer*.)

If our students of astronomy have some linguistic knowledge, they would spot that the *names* of some constellations appear in the text. James and John leaving their father with "the hired men" (Mark 1:20) is an allusion to Aries, called Lu Hunga, *The Hired Man*, by the Babylonians.[17] The Greek names of both Gemini (Mark 4:30) and Libra (Mark 10:7) appear in Mark, and the non-zodiacal constellations Ara (Mark 11:21) and Ophis (Mark 16:18) are also mentioned.

They would no doubt notice that the names of individual stars appear, as well. Fomalhaut, one of the so-called Royal Stars, whose name means

---

[17] See White, p. 28.

'*The Fish's Mouth*,'[18] is possibly alluded to in the instruction Jesus gives to Peter to catch a fish and find a coin in its mouth (Matthew 17:27), and Ma Alaph in Cancer, which is said to mean *Assembled Thousands*,[19] could well be referenced in the stories of the Feeding of the Five Thousand (Mark 6: 30-44) and the Feeding of the Four Thousand (Mark 8:1-9).

The student of astronomy would possibly be struck by the numerous references to fish, fishing, and fishermen which occur in the Gospels,[20] and may conclude that the Gospels seem to have some connection with the constellation Pisces, the Fish.

Ptolemy catalogued 48 constellations, and our astronomically literate, mythologically aware linguist would notice that about half of them make an appearance in one form or another in Mark's text. But what he or she would find even more remarkable is that *they appear in the precise order that they are found in the sky*. There's nothing serendipitous about such a sequence.

Connections and Correlations

This astronomical schema is remarkable enough, but what is even more remarkable is the way in which *astrological* elements are incorporated into the text. The ancients didn't distinguish between astronomy and astrology. The observable, chartable *celestial* patterns (astronomy) and what were considered to be their analogically related *terrestrial* correlates (astrology), formed one unified area of study.

---

[18] Allen, p. 345.
[19] Seiss, p. 125.
[20] There are four references to 'fish' in Mark and twenty-one in the other three Gospels (Six in Matthew, six in Luke, and nine in John) and 'fishermen' are mentioned five times. But, with the exception of one reference in 1 Cor. 15:39, there are no 'fish' references in the rest of the New Testament.

Nor did the ancients live in an atomised world of separate, discrete, entities as we do.[21] They perceived, in the words of the English poet, Francis Thompson, that:

> All things by immortal power,
> Near or far,
> Hiddenly
> To each other linkéd are,
> Thou canst not stir a flower
> Without troubling of a star...[22]

For them, astrology was the study of this link. It was concerned with *correspondences and connections*, in which things are related to each other, either directly or analogically, because they share a common essence or function

Each of the seven 'wanderers'—Sun, Moon, Mercury, Venus, Mars, Jupiter, and Saturn—generated its own series of correspondences based upon its size, colour, the speed of its apparent orbit around the earth, its seasons of prominence, and so on. The presence in our language of the words *mercurial, venereal, martial, jovial* and *saturnine* testify to this perceived connection between planets and people. The table below will help explain how these correspondences are derived.

Sun	Moon	Mercury	Mars	Saturn
gold	silver	Quicksilver	iron	lead
heart	stomach	nerves	genitals	bones
vitality	emotions	communication	action	restriction
maturity	infancy	childhood	youth	old age
lion	cow	monkey	scorpion	owl

---

[21] Although modern science seems to be showing the wisdom of the ancient view.
[22] From *The Mistress of Vision* by Francis Thompson, (1859-1907).

Reading horizontally, we can readily detect six distinct groups: celestial bodies, metals, body parts, and so on. But there is another way of grouping these things which is quite foreign to us but which is basic to astrological thinking: by reading vertically we perceive five different groups. The relationships that exist among the members of these new groupings are not so immediately apparent, and some imagination may be required to discern them, but the individual elements which comprise each group are not as disparate as they may at first sight appear. Mercury, for example, as the fastest moving planet, is associated with the lightning responses of the body's nervous system and, by analogy, with an individual's need for communication. Quicksilver, or mercury, is the only 'mobile' metal; early childhood is the time of initial explorations, when we learn language; monkeys are known for their mercurial qualities of mimicry, mischievousness, and inquisitiveness.

These lists can be extended indefinitely to incorporate flowers, birds, plants, insects, jewels, countries, cities, colors, and so on. In each case, some feature of the creature, object, or place will indicate its planetary or zodiacal 'signature.' So, the lion is associated with the Sun: one 'rules' the solar system, the other 'rules' the jungle, and both then become natural symbols of kingship, pride, glory, power. We almost instinctively acknowledge the appropriateness of such relations and we cannot fail to observe them. For example, here's how the fifth century Neo-Platonist writer, Macrobius, views the relationship between the lion and the Sun:

> This beast seems to derive his own nature from that luminary (the Sun), being in force and heat as superior to all other animals as the Sun is to the stars. The lion is always seen with his eyes wide open and full of fire, so doth the Sun look upon the Earth with open and fiery eye.[23]

The Moon, whose shape constantly changes, whose rhythms reflect and even influence female *men*strual cycles becomes associated with change and inconstancy, with fluctuating emotions, and, as the 'star' of

---

[23] Quoted in Brown, p. 62.

the night, with dreams, and visions. Shakespeare, who lived at a time when such ideas still had currency, has Cleopatra declare:

> I am marble constant: now the fleeting moon
> No planet is of mine.[24]

Such thinking has given rise to the doctrine of 'correspondences' or 'sympathy', according to which things are related to each other because they are thought to share a common property. The lion, the Sun, gold, the heart, and the king, all seem to belong together, to reflect each other, to display a commonality of function or essence which links them although they belong to radically different categories of being.

The Zodiac

> The man in the street does not know a star in the sky. The solstice he does not observe, the equinox he knows as little; and the whole bright calendar of the year is without a dial in his mind.
> —Ralph Waldo Emerson

The symbolism of the signs of the zodiac was derived from the yearly cycle of the Sun in the sky and the interplay of light and darkness which this occasions. Especially important were the two equinoxes and the two solstices. In the northern hemisphere, the spring equinox marked the beginning of the solar year, when day and night are equal, but when the light—symbolic of individuality—begins to dominate. The autumn equinox marked the point at which the two are equal once again, but now the darkness—symbolising the collective—begins its period of supremacy.[25] The summer solstice marked the point of the Sun's highest elevation in the sky and the winter solstice marked its lowest.

---

[24] Antony and Cleopatra, Act V, Scene 2.
[25] *The Pulse of Life* (Shambhala, 1970) by Dane Rudhyar explains the symbolism of the interplay of light and darkness in the yearly cycle.

These four points were designated 'Cardinal' or initiatory, and were followed by 'Fixed' or stable signs which in turn preceded 'Mutable' or changeable signs. The Mutable signs were said by Manilius to be 'disōma,' two-bodied, since the Sun transits them between the seasons. Each sign was 'ruled' by one of the planets, and was also associated with one or other of the four Elements—Fire, Earth, Air, and Water—giving us the following schema.

Aries	♈	Fire	Cardinal	Ram	Mars
Taurus	♉	Earth	Fixed	Bull	Venus
Gemini	♊	Air	Mutable	Twins	Mercury
Cancer	♋	Water	Cardinal	Crab	Moon
Leo	♌	Fire	Fixed	Lion	Sun
Virgo	♍	Earth	Mutable	Virgin	Mercury
Libra	♎	Air	Cardinal	Scales	Venus
Scorpio	♏	Water	Fixed	Scorpion	Mars
Sagittarius	♐	Fire	Mutable	Centaur	Jupiter
Capricorn	♑	Earth	Cardinal	Mountain Goat	Saturn
Aquarius	♒	Air	Fixed	Water-Bearer	Saturn
Pisces	♓	Water	Mutable	Two Fish	Jupiter

The human being was considered to be a universe in miniature, a microcosm within the macrocosm, and so each part of the human body was correlated with one or other of the zodiacal constellations.

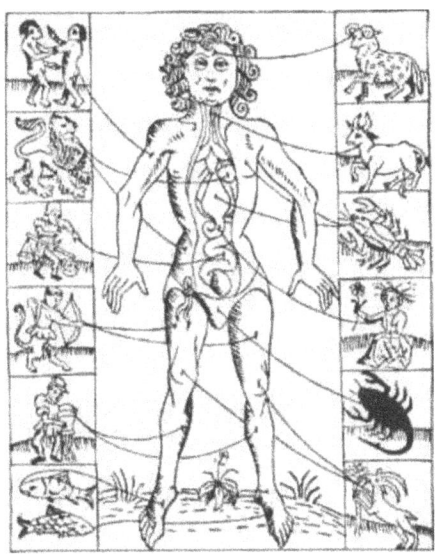

The Zodiacal Man

'Aries,' where the Sun is placed as the year begins at the spring equinox, can be correlated with, and therefore can symbolise, beginnings, newness, lambs, and reviving life; and, since it is generally assumed that things begin at the top, it can also be linked with the heads of things, and so with leaders and even roofs, ceilings, and mountaintops.

Just as the first sign, Aries, is associated with the head and with beginnings, the final sign, Pisces, in which the Sun 'dies' before being reborn at the spring equinox, is associated with decline, weakness, endings, and the feet. Each of the other signs has its own matrix of associations, conceived and delineated in the poetic imaginations of antiquity's 'watchers of the skies,' but derived principally by analogy from the annual journey of the Sun, the changing seasons, and the interplay of light and darkness. These associations can be gleaned from the ancient writers, and, since astrological tradition changes little, from more modern ones.[26]

---

[26] Ancient writers include Manilius, a contemporary of Mark, who wrote his *Astronomica* in Latin during the first century CE; Aratos, who wrote *Phaenomena* in

Part 2

Valentinus was Right

Why did not somebody teach me the constellations, and make me at home in the starry heavens, which are always overhead, and which I don't half know to this day?

—Thomas Carlyle

The Zodiacal Divisions of Mark's Gospel

As Valentinus observed, Mark's Gospel follows the yearly cycle of the Sun. Here are the zodiacal sections.

Aries	1:1-3:35	"…beginning…"
Taurus	4:1-4:34	"Again, Jesus began to teach by the lake…"
Gemini	4:35-6:29	"That day, when evening came…"
Cancer	6:30-8:26	"The apostles gathered round Jesus and reported to him…"
Leo	8:27-9:29	"Jesus and his disciples went on to the villages…"

Greek c300 BCE, and Ptolemy who wrote in Greek in the mid second century CE, but whose work *Tetrabiblos*, faithfully transmits the astrology of antiquity. Vettius Valens (120-175) a younger contemporary of Ptolemy, produced (in Greek) a very comprehensive treatise on Hellenistic astrology. Translations of Valens in book form are not easy to come by but a translation by Professor Mark Riley is available at: https://www.csus.edu/indiv/r/rileymt/Vettius%20Valens%20entire.pdf. The first seven pages are relevant to our present study.
Any modern astrological text-book will give the customary associations. A comprehensive list can be found in *The Astrologer's Manual* (pages 69-87) by L.K. Green. This website gives lists of relevant keywords and zodiacal associations: http://bonnierobson.com/index.htm.

Virgo	9:30-9:50	"They left that place and passed through Galilee…"
Libra	10:1-10:31	"Jesus then left that place and went into the region of Judea…"
Scorpio	10:32-10:52	"They were on their way up to Jerusalem…"
Sagittarius	11:1-11:26	"As they approached Jerusalem and came to Bethphage…"
Capricorn	11:27-12:44	"They arrived again in Jerusalem…"
Aquarius	13:1-14:16	"As Jesus was leaving the Temple…"
Pisces	14:17-16:18	"When evening came, Jesus arrived with the Twelve…"

Notice that these are *distinct* sections. Each section is introduced by a *significant* change of location or time. Note, too, that the zodiacal sections are not watertight! For example, 'twos' appear in Gemini, but they appear elsewhere; 'food' appears in Cancer, but it appears elsewhere. The sections are not related to a zodiac sign by a single reference but by a number of references—the Gemini section, for example, has *twenty* indications of Gemini, and the Cancer section has at least *a dozen* indications of Cancer.

The sections are of different lengths, which may be just as the author of the Gospel wanted it, or (more probably) it may suggest that the text we now possess is an edited version of a longer document.

In addition to the twelve zodiacal constellations, Mark makes reference to a number of the so-called 'decans' or 'faces,' thirty-six constellations which are associated with the zodiacal constellations (three to each constellation) because they 'come upon the meridian line or close along the meridian line' at the same time as their associated zodiacal constellation.[27] These were formulated by the Arabic astronomer, Albumazer (787-886 CE), but it is likely that Albumazer was reproducing a tabulation which originated in the remotest antiquity.[28] (See Appendix 1 for a list of these decans.)

Aries—Mark 1:1-3:35

Aries is the sign of the spring equinox, when the solar year begins. It is the Cardinal Fire sign and is associated with the Ram, Mars, lambs, beginnings, initiation, newness, fire, fever, burns, simplicity, austerity, the head, the leader, the top, the roof, impulsiveness, confrontation, challenge, deserted places, wildness, the wilderness, mountain tops.[29]

The public ministry of Jesus began in the spring, says the Clementine Homilies;[30] and themes of 'newness' and 'new life' pervade this section. The word 'new' appears *five* times (1:27; 2:21, 2:22), twice as νέος (*neos*), meaning 'new in time,' and three times as καινός (*kainos*), meaning 'new in quality.'

The very first word of the Gospel is 'beginning' (ἀρχὴ). It doesn't even have a definite article to stop it from being the first word!

Both John the Baptist and Jesus preach "repentance," *beginning again* from the Greek μετανοέω (*metanoeō*), which means 'to change one's mind, to think differently afterwards' (Mark 1:4, 1:14).

Jesus is baptized by John. This is a sign of *initiation*, the beginning of a new chapter in Jesus' life.

Levi is the son of *Alphaeus* (Mark 2:14), a name which derives from the Hebrew חלף meaning 'a swift transition, a hurried traversal or change or renewal.'[31]

---

[27] Seiss, p. 18.
[28] See Appendix 1 for a list of these decans.
[29] Relevant Decans: Cassiopeia (*The Reclining Woman*), Perseus (*The Bridegroom*).
[30] Section 20. See Full Text of The Clementine Homilies at Internet Archive.
[31] Abarim.

The Twelve Apostles are the 'new Israel' and are called "on a mountain" (Mark 3:13).

Aries' association with the head and to the tops of things in general is reflected in the curious detail of the "paralyzed man" being lowered down through "the roof" to Jesus (Mark 2:1-12).

Another telling detail occurs in the passage describing how James and John leave their father "with the hired men" (Mark 1:20). As White informs us, 'The Hired Man' was the Babylonian name for Aries:

> Contrary to its name, the Hired Man was represented in the heavens by the familiar ram or lamb of Aries. As a seasonal symbol the lamb reflects the fact that a majority of newborn lambs, kids and calves appear in the cattle-fold in the springtime.[32]

Jesus revives three men from conditions which imply powerlessness—leprosy (Mark 1:40-45), paralysis (Mark 2:1-12), and a withered hand (Mark 3:1-5)—thus giving them *new life*.

John the Baptist, dressed *simply* and eating an *austere* diet, appears "in the wilderness" (Mark 1:4-8). Eventually—in what is a narrative flashback—John will lose his head (Mark 6:14-29). According to Ptolemy, Algol, a prominent star in the nearby constellation, Perseus, was associated with beheading (αποκεφλιζομνους).[33] It was known as 'Rosh ha Satan' *Satan's Head* by the Hebrews.[34] Josephus mentions the death of John the Baptist at the hands of Herod but he doesn't say he was beheaded.[35]

In the Fourth Gospel, John the Baptist calls Jesus "the lamb of God" (John 1:29).

Jesus goes into "the wilderness," among "the wild animals," to be tempted by Satan (Mark 1:12-13).

---

[32] White, p. 28.
[33] Tetrabiblos, IV, 9.
[34] Allen, p. 332.
[35] *Antiquities*, 18: 5, 2.

In Matthew (3:11) and Luke (3:16), John the Baptist says that one coming after him will be baptized "with the Holy Spirit and fire." The 'fire'—appropriate to Aries—is strangely absent from Mark. This is the first of a number of occasions on which another Gospel is more 'astrological' than Mark.

Both Matthew (8:19-22) and Luke (9:57-62) report Jesus saying that the "Son of Man has no place to lay his head" and to "let the dead bury their own dead." Both of these sayings are appropriate to Aries, but are absent from Mark.

Aries is associated with *impulsive behaviour*. Simon, Andrew, James, John, and Levi follow Jesus without a second thought (1:16-20, 2:13-17).

Aries, 'ruled' by Mars, is associated with daring, defiance, confrontation. Jesus so antagonizes the Jewish authorities that they conspire to kill him (Mark 3:6).

Nearby Aries, is the famous and easily identifiable constellation, Cassiopeia, *The Reclining Woman*. Simon's mother-in-law is said to be *reclining* (κατέκειτο) with that most Arien of conditions, "a *fever*" (Mark 1:30). The words translated 'fever' are from the Greek root 'πύρ (*pur*) which means 'fire.' (πυρετός, οῦ, ὁ means 'fiery heat, scorching heat.')[36] She was 'burning up' and so no doubt had a rose-coloured face, which is what the name 'Cassiopeia' is said to mean in Phoenician.[37]

---

[36] Thayer's Greek Lexicon.
[37] https://astronomyisawesome.com/galaxies/7-most-beautiful-constellations/
There is also a possible derivation from the Greek words αἴθω + ὤψ (aitho "I burn" + ops "face") i.e. Burnt-face.

Cassiopeia
The Reclining Woman, The Rose-Colored Face

In Matthew's Gospel, she is "*Peter's* mother-in-law" (Mathew 8:14). This is even more clearly faithful to the astronomy and the mythology than Mark's version. 'Peter' (Πέτρος) means 'rock,' so Peter's wife is 'chained to the rock' (i.e. she's married to Peter!), just as Cassiopeia's daughter, Andromeda, is 'chained to the rock' (literally!) before being rescued by Perseus who married her. Perseus thus became the constellation which Aratus referred to as *the Bridegroom* (γαμβρος),[38] and which Jesus mentioned when he said, 'Can the wedding guests fast while *the bridegroom* is with them?' (Mark 2:19).

Andromeda, *'Chained to the Rock'* Théodore Chassériau, 1840

---

[38] Aratus, line 248.

Taurus—Mark 4:1-20

Taurus is the Fixed Earth sign and is associated with the Bull, Venus, the Earth, the neck, persistence, stubbornness, farming, growth, and light. The Sun enters Taurus in late April, when spring has really taken hold and growth, colour, and profusion of plants are in evidence.

Taurus is the first Earth sign, and the Greek word for 'earth' (ἡ γῆ) is used *nine* times in this section; and nowhere else in the Gospel do we find such a wealth of agricultural imagery and vocabulary. The Roman astrological poet, Manilius, equates this constellation with farming in general.

> Dull honest Plowmen to manure the Field
> Strong Taurus bears, by him the Grounds are till'd'
> ......
> He takes the Yoke, nor doth the Plough disdain,
> And teacheth Farmers to manure the Plain…[39]

It is appropriate, then, that in this section we find the Parable of the Growing Seed (Mark 4:26-29) and the Parable of the Mustard Seed (Mark 4:30-32). The Pleiades, a beautiful asterism in Taurus, was connected with seeding-time. Virgil alludes to this in his First Georgic:

> Some that before the fall o'th' Pleiades
> Began to sowe, deceaved in the increase
> Have reapt wilde oats for wheate.[40]

The Pleiades was called 'A Hen with her Chickens' by numerous cultures throughout the ancient world:

> A common figure for these stars, everywhere popular for many centuries, is that of a Hen with her Chickens—another instance of the

---

[39] Manilius, p. 124.
[40] Allen, p. 401. See Virgil's *First Georgic*, lines 219-216.

constant association of the Pleiades with flocking birds, and here especially appropriate from their compact grouping.[41]

Mark does not have this saying, but it is found in both Matthew (23:37) and Luke (13:34). In Luke it occurs close by his version of the parables of the Mustard Seed and the Yeast, possibly indicating that it was originally associated with the parables of growth which appear in the Taurus section of Mark.

Because Taurus is the most spectacular of the zodiacal constellations, (it contains two beautiful asterisms—the Hyades and the Pleiades—plus Aldebaran, the ninth brightest star in the heavens), it was associated with light by the ancients. The Hindus pictured the Pleiades as a Flame 'and held their great star-festival Diwali, the Feast of Lamps, in the Pleiad month, Kartik.'[42] Hence the Parable of the Lamp occurs in this section (Mark 4: 21).

One of the stars of the Pleiades was said to be 'hidden,' some people saying they could see six stars, others saying they could see seven. Erastosthenes called the Pleiades Pleias Eptasteros, the 'Seven Starred Pleiad,' although he said that one of them was panaphanes—'all invisible' (παναφανης).[43] Hence Jesus' saying, 'Nothing will be hidden that will not be revealed (φανερωθῇ)' (Mark 4:22).

Taurus is associated with abundance: 'Some other seed fell on good soil. It came up, grew and produced a crop, some multiplying thirty, some sixty, some a hundred times' (Mark 4:8).

The Greeks called Taurus' principal star, Aldebaran, 'Lampadias' (λαμπαδιας)—the Torch Bearer, a name derived from the Greek verb λάμπω (lampō) 'to shine.' Matthew's version of these sayings about lamps and light uses this verb twice.

You are the light of the world. A city on a hill cannot be hidden. Neither do people light a lamp and put it under a bowl. Instead they put

---

[41] Allen, p. 399.
[42] Allen, p. 393.
[43] Allen, p. 411; Also see Liddell and Scott, p. 874.

it on a stand, and it gives light (*lampei*) to everyone in the house. In the same way, let your light shine (*lampsatō*) before men, that they may see your good deeds and praise your Father in heaven (Matthew 5:14-16).

Since Aldebaran was called Oculus Tauri or The Bull's Eye, and even God's Eye, it is interesting to note that immediately after his version of the Parable of the Lamp, Luke adds:

Your eye is the lamp of your body. When your eyes are good, your whole body also is full of light. But when they are bad, your body also is full of darkness. See to it, then, that the light within you is not darkness. Therefore, if your whole body is full of light, and no part of it dark, it will be completely lighted, as when the light of a lamp shines on you (Luke 11: 34-36).

Gemini – Mark 4:35-6:29

The Twins, associated with Mercury, air, the wind, duality, halves, fragmentation, brothers and sisters, close relatives, vacillation, speech, reporting, preaching, communication.[44]

In these 78 verses, there are *over 20* indications of Gemini. The section opens with the Calming of the Windstorm (Mark 4:35-42). This passage is obviously inspired by Psalm 107, and may owe something to Homer's story of Aeolus' bag of winds in the Odyssey,[45] but it is placed here to reflect the mythology of Castor and Pollux, the twin stars of Gemini, considered to be the patrons of seafarers. One of the Homeric Hymns is dedicated to these twin deities on whom sailors would call when in distress. Here's a more modern account from Macaulay's *The Lays of Ancient Rome*:

Back comes the chief in triumph,

---

[44] Relevant Decans: Orion, Canis Major (*Big Dog*), Canis Minor (*Little Dog*).
[45] *Odyssey* 10:1-69. See MacDonald, pp. 61-2.

> Who, in the hour of fight,
> Hath seen the great Twin Brethren
> In harness on his right.
> Safe comes the ship to haven
> Through billows and through gales,
> If once the great Twin Brethren
> Sit shining on the sails.[46]

Matthew, in his parallel passage (Matthew 4:24), uses the term seismos (σεισμὸς) to identify the type of storm the apostles experienced. Seismos means 'earthquake.' Mark uses the word *laelaps* ((λαῖλαψ), which, according to Aristotle, 'is a whirlwind revolving from below upward.'[47] In addition, 'Laelaps' is the name of the faithful dog of Orion, a constellation close by Gemini.

Matthew and Luke simply say that Jesus 'rebuked' the wind, but Mark gives the actual word he used: Σιώπα (siōpa) (Mark 4:39), which means 'Quiet!' or 'Be still!' This echoes the Doric Greek name for Gemini το σίω (siō) which is the dual form of the word for 'god' (i.e. Gemini, 'the two gods').[48]

Gemini's association with multiplicity and fragmentation is reflected in the story of the Gerasene Demoniac (Mark 5:1-20). The demon-possessed man says, "My name is Legion, for we are many" (Mark 5:9).

In his parallel passage, Matthew says there were "*two* demon-possessed men" (Matthew 8:28).

There are five indications of Gemini's association with proclaiming, preaching, announcing, reporting, and teaching, the most significant being the sending out of the apostles to *proclaim* (κηρύσσειν) the message of the kingdom (Mark 5:7-13). The apostles are sent out '*two by two*' and ordered not to take *two* coats. The demons from Legion enter *two* thousand pigs (all the more significant since a Roman legion was normally

---

[46] Thomas B. Macaulay, *Lays of Ancient Rome*, "The Battle of The Lake Regillus." (2009; Originally published in 1842).
[47] Thayer's Greek Lexicon.
[48] See Liddell and Scott, p. 1392.

between four and six thousand strong). Herod offers Herodias *half* his kingdom. Herod is shown to be in *two minds* about John.

The story of Jairus' Daughter and the Woman with the Flow of Blood (Mark 5:21-43) *is the only 'double' miracle in the Gospels.*

> What we have here is without precise parallel in the Gospel—an incident broken into by another incident which takes place in the middle of it.[49]

Immediately following his account of this dual miracle, Matthew tells two more stories which are not found in Mark but which express the Geminian theme: The Healing of the *Two* Blind Men (Matthew 9:27-31), and the Cure of the Mute (Matthew 9:32-34). Geminian duality is obvious in the first; the second relates to Gemini's association with speech and communication generally.

Gemini is associated with *relatives,* especially brothers and sisters. Jesus' relatives have been mentioned before (Mark 3:20-34), but this is the only time they are named (Mark 6:3).

The man who had been demon-possessed is told by Jesus to go home and tell *his own people* (τοὺς σούς) what the Lord had done for him (Mark 5:19), and *brother, wife, sister-in-law, daughter, and niece* all feature in the story of John the Baptist's beheading (Mark 6:21-29).

Cancer—Mark 6:30-8:26

Associated with the Crab, the Moon, water, traditions, the nation, the clan, the shell, the stomach, food. When the Sun enters Cancer, it begins to reverse its direction and starts to move south.[50]

Cancer and its 'ruler,' the Moon, are associated with the *stomach and with food.* This section contains The Feeding of the Five Thousand (Mark

---

[49] Nineham, *St. Mark*, Pelican Gospel Commentary.
[50] Relevant Decans: Ursa Major (*Big Bear*), Ursa Minor (*Little Bear*), Argo (*The Ship which Conquered the Waters*).

6:30-44) and the Feeding of the Four Thousand (Mark 8: 1-13). Close by Cancer are Ursa Major and Ursa Minor, the two 'bears,' the Great Bear and the Little Bear. Ancient commentators saw these two constellations as 'flocks' (דברים), not 'bears' (דבים).[51] Jesus feeds two flocks, one bigger than the other.

The constellation Cancer contains a star called *Ma'Alaph*, which means 'Assembled Thousands.'[52]

Cancer concerns *traditions and customs*. This section contains a lengthy piece in which Jesus questions the food and hand-washing traditions of the Pharisees (Mark 7:1-23) and their tradition of declaring money or property "Corban" in order to escape their responsibilities to their parents (Mark 7:11-12).

Jesus walks on the *water* in this section (Mark 6:45-52). Walking on Water demonstrates mastery over the emotions, which, because of their inconstancy and instability, were associated with water by the ancients. In addition, one of the decans of Cancer is the constellation Argo, Jason's ship, said by Manilius to be the ship "*that conquered the water (quae vicerat aequor).*"[53]

Cancer is associated with the home, the fatherland (or motherland), with closing oneself off (like the crab's shell) from the foreign and the strange, with *'clannish'* behaviour. Jesus is shown exhibiting just such clannishness in his treatment of the Syrophoenician Woman who asks him to help her daughter. 'It's wrong to give the children's food to the dogs' (Mark 7:27), he says. 'Yes, but the dogs can eat the children's crumbs,' says the woman (Mark 7:28). This image is taken straight from the constellation patterns, from the area between Gemini and Cancer. Sirius is The *Dog Star* and can be found in the constellation Canis Major (the *Big Dog*) and Procyon which means *'Before the Dog'* (i.e. rising before Sirius) is in Canis Minor (the *Little Dog*).

---

[51] Allen, p. 449.
[52] Seiss, p. 125.
[53] Manilius, Book 1, line 623.

Above Procyon are the stars of Castor and Pollux, the Twins—... Sometimes this rectangle is seen as a table at which Castor and Pollux are eating; the two dogs (Sirius and Procyon) are waiting patiently for the table crumbs. These crumbs can be seen as very faint stars of magnitude 5 or 6, scattered between Gemini and Procyon.[54]

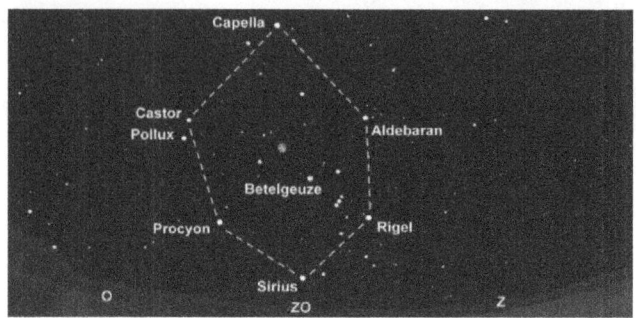

Jesus' strange journey is only found in Mark:

Καὶ πάλιν ἐξελθὼν ἐκ τῶν ὁρίων Τύρου ἦλθεν διὰ Σιδῶνος εἰς τὴν θάλασσαν τῆς Γαλιλαίας ἀνὰ μέσον τῶν ὁρίων Δεκαπόλεως.

'Leaving the region of Tyre, he went through Sidon to the Sea of Galilee, up through the middle of the Decapolis' (Mk 7:31).

---

[54] Staal, *Patterns in the Sky*, page 86. There are a number of 'dogs' in this part of the sky. Even the two 'bears' (Ursa Major and Ursa Minor, both close by Cancer) have been associated by some ancient commentators with dogs. See Allen, page 450.

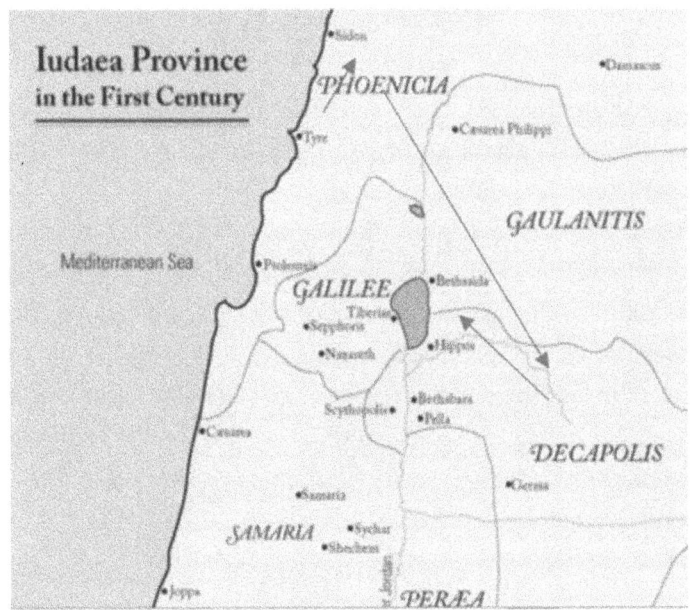

Jesus' Strange Journey

This has been likened to travelling from London to Cornwall via Manchester. It describes what airline pilots call 'crabbing,' that is, pointing the vessel in one direction while moving in another. *Crabs don't walk in straight lines.*

> Anyone who has watched a crab on the beach must have noticed its peculiar sideways walk, its sudden forward movements, and its occasional circles—as though it cannot make up its mind where to go.[55]

This is an ingenious reference to Cancer. It is not, as the commentaries tell us, an indication that Mark didn't know his geography very well!

---

[55] Staal, pp. 146-147.

Leo—Mark 8:27-9:29

Associated with the Lion, the Sun, royalty, 'divine splendour,' glory, the heart, faith, self-importance. Leo is the sign of the summer when the Sun's heat is fiercest.

The Leo section contains the Transfiguration (Mark 9:2-7), when Jesus demonstrates his divine nature to his disciples. Leo, the only sign said to be 'ruled' by the Sun, has been called 'the sign of divine splendor.'[56] Although Mark says that Jesus' clothing shone with intense whiteness, Matthew, in his corresponding account, says that his garments "*shone like the Sun*, and his clothes became as white as light" (καὶ μετεμορφώθη ἔμπροσθεν αὐτῶν, καὶ ἔλαμψεν τὸ πρόσωπον αὐτοῦ ὡς ὁ ἥλιος, τὰ δὲ ἱμάτια αὐτοῦ ἐγένετο λευκὰ ὡς τὸ φῶς) (Matthew 17:2).

Here, once again, Matthew is more 'astrological' than Mark.

The names of some of Leo's stars reflect the Transfiguration. The principal star of the constellation is Regulus—*the Little King*; the second star is Al Giebha, said to mean *the Exalted, the Exaltation*, and Zosma in the lion's tail means, *the Shining, the Epiphany*.[57]

Catholics celebrate the Feast of the Transfiguration on 6th August, when the Sun is in the very centre of Leo.

Leo, like all the Fire signs (Aries, Leo, and Sagittarius) is associated with *faith*, the virtue extolled by Jesus in the account of the healing of the dumb boy (Mark 9:14-29).

---

[56] Charles Carter, *Essays on the Foundations of Astrology*. (Fowler, London, 1961), p. 71.

[57] Seiss gives these meanings in *The Gospel in the Stars*, page 134. I cannot vouch for the meanings of Al Giebha and Zosma, but they seem remarkably appropriate, particularly since Seiss is not mentioning them in connection with the Transfiguration.

Virgo—Mark 9:30-9:50

Associated with: the Virgin, Mercury, humility, service, simplicity, purity, perfectionism, children, innocence, details.

Virgo is the sign of the harvest, hence its symbol, the maiden with a wheat-sheaf. As the harvest sign, Virgo is the House of Bread, known in Hebrew as Bethlehem (בַּיִת - house, לֶחֶם - bread).[58]

Virgo is associated with modesty. Manilius tells us:

> But modest Virgo's rays give polished parts
> ...But bashful modesty casts down their eyes.[59]

In this (short) section, we read of the apostles arguing about who was the greatest among them. Jesus tells them, 'If anyone wants to be first, he will be last of all, and the servant of all' (Mark 9:35).[60]

Jesus warns the apostles against the besetting fault of Virgo—*perfectionism* (Mark 9:39-40). "Whoever is not against us is for us," he says. Sometimes, "near enough" is good enough!

In Egypt, Virgo was associated with the goddess, Isis, who is often depicted carrying the infant, Horus. Here, Jesus takes a child in his arms (Mark 9:36) to illustrate innocence and humility.

Virgo is associated with small gestures rather than grandiose ones. Hence, "Whoever gives you a cup of cold water to drink because you bear the name of Christ won't go unrewarded" (Mark 9:41).

Close by Virgo is the constellation Coma Berenice. Although it wasn't mentioned as a separate constellation by Ptolemy, its stars have (since at least the third century BCE) been associated with Berenice's Hair. Queen Berenice of Egypt cut off her hair, of which she was extremely proud, in

---

[58] Relevant Decans: Coma Berenice (*the Infant*), Boötes (*the Shepherd or Herdsman*).
[59] Manilius, *Astronomica*, p. 125.
[60] This saying is appropriate to Virgo for another reason: in the ancient world, it was customary to start the constellational circle with Virgo. See Cyril Fagan, *Zodiacs Old and New*, page 30.

thanksgiving for the safe return of her husband from a perilous journey. Mark 9:42-48, which deals with cutting off certain body parts, could well echo this tale.

Jesus mentions salt (ἅλας, ατος, τό) in this section (Mark 9:50). Salt is a symbol of cleanliness and purity, and Strong's Exhaustive Concordance says that it relates figuratively to that most Virgoan of attributes, *prudence*. Salt also demonstrates how tiny grains of pretty ordinary stuff can exert a powerful influence.

The Virgo section of Mark is short, but Matthew's treatment of the same themes (Chapter 18) is longer and includes the Parable of the Lost Sheep (Matthew 18:12-14) which has a very Virgoan flavour (looking after the details). It also reflects the nearby constellation Boötes, *the Shepherd* or *the Husbandman*. Luke adds the Parable of the Lost Coin, which makes much the same point (Luke 15:8-10). Luke also has Jesus' comments about the labourers and the harvest (Luke 10:2) just after Jesus has set a child before the disciples (Luke 9:46-48), possibly indicating that this originally belonged to the Virgo section.

The Catholic Church celebrates the birthday of the Virgin Mary—who embodies the Virgoan virtues set out above—on 8th September, when the Sun is in the centre of Virgo.

Libra—Mark 10:1-10:31

Associated with: the Scales, Venus, relationships, marriage, 'weighing in the balance.'[61]

Libra is the sign of the autumn equinox, when day and night are equal. It is symbolised by the Balance, and so is associated with relationships, marriage, and 'the primitive urge for unity and relatedness with others.'[62] In this section, Jesus gives his teaching on marriage and divorce.

---

[61] Relevant Decans: Crux (*The Cross*), Lupus (*The Wolf* or *The Victim*), Corona (*The Crown*).
[62] Jeff Mayo, *Teach Yourself Astrology*. (E.U.P. London, 1964), p. 63.

The Greeks called Libra 'Zugos' (ζεῦγος) *the Yoke*, and it is a word *formed from this very root* which Jesus uses to describe how man and woman are 'yoked' together (συνέζευξεν) in marriage (Mark 10:9).

In Egypt, Libra was associated with the goddess Ma'at, who weighed the hearts of the dead against a feather. Those who passed her test were said to be 'light-hearted,' while those who failed were 'heavy-hearted.' The rich young man walks away from Jesus in great sorrow (λυπούμενος) 'heavy-hearted' (Mark 10:22). Strong's Exhaustive Concordance defines the root verb λυπέω (*lupeo*) as: 'to distress; reflexively or passively, to be sad—cause grief, grieve, *be in heaviness*, (be) sorrow(-ful), be (make) sorry.' Mark's use of this verb also reflects the nearby constellation Lupus. It is a clever cross-language pun: *Lupus* is a Latin noun, *Lupeo* is a Greek verb.

Libra's other decans—the Cross and the Crown—both feature in the Gospel's final episodes.

Scorpio—Mark 10:32-10:52

Associated with the Scorpion, Mars, depth, power, sex, the sexual organs, death and regeneration, expiation, purgation, mystery.[63]

Scorpio is about 'depth,' and so the location of this section around Jericho is appropriate: Jericho is the lowest inhabited place on earth, 825 feet below sea level. Before the ascent to Jerusalem (2,500 feet above sea level), comes the descent into Jericho.

At this point, James and John ask Jesus to 'allow one of us to sit on your right hand and one on your left hand in your glory' (Mark 10:35-45). They want power—a very Scorpionic desire.

A passage purporting to be from a longer version of Mark, which Professor Morton Smith claimed to have discovered in 1958, is said to be

---

[63] Relevant Decans: Ophiuchus (*The Serpent Holder*) and Serpens (*the Snake*).

located in this section,[64] and since the themes of this passage are clearly Scorpionic (death, regeneration, mystery, with just a hint of sex),[65] there is at least a chance that it is an authentic part of original Mark. It may have been excised because of the possible sexual element.

The constellation Ophiuchus *the Serpent Bearer* (associated with Asclepius, *the Healer*, and Serpens, *The Snake*), which the Greeks called Ophis (ὄφις) lies between Scorpio and Sagittarius. It is quite possible that some verses from a disputed ending of Mark (Mark 16:17-18), verses which tell us that believers will pick up snakes (ὄφεις), drink deadly poison, and place their hands on sick people to make them well, really belong in this section of the Gospel.

Sagittarius—Mark 11:1-11:26

Associated with: the Centaur, Jupiter, horses, zeal, travel, foreigners, religion, arrows, the thighs, faith. Relevant Decan: Ara (*The Altar*).

In Mark (and Luke), Jesus rides into Jerusalem on a *young horse* (πῶλος), and *not a donkey.* This is an image of the Centaur, half man, half horse, the pictogram of Sagittarius. By sedately riding on an *unbroken* horse ('a horse on which no one has ever sat'—Mark 11:2), Jesus is showing mastery over the Element Fire.

---

[64] 'After this follows the text, "And James and John come to him and all that section..."' (Barnstone, p. 342).

[65] Here is the relevant passage: "And they come into Bethany. And a certain woman whose brother had died was there. And, coming, she prostrated herself before Jesus and says to him, 'Son of David, have mercy on me.' But the disciples rebuked her. And Jesus, being angered, went off with her into the garden where the tomb was, and straightway a great cry was heard from the tomb. And going near Jesus rolled away the stone from the door of the tomb. And straightway, going in where the youth was, he stretched forth his hand and raised him, seizing his hand. But the youth, looking upon him, loved him and began to beseech him that he might be with him." (Barnstone, p. 342).

Jesus' ride into Jerusalem on a horse echoes Psalm 45, a psalm which contains Sagittarius related elements—the horse, the arrows, and even the thigh (Hebrew יָרֵךְ), the body-part associated with Sagittarius.⁶⁶

Sagittarius is said by Ptolemy to be 'bi-corporeal,' two-bodied, just like Gemini. In Gemini, we had two miracles, one in the middle of the other; in Sagittarius we have a miracle in two parts—the cursing of the fig tree (Mark 11:14) and its discovery as a withered plant (Mark 11:20-21). Cursing the fig tree shows Jesus' mastery over the Element Earth. The 'bi-corporeal' nature of Sagittarius is also shown by the place the apostles are to find the horse (Mark 11:4). It is 'the place where two roads meet' (ἐπὶ τοῦ ἀμφόδου).

A constellation close by Sagittarius is Ara. In Latin, this means 'Altar,' but in Greek it means 'Curse.' 'The fig tree you cursed (κατηράσω— *kateraso*) has withered.'

Jesus overturns the chairs of those who sold pigeons (Mark 11:15). The two stars in the tip of the Archer's arrow have been compared to an overturned chair.⁶⁷

Sagittarius is associated with travel, foreigners, *internationalism*. "Isn't it written, 'My house will be called a house of prayer *for all nations*?'" asks Jesus (Mark 11:17). Manilius says that 'Ara' represents the *mundi templum*, the temple of the world.⁶⁸

The Fourth Gospel's account of this incident (John 2:17) has the apostles remembering the words of Psalm 69, "Zeal for your house will consume me," reflecting the Sagittarian association with fervour.

---

⁶⁶ Gird your sword upon your thigh, O mighty one;
With your glory and majesty.
And in your majesty ride prosperously
Because of truth, humility, and righteousness;
And your right hand shall teach you awesome things.
Your arrows are sharp in the heart of the king's enemies;
The peoples fall under you. (Verses 3-5, NKJV.)
⁶⁷ Allen, p. 355.
⁶⁸ Allen, p. 63.

Capricorn—Mark 11:27-12:44

Associated with: The Mountain-Goat, Saturn, authority, the father, structure, convention, propriety, traditions.

The question of authority dominates this section. It opens with the question, 'By what *authority* do you do these things?' (Mark 11:28). Jesus assesses the various sources of spiritual authority within Judaism (Pharisees, Sadducees, Scribes etc.) and finds them wanting. He tells a parable about their inadequacies (Mark 12:1-12). He comments on the legitimacy of the state's authority (Mark 12:13-17). He even comments on the authority of the Jewish Scriptures (Mark 12:35-37).

Jesus asks his questioners to produce a denarius (Mark 12:15), *not just any coin*.[69] Augustus had a denarius minted which showed his head on one side and Capricorn (the sign in which his Moon was placed) on the other, and so did the emperor, Titus, whose Sun was in Capricorn (born on 30th December 39 CE). As far as I am aware, *Capricorn is the only zodiac sign to appear on a Roman denarius*. Below is the Titus denarius, minted about CE 79.

A Denarius, showing Titus and his Birth-Sign, Capricorn

---

[69] Matthew uses the word *nomisma* (νόμισμα) which just means 'a coin' or 'lawful money.' Luke follows Mark and has Jesus ask specifically for a denarius (Luke 20:24).

In the Capricorn section of his Gospel, Mark has a lengthy condemnation of hypocrisy, a vice associated with Capricorn. Charles Carter writes: "the New Testament does contain condemnations of the leaders of Jewry that certainly sound like attacks upon the traditional Capricorn—the love of high places, hypocritical formalism in religion, the desecration of holy places in pursuit of gain."[70]

In Matthew's much longer condemnation of hypocrisy (Chapter 23), he adds: "They love to be greeted with respect in the marketplaces and to be called 'Rabbi' by others. But you are not to be called 'Rabbi' for you have one Teacher, and you are all brothers. And do not call anyone of earth "father," for you have one Father, and he is in heaven" (Matthew 23:7-9). This is a clear reflection of Capricorn's association with *fatherhood*. Yet another example of Matthew being more astrological than Mark.

Aquarius—Mark 13:1-14:16

Associated with: The Man Carrying a Jar of Water, Saturn, friendship, altruism, anarchy, political and social upheaval, drastic change, future hopes and wishes.

The Man Carrying a Jar of Water (Mark 14: 13-16) is one of the clearest zodiacal references.

> "This constellation has been represented, even on very early Babylonian stones, as a man, or a boy, pouring water from a bucket or urn."[71]

---

[70] Carter, Essays on the Foundations of Astrology, p. 83.
[71] Allen, p. 45.

Immediately before this, Jesus is anointed by an unnamed woman altruistically breaking open another jar (Mark 14:1-9).[72] Male and female together are offering their gifts to humanity.

Aquarius, ruled by Saturn, is associated with anarchy, political and social upheaval, drastic and radical change. The whole of Mark Chapter 13 is devoted to these very themes. "At that time they will see the son of man coming in clouds ('water-bearers'!) with great power and glory" (Mark 13:26).

In a parallel passage, Matthew has, "*the sign* of the Son of Man will appear in the sky…" (Matthew 24:30). This is a reference to the coming Age of Aquarius. (Aquarius is the only single human figure in the zodiac.) Once again, Matthew is more 'astrological' than Mark.

Pisces—Mark 14:17-16:18

Associated with: the Fish, Jupiter, secret enemies, betrayal, cowardice, sleep, dreams, endings, the feet.[73]

Pisces is the sign in which the sun 'dies' before being 'born anew' at the spring equinox, when it enters Aries once again.

Pisces was not held in high regard by the ancients. According to Allen, it "was considered…a dull treacherous and malignant sign"[74] and was associated with treachery (Judas betrays Jesus to the authorities in Mark 14:43-45); and lying ("some stood up and gave false testimony against him" – Mark 14:57); and cowardice (Peter repeatedly denies Jesus in Mark 14); and sleep (the apostles sleep in the Garden of Gethsemane in

---

[72] It's a version of the story told in Jn 12 and Luke 7 where Mary Magdalene (in John) or 'a sinful woman' (in Luke) anoints Jesus's *feet*. Mark wants the story in the Aquarius section (to indicate altruism), so he can't mention the feet, since this would confusingly associate it with the very next sign, Pisces. In addition, 'head' and 'feet' have very different symbolic values.

[73] Relevant Decans: Cepheus (*The Crowned King*), Andromeda (*The Sacrificed and Chained Woman*).

[74] Allen, pp. 339-340.

Mark 14:40); and alcohol and narcotics ("They gave [Jesus] wine mingled with myrrh" – Mark 15:23).

Pisces was also associated with dreams and premonitions. Mark does not mention dreams, but Matthew has an account of Pilate's wife's premonitory dream (Matthew 27:19).

The myth of Cepheus (*the Crowned King*) is clearly referred to in the story of the scourging of Jesus (Mark 15:16-20). The constellation Cepheus is close by Pisces.

The story of Andromeda (*The Sacrificed Woman*), is also alluded to in this section. Manilius wrote of Andromeda, "on the virgin cross hung the maid about to die (*et cruce virginea moritura puella pependit*)."[75] Andromeda, too, is close by Pisces.

Pisces is also connected with the feet. In John's Gospel, Jesus washes the feet of his disciples at the Last Supper (John 13ff), and Mary Magdalene washes Jesus' feet and dries them with her hair (Aries to Pisces, Head to Feet).

The Gospels have strong Piscean connections. One wonders, in the light of Pisces' bad reputation, why the early Christians chose the Fish as a symbol of Christ. As Strachan comments, "It is impossible to explain how such a 'cold-blooded, apathetic creature of the waters could come to symbolise the noble and exalted Saviour without reference to astral symbolism."[76]

The Fish – Early Christian Symbol

---

[75] Manilius, Book V, line 552.
[76] Strachan, *Christ and the Cosmos*, p. 42; See Appendix 2.

Among the four Gospels, only Mark has a zodiacal structure, but, as we have seen, there are a number of occasions on which another Gospel (usually Matthew) is more 'astrological' than Mark. If all these elements were present in canonical Mark, the zodiacal structure would be so glaringly obvious that not even Irenaeus would dare to deny it! Why, we might ask, are they not there? I leave the reader to judge the implications of these omissions.

Part 3

Mark as a Guide to the Spiritual Life

A dialectical soul-constitution can make nothing of the Gospels, which in the hands of scholars have become just a well-picked carcase.

—Rudolph Steiner

This constellation-based schema—clear, consistent, irrefutable—prompts a number of questions about the nature of Mark's Gospel, the most important one being, 'What kind of document is this?' It is certainly not a hastily compiled, rudimentary biography of Jesus, which Matthew and Luke added to and improved upon, as many believe; still less is it likely to be a series of random reminiscences made to the author of the Gospel by the Apostle Peter and presented 'in no particular order' as Papias claimed in the second century, and which some branches of orthodoxy still teach. Scholars have found this particular statement by Papias quite puzzling, because Mark seems to have a reasonably coherent chronological order. But Papias is no doubt denying a *zodiacal* order because such an order would undermine his claim (a claim made by generations of scholars and preachers) that Mark's story is basically history.

But nobody writes history or compiles reminiscences in this way. Nobody writes a biography, however sketchy, which says nothing about the appearance or education of the subject, little about their family, and which recounts the events of just one year of the subject's life.

On the other hand, Mark's Gospel is not 'myth.' Of course, it can be considered a myth in the way this term is (mis)used currently (i.e. to mean 'an untruth' or 'something that never actually happened'). But then again, so can most of the world's literature. Although mythic elements are incorporated into the text, the Gospel does not fully satisfy any of the more scholarly and comprehensive definitions of myth.[77] To ask, 'is the Gospel of Mark history or myth?' is to present us with a very unsatisfactory choice: it is neither, although it contains elements of both.

Mark's Gospel is a unique *literary* creation. It has no doubt undergone a number of revisions, but the version we now possess preserves the structure of a much longer document, which probably originated in an esoteric or Gnostic school. It was written to provide spiritual guidance for the coming age of Pisces. (See Appendix 2.) Its primary aim was *pedagogical*, not historical.

The astrological schema is neither ornamental nor merely functional. In each zodiacal section, the astrological meaning of the sign *informs and defines* the nature of the lesson(s) we need to learn from that section. All the component parts of a section—miracles, oral teaching, actions—are linked by their zodiacal context. The stories are not 'remembered incidents' randomly strung together, but *deliberately constructed narratives* (some of them inspired by episodes in the Hebrew Scriptures, some by episodes in mythology, some springing directly from the imagination of the author), designed to provide material for meditation and reflection to spiritual aspirants in a wisdom school.

The zodiac—the apparent annual path of the Sun in the sky—is a natural symbol of the path of life, and in each of the zodiacal sections we are presented with an important issue which every human being has to face. Just as Hercules has to complete twelve tasks on his way to find the golden apples,[78] so the aspirant must complete twelve spiritual tasks on

---

[77] E.g. 'A usually traditional story of ostensibly historical events that serves to unfold part of the world view of a people or explain a practice, belief, or natural phenomenon.' (Merriam-Webster)

[78] See *The Labours of Hercules*, by Alice Bailey.

his/her way to 'resurrection' or self-transformation. As we learn from Acts, Christianity was originally called 'the Way' or 'the Path' (Acts 9:2). The Greek word for 'path' is *hodos*,[79] and this word is a possible root of the word 'zodiac.'[80] In the Gospel of John, Jesus himself is the way (ὁδός), the truth, and the life (John 14:6).

The miracle stories are not assigned to a section randomly. For example, three healings of specified diseases in the Aries section belong together because each one illustrates in its own way the necessity and the possibility of grasping the new life symbolised by the spring. "The leper" (Mark 1:40-45) is one of the 'living dead;' "the paralysed man" has been rendered powerless because he is crippled by his past (his "sins") (Mark 2:1-12), and the man with the "withered hand" (Mark 3:1-5) is operating on half his potential power. In Matthew's Gospel, these stories are scattered around (Matthew 8:1-4; 9:1-8; 12:9-14) and so, lacking a unifying context, they can only be seen as yet more isolated examples of Jesus' amazing power. However, by placing them close together and linking them thematically with other images of beginnings and newness, Mark gives them a symbolic power which they lack when separated.

The *specified* diseases from which people are cured in the Gospels—blindness, deafness, demonic possession, leprosy, paralysis, high-fever—are all capable, without too much imagination, of being related to spiritual conditions. Jesus doesn't cure anyone of piles or toothache, because, distressing though these conditions may be,[81] they cannot easily provide images for spiritual ailments. But spiritual blindness is easy to grasp, as is spiritual deafness, spiritual possession, spiritual paralysis and, since leprosy was a kind of living death, spiritual leprosy is not a difficult concept to understand either. These are conditions which afflict us all, and if we

---

[79] ὁδός, οῦ, ἡ

[80] The word 'zodiac' comes from the primitive root *zoad*, 'a walk, way, or going by steps', and is related to the Greek word *hodos*, 'road', and the Sanskrit *sodi*, 'path.' (Seiss, p. 17.)

[81] British comedian Spike Milligan famously declared that it's difficult for a man with piles to believe in God, and Thomas de Quincy said that three-quarters of the world's pain is caused by toothache.

shift our focus away from the literal, we can avoid the interminable debate about the historical authenticity of these miracle stories.

Jesus' Strange Behaviour

On four occasions, Jesus behaves in ways that don't fit with the 'perfect man' image we have built for him over the centuries. At the end of Mark 3 (verses 31-35), Jesus seems to speak disrespectfully of his family; in Chapter 7 (24-30), he behaves towards the Syrophoenician woman in a way that appears to be racist; and in Chapter 11 (12-14) he speaks spitefully to the fig tree. In the same chapter (15-17), he violently casts out the traders and money-changers from the Temple. In each case, the evangelist's purpose is to show Jesus teaching an extremely important spiritual principle by means of dramatic behavioural inconsistencies. This, no doubt, was (is) a popular method of instruction within esoteric schools, and the fact that Mark employs it underlines the *pedagogical* nature of his Gospel. The Sufi writer, Idries Shah, tells the following story which illustrates the method.

> The Sufi, Bahaudin El Shah, was teaching some disciples in the square of Bokhara when another Sufi joined the crowd. Bahaudin questioned the newcomer: "Where do you come from?"
> "I have no idea," said the other, grinning foolishly.
> Some of Bahaudin's disciples murmured their disapproval of this disrespect.
> "Where are you going?" persisted Bahaudin.
> "I do not know," shouted the dervish.
> "What is Good?"
> By now a large crowd had gathered.
> "I do not know."
> "What is Evil?"
> "I have no idea."
> "What is Right?"
> "What is good for me."

"What is Wrong?"

"Whatever is bad for me."

The crowd, irritated beyond its patience by this dervish, drove him away. He went off, striding purposefully in a direction which led nowhere, as far as anyone knew.

"Fools," said Bahaudin, "this man is acting the part of humanity. While you were despising him, he was deliberately demonstrating heedlessness as each of you does, all unaware, every day of your lives."[82]

A Summary of Mark's Twelve Spiritual Tasks

The principal lesson of **Aries**, the springtime sign, concerns our relationship with the past and our resolve for the future. We are not to let the past with its sins, its guilt, and its failures paralyse our present. 'Your sins are forgiven,' says Jesus to the paralysed man (you and me!) 'so pick up your bed and walk!' This first section teaches that embarking on the process of personal transformation (which is what is meant by 'living a spiritual life') requires courage and a willingness to break free from debilitating personal habits of thought and behaviour, and from social and family relationships which hinder our resolve. It warns us against procrastination.

In the **Taurus** section we learn that steadfastness, sticking to our resolve, is vital to our spiritual growth; we must not be like the seed that grows well for a while but which then is choked by thorns—the physical appetites, and the cares and concerns of the world. Taurus also teaches us that light will come to us and hidden things will be revealed to us, if only we persevere

Gemini, the Twins, highlights the importance of calming the turbulence of our scattered and confused mental processes by awakening the 'master' who lies sleeping within each of us. Here we learn about the

---

[82] Slightly adapted from Idries Shah, *Wisdom of the Idiots*, p. 12.

fragmented nature of the psyche; that in each of us there is a whole crowd ('Legion') of personalities jostling for attention.

This section also teaches us that in our ordinary state we are asleep, reacting to circumstances rather than choosing our actions. Waking up from this sleep—as Jairus' daughter is awakened by Jesus—is a necessary step on the way to wholeness. We are alerted to the importance of reincorporating the feminine—the neglected, moribund polarity—into our religious life.

Cancer: See below for an extended analysis of this section.

In **Leo**, which includes the scene of the Transfiguration, we are taught about the true nature of the human being. We are all children of God. Each of us is a glorious emanation from God with a vital and unique part to play in the drama of the universe. "We are stardust, we are golden," sang Joni Mitchel.

However, no sooner are we apprised of our elevated status than we are taught the virtues of humility and service, the great lessons of **Virgo**. 'Don't get above yourself,' says Jesus to his apostles. 'Never mind arguing with each other about who is the greatest. Serve one another and cultivate the mind of a child to perceive the world afresh.'

The equinoctial sign of **Libra**, which the Sun enters when day and night are equal, carries the lessons of mutuality and reciprocity, of entering into caring and supportive relationships with people. Here we learn about the 'sacred marriage', the union of male and female, of yang and yin, within the individual psyche. We are taught, too, that wealth can be a severe hindrance to our spiritual progress, deflecting us from the life of the spirit by fostering self-indulgence and distraction.

In the **Scorpio** section, which comes as Jesus and the apostles approach Jericho, the lowest inhabited place on earth, we are warned not to seek power over others, and taught about those hidden connections which bind us one to another, so that no individual acts to and for himself alone; our actions, for good or ill, have consequences for ourselves and for others.

At the beginning of the **Sagittarius** section, Jesus rides into Jerusalem on an unbroken horse, symbolising the mastery of the bestial by the divine, mastery which each of us is called to attain. Each of us is a 'place where two roads meet.'[83]

In this section we also learn about the power of prayer and of faith to bring about remarkable changes in our world.[84]

In **Capricorn** we learn about the attitude we should cultivate towards all religious authority—bishops, priests, ministers, traditions, church councils, holy books, and the like. We must not cravenly follow the lead of others. We must take responsibility for our own spiritual progress.

The **Aquarius** section teaches the importance of standing out from the crowd, and of being willing to offer our unique gifts to society. We also learn that coming to a state of enlightened transformation will turn our interior universe upside down. Jesus teaches us that at the end of each of the astrological ages[85] we can expect to experience global chaos.

Finally, in the lengthy **Pisces** section, we see a dramatic presentation of the crucifixion of the false self which has kept us enslaved in our own egotism and craving but which has never been able to deliver the happiness it has constantly promised. We also learn that each of us is crucified between two thieves, the past and the future, which steal away our life.

In the final few verses of the Gospel of Mark, we read about the Resurrection, the empty tomb, which happens on the first day of the week—Sunday—just as the Sun has risen. These references to the Sun are not accidental or peripheral. The yearly journey of the Sun in the sky reflects

---

[83] I.e. the animalistic and the angelic

[84] In Mark, Jesus cleanses the Temple towards the end of his career because this event fits perfectly with the Sagittarian nature of the action. Jesus has just ridden into Jerusalem on *an unbroken h*orse, symbolically demonstrating his mastery of the animal passions. He cleanses the Temple *after this*, suggesting that his actions in the Temple are not the result of the red mist of blind rage, but the justifiable anger required to rectify an obvious wrong. The Fourth Gospel uses the same basic story but for a different purpose, placing it at the beginning of Jesus' ministry and relating it specifically to the Passover. To ask, 'Did it happen at the beginning or the end of Jesus' ministry?' is to ask a pointless historical question of a deeply symbolic story. It is just a silly pedantic diversion. We must always ask about the *function* of a particular story *in its context* before we even consider its historicity or even its provenance.

[85] See Appendix 2.

the life journey of the spiritual aspirant. Just as the Sun is 'resurrected' each year at the equinox, and each day at dawn; just as winter is transformed into spring; just as the caterpillar is transformed into the butterfly, so the spiritual journey outlined by Mark results in the birth of a new creature, a resurrected creature, someone who has overcome the sleep of the unlived life and who is now prepared to enter into life with new attitudes, new visions, new hopes. Such a 'resurrected' person has not tasted death but has seen the kingdom of God come with power, just as Jesus promised (Mark 9:1).

Jesus' disciples are to meet him in Galilee, that is, back where it all started. Galilee comes from the Hebrew word *galal* which means 'to roll, to encircle.'[86] Resurrection doesn't take us away from the cycle of ordinary life, it sends us back on to it once more, but this time, in the words of T.S. Eliot, "we'll know the place for the first time."

All valid religion is a call to resurrection. Not to life after death, but to a new kind of life *achievable now*. As Balzac says, at the end of his novel *Louis Lambert*, 'The resurrection is brought about by the winds of heaven which sweep the worlds. The angel borne upon the blast does not say, "Arise, you who are dead!" but "Arise, you who are living!"'[87]

This is the sublime message of the work of genius that we call the Gospel of Mark.

The Cancer Section—Mark 6:30-8:26

As an extended example of how the various components of a zodiacal segment fit together, let us look more closely at Cancer. *Food, ancestry, traditions, emotions, clannishness, nurture*; these are all associated with the sign Cancer, and these are the principal themes of this section of Mark's Gospel as even a cursory glance will show.

---

[86] גלל A noun from this root גיל (gil) describes a circle or time: an age (Abarim)
[87] La résurrection se fait par le vent du ciel qui balaie les mondes. L'ange porté par le vent ne dit pas: – Morts, levez-vous! Il dit: – Que les vivants se lèvent!

Cancer, along with its associated planet, the Moon, is said to 'rule' the stomach, and one of the dominant themes of this whole section is food. It begins with the account of the Feeding of the Five Thousand and it goes on to discuss the Jewish obsession with dietary laws, the tradition of ritual cleansing before food, and later it deals with the Feeding of the Four Thousand and 'the leaven' or yeast of the Pharisees.

There are two feeding stories. This has given headaches to traditional commentators for many years, some scholars suggesting that Mark included two accounts of the same event, showing him to be less than a competent historian—just as Jesus' strange journey shows him to be a poor geographer. Liberal scholars who view the Gospel as 'exaggerated history' will often explain these stories by saying that all the people really had food hidden away, but they were too mean to advertise the fact. After listening to Jesus, they were ashamed of their selfishness and willingly shared what they had, and everyone was satisfied. But this kind of explanation—harmless enough in its way—is rather patronising to the Gospel's author, implying that he allowed evangelistic piety to cloud his judgement.

But the author of this Gospel was no fool to be patronised, still less was he a poor historian or a poor geographer. The author knew perfectly well what he was doing. He deliberately has *two* feeding stories because he wants to make a very important point relating to Jewish clannishness. The stories are indeed the same except for a few details. But the details are crucial to a proper understanding of their meaning: the feeding of the Five Thousand takes place in Jewish territory, the feeding of the Four Thousand occurs in a predominantly Gentile area (the Decapolis). So, the two stories show that God's spiritual 'manna' is to be distributed to all people, not just to the Jews, and, read together, they constitute an attack on the narrow exclusivism and parochialism which characterised much Jewish thinking at the time the Gospel was written, and which have characterised much religious thought and practice before and since that time.

The traditions we inherit and pass on, the prejudices we develop, our natural instincts, act like the crab's shell to cut us off from what we consider to be alien or strange. It is probably a survival mechanism, built into our genes, but one objective of the spiritual life is to identify and then try to overcome those instinctive factors which work to give us short term survival advantages, but which have now outlived their usefulness and which actually impede our development as a species

The visceral—'gut'—reactions, which all human beings exhibit in the presence of the unfamiliar, are a feature of our emotional life. They come unbidden, up from the depths, and we have little immediate or conscious control over them. We instinctively prefer those people who look like us, talk like us, and who share our assumptions and our outlook. This is why the story of Jesus walking on the water is so appropriate in the Cancer section of the Gospel. It is astronomically appropriate because one of the decans of Cancer is Argo, the mythical and magical ship of the Argonauts which, according to the Roman writer Manilius, was the ship "which conquered the waters." But this story is also related to the idea of overcoming our emotional reactions to things, because water has perennially symbolised the turbulent emotional life of the individual and, by walking on the water, Jesus is demonstrating his mastery over those instinctive responses to life which will often override our intellectual convictions and which are the cause of so much emotional turbulence. Walking on the water is not a marvellous demonstration of the uniqueness of Jesus, a proof of his divinity; nor is it a misapprehension on the part of eye-witnesses who saw Jesus walking on some kind of rocky outcrop and mistook it for a miracle. It is, rather, something we are all called upon to do: we, too, must strive to conquer the internal emotional turmoil which militates against any genuine acceptance of unfamiliar customs and people.

There are three more miracle stories in this section, and although they seem like unrelated incidents, they must be taken together to get the full impact of the lesson the Gospel writer is trying to teach us.

The first one is the story of the woman who asks Jesus to cast out a demon from her daughter. It is important to remember that this woman is a Gentile—a non-Jew—and it is for this very reason that Jesus initially refuses her request. 'It's not right to give the children's food to the dogs,' he says. This, of course, is a terrible insult, and the fact that it is uttered by Jesus himself has proved quite embarrassing to conventional commentators, who try to soften it a little by saying that the word used was rather an affectionate term for a dog, and anyway, Jesus was really only testing the woman's faith. Does Jesus really come out of it better if we assume that he is playing some sort of game with this distressed woman? If she had been unable to respond cleverly to his insult would he have refused to heal her daughter?

Considered as literal history, as an actual event in the life of Jesus, this incident is quite despicable. However, considered as an *enacted parable*, in which Jesus plays the part of humanity, it is a powerful demonstration of 'the heedlessness' we all show in our dealings with strangers.

To appreciate the significance of this story, we must read it in conjunction with the story of the deaf man, which follows. After putting his fingers in the man's ears and touching his tongue with spittle, Jesus says the Aramaic word *Ephphatha*, and the man finds himself able to hear properly and to speak coherently.

It is unusual to find Aramaic words or phrases in the Gospels. Aramaic was the first language of the Palestinian Jews, and so would have been the language of Jesus and the apostles, and commentators regularly point out that it is present in the Gospels—which were all originally written in Greek—because these would have been the actual words that Jesus said. But Aramaic is almost certainly used *for emphasis* in the Gospel of Mark. The Gospel writer is saying, 'I'm writing this word in another language, so pay attention to it. It's important.'

The word *Ephphatha* means 'Open up!' What Jesus is saying to this deaf man's ears is the Gospel's message to you and me. Our ears are closed to the entreaties of those who live in foreign countries, whose skin colour is different from our own, whose way of life does not correspond with ours. We are deaf to the words even of those who live in close proximity to us, but whose traditions are different from ours. The Jewish exclusiveness displayed by Jesus in his encounter with the Gentile woman dramatically illustrates our own clannishness, our instinctive conviction that 'blood is thicker than water', that 'charity begins at home.' It's a shocking reminder of our own refusal to listen attentively to the unfamiliar voices. It is only when we are prepared to open up that our prejudices can be eroded; and only then that the impediment in our speech will be removed and our opinions will be worth listening to. We have to break the shell of our own tribalism.

This theme is explored further in the final scene of this section, the Cure of the Blind Man. As Jesus enters Bethsaida a blind man is brought to him and, in response to the man's entreaties, Jesus restores his sight. This seems to be just another example of Jesus' amazing power to heal. But the story is different from all the other miracles recounted in the Gospels, because it is the only one in which Jesus is shown failing at his first attempt. He takes the man to one side, rubs spittle on his eyes, and asks him, 'What do you see?' 'I see men but they look like walking trees,' the man replies. Jesus rubs the man's eyes again, and this time his sight is restored and he can see everything clearly.

The blind man is you and me. We have received the first rub of the spittle, and we can see—that is, we have the sense of sight—but we don't quite see people, we see walking trees—or, in contemporary language, ciphers, zombies, humanoids. We recognise their general shape and their mobility, but we have yet to grant them fully human status. What we need is a second metaphorical rub of the eyes to correct our vision, to remove the residual film which prevents us seeing people as they really are, as ends in themselves, and not as means to our own ends. Einstein expresses the same sentiment as Mark, but less dramatically and more philosophically, as follows:

> A human being is part of a whole called by us 'universe', a part limited in time and space. He experiences himself, his thoughts, and feelings as something separated from the rest, a kind of optical delusion of his consciousness. This delusion is a kind of prison for us, restricting us to our personal desires and to affection for a few persons nearest to us. Our task must be to free ourselves from this prison by widening our

circle of compassion to embrace all living creatures and the whole of nature in its beauty.[88]

The function of all spiritual practice—from whatever tradition it comes—is to help us to narrow the gap between self-awareness and other-awareness, to remove that residual film from our eyes which is deluding our sight.

Each of the zodiacal sections can (and should) be analysed in the same way. When we stop asking irrelevant—and distracting—'historical' questions of the text, we can begin to see what its real purpose is, and we can begin to see something of the genius behind it.

Appendix 1

The Constellations and their Decans According to Albumazer (See Fiorello, page vii-ix)

Aries – Cassiopeia, Cetus, Perseus
Taurus – Orion, Eridanus, Auriga
Gemini – Lepus, Canis Major (Sirius), Canis Minor (Procyon)
Cancer – Ursa Major, Ursa Minor, Argo
Leo – Hydra, Crater, Corvus
Virgo – Coma, Centaurus, Boötes
Libra – The Cross, The Victim, The Crown
Scorpio – The Serpent, Ophiuchus, Hercules
Sagittarius – Lyra, Ara, Draco
Capricorn – Sagitta, Aquila, Delphinus
Aquarius – The Southern Fish, Pegasus, Cygnus
Pisces – The Band, Cepheus, Andromeda

---

[88] Goldstein, page 26.

Chapter 9: The Mythic Power of the Atonement
By Robert M. Price

If Jesus Christ should turn out to have been a purely mythic or literary figure, would that stultify all talk of his atonement? I hope to show that the same question arises (or should) for theologians who do not espouse (or who even reject) the Christ Myth theory but nonetheless understand the language of the atonement as a mythical clothing or depiction of an underlying truth. The power of the atonement may turn out to be mythic in character even if it is based on the death of a historical individual. To anticipate, it boils down to the unstable relationship between the historian and the believer within each mind. If faith admits it has no right to pretend certainty about a historical Jesus (what he was like if he existed), then uncertainty becomes a structural, almost defining, feature of the Jesus available to faith, and this is practically tantamount to favoring the Christ Myth theory. The result is the same. Finally, I want to outline the possible continuing significance of a mythic atonement, based on an updating of the significance it had in three mythic systems that combined to form Christianity as we know it.

The Gospel Jesus: Picture, Not Window

Two of the twentieth century's greatest theologians, Paul Tillich and Rudolf Bultmann, rejected the Christ Myth theory as so improbable as to count as Cartesian hyperbolic doubt: "Of course the doubt as to whether Jesus really existed is unfounded and not worth refutation. No sane person can doubt that Jesus stands as founder behind the historical movement whose first distinct stage is represented by the oldest Palestinian community."[1] That is, neither man took it seriously as a historical hypothesis, but both did find the notion somewhat useful as a hypothetical foil with which to pursue the question of faith and historical method. Is Christian faith inherently unstable if it admits the tentative, provisional character of all historical judgments? Must the would-be Christian historian either secretly fear that fatal evidence against his Christ of faith might one day appear, or else let the will to believe foreclose that possibility? The first alternative seems to vitiate faith, veiling it in doubt; the second seems to sacrifice intellectual honesty in the interest of dogmatic certitude, thus corrupting faith in a different way. I mean to suggest that such reasoning opens the door through which neither Tillich nor Bultmann stepped, but which we might find a handy escape route if we found (as I have) that the evidence makes a historical Jesus unlikely.

The view of Martin Kähler, Wilhelm Herrmann, and Paul Tillich, that it is the "picture of Jesus Christ" in the gospels that communicates God-consciousness, seems almost perfectly designed for the Christ-Myth theory (and is perfectly compatible with it). It is true that Tillich said there must have been a historical Jesus.[2] But take a closer look: He said there had to be a first link in the chain when the New Being appeared among mankind. It started with someone, even if we cannot confidently assign him the name "Jesus."

> [P]articipation, not historical argument, guarantees the reality of the event upon which Christianity is based. It guarantees a personal life in which the New Being has conquered the old being. But it does not guarantee his name to have been Jesus of Nazareth. Historical doubt concerning the existence and the life of someone with this name cannot be overruled. He might have had another name. (This is a historically absurd, but largely necessary, consequence of the historical method.)…The power which has created and preserved the

---

[1] Rudolf Bultmann, trans. by Louise Pettibone Smith and Erminie Huntress Lantero, *Jesus and the Word*. (NY: Scribner's, 1958), p. 13.
[2] Though oral tradition tells us he once said it wouldn't matter after all.

community of the New Being is not an abstract statement about its appearance; it is the picture of him in whom it has appeared. No special trait of this picture can be verified with certainty. But it can be definitely asserted that through this picture the New Being has power to transform those who are transformed by it.[3]

Think of what Rousseau said—if the gospel Jesus was a fiction, then whoever created him is greater than Jesus: "The Gospel has marks of truth so great, so striking, so perfectly inimitable, that the inventor of it would be more astonishing than the hero."[4] Similarly says F.F. Bruce: "To the question whether the discourses in this Gospel [John] are genuine words of Christ, not a few would reply that, if they are not, than a greater than Christ is here."[5] And I think that is saying the same as Tillich. Such a Jesus-creator would count as the real Jesus: it wouldn't really matter!

Here one may observe a strong similarity between Tillich on the one hand and his teachers Wilhelm Herrmann and Martin Kähler on the other, despite the real differences between the three. Tillich notes appreciatively Herrmann's attempts to approach Christ by the avenue of Christian experience. Herrmann, too, seems to work backward from the believer's experience of Jesus Christ thanks to the gospel portrait of him to the substantial reliability of that picture in portraying Jesus.

> [W]hen we speak of the historical Christ we mean that life of Jesus which speaks to us from the New Testament, as the disciples' testimony to their faith, but which, when we perceive it, always comes home to us as a miraculous revelation. That historical research cannot give us this we *know*. But neither will it ever take this from us by any

---

[3] Paul Tillich, *Systematic Theology II: Existence and the Christ*. (Chicago: University of Chicago Press, 1958), p. 114.
[4] Quoted in W. Woodhouse Nicoll, *The Church's One Foundation*. (Hodder & Stoughton, 1901), p. 41; reproduced in J.N.D. Anderson, *Christianity: The Witness of History*. (London: Tyndale Press, 1969), p. 35.
[5] F.F. Bruce, *The New Testament Documents: Are They Reliable?*. (Grand Rapids: Eerdmans, 1960), p. 47.

of its discoveries. This we *believe*, the more we experience the influence that this picture of the glory of Jesus has upon us.[6]

Kähler disagrees with Herrmann in making a psychological sketch of Jesus the basis for the origin and transmission of faith in Christ. Yet he joins him in talking in terms of the effectiveness of the biblical picture of Christ as the catalyst for faith, as well as its ultimate origin in Jesus himself.

[W]hat was the decisive influence that Jesus had upon posterity? According to the Bible and church history it consisted in nothing else but the faith of his disciples, their conviction that in Jesus they had found the conqueror of guilt, sin, temptation, and death. [...] If now, with the due recognition given to their differences, the first eyewitnesses were nevertheless in agreement on the picture of Christ which they handed down...then this picture must have been impressed upon their hearts and minds with an incomparable and indelible preciseness rich in content.[7]

For Kähler, like Tillich, this picture is that of the New Testament gospels, not some "historical Jesus" reconstruction. Tillich said of Kähler's work: "I do not believe that Kähler's answer to the question of the historical Jesus is sufficient for our situation today."[8] But despite his declaration of disagreement with Herrmann and Kähler at some points, Tillich's position is fundamentally similar. All three begin with the Christian's experience of the New Being (freedom from sin, etc.) as mediated by the New Testament picture of Jesus, which experience in turn guarantees the substance of that picture as a portrayal of Jesus' effect on the original disciples and evangelists. All three seem to feel they have paid adequate tribute to historical criticism by allowing that any particular detail of the Jesus

---

[6] Wilhelm Herrmann, trans. by J. Sandys Stanyon, *The Communion of the Christian with God: Described on the Basis of Luther's Statements*: Lives of Jesus Series. (Philadelphia: Fortress Press, 1971), pp. 77-78.
[7] Martin Kähler, trans. by Carl E. Braaten, *The So-called Historical Jesus and the Historic Biblical Christ*. (Philadelphia: Fortress Press, 1970) pp. 63, 88.
[8] Paul Tillich, Preface to Kähler, p. xii.

picture may be questioned. Yet have they paid the devil his due? Or are they still in danger of having their faith undermined by historical delving?

Van A. Harvey contends that such schemas as these remain dependent on a historical judgment that the New Testament picture of Jesus must represent a real person and not, say, an abstract allegorical character or a wholly fictive protagonist. And does this not maintain the guilty conscience of the believer who needs some sort of historical Jesus and must pretend he knows he has one? Kähler anticipates this criticism and contends that sinful men could not invent such a portrait of a sinless Jesus.[9] Herrmann is content to let the overpowering experience of Jesus' inner life (as conveyed by the biblical picture of him) overrule any doubts that the believer is dealing with a total abstraction instead of a real person. What artificial abstractions have been added to the gospel portrait are of the same character as the reality itself and only tend to reinforce it.[10] That is, people would have been tempted to embroider the Jesus tradition only with sayings or stories that rang true to the historical Jesus, even if some of those things he didn't actually say or do.

Tillich certainly seems to leave himself open to Harvey's criticism. Tillich admits that if the portrait of Jesus were a created fiction, or an abstraction, this would be insufficient.

> Without the concreteness of the New Being, its newness would be empty....A picture imagined by the...contemporaries of Jesus would have expressed this untransformed existence and their quest for a New Being. But it would not have been the New Being.[11]

---

[9] Kähler, p. 79. Cf. Descartes' insistence that, as an imperfect mind, he could never have dreamed up the shape of a perfect circle, so it must have an independent existence outside his mind, etc.

[10] Herrmann, p. 75.

[11] Paul Tillich, *Systematic Theology*, Vol. II. *Existence and the Christ*. (Chicago: University of Chicago Press, 1958), pp. 114, 115. One is reminded of Bultmann's contention that one may know *about* love from reading romance novels, but one can know love for oneself only by entering into a relationship with another, and so with authentic existence. The secular existentialist may grasp the idea, but only the Christian may experience it.

In other words, even if his name turned out not to be "Jesus," the existence of an individual corresponding to the New Testament portrait is necessary to Christian faith. Tillich admits that even the barest theoretical possibility that the Jesus of the biblical records did not exist would be "destructive for the Christian faith."[12] It seems that Harvey is correct in charging that Tillich has not succeeded in bridging the gap of uncertainty. The place of Jesus in Christian faith remains dependent on a probabilistic historical judgment, i.e., that the gospels' picture of Jesus actually represents a real historical individual of whatever name.

In addition, Harvey points out, the contours of this picture of Jesus may well vary with the exegete who tries to present it (shades of the quest for the historical Jesus!). "Even this 'picture of Christ' in the New Testament, of which Kähler and Tillich speak as though it were independent of criticism, can be abstracted only by an act of historical imagination."[13]

Harvey proposes his own alternative, drawing on the thought of H. Richard Niebuhr. He suggests that an image of Jesus may function as a revelatory paradigm, an image "cast up" by the original event (whatever that may have been, and Harvey admits we cannot know). This image "does illuminate our experience and our relationship to that upon which we are absolutely dependent....The power of the Christian message is mediated through the image of Jesus. It is this image which the Christian finds to be a reliable one for relating himself to the Beings around him and to the power acting in and through all Beings."[14] To be thus effective, the image need have no connection with historical facts, though there may be reasons for thinking it does.

It seems to me that Harvey's alternative is more consistent with Tillich's desire to deliver faith from the threatening tentativeness of historical judgments than is Tillich's own answer. In fact, Harvey's model naturally follows from Tillich's statement that all faith can guarantee is its own

---

[12] Paul Tillich, *Systematic Theology*, p. 113.
[13] Van A. Harvey, The Historian and the Believer: An Essay in the Morality of Historical Knowledge. (NY: Macmillan, 1972), pp. 282, 293.
[14] Ibid. p. 249.

experience of the New Being mediated by the picture of Jesus Christ. To go any further, as Tillich tries to do, and to conclude that this picture must represent a historical individual is to make faith responsible for a theoretically debatable historical judgment. And as long as faith guarantees that its own experience is truly that of the New Being under the conditions of human finitude, isn't this enough? Does faith somehow need to believe that the effective catalytic picture also came from a factual experience of the New Being in conditions of finitude, that of a historical Jesus? Tillich himself hints that such a belief is not a necessary implication of the experience of the New Being. He indicates this when he allows that the New Being is at work even where Jesus is not known at all.[15] I believe that Tillich's thinking would be compatible with a denial of a historical Jesus (which some[16] aver that in private he admitted).

It may seem odd for Tillich to sound so concerned to find some way of hermetically sealing off faith from tormenting doubt. Isn't he famous for claiming that faith includes doubt and is by no means antithetical to doubt? Indeed. He has no respect for *skeptical doubt*, that cynical *ennui* that cares not to commit itself to any belief or cause, whether because of prior disillusionment or just laziness. He has great respect for *methodological doubt*, the epistemological tool of both scientific and historical investigation.[17] He believes, of course, that faith neither faces a threat from such scrutiny nor has any right to suspend such doubt (and in the former case, we would be dealing with the *intellectualistic distortion* of faith, while in the latter we would be suffering from the *voluntaristic distortion* of faith).[18] The only kind of doubt relevant to faith is *existential doubt*, the nagging uneasiness that one's commitment to a concern as one's ultimate concern may possibly prove to have been idolatrous, as when an idealistic

---

[15] Tillich, *Systematic Theology*, p. 164.
[16] A professor of mine, Adele McCollum, heard Tillich say this.
[17] Paul Tillich, *Dynamics of Faith*. (NY: Harper & Row Torchbooks Cloister Library, 1958), pp. 18-21.
[18] Ibid. pp. 30-40.

campaign worker for a reformist candidate finds he has wasted his efforts on one more corrupt politician.

It seems to me that the sort of doubt relevant to the historical Jesus problem would be existential doubt, and it would take this form: do our hearts condemn us as we examine our own ostensible experience of the New Being? When we look to the examples of our co-religionists and forbears in the New Being, in the Christian community, do we really behold evidence of a New Being, or are we allowing slogans to substitute for reality? The relevant (and perhaps terrifying) element of doubt occurs not on the *far* end of the historical/experiential corridor, the long chain which stretches between our experience and the gospel portrait of Jesus as the Christ, but rather on the *near* end. Tillich took for granted that we have a transforming experience of the New Being based on an encounter with the Jesus-picture (Galatians 3:1); doubts began to arise as to whether this portrait was historically sound. And the threat (which faith, by its nature as ultimate concern, should not have to fear) was that of methodological doubt. Tillich sought to quiet that doubt by reasoning backward from the supposedly sure experience of the believer to the powerful efficacy, hence historical soundness, of the first cause of our experience, the portrait of Jesus. He ought rather to have located the threat of doubt in the eye of the beholder of the Jesus-portrait: are we sure we have contracted the happy contagion of the New Being? Perhaps Christ is not our ultimate concern, despite our protestations of devotion. Or perhaps the Christian confession is not what it is cracked up to be, hence an idol. These would be appropriate existential doubts.

Theology and Mythology

Rudolf Bultmann, a friend and colleague of Paul Tillich, shared many views with him. At least there was similar thinking at many points. Both decried the danger of mythology. Though it remains irreplaceable as the language of religion, it does its job of confronting us with the divine address only when the myth is "broken," "deliteralized" (Tillich) or "demythologized" (Bultmann). Myth tends logically to objectify the Transcendent Reality which we point to with the term "God." That is, the fanciful stories of the Bible depict God as an individual person (even if a disembodied intelligence) with anthropomorphic traits including love, wrath, will, and vulnerability to outrage and indignity. But the *infi*nite cannot be de*fin*ed, and to do so is to substitute a god for God, God for Being itself.

> As in the conception of heaven the transcendence of God is imagined by means of the category of space, so in the conception of the end of the world, the transcendence of God is imagined by means of the category of time.[19]

So Bultmann, like Tillich, sought to "break open" the myths. One inevitably wonders how far he will go in that process.

> Very soon the process of demythologizing began...The decisive step was taken when Paul declared that the turning point from the old world to the new was not a matter of the future but did take place in the coming of Jesus Christ.[20]

Bultmann, too, comes very close to the Christ Myth theory. If the saving Jesus Christ was raised into the Kerygma, I cannot see what difference it would make if he had been similarly *incarnated or born* into the Kerygma. All that matters is the Proclaimed, not the Proclaimer. In fact we might even wonder if an insistence on a historical Jesus should not be considered a case of mythical objectification of the Christ event, an "event" that really occurs in the preaching of the gospel, as Tillich and the others knew. Karl Jaspers certainly thought so:

> You say that...the purpose of demythologization...is to eliminate objective fixation...But above all, it seems to me that by asserting God's summons to decision, or the encounter, still takes place by way of that miracle of about 1950 years ago, you retain the objectivity of the

---

[19] Rudolf Bultmann, *Jesus Christ and Mythology*. (NY: Scribner's, 1958), p. 22.
[20] Ibid. p. 32.

revelation. You say that it is only an event, the word of God conceived of "as my God, who here and now speaks to me through the mouths of men"; but you also say that this event is bound to a tradition and to "its figure and history," which provide us with "evidence of the word of God." This implies that the word of God is bound to the actual words of the New Testament, that is to say, to a completely frozen objectivity...So far as I can see, this is in contradiction with your intention to abolish the objective fixation.[21]

When Bultmann insists on the preaching moment as the event of revelation, doesn't that demythologize the *past in just the same way* as he says Paul, John, and the Gnostics demythologized the future? It is a matter of existential engagement in the now! *We can no more know for sure whether he came in the past than when he might come in the future!* [Revelation] can never become merely an event in the past that one simply perceives; rather even as it remains ambiguous and therefore can be understood merely as such a past event—even as one can inquire about the "historical Jesus" or "Christ according to the flesh" (II Cor. 5:16)...— even so it is understood in its true character only when it is understood as something that takes place in the present, in my particular present. The way in which it is made present... is through preaching... Thus there is also no way whereby the hearer of the preaching can get behind it, whether in order to find a "historical Jesus" or to find some cosmic process that has occurred in a certain place and at a certain time. Rather everything that is decisive for him takes place in his present; *"now* is the day of salvation."[22]

In his seminal essay on demythologizing, Bultmann pulled no punches: "What a primitive mythology it is, that a divine Being should become incarnate, and atone for the sins of men through his own

---

[21] Karl Jaspers, "The Issues Clarified." In Karl Jaspers and Rudolf Bultmann, *Myth and Christianity: An Inquiry into the Possibility of Religion without Mythology.* (NY: Noonday Press/Farrar, Strauss & Giroux, 1958), pp. 76-77.
[22] Rudolf Bultmann, trans. by Schubert M. Ogden, "The Concept of Revelation in the New Testament" in Bultmann, *Existence & Faith: Shorter Writings of Rudolf Bultmann.* (NY: Living Age Books/Meridian Books, 1964), pp. 78-79.

blood!"[23] And what is primitive about mythology? [It] speaks of gods as if they were men and of their actions as human actions, although it conceives of the gods as endowed with superhuman power and of their actions as incalculable, as capable of breaking the normal, ordinary order of events. It may be said that myths give to the transcendent reality an imminent, this-worldly objectivity. Myths give worldly objectivity to that which is unworldly.[24]

Must we not ask whether Bultmann, having demythologized so much (and historically debunked so much) of a historical Jesus, ought not have gone the whole way and dispensed with Jesus altogether, retreating to secular existentialism? "It might well appear as though the event of Christ were a relic of mythology which still awaits elimination."[25] Indeed it might.

Is Bultmann consistent methodologically when he insists that a historical individual must be the magnet to which legends and myths have been attracted? David Friedrich Strauss made a signal point about the criticism of biblical myth:

> Every narrative, however miraculous, contains some details which might in themselves be historical, but which, in consequence of their connexion with the other supernatural incidents, necessarily become equally doubtful.[26]
> It is moreover inconsistent and arbitrary to refer the dress in which the events of the Old Testament are clothed to poetry, and to preserve the events themselves as historical; much rather do the particular

---

[23] Rudolf Bultmann, trans. by Reginald H. Fuller, "New Testament and Mythology." In Hans Werner Bartsch, ed., *Kerygma and Myth*. (NY: Harper & Row Torchbooks, 1961), p. 7.
[24] Bultmann, Jesus Christ and Mythology, p. 19.
[25] Bultmann, "New Testament and Mythology," p. 23.
[26] David Friedrich Strauss, trans. by George Eliot [Mary Ann Evans], *The Life of Jesus Critically Examined*, Lives of Jesus Series. (Philadelphia: Fortress Press, 1972), p. 90.

details and the dress in which they appear, constitute a whole belonging to the province of poetry and mythus.[27]

That is, once we have identified the story as a whole as mythical, we have no business trying to hold onto this or that non-miraculous detail of the story as residually factual. We can never be sure such elements are more than window-dressing for the myth, and there is no reason they should be. Why believe Elisha's disciple had actually borrowed an axe if we have dispensed with Elisha causing it to float to the surface? Why is not a hypothetical historical Jesus such a gratuitous possible left-over once Bultmann has demythologized everything else?

The notion of a timeless salvation not occurring at a moment in history but rather being revealed at such a juncture even surfaces for a moment in the New Testament itself. Revelation 13:8 locates the death of Jesus in primordial Sacred Time, before history. 1 Peter 1:18-20 similarly speaks of the sacrificial bloodshed of Christ destined in the remote past and, not occurring, but being manifested in recent days. Do we not here have intimated the notion of an eternal fact or condition of divine atonement manifest in the lower, temporal world? And that is mythical, a sequential narrative story depicting for temporal creatures an eternal condition or reality. "This interpretation of the cross as a permanent fact rather than a mythological event does far more justice to the redemptive significance of the event of the past than any of the traditional interpretations."[28]

But even such a disclosure, without an accompanying "saving event," can be said to be an event in its own right, a catalyst, just as Bultmann characterizes the "revelatory" import of gospel preaching. As Tillich says:

> [I]n the Cross of the Christ the divine participation in existential estrangement becomes manifest…[But] it must be stressed that it is a basic distortion of the doctrine of atonement if, instead of saying "becomes manifest" one says "becomes possible." On the other hand,

---

[27] Strauss, The Life of Jesus Critically Examined, p. 55.
[28] Bultmann, "New Testament and Mythology," p 37.

"becomes manifest" does not mean only "becomes known." Manifestations are effective expressions, not only communications. Something happens through a manifestation which has effects and consequences. The Cross of the Christ is a manifestation in this sense. It is a manifestation by actualization.[29]

And what is revealed? It is "the divine paradox of the appearance of the eternal God-man unity within existential estrangement."[30] Tillich and Bultmann, it seems to me, are verging perilously close to the edge of Strauss' Hegelian reading of the gospel:

> Faith, in her early stages, is governed by the senses, and therefore contemplates a temporal history; what she holds to be true is the external, ordinary event, the evidence for which is of the historical, forensic kind—a fact to be proved by the testimony of the senses, and the moral confidence inspired by the witnesses. But mind having once taken occasion by this external fact, to bring under its consciousness the idea of humanity as one with God, sees in history only the presentation of that idea; the object of faith is completely changed; instead of a sensible, empirical fact, it has become a spiritual and divine idea, which has its confirmation no longer in history but in philosophy. When the mind has thus gone beyond the sensible history, and entered into the domain of the absolute, the former ceases to be essential; it takes a subordinate place, above which the spiritual truths suggested by the history stand self-supported; it becomes as the faint image of a dream which belongs only to the past.[31]

The Book of Mormon has such a notion. In it, the death of Christ is such a metaphysical *fait accompli* that temporally, historically pre-Christian Nephites are nonetheless already believing Christians, knowing in advance (as many Christians always thought of Old Testament "believers") the details of the crucifixion and resurrection thanks to explicit

---

[29] Tillich, *Systematic Theology*, p. 175.
[30] Ibid. p. 159.
[31] Strauss, The Life of Jesus Critically Examined, pp. 780-781.

prophecy (which, again, Christians popularly supposed existed in the Old Testament). When Jesus did finally come to Southwest Asia to die and rise, it was almost superfluous, as when we know our favorite line in a movie or a song is coming up, and we anticipate it so clearly and remember it so distinctly, there is really no new event when it is said or sung. It has overtaken us before we are aware of it; we are unable to pick it out of the line-up of moments before us. We almost do not notice it has "happened," because, in a real sense, it hasn't. Augustine used just such an analogy in conveying God's ability to see the future though it hasn't happened yet: picture an observer high in a tower viewing a parade below. He can see the beginning and the end of the procession, and even though technically the approaching marchers have not reached the point above which the observer is standing, he sees them coming up, and it is all the same thing. With this Augustine compares the experience of reciting a familiar Psalm. One knows it so well, it is practically present as a whole in the present moment of consciousness, though technically, almost superfluously, it does come present to the reciter's lips at a particular, slim slice of time, and then is remembered just as clearly as it had been both anticipated and perceived. So with the atonement. It has already happened in mythic, Sacred Time, but it is re-presented whenever the gospel is preached or the gospels are read. And again it works its wonders.

The Threefold Cord

My studies have led me to the working hypothesis that our familiar Catholic-Orthodox Christianity was not only not "the" single, original form of the faith, but that it was not even one of the earliest versions. I reject the oft-heard notion of a "proto-orthodoxy" as an attempt to preserve some vestige of the primary character of Catholic-Orthodox Christianity as at least being there on the ground floor. Instead, it seems to me that this form of the Christian religion represents an amalgam of three of the no doubt many disparate movements that eventually combined, perhaps as certain of these sects threatened to peter out, as failing congregations do today.

I follow Harnack[32] in thinking it most likely that *Gnosticism* was the source of the basic notion of a cosmic Christ-Spirit appearing for a while on earth, whether in actual flesh or the semblance of it. Gnosticism posited a pre-cosmic crisis. The Ultimate Father emitted from himself a series of "syzygies," paired entities ("Aions"), each set flowing from the last like the levels of reality cascading from the One in Neo-Platonism. At the end of the chain of emanation there occurred the divine Dame Wisdom, who was acutely aware of her singularity and wished desperately to bear another entity. It was metaphorical for the fact that, being on the rim of the Divine Fullness (Pleroma), she could not "conceive" the truth at the heart of God and thus went astray. Her child, Ialdabaoth (identified with Yahweh Sabaoth) was egotistical and jumped to the conclusion that he was the sole deity. Pathetically ignorant of the divine Fullness above him, he was humiliated by the scornful derision of the Aions. He then undertook to emulate the work of the True God by creating the Archons ("rulers"), debased counterparts to the divine Aions. The Archons were equal to the elemental spirits of Stoicism and the planetary gods of Persia. They were malevolent henchmen-angels. Then he created the world of matter, complete with an inert clay man, Adam, earthly counterpart to the heavenly Man of Light. The whole creation was inert until the Archons managed to steal the sparks of light from the Pleroma, dismembering the Man of Light, one of the Aions. These "photons" they employed, as we might say, as replicating DNA to get the mud-ball world up and running.

It worked, with the result that a select few (reincarnating) humans possessed at their core a spark of light, a true soul. They were ill at ease in a world in which they did not properly belong, though the rest of

---

[32] Adolf von Harnack, *Lehrbuch der Dogmengeschichte, Die Entstehung des christlichen Dogmas*. (Tubingen, 1909), vol. I p. 286, n. 1, 287; Note, in Kurt Rudolph, trans. by Robert McLachlan Wilson, P.W. Coxon, and K.H. Kuhn, *Gnosis: The Nature and History of Gnosticism*. (San Francisco: Harper & Row, 1983), pp. 162, 372.

animated humanity fit in just fine. These worldlings were of two types: the hedonistic rabble were little more than two-legged animals. The higher sort could be found populating the pews of conventional biblical religion, whether Judaism or Christianity, oblivious of the fact that, in keeping the commandments and worshipping Yahweh, they were dupes and slaves of the Archons who had created conventional religion in the first place. As for the pneumatic elite, they might be awakened to their divine origin and destiny by the Gnostic Revealer (like Morpheus in *The Matrix*), manifested on earth in various mystagogues and gurus like Simon Magus and Dositheus of Samaria. These taught their recruits (if you were intrigued by what they said, you must be one of the elect, as Calvinists still say today) that they could end reincarnation in this hell-hole by learning how to slip past the archontic guardians (like patrols along the Berlin Wall) at death and return to the Light-World of the Pleroma. In this way, combining their long-lost fragments of the Primal Man of Light, they would be restoring or resurrecting him.[33]

Eventually leaders of one of these sects thought to establish their authority over and above the wild diversity of Gnostic speculations by positing a historical founder who had passed on his teaching along official channels. Both Gnostics and Catholics began to claim that they had learned the true teachings of Jesus from those who sat at his feet and took notes. Otherwise, it would be a deadlocked dispute over whose subjective "revelations" from the heavenly Christ were genuine. (Of course, competing claims of apostolic succession canceled one another out, resulting in the same stalemate!) This required historicizing the destruction of the Primal Man by the Archons (Colossians 2:15; 1 Corinthians 2:7-8), making it into an event that took place on earth, engineered by *earthly* authorities (Pilate and the Sanhedrin). It must be posited as having happened in recent history in order to shorten the chain of succession between this

---

[33] Wilhelm Bousset, trans. by John Steely, Kyrios Christos: A History of the Belief in Christ from the Beginnings of Christianity to Irenaeus. (NY: Abingdon Press, 1970), pp. 197-198.

founder and the present leaders of the sect.[34] The death was salvific in that it did at least vivify the creation, bringing life to all beings, much like the kindred myth of the Cosmic Man Purusha in the *Rig Veda* (X. 90). Purusha was a giant entity whose body filled the heavens (cf. Ephesians 4:10) until he offered himself as a cosmic sacrifice, the members of his body becoming the various parts of the universe, including the four castes, the scriptures, etc. This, I think, is the ultimate origin (or at least an ancient parallel) of the "Celestial Christ" theology posited by Jesus Mythicists.

Gnostics believed that the Demiurge created the world of matter but could not breathe life into it till his henchmen, the Archons, ambushed the Primal Man, the Man of Light, disintegrating him in order to use his photons (as we would call them) as a kind of self-replicating DNA. In other words, the Man of Light's death gave life to the world, and he did it at the dawn of time. Gnostics shared the widespread ancient interest in astronomy, and this explains how there could be a "crucifixion" in the heavens ("outer space"), locating the assault on the Primal Man at the intersection of the sun's ecliptic and the celestial equator at Pisces, the celestial cross.

The crucifixion of the divine man was said to be preceded by a period of public and esoteric teaching, the Revealer telling one thing to the conventionally pious, another to the elect, a plan of salvation for each. This portrait was based on the role and activities of the Gnostic gurus themselves.[35] So in the historicized version, the death of the Primal Man was drawn forward from the remote past, and his restoration/resurrection was drawn back from the remote future, originally the eschatological harvest of Pleromatic sparks. Thus began the Gnostic Christian myth of the atoning death and resurrection of Jesus Christ. The notion of a historical,

---

[34] Arthur Drews, trans. by C. Delisle Burns, *The Christ Myth*, Westminster College-Oxford: *Classics in the Study of Religions*. (Amherst: Prometheus Books, 1998), pp. 271-272.
[35] Walter Schmithals, trans. by John E. Steely, *The Office of Apostle in the Early Church*. (NY: Abingdon Press, 1969), pp. 175-176.

incarnate Jesus would have arisen as an attempt to consolidate ecclesiastical authority for one's teachings.

If there was no incarnation, no historical Jesus, then there was no Roman crucifixion of Jesus on Golgotha—and thus no saving sacrifice? No forgiveness of sins for the human race? That does not follow. For one thing, there seems to be little difference between looking back gratefully two thousand years into the past to a Roman crucifixion and looking back to a "prehistoric" crucifixion. Even the traditional understanding of the atonement creates a puzzling paradox: how could Jesus' sacrifice have availed to forgive sins that had not yet been committed? Early Christians seem to have believed that the Cross took care of sins committed up to that time, and that subsequent sins would place one in peril all over again. Hebrews 6:3-6 and 10:26-31 warn that new sins could not be forgiven unless Christ were to go to the cross again—which he is not going to do!

This is why many ancient Christians, like the Emperor Constantine, delayed baptism till their deathbed.[36] This is why it was such a big deal when, in the second century, the Angel of Repentance told Hermas to proclaim a "second repentance," a special, one-time, not-to-be-repeated amnesty for sins committed since baptism. This sort of perfectionism was possible only because the early Christians expected the Second Coming in the very near future, so they figured they could hold on till then, refraining from sin, but this became more difficult as time went on. None of this would have been a problem if they understood the sacrifice of Christ to cover all future sins committed by then-living and future sinners. And if you're going to believe the Cross covered all future sins, you might as well place the "Cross" all the way back to the beginning of time, a la 1 Peter 1:20 and Revelation 13:8: "…the Lamb slain from the foundation of the world."

How drastic a readjustment would it entail if Christianity were to move the saving work of Christ from earth to heaven? The New Testament already places much of Jesus' ministry on our behalf in the heavens.

---

[36] "We're taking an awful risk, Vader!"

Romans 8:34, 1 John 2:1, and Hebrews 7:25 all speak of Jesus' continuing intercession on our behalf in heaven, something that seems to suggest that for Jesus to say, "It is finished" (John 19:30) may have been a bit premature, for does it not imply that Jesus plays the role of Moses in Exodus 32:9-14, beseeching God to stay his avenging hand from his people when they sin? Hebrews 10:1-4, though its author denigrates the Old Testament sacrificial system as ineffective, otherwise it would not require repetition, seems to envision Christ's perpetual offering of his own shed blood in the heavenly tabernacle (Hebrews 9:11-14) as open to the same criticism. Why does he have to keep doing it? But the point is, even traditional Christian soteriology is already accustomed to a belief in a saving work of Christ in heaven, far above the earth. If heaven was, as Mythicists contend, the *only* location of Christ's sacrifice as originally conceived, what difference would it make?

I Love a Mystery

I think the sacramental system of Christianity derives from the Mystery Religion of Jesus, in which Jesus was a typical *Kurios* and *Soter*.[37] What were Mystery Religions? These faiths began in agrarian regions as a kind of nature worship. The changing of the seasons was symbolized under the form of a god who embodied nature's vitality. As the year declined, and with it the productivity of the soil, so the god was believed to have lost his vigor. When winter came, it marked the death of the god. But spring signaled/brought his resurrection.[38] The people performed rituals either to observe or actually to bring about the renewal of nature/the god. The

---

[37] Wilhelm Bousset, p. 223; Rudolf Bultmann, trans. by Kendrick Groebel, *Theology of the New Testament*. Complete in One Volume. Scribner Studies in Contemporary Theology. (NY: Scribner's, 1951, 1955), vol. 1, p. 124; Ferdinand Hahn, trans. by Harold Knight and George Ogg, *The Titles of Jesus in Christology: Their History in Earliest Christianity*. (NY: World Publishing Company, 1969), p. 111.

[38] For us to mark Easter with rabbits, eggs, and flowers is a clear survival of the same thinking; the Easter Bunny is no interloper on, no usurper of, the holiday's "real" meaning.

king renewed his power and divine mandate by undergoing a ritual humiliation at the hands of the priest or shaman, then protesting his innocence, then receiving back the tokens of his authority. He would perhaps engage in mock battle (like Tibetan religious dances today) with a dragon (men in a dragon suit) in which he might drop to the ground as dead, slain by the dragon, then rise again and defeat the foe, to his subjects' acclaim. And the crops would return. It seems likely that, originally, the king, earthly vicar of the god, was ceremonially executed for real, but that eventually a "fool king" (a poor man or a condemned prisoner) was substituted for the real king and given a royal send-off of banqueting and concubines. He stood in for the king in death, and the king himself returned, "resurrected," along with nature. It marked the Eternal Return, the cyclical replay of Sacred Time, bringing back, for a crucial moment, the Primordial pre-time of Creation in order to renew the world.[39] Part and parcel of the pre-cosmic drama was the death and resurrection of nature's god, call him Baal, Marduk, Osiris, whatever.

Such were the Mystery Religions. How did they become Mystery *Cults*? It seems to have been a result of the cosmopolitanism of the Hellenistic world after Alexander the Great. Great numbers of people relocated throughout the Mediterranean world as slaves, prisoners of war, soldiers, merchants, or colonists. When these people left their rural homes and settled instead in faceless cities, their link with the old religions was severed, or would be unless they were reinterpreted for the new circumstances. Local assemblies dedicated to the worship of the old nature deities served as gathering points for those of a common ethnicity amid the anonymity (like a Black Students Union or a Sons of Italy Hall). But in the urban setting the agricultural connection was lost. The rituals now took on a new purpose: they functioned as rites of passage for the spiritual rebirth of the individual. The inner world substituted for the outward.

---

[39] Mircea Eliade, trans. by Willard R. Trask, *The Sacred and the Profane: The Nature of Religion*. (NY: Harcourt, Brace & World, 1959); Eliade, trans. by Willard R. Trask, *Cosmos and History: The Myth of the Eternal Return*. (Harper Torchbooks; Bollingen Library; NY: Harper & Row, 1959).

All cultures have rites of passage,[40] and puberty rites always include initiation into the sacred arcana that only adults know. The Mystery Cults (a cult being an old religion transplanted into a new cultural context) added a second rebirth: a divinization, the promise of immortality. Like Gnosticism, with which there was significant overlap (these things are only sealed off from each other as textbook typologies, ideal types, not in reality), the Mystery Cults provided a visionary ascent past the celestial spheres and their guardians as well as sacraments of rebirth, often including a sacred meal. In these elements, the initiate, like the king of the old days, was made one with the savior and his fate, triumphing over misfortune and/or death. Even people to whom these newly transplanted religions were alien found them intriguing and attractive for that very reason, and joined up. One could hedge one's bets by joining as many such cults as one could afford, and in this way mythemes and rituals began to flow between religions, so that, e.g., the Tarsian/Persian Mithras would be depicted wearing the Phrygian shepherd's cap of Attis. And as members of these faiths converted to the new Christian religion(s), the same assimilation of details must have occurred.[41]

Whence came the Mystery Cult of the Kyrios Jesus?[42] There may have been more than one such movement, and these may have merged, as rival Melchizedek sects did later. One such religion might have been a Jewish version of any of the dying and rising god religions long known in Israel, whether that of Marduk, Tammuz, Osiris, or Dionysus. The Osiris faith, of which the story of the Patriarch Joseph already seems to be a variant, must have been familiar from the long-ago days of the third millennium

---

[40] Arnold van Gennep, trans. by Monika B. Vizedom and Gabrielle L. Caffee, *The Rites of Passage*. (Chicago: University of Chicago Press, 1960).

[41] Richard Reitzenstain, trans. by John E. Steely, *Hellenistic Mystery-Religions: Their Basic Ideas and Significance*. Pittsburgh Theological Monograph Series 15. (Pittsburgh: Pickwick Press, 1978), p. 149.

[42] I am not arguing that some more primitive, apocalyptic version of Christianity moved out of Palestine and absorbed Hellenistic mythemes in order to make the gospel palatable to potential Gentile converts. That may have occurred, too, but I am thinking of a more "home grown" Jesus Mystery Cult.

BCE when Egypt controlled Canaan. Ezekiel bemoans the Jerusalemite women's mourning for Tammuz (Ezekiel 8:14). During the Hellenization of Jews against which the Hasmoneans fought, many Jews converted to the rites of Dionysus (2 Maccabees 6:7),[43] whom many in the ancient world believed was the same as Yahweh anyway. All it would have taken for a Jesus version to be born would have been the reverent substitution of the epithet "Yeshuah," denoting "savior," for the actual name of the god, as happened in India when Rudra eventually became known as "Siva," formerly a title: "Auspicious One."[44]

Or "Yeshua," "Yehoshua," literally "Yahweh is Salvation," may have denoted a theophany of the god Yahweh, sent by his Father, El Elyon, the Ancient of Days. (As Margaret Barker[45] argues, popular Jewish religion seems never to have accepted the attempt of the high-handed Deuteronomic elite to merge the ancient gods El and Yahweh, any more than they forgot about archaic Leviathan (Revelation 12). And, as Geo Widengren[46] maintains, Yahweh had long been understood as a dying and rising deity, called back from death by his worshippers' cultic shout, "Yahweh lives!" (Psalm 18:46-47). Here already were the saving (world-enlivening) death and resurrection of the divine Jesus. The gospels merely historicized the myth by bringing it forward into roughly contemporary times. Kyrios Christos had, his devotees believed, suffered in a supernatural, mythic struggle and risen in subsequent victory.

---

[43] The author of 2 Maccabees would prefer to think Jews embraced the Bacchanalia under duress, but it seems clear it was a voluntary conversion to Hellenic ways, the very sort of thing that led the Hasmoneans to rise up and take action. The crisis was less the pagan attempt to eradicate Judaism then the shocking spectacle of Jews converting to Hellenism.
[44] W.J. Wilkins, *Hindu Mythology, Vedic and Puranic* (2nd ed., 1882, rpt. Calcutta: Rupa, 1989), p. 266; Mahadev Chakravarti, *The Concept of Rudra-Siva Through the Ages* (Dehli: Motilal Banarsidass, 2nd rev. ed., 1994), p. 28.
[45] Margaret Barker, *The Great Angel: A Study of Israel's Second God* (Louisville: Westminster/John Knox, 1992).
[46] Geo Widengren, "Early Hebrew Myths and their Interpretation" in S.H. Hooke, ed., *Myth, Ritual and Kingship: Essays on the Theory and Practice of Kingship in the Ancient Near East and in Israel.* (NY: Oxford University Press, 1958), p. 191.

"Mystery" is simply the Greek equivalent to the Latin *sacramentum*, referring to an oath of initiation. Sacramental rituals automatically make Christianity a mystery religion. Ritual washing (baptism) is universal, but Holy Communion just has to be derived from Dionysus worship or something similar, for whose body is the bread, whose blood is the fruit of the vine? To use James Frazer's term,[47] it must be the Corn King. It has nothing to do with Passover as anyone can see.

Hero Worship

The third element was that of the *hero cult* of Jesus the divine man (*theios aner*). From this type of Jesus-devotion stems the novelistic character of the gospels as aretalogies, glowing hagiographies of heroes like Apollonius of Tyana and Pythagoras. The gospel genre, as Charles H. Talbert[48] has shown (following in the footsteps of Clyde Weber Votaw),[49] is certainly to be considered a subset of the aretalogy as it morphed into a novel. The Hellenistic Romances[50] often featured the vicissitudes of comatose heroines accidentally entombed alive, only to be rescued by tomb robbers seeking the rich funerary tokens heaped by the body. The woman's husband or suitor, in pursuit of her after the robbers kidnap her, winds up getting crucified but surviving it, followed by a reunion with his beloved whom he had given up hope of finding alive; the lovers first think each other to be ghosts, disbelieving for joy. Our gospels contain traces of such features which are after all genre conventions.

---

[47] Probably better known nowadays from C.S. Lewis, *Miracles: A Preliminary Study*. (NY: Macmillan, 1974), pp. 116-117.
[48] Charles H. Talbert, *What Is a Gospel? The Genre of the Canonical Gospels*. (Philadelphia: Fortress Press, 1977).
[49] Clyde Weber Votaw, *The Gospels and Contemporary Biographies in the Greco-Roman World*, Facet Books Biblical Series 27. (Philadelphia: Fortress Press, 1970).
[50] B.P. Reardon, ed., *Collected Ancient Greek Novels* (Berkeley: University of California Press, 1989). See particularly Chariton's *Chaireas and Callirhoe* and Xenophon's *An Ephesian Tale*.

Hero cults sometimes featured initiation rites, as in the case of Hercules, whose initiates donned the lion's mane to identify with the son of Zeus' victory over the Nemean Lion. The Mystery Lord Mithras represented a conflation between the Vedic Mitra and the Greek demigod hero Perseus. His initiates participated in his similar victory over the Cosmic Bull. But, aside from this, was there a redemptive dimension to the hero cult, or was it just partisan fan loyalty ("I am of Paul! I am of Cephas! I am of Apollos!")?

As Bruno Bauer, a Christ Myth pioneer, showed, there was a tendency among Hellenistic philosophers to internalize the adulation of the ancient heroes for the sake of one's own character growth. One made a hero into a kind of imaginary friend who could act as one's conscience, looking askance at temptations. Bauer quotes Epicurus: "We must select some noble man whom we always have before our eyes so that we live as if he looks at what we do, and act as if he sees it" (Epistle 11).

> [Seneca, Bauer says,] finds it useful and wholesome (*salutarem*). "We need," he continues, "a guard and teacher. A great number of sins are eliminated when the stumbling person (*peccatoris*) has at his side a witness. The spirit must have somebody whom it reveres with an awe to which is added also his most secret inner being (*sanctius facit*). The mere thought of such a helper has regulating and improving power. He is a guard, an example and a norm without which one will not restore to balance whatever is wrong." "Put on (*indue*)," it says in Epistola 67, "the spirit of a great man"—the same as in the New Testament: "Put on the Lord Jesus Christ" (Romans 13:14) or "You have put on Christus" (Galatians 3:27).[51]

> Often Seneca takes characteristics for the picture of his ideal from Cato's experiences. What will the wise man do, he asks e.g., (*Constant. sap chpt.* 14) when he is struck on the cheek? What Cato did, is the answer, when he was hit in the face. He did not get angry, he did not

---

[51] Bruno Bauer, *Christ and the Caesars: The Origin of Christianity from Romanized Greek Culture*. Trans. Frank E. Schacht. (Charleston: Alexander Davidonis, 1998), p. 41.

take revenge for the offense. He did not forgive the offender but simply stated that no offense had been given him... "To be crucified, put in chains, maimed to offer oneself as a sacrifice" (*Provid*, chpt. 5) belongs to the marks of the virtuous who labor for the large community of humanity.[52]

This notion was a major element in the evolution and cross-fertilization of Hellenistic Jewish, Oriental, and Roman ideas that Bauer believed crystallized in Christianity. In effect, Mark the evangelist sought to fill out the picture of an ideal wise man by crafting the fictional hero Jesus Christ.

There was significant overlap between these three forms of faith, Gnosticism, Mystery Cults, and hero worship, and this fact facilitated the eventual fusion of all three. The result is our familiar religion of the Son of God who had existed in celestial form for ages past, only lately touching down among men and leaving behind a set of miracles and of sacraments of salvation.

The Power That Perdures

Is not the brief survey we have just made little more than a tour of dusty museum relics, of interest only to antiquarians? Is not the whole thing a rationalization for debunking and denying the atonement of Christ? I think not. Rather, I suggest, all three ancient, mythic roots of Christianity still hold the power to redeem and to transform, once we understand them.

What has Gnosticism to teach us? How can it save us? I will return to Carl Jung presently, in connection with the efficacy of ritual, but here let me just remark on the centrality of ancient Gnostic insights to Jung's exposition of the process of Individuation, i.e., psychological healing and maturity, culminating in a Christlike egoless love of all people. As Stefan A. Hoeller shows, Jung used Bultmann's demythologizing hermeneutic

---

[52] Bruno Bauer, *Christ and the Caesars*, p. 42.

on the Gnostic myths to great (and still relevant) effect.[53] But mainly I want to show that Gnostic doctrines of salvation as enlightenment and superior insight have been vindicated by the modern field of Sociology of Knowledge, especially as set forth by Peter L. Berger and Thomas Luckmann,[54] contemporary sociologists in the tradition of Durkheim. They observe that, while animals are born with instinctive patterns of behavior which order their environment and govern their activity, we humans are not so "lucky." We have more brain space, and it gives us intelligence, but at the cost of instinct. As a result, there is an important aspect of our environment that we must create, invent, that is *not a given of nature*. And that is the symbolic, cultural, spiritual world of *meaning*.

In that our worlds of meaning are human creations, they are *products of history, not of nature* (or of culture rather than nature). But for them to seem real enough to do the job we want them to do (to provide order, meaning, comfort, and guides for behavior), we must hide the fact of their human-createdness and make them seem instead the product of nature—or of divine creation. Thus meaning systems, cultures, are traditionally *religious*. This process has four phases: *objectification, reification, internalization*, and *alienation*.

Objectification: the first founders/framers of our culture/social order/worldview presumably created an *ad hoc* "social contract" to lend order to their society. They knew it was their human creation. They knew they could go "back to the drawing board," and they may have done so more than once. They may have consciously invented supernatural sanctions to keep people in line. They may have invented the claim that Moses or Hammurabi or Manu received their laws directly from heaven. But this need not have been the case, as we shall shortly see. The simple fact that

---

[53] Stephan A. Hoeller, *The Gnostic Jung and the Seven Sermons to the Dead* (Wheaton: Quest Books/The Theosophical Publishing House, 1982).
[54] Peter L. Berger and Thomas Luckmann, The Social Construction of Reality: A Treatise in the Sociology of Knowledge. (Garden City: Doubleday Anchor, 1969); Peter L. Berger, The Sacred Canopy: Elements of a Sociological Theory of Religion. (Garden City: Doubleday Anchor, 1969); and Thomas Luckmann, The Invisible Religion: The Problem of Religion in Modern Society. (NY: Macmillan, 1967).

the society's rulers are themselves subject to the laws they have created already objectifies the order they have created.

Reification is the end result of objectification. It is when human-created institutions take on a life of their own. They take priority over their human creators. This happens by token of the fact that the founders bequeath their creation to the next generation, and the new generations do not experience the institutions as a human creation—because *they* did not create them. The institutions do in fact predate them and thus possess a "givenness" they did not have for the founding generation. Their elders' institutions take on some measure of the infallibility we first ascribe to our parents. The founders may become deified (perhaps via ancestor worship, perhaps by euhemerism). Or they are thought to have been in direct touch with God. The New Testament belief in the Principalities and Powers[55] is an acute mythic symbol for these: superhuman, impersonal entities no longer amenable to human correction. They oppress us, and yet we need them in place to stem the tide of chaos. (Reification is also *mystification*, when the human becomes suffused by the illusory haze of "the divine.")

Internalization occurs when the social order/worldview/value system becomes, a la Jeremiah, "a law written upon the heart" by means of *socialization* and *indoctrination*. One learns to do as the Romans do, and one has to obey parents. By internalization, one comes to have an internal monitor (society/family/peers internalized in an imaginary way) whose scrutiny one cannot escape. The mystification of sanctions of behavior proceeds from threats of punishment by society if caught, to threats of divine retribution if not caught. With maturity one grows from barely internalized threats of externally imposed divine retribution, to an

---

[55] G.B. Caird, *Principalities and Powers: A Study in Pauline Theology*, The Chancellor's Lectures for 1954 at Queen's University, Kingston, Ontario. (Oxford at the Clarendon Press, 1956); Heinrich Schlier, *Principalities and Powers in the New Testament*, Quaestiones Disputatae 3. (NY: Herder and Herder, 1961); H. Berkhof, trans. by John Howard Yoder, *Christ and the Powers*. (Scottsdale: Herald Press, 1962).

internalized *shame* ("How would people regard me if they knew what I was doing?") to internal jealousy for one's own integrity ("How could I live with myself if I did this?").

Alienation is the subjection of one's self, behavior, and opinions to heteronomous standards and leads to personal *inauthenticity*. We may even desire this, to lay down the burden of individual responsibility (as Dostoyevsky described so well in his parable of *The Grand Inquisitor*). But the more one chafes at the community's imposition of a false self (false consciousness) the greater will be one's zeal to obey and to stifle this impulse to rebel. Religious fanaticism is one result. The fanatic is trying to silence his own doubts, and it will not work forever. But he is "safe" as long as he is ensconced amid a congenial *plausibility structure*, a social arrangement wherein one is surrounded by an atmosphere conducive to reinforcing one's beliefs. There one rejoices in the reassuring presence of many fellow believers. The ruse is successful: what is actually the work of human imagination in history has been disguised as a fact of nature (or divine revelation).

He who knows this knows what the ancient Gnostic knew: conventional religion with its warnings against heresy and Thoughtcrime, with its prepackaged rules, its demand for abject conformity and "the obedience of faith"—is not the divine creation it claims to be but rather an artificial product of lesser (fellow human) beings who would arrogate our worship to themselves. No institutions or doctrines are founded upon the rock of superhuman revelation. Once we see the man behind the curtain manipulating the special effects, we are free of his bullying and tyranny. The ancient Gnostics experienced that as liberation. So does the modern intellectual, though he needs no metaphysical myths to attain that perspective. The hermeneutic of suspicion is enough. This is why the ancient Gnostics revered the Edenic Serpent as a paragon of wisdom when he posed the Socratic question, "Yea, hath God said?"

Ritual Icons

I believe, from experience, that knowledge of the mythic origins of the atonement enhances the sacramental experience. It is a case of Derrida's iteration paradox: the ostensible uniqueness of a thing vanishes when we find we are able to place it within a larger category with other similar phenomena.[56] But only in this way can we come to grasp what kind of thing it is: "Ah! One of *those*!" When I come forward to receive the Eucharist, I often think how I am doing what not only the ancient Christians but all the ancient mystery faiths did. It establishes a long, long chain reaching back through the remote past to the mythic Sacred Time of origins. How does this work? Here I draw upon Jung.

Carl Jung sought to plumb the Stygian depths of what he called the Collective Unconscious. Some take Jung to mean something like a shared racial memory, but I accept Don Cupitt's interpretation that the Collective Unconscious is simply the common template for the way all human minds are hard-wired.[57] It is a matter of brain structure, nothing spooky. It just means that we all have built-in images, whether numerical, geometrical, various human faces, plot elements, narrative roles like the hero, the crone, the king, the counselor, etc. These Archetypes[58] cannot help manifesting themselves to our conscious minds through various channels, such as dreaming. We need to experience these Archetypes if we are to progress along the path to maturation, what Jung called "Individuation." The Archetypes are like computer screen icons. We must click on these images if we want to plumb more deeply the capabilities of our computers and become expert users, drawing on the full potential of the machines.

---

[56] Jonathan Culler, *On Deconstruction: Theory and Criticism after Structuralism*. (Ithaca: Cornell University Press, 1982), p. 120.
[57] Don Cupitt, *The Sea of Faith: Christianity in Change*. (London: British Broadcasting Corporation, 1984), pp. 75-77.
[58] Carl Jung, trans. by R.F.C. Hull, *The Archetypes and the Collective Unconscious*, *Bollingen Series XX. The Collected Works of C.G. Jung*. (Princeton: Princeton University Press, 1980), vol. 9, pt. I.

We must activate the potential that is programmed genetically into us by beholding the Archetypes, then "clicking on" them, which in our case means that we must find a way to *step into* the archetypal image. Religions take these images and make them into holy epics and myths. Religion also crafts rituals in which we can act out the myths. It is a very powerful, transformative experience. That is true even of secular acting. One assumes for a while a different character and persona, and one is in some measure transformed by it. Religious rituals, then, are the main way we click on the icons to bring more and more of our pre-programmed potential on line. Thus we mature (if we do). It involves no faith, no pretending to believe what we do not.

The Personal Savior

I said that Bruno Bauer believed that one of the chief factors in crystallizing the mythic Jesus Christ was the Hellenistic notion of creating an imaginary companion, a paragon of the virtues which one would like to live out ("What would Jesus do?"), and to imagine his constant scrutiny of our every thought and action. Mark, Bauer said, designed his Jesus for just this purpose. Well, one can only say that Mark's experiment has succeeded beyond all expectation since here, two millennia later, millions of people experience just such a Jesus, just such an imaginary friend, their conscience with a face (and sandals). Ironically, the notion of every Christian "having a personal relationship with Jesus Christ" is, as far as I can see, wholly absent from the New Testament (despite the preaching of some who would have us believe it is the sole theme of the Bible!). It stems from German Pietism of the eighteenth century. But it certainly parallels the original function of the hero Jesus as Bauer understood it. Compare the musings of Count Zinzendorf with Bauer's quotes from Epicurus and Seneca above.

> One has the Creator of all things, the fatherly Power, the God of the entire world, standing in his suffering form, in his penitential form,

in the form of one atoning for the whole human race—this individual object stands before the vision of one's heart, before the eyes of one's spirit, before one's inward man.[59]

For every loving look from the Savior indicates our morality to us throughout our whole life: One dissatisfied, one sorrowful, one painful look from the Savior embitters and makes loathsome to us everything that is immoral, unethical, and disorderly, all fleshly-mindedness, as often as it is necessary.[60]

How significant that, here, at the birth of the "personal savior" spirituality, we find it described as an exercise in the imagination and not yet as a genuine extra-mental transaction with the ascended Christ. The former conception appears to have hardened into the latter, just as the Yogic charkas started out as merely a mental picture to facilitate meditation but was eventually taken literally, as it still is, as a kind of invisible quasi-physical spinal cord.[61] It is yet another case of what Bultmann said would happen any time a helpful myth is taken literally: it subverts itself. The cross as the agency of God's forgiveness makes sense only as a myth or a symbol. Once taken literally, the cross suggests that God cannot do what the symbol was trying to say that he does: freely forgive. No, the literal interpretation implies that, a la Plato's *Euthyphro* dialogue, God is subservient to higher rules of justice and has no choice but to exact punishment for sin as long as *some*one suffers for it. In the same way, if one stuck close to Seneca's version of the pose of having an imaginary confidant, one might find it as powerful as Count Zinzendorf did. But taking it literally produces puerile absurdities such as positing Jesus having private one-on-one conversations with millions of individuals at the same time, like Santa Claus visiting every house on earth in the space of a single night. But the

---

[59] Nicolaus Ludwig Zinzendorf, "On the Essential Character and Circumstances of the Life of a Christian" (1746). In Peter C. Erb, trans. & ed., *Pietists: Selected Writings*. Classics of Western Spirituality. (NY: Paulist Press, 1983), p. 319.
[60] Erb, Pietists: Selected Writings, p. 321.
[61] Agehananda Bharati, *The Tantric Tradition*. (Garden City: Doubleday Anchor, 1970), p. 291.

power of the Jesus hero cult, as Bauer understood it, remains available if one wants to go that route.

Someone will say, "Yes, but what does that have to do with the atonement?" In return, I might ask what the standard fundamentalist belief in the personal relationship with Christ has to do with the cross. As far as I can see, it is a logically self-contained spirituality exactly analogous to Bhakti mysticism in both Hinduism and Buddhism, where one chooses a divine patron and serves him (Siva, Krishna, Avalokitesvara, Ram) or her (Kali, Kwan Yin) with one's emotional devotions. But in fact there is a *bit* of a link in that part of the heroism of Jesus is his unflinching martyr's death. In fact, the most explicit gospel invitation to emulate the hero Jesus is the summons to take up one's cross and follow in his footsteps.

Once, many years ago, I happened to be watching *Saturday Night Live*, and Bob Dylan was the musical guest. It was during his "born again" phase, and he was singing his song, "Gotta Serve Somebody."[62] It occurred to me very clearly that, my doubts and questions about the historical Jesus notwithstanding, the outlines of the way of discipleship were pretty clearly set out in the gospels. It was an open door, and the Jesus on the page was beckoning me to step through. It seems perverse to imagine that the academic question of whether Jesus ever existed in history could be germane at all in making that decision. It still does.

---

[62] The song sounds like an unwitting paraphrase of Larry Norman's "Righteous Rocker," don't you think?

Chapter 10: A Sacrifice in Heaven
The Son in the Epistle to the Hebrews
By Earl Doherty

Part 1

A New Son and Covenant

More than any other New Testament document, the Epistle to the Hebrews contains all the elements needed to understand the general nature of early cultic Christianity. This, despite the fact that it is often styled an anomaly, even "an alien presence in the New Testament"[1] since its presentation of Christ is so unique.

Who the writer is, where he writes, whom he is addressing remain unknown. But in this carefully crafted treatise, the author of Hebrews is speaking to a group which has been founded on a revelatory experience at some time in the past (Hebrews 2:3-4), a group which now shares a distinctive Christology and sectarian outlook. They expect the end of the present world to arrive shortly (Hebrews 1:2, 3:14, etc.). The community has known persecution (Hebrews 10:32f) and is perhaps in danger of losing its faith or fervor, thus prompting this treatise. The thought world of the epistle is strongly Jewish (though of a variety outside the mainstream and with Hellenistic elements), and if, as some suggest, the writer is part of a Gentile community, then it is one which has fully absorbed and adopted a Jewish identity. The epistle tends to be dated fairly early,

---

[1] L. D. Hurst, *Hebrews: Its Background and Thought*, p.1.

between 60 and 90, and many lean toward locating it before the destruction of the Temple in 70, since nothing of that event surfaces in the author's focus on the sacrificial cult.

Those elements in Hebrews which reveal the nature of incipient Christianity lie surprisingly clear to the eye, and they begin at the very head of the epistle. Here are the opening four verses, courtesy of the New English Bible:

> [1]When in former times God spoke to our forefathers, he spoke in fragmentary and varied fashion through the prophets. [2]But in this final age (literally, these last days) he has spoken to us in the Son (en huio), whom he has made heir to the whole universe, and through whom he created all orders of existence: [3]the Son who is the effulgence of God's splendor and the stamp of God's very being, and sustains the universe by his word of power. When he had brought about the purgation of sins, he took his seat at the right hand of Majesty on high, [4]raised as far above the angels as the title he has inherited is superior to theirs.

The fundamental theology of this community is a belief in the Son, and here the author defines this entity. His concept fits into the widespread Hellenistic doctrine of the "Logos"—though the word itself does not appear anywhere in the epistle in this sense—and the language closely resembles that used of Jewish personified Wisdom in *The Wisdom of Solomon* (as in Hebrews 7:26), an important document of Hellenistic Judaism written most likely in Alexandria early in the first century CE. Here Wisdom has been cast in a Logos mold.

Hebrews' "Son" reflects the dominant religious philosophy of the age, that the ultimate God emanates a force or secondary divinity that constitutes his image, one who has served to effect creation and who provides the ongoing sustaining power of the universe. The Son is also an intermediary channel between heaven and earth, and for this group, as for so many others on the Christian cultic scene,[2] he conforms to another aspect of personified Wisdom in that he serves as the voice of God to humanity,

---

[2] Compare to 1 John 5:20.

revealing knowledge about the Deity and the availability of salvation. Finally, in a feature shared by not quite so many early Christian groups, this sect regards the Son as an agent of salvation through a sacrifice for sin.

This doctrine is what the writer will concentrate on throughout the epistle. He will cast it in a unique setting and Christology which lies outside standard Logos concepts and takes up residence in that most ancient of Jewish institutions: the sacrificial cult of the Temple as it became embodied in the legends of the Exodus and the establishment of the first covenant on Mount Sinai. For the community of Hebrews, the Son Jesus Christ is the spiritual High Priest whose sacrifice in heaven has established a new covenant to supplant the old.

A Missing Equation and a Silent Voice

For all that is said about the Son here and throughout this longest of the New Testament epistles after Romans, we should immediately note what is *not* said. First, no equation is ever made of this divine figure with the human man Jesus of Nazareth, known to later Christianity from the Gospels. As we shall see, the Son inhabits not an earthly setting, but a higher world revealed by scripture; more than one passage tells us, in fact, that he had never been to earth.[3] In the opening verses of Hebrews quoted above, the writer alludes to the Son's work of salvation, a bare statement that he had "brought about the purgation of sins" (Hebrews 1:3). Not only does this lack any context of a life on earth, the act itself will be placed by the writer in a heavenly sanctuary, a spiritual world setting of a Platonic type. Here we can see that the earliest expression of Christ belief had nothing to do with a reaction to an historical preaching sage and everything to do with the heady expressions of contemporary Greek and Jewish philosophy, about the unseen realm of heaven and the various manifestations of Deity which existed there.

---

[3] See Epilogue.

In that unseen reality, the writer is concerned with establishing certain things about the Son. If we go on from Hebrews 1:3 above, we find that one of these is that he is "superior to the angels" (Hebrews 1:4). To prove this, the writer quotes several passages from the Psalms and elsewhere, comparing what God says about the angels with what he says (as the writer sees it) about the Son. The latter includes Psalm 2's famous verse: "Thou art my Son; today I have begotten you" (Psalm 2:7). In quoting Psalm 45:6, the writer seems to regard the Son as being addressed by the term "God." Psalm 102's declaration that through the Son was the Earth's foundation laid, and Psalm 110's invitation to the Son to sit at God's right hand, proves for the writer that he is "superior to the angels." But should we not wonder why the writer did not think to appeal to the Son's incarnation, to his life and ministry on earth, to his rising from the tomb, to prove such a superiority? In fact, one of the glaring silences in this epistle is the failure to mention the resurrection at all! For that, Jean Héring calls this work "an enigma."[4]

What the writer is doing, of course, is using scripture to cast light on the workings of the higher realm. Jesus the Son, together with the angels, are exclusively spiritual figures, part of the paraphernalia of heaven, with Jesus defined (as in Psalm 1:3) in thoroughly mythological terms. The writer needs to rank the heavenly Christ above the angels because he regards him as the agency of the new covenant, whereas the angels have been associated with the delivering of the old covenant, now superseded. Christ's proven superiority will support the superiority of this new covenant and the validity of the community's covenant theology. In the face of such a need, it is unthinkable that all aspects of the Son's nature and activities would not be appealed to. Héring's "enigma" is a pale judgment on the pervasive and inexplicable silence in this epistle about every aspect of Jesus' career on earth. (Those handful of references which scholars like to point to as allusions to Gospel details are better seen as dependent on scripture and will be dealt with later in this chapter.)

---

[4] Jean Héring, *Hebrews*, p. xi.

Our second focus on what is *not* said in Hebrews proceeds from the opening declaration, that in this final age God has "spoken to us in (or through) the Son." Is it feasible that, after expressing such a sentiment, the writer would go on through thirteen chapters and never once give us a word of what this Son spoke on earth? Not a single Gospel saying is introduced, not even a reference to the fact itself that Jesus had taught in a human ministry. Hebrews 2 begins with the idea that "we must pay heed to the things we were told" (Hebrews 2:1), but this is evidently not to include the words delivered by the Son while on earth, since they are never presented. And when the writer goes on to refer to the experience which lay at the inauguration of the sect, the "announcement of salvation through the Lord" (Hebrews 2:3-4), this is clearly a revelatory event he is describing, and not any ministry of Jesus. In Hebrews, the "voice" of the Son comes entirely from scripture, and it is a voice which speaks in the present, not from the past. When the author first quotes the Son's perceived words in the Psalms and Isaiah, he introduces them in the present tense: "he says" (Hebrews 2:12-13).[5] The Son is an entity who is known and communicates now and today, through the sacred writings.

The words in these particular quotations are used to illustrate the contention that the Son is not ashamed to call believers his brothers. Yet more than one commentator has wondered why, instead of going to the Old Testament to prove his point, the writer does not draw on any of Jesus' several statements on the subject, as recorded in the Gospels. Why not Luke 8:21 (and parallels): "My brothers are those who hear the word of God and act on it." Or Mark 3:35: "Whoever does the will of God is my brother." Or Matthew 25:40: "Anything you did for one of my brothers...you did for me." Even John 20:17 might have served: "Go to my brothers and tell them that I am now ascending to my Father..." Does the writer lack all knowledge of such sayings by Jesus in an earthly ministry?

---

[5] "He says" – the Greek present participle *legon*.

Graham Hughes, in his study of Hebrews, shows to what bizarre lengths scholars can go in order to account for such silences.[6] He questions why the writer did not draw on those Gospel sayings which "coincide" with the Old Testament verses he actually uses. Hughes' first assumption is that such sayings *were* well known to the author. So much so, he says, that he regarded the Old Testament quotations as "forms" of the Gospel sayings. Thus, "the former can now be appropriated to give expression to the latter." Once the brain stops spinning, the reader may well ask: why should the author pass up quoting Jesus' sayings themselves in favor of quoting Old Testament verses which 'stand for them'? If he wants to "give expression to" the sayings, why not just quote the sayings? This is a good example of a common scholarly practice of defining something as its opposite: the absence of any Gospel sayings in Hebrews is really a quotation of those sayings through their Old Testament prefigurations!

In actuality, all we have in Hebrews are those Old Testament verses. They show that the voice of the Son through which God speaks in this final age is the voice heard in a new interpretation of the sacred writings, that for sects like the one which produced this epistle, scripture provides a window into the higher world where God and the Son do their work and communicate with humanity.

A Spirit World Body

If we go on to Hebrews 10:5-7, things become even clearer. Here the Son speaks in what might be styled a "mythical present" through a passage from Psalm 40 (actually, from the Septuagint version, No. 39, showing that the community lives in a Hellenistic milieu, not a Hebrew one):

> That is why, at his coming into the world, he says:
> "Sacrifice and offering thou didst not desire,
> But thou hast prepared a body for me.

---

[6] Graham Hughes, *Hebrews and Hermeneutics*, (Cambridge University Press, 2004), p.62.

> Whole-offerings and sin-offerings thou didst not delight in.
> Then I said: 'Here am I: as it is written of me in the scroll,
> I have come, O God, to do thy will.'"

How do scholars approach this seemingly odd mode of expression? The writer presents Christ as speaking in the present ("he says"). Yet this speaking is "at his coming into the world," which must also be in the same present. Such actions are placed not in history, but in scripture, in whatever the writer regards as represented by the words of the Psalm. Nor does he show any sense of confusion between this "coming" and any recent coming of Jesus into the world in an historical sense, at Bethlehem or on earth generally.

But confusion among commentators abounds. Héring simply translates the verb into the past tense, without comment.[7] Hugh Montefiore suggests that the coming into the world refers to Christ's "human conception or his human birth," and that the writer regards the Psalm as reporting Jesus' words to the Father at such a moment.[8] Paul Ellingworth assumes that the writer hears Christ speaking through scripture prior to his human incarnation. All this is something that has to be read into the epistle's words, for of birth and incarnation in an historical setting it has nothing to say.[9]

Ellingworth points to a promising interpretation of the "he says," calling it "a timeless present referring to the permanent record of scripture."[10] We are skirting Platonic ideas here, with their concept of a higher world of timeless reality. Why not suggest, then, that the writer views scripture as presenting a picture of spiritual world realities, and it is in this spiritual world that Christ operates? The writer of Hebrews has gone to the sacred writings for the story of Christ, the newly revealed "Son." In that case, the "he says" (here and throughout the epistle) becomes a mythical present,

---

[7] Héring, *Hebrews*, (Cambridge University Press, 2004), p. 84f.
[8] Hugh Montefiore, *Epistle to the Hebrews*, p. 166.
[9] Paul Ellingworth, *New International Greek Testament Commentary, Hebrews*, p. 499.
[10] Ibid. p. 500.

reflecting the higher world of myth, which seems to be the common universe of so many early Christian writers.

In this passage, we can see the type of source which could have given rise to the idea that the spiritual Son had taken on or entered "flesh," as well as the idea that he had undergone sacrifice. At first this was envisioned as taking place within the lower celestial realm. For the writer of Hebrews, this would have placed the Son "for a short while...lower than the angels" (Hebrews 2:9). Into this mythological realm Christ had "come" to receive the body prepared for him, to provide a new sacrifice and a new covenant to supplant the old one with its animal sacrifices which God no longer wanted. (As we shall see, the writer's concept of exactly where the divine death itself had taken place is somewhat vague. Instead, he focuses on Christ's subsequent actions in the heavenly sanctuary, offering his blood to God in a higher world parallel to the earthly sacrificial cult.)

Part 2

Before going on to examine how the author of Hebrews presents the sacrifice of the Son, we should look at a handful of passages which could be said to constitute cryptic references to incidents portrayed in the Gospels. Commentators, in a show of enthusiasm over this, often pronounce Hebrews to be the epistle which "most displays an interest in the historical Jesus." In fact, these few references can be shown to be based on readings of scripture and can be placed within the mythological world to which Hebrews 10:5 points. In the process, we will also look at a couple of Gospel features which are notably conspicuous by their absence.

Outside the Compound

The first to consider is Hebrews 13:11-13:

¹¹Those animals whose blood is brought as a sin-offering by the High Priest into the sanctuary have their bodies burnt outside the camp, ¹²and therefore Jesus also suffered outside the gate, to consecrate the people by his own blood. ¹³Let us then go to meet him outside the camp, bearing the stigma that he bore.

The first thing to note is that the name of Jerusalem is not used. Only the Gospel story would lead us to identify the author's thought about a gate with that city. Nor does the name of Calvary or Golgotha ever appear.

Note, too, that the flanking verses above use the word "camp." Here we need to look at the Greek word "*parembole.*" It means a fortified military camp, and it is used in Exodus and Leviticus to refer to the Israelite camp in the wilderness of Sinai. Hebrews, in its presentation of the cultic rituals of sacrifice, seems to have this ancient 'historical' setting in mind rather than any contemporary Herodian Temple. The present passage, then, lies far from the site of Jerusalem in the writer's mind; and all of it has the mark of symbolic significance. Jesus suffering "outside the gate" is an element which is dependent, not on some historical record, but on the idea in the previous phrase. Jesus did this *because* bodies of sacrificed animals were burned outside the camp.

For this writer, everything to do with Christ and his sacrifice must be modeled on the sacrificial cultus of the Jewish religion, as described in scripture. Scripture determines the picture he creates of Christ and his activities in the spiritual world, and if animals were sacrificed outside the boundaries of the camp at Sinai, then Jesus had to undergo the same thing, in a higher world mythic parallel to the earthly copy. The idea of "outside the gate" also provides a symbolic parallel to the experiences of the believers, as we see by the succeeding verse which suggests that the author saw both Jesus and his own sect as rejected outsiders, living 'beyond the pale' with no permanent home. This is suggestive of the paradigmatic relationship between earthly and heavenly counterparts. Thus we can discount any necessary reference in this passage to Jerusalem or an historical event.

In any case, we have strong indication from an earlier passage (Hebrews 7:1-3) that the writer of Hebrews possesses no concept of Jesus ever having been in or near Jerusalem. Jesus in his role as heavenly High Priest finds his archetype, his scriptural precedent, in Melchizedek. This figure was "king of Salem and priest of God Most High," who is mentioned briefly in Genesis 14:18-20. (There is an even briefer reference to him in Psalm 110:4.) In comparing Melchizedek to Jesus, the writer is anxious to milk everything he can from this shadowy character; one who serves the role of prototype for Jesus the new High Priest. And yet he fails to make the obvious point that Melchizedek had officiated in the same city where Jesus later performed his own act as High Priest, the sacrifice of himself. This is only one of many unthinkable omissions in this epistle.

"In the Days of His Flesh"

The philosophy of the period regarded the upper spiritual portion of the universe as containing the primary and ideal counterparts of material world things, giving savior gods like Christ features which sound like human attributes. Not only could the Lord be "sprung from Judah" (Hebrews 7:14) because scripture indicated that this would be the Messiah's lineage, but he could also be said to possess the *likeness* of "flesh" and "blood" and to undergo sacrifice. Says Hebrews 2:14: "Since (Christ's children) have blood and flesh, he too shared the same things *in a like manner* (the Greek word means "similar, near to," not "identical"), so that through death he might break the power of him who had death at his command." This is a classic expression of the parallel between the higher world paradigm and the believers linked to him on earth.

If "flesh" could refer to the lower celestial regions, or more generally to the counterpart spirit world of myth where all the activities of savior gods and goddesses took place, then Hebrews 5:7 can readily be placed in such a context:

In the days of his flesh (*en tais hemerais tes sarkos autou*) he offered up prayers and petitions, with loud cries and tears, to God who was able to deliver him from death (literally, out of death). Because of his humble submission his prayer was heard.

Scholars regularly claim that this passage is a reference to an incident in the earthly life of Jesus, namely the Passion scene in the Garden of Gethsemane. But is it? Some recognize the problems in such an interpretation. At Gethsemane, Jesus' anguished plea that the cup of suffering should pass him by was in fact not answered by God, which contradicts the point the writer wishes to make. From Hebrews 4:14 on, he is anxious to show that Jesus is qualified to be High Priest for human beings, and one of his tasks, like the earthly high priest, is to petition God on their behalf. The reference in Hebrews 5:7 is designed to show that on the latter score Jesus has already proven himself. For "in the days of his flesh" his prayers to God on his own behalf were answered. Not that the writer of Hebrews envisions his Jesus as having successfully avoided death through prayers to God for such a thing; those prayers were rather that Jesus be delivered out of death (that is, brought up from it) and that he be perfected through suffering and obedience in order to serve as the source of humanity's salvation (cf. Hebrews 2:10).[11] And in fact, says the writer, this request was granted.

Any tradition about Jesus at Gethsemane which bore a resemblance to the Gospel account would not fit Hebrews' idea here, for the Gospel Jesus had prayed, in a moment of human weakness, that the cup be removed. This writer would never want to suggest that such a prayer was in any way answered, or was even a worthy one, much less that it made Jesus qualified to be the ideal High Priest. Scholars who squarely face this discrepancy usually downplay the link to Gethsemane. This does not include Montefiore who declares that "this historical incident evidently made a deep impression upon the author."[12] So deep, that he can only refer to it

---

[11] Compare to Hebrews 2:10.
[12] Montefiore, *Epistle to the Hebrews*, p. 97.

cryptically, making no connection to a specific moment in Jesus' earthly life. (What would have prevented him from actually saying "in the Gethsemane garden"?) And he misapplies it to the point he is making.

Where then did the idea in Hebrews 5:7 come from? In the case of this epistle, we know the answer by now: from scripture. G. A. Buchanan suggests that "offering up petitions" is drawn from Psalm 116:1, which uses the same words (in the Septuagint version).[13] And Montefiore, while fussing over the fact that it does not appear in the Gospel description, sees the phrase "loud cries and tears" as an enlargement on Psalm 22:24: "when I cried to him, he heard me" (again in the wording of the Septuagint). Reflecting scholarship in general, Ellingworth admits that Hebrews 5:7 represents "a generalized use of the language and pattern of Old Testament intercession."[14] He allows that the words do not refer to Gethsemane—though he considers that they must refer to *some* historical event.

It is clear that the picture of Jesus' "days in flesh" is being built up through the course of the first century from passages in scripture which supposedly supply details of those activities. For early writers like that of Hebrews, such activities were mythical ones, taking place in the spiritual world of true reality. This "supernatural incarnation" (using Pfleiderer's phrase) is characterized almost universally in early Christian writers by the word "flesh" (*sarx*) in some form or other (*kata sarka, en sarki*, etc.). When it came time to envision the Christ as having entered the flesh of the material world, the step was a simple one. (It may have been one small step for a god, but it was a giant leap for Western mankind.)

Gone Missing: The Last Supper...

But these few gleanings from Hebrews which scholars have attempted to link to incidents contained in the Gospels are overshadowed by two

---

[13] G. A. Buchanan, *Anchor Bible, Hebrews*, p. 98.
[14] Ellingworth, *New International Greek Testament Commentary, Hebrews*, p. 285.

startling voids in the thought of this writer. Commentaries never lack for expressions of astonishment and a scramble for explanation on the subject of the Eucharist and the Resurrection, both of which are missing in this epistle. The former at least, should be a centerpiece.

The core of Hebrews' attention is focused on the concept of sacrifice. The Jewish sacrificial cult as expressed in the ritual of the Day of Atonement and at the inauguration of the old Mosaic covenant is set against the sacrifice offered up by the new High Priest Jesus which has established a new and superseding covenant. In the Gospels, Jesus' act of institution at the Last Supper places a sacramental significance on the atoning sacrifice he is about to undergo, and is presented by Jesus himself as the establishment of a new covenant. If such a thing had existed within the tradition of the author of Hebrews, there are few statements in the entire field of New Testament research which could be made with more confidence than that he would not have failed to bring in Jesus' establishment of the Eucharist for the closest examination.

And yet we read in Hebrews 9:15-22:

> And therefore he (Christ) is the mediator of a new covenant…to bring deliverance from sins…The former covenant itself was not inaugurated without blood. For when Moses had recited all the commandments to the people, he took the blood of the calves…saying, "This is the blood of the covenant which God has enjoined upon you."…And without the shedding of blood there is no forgiveness.

This passage cries out for a detailed comparison with the establishment of the Christian Eucharist at the Last Supper. There Jesus inaugurated the new covenant as Moses had the old; the words of Jesus (e.g., Mark. 14:24: "This is my blood of the covenant, shed for many") were spoken in parallel to Moses' own; Jesus' blood was shed "for the forgiveness of sins" (Matthew 26:28), the same purpose for which the Law of the old covenant had required the shedding of blood. Can there be any feasible explanation for why the author of Hebrews would ignore the entire tradition of Jesus' establishment of the Eucharist with all these important features—other than the inescapable conclusion that he could have known of no such thing?

Again, there's a clincher. It was pointed out above that the writer is eager to take as much as he can from the meager data available in Genesis and Psalm 110 about the figure of Melchizedek, king and priest of Jerusalem in the time of Abraham. But there is more than the one omission described earlier in his use of Genesis 14:18-20. Verse 18 begins: "Then Melchizedek king of Salem brought food and wine."

A writer whose main occupation is making parallels between his own brand of Christian theology and its embodiment in the sacred scriptures, fails to point to Melchizedek's "food and wine" as a prefiguring of the bread and cup of the eucharistic sacrament established by Jesus! Another unthinkable omission.

How do scholars deal with Hebrews' stunning silence on the Eucharist? Most of them seize on the observation that the author, when quoting Moses in Hebrews 9, has made a "subtle change" of one of the words from Exodus 24:8, substituting another which appears in Mark's account of Jesus' words at the Supper. (Instead of "Behold the blood..." he writes: "This is the blood...") This "change" is supposed to indicate that the author knew of the Supper scene and had Jesus' words in mind, if only subconsciously. He can have them sufficiently in mind to alter a word, but not sufficiently to give us any discussion of the very act and sayings of Christ which lie at the core of his new covenant theology. Montefiore notes that the author of Hebrews "is not concerned in this epistle with the Christian Eucharist,"[15] which hardly explains the matter nor alleviates the perplexity of it.

Few other features of the documentary record so clearly reveal the fragmented and uncoordinated nature of the early Christian movement. Hebrews provides strong evidence that independent expressions of belief in the existence of a divine Son and his role in salvation were to be found all over the landscape of the first century, with no central source or authority

---

[15] Montefiore, *Epistle to the Hebrews*, p. 158.

and little common sharing of doctrine and ritual. Just where the community which produced Hebrews was located, or the year in which this unique document was written, is impossible to tell, but that it owed its genesis to any historical events in Jerusalem, or anywhere else, is very difficult to support.

...and the Empty Tomb

The second of those startling voids in Hebrews is the absence of any concept of a resurrection for Christ, either in flesh or for a period on earth. Héring, in addition to labeling the epistle an "enigma" on this account, observes that the writer seems to have no regard for the Easter miracle, since "events unroll as though Jesus went up to heaven immediately after death,"[16] an idea found in more than one early Christian document. After "enduring the cross" (a reference which can easily fit into the mythical setting, as discussed above), Jesus takes his seat at the right hand of the throne of God (Hebrews 12:2).[17] A similar process is described in Hebrews 10:12: "But Christ offered for all time one sacrifice for sins, and took his seat at the right hand of God." This mimics the sequence in Hebrews 1:3 as well, noted above. Finally, in Hebrews 13:20, in a passage which has in any case been questioned as authentic to the original epistle, the writer speaks a prayer which begins: "May the God of peace, who brought up from the dead our Lord Jesus, the great Shepherd of the sheep..." Here the Greek verb is *"anago,"* meaning to "lead up," not the usual word applied in other New Testament passages to the idea of resurrection. Not surprisingly, the whole phrase is modeled on an Old Testament passage, Isaiah 63:11 (Septuagint): "Where is he that brought up from the sea the shepherd of the sheep?" Once again, we see that ideas about Jesus and his activities are derived not from history, but from scripture.

---

[16] Héring, *Hebrews*, p. xi.
[17] If you can have a throne in heaven, why not a cross? (Editor's note.)

W. D. Davies would like to suggest that "brought up" includes within itself the idea of both resurrection and ascension (including the standard 40-day interim, no doubt),[18] which is yet another case of solving a problem by letting a silence stand for the very thing which is not in evidence. But it is difficult to believe that this writer could have had any concept that Jesus had overcome death in some way which would be meaningful to human hopes. In Hebrews 7:16, the author extols Jesus as one who owes his priesthood "to the power of a life that cannot be destroyed." Is this founded on Jesus' conquest of death through his resurrection from the tomb? No such idea is hinted at. Instead, the statement is based—once again—on an interpretation of a scriptural passage, the one in Psalm 110 which declares: "Thou art a priest forever."

James Moffat, in his study of Hebrews, would have us believe that the author could not make use of the idea of Jesus' resurrection because he was confining his High Priest analogy to the biblical prototype of sacrifice on the Day of Atonement, and there was no "slot" for it![19] Can we believe that *any* literary consideration would lead a Christian writer to reject the rising of Jesus from his tomb as 'unusable' and ignore it for thirteen chapters?

Part 3

A High Priest in a Heavenly Sanctuary

The picture of Christ in the Epistle to the Hebrews is unlike any other in the New Testament. Scholars have often asked themselves what led its author to even think of portraying Jesus in this manner, as the heavenly High Priest whose blood sacrifice, offered in the heavenly sanctuary, is the higher world counterpart of the Day of Atonement sacrifice performed by the high priest in the sanctuary on earth. It is the more perfect

---

[18] W. D. Davies, *Hebrews*, p. 137.
[19] James Moffat, *International Critical Commentary, Hebrews*, p. xxxviii.

embodiment of the earthly cult, and it has established a new covenant which ushers in the final age.

Nor is this writer some isolated theologian, for behind him (as we can see from the epistle) lies some form of community whose views he is representing and to whom he is addressing himself. Of course, scholars ask this question within the context of orthodox assumptions. They ask what led such a group to deviate so radically and with such "fresh creative thinking"[20] from what must have been the more standard Christian message about Jesus, from the theological and historical picture they must have received through the apostolic channels by which they were converted. Cast in this way, the question is indeed a challenging and perplexing one.

But in the epistle itself, no sign of such a deviation can be detected. Such a question is never addressed. The writer and his community seem to move in their own world, a world exclusively dependent on scripture and its interpretation. The handful of seeming allusions to some "earthly" experience of their divine Christ are, as we have just seen, ambiguous and cryptic, and can more easily be explained as proceeding from scripture than from any traditions of a historical Jesus of Nazareth, a figure who is never explicitly mentioned.

As noted above, Hebrews provides perhaps the best example in the New Testament of how Christ belief arose spontaneously out of currents and trends of the day, in independent expressions, each taking on its own characteristics as a result of the local conditions and the people involved. The epistle is what it is because a distinct group formulated their own picture of spiritual realities. They searched scripture for information and insight about the Son of God, under the influence of the wider religious and philosophical atmosphere of the first century, especially Alexandrian Platonism, and this is what they came up with. Their mediator between heaven and earth has been cast in the mold of the Jewish sacrificial cult. But they are not reinterpreting an apostolic message, they are not giving

---

[20] Montefiore, *Epistle to the Hebrews*, p. 96.

an against-the-grain twist (for reasons which would be difficult to explain) to the story of some recent man. No bow is made in the epistle to any wider Christian movement, nor to any standard from which they are deviating. The sectarian community represented by Hebrews is self-sufficient, and it, too, like all other expressions of Christ belief of the day, from Paul to the enigmatic Johannine community, professes its dependence on, and defines its origins in, divine revelation and the sacred writings. Nothing else is in evidence.

It is illuminating that Montefiore, in trying to answer the question of why the writer of Hebrews interpreted Jesus in his own peculiar way, instinctively draws on Gospel details. He points to Jesus' words about his sacrificial death,[21] his saying about building a temple not made with hands, the high priestly prayer quoted in John 17. But why is this natural instinct of the post-Gospel Christian exegete not mirrored in the document itself? In Hebrews, there *are* no sayings of Jesus quoted; there *are* no events of his life as recorded in the Gospels which the writer draws on to explain his interpretation of Jesus as High Priest. Not even the central concept of Jesus' sacrifice as the establishment of a new covenant has been illuminated by the slightest reference to the Last Supper or to the words Jesus is said to have spoken on that occasion inaugurating such a covenant. Montefiore has only succeeded in highlighting the perplexing, maddening silence of it all.

A Blood Offering

To examine the mythical world of Hebrews, we will jump into the very middle of the epistle and the center of the writer's thought: the sacrifice of Christ in the heavenly realm as laid out in Hebrews 8 and 9. The structure of this thought is thoroughly Platonic, though it mirrors some longstanding Jewish ideas as well. I will quote Marcus Dods from his 1910

---

[21] Montefiore, *Epistle to the Hebrews*, p. 95f.

commentary on Hebrews in the *Expositor's Greek Testament*, for he lays out the Platonic principle very succinctly:

> (The author's focus on the "heavenly" represents) the contrast of this world and heaven, between that of the merely material and transient, and the ideal and abiding. Things of this world are material, unreal, transient; those of heaven are ideal, true, eternal. Heaven is the world of realities, of things themselves, of which the things here are but copies.[22]

One side of this Platonic duality is the earthly sacrificial cult of the Temple, performed by the priests. Strictly speaking, the author presents it in its pre-Temple setting, when the early priestly ministry was conducted in a movable tent complex during the wanderings in the wilderness (or so legend had it). This places him directly in the world of the scriptures, in the company of Moses at the time of the Exodus. The day-to-day offerings and sacrifices take place in the outer tent, but once a year. On the Day of Atonement, the high priest passes through the curtain which closes off the inner tent, the Most Holy Place or sanctuary where stands the ark of the covenant (Hebrews 9:4). On this day, the high priest enters the sanctuary with the blood of special sacrifices "which he offers on his own behalf and for the people's sins of ignorance" (Hebrews 9:7).

Here is the earthly, transient manifestation: a material sanctuary involving goat and bull sacrifices of limited efficacy, part of an old covenant which has proven itself faulty (Hebrews 8:8). And what is the other side of the Platonic equation? This is "the real sanctuary, the tent pitched by the Lord and not by man" (Hebrews 8:2). The tent of Christ's priesthood "is a greater and more perfect one, not made by men's hands, not part of the created world" (Hebrews 9:11). In other words, it lies in the upper world of the real and eternal.

Here, despite attempts to claim the contrary, there can be no denying that Hebrews' thought world is fundamentally Platonic. This is a divided, dualistic universe of realms heavenly and earthly, genuine and imitation.

---

[22] Marcus Dods, *Expositor's Greek Testament* (1910), p. 271.

Christ enters "not that sanctuary made by men's hands which is only a symbol of the reality, but heaven itself" (Hebrews 9:24). In classic fashion, the upper world contains the "archetype," the lower world the "antitype" or copy.

Christ as heavenly High Priest is infinitely superior to the high priest on earth who officiates in the earthly tabernacle. The blood of the sacrifice Christ offers is his own blood, so much greater in power than the material blood of animals that it has "secured an eternal deliverance" (Hebrews 9:12), a forgiveness of sins which the earthly sacrifices could never achieve.

But the writer of Hebrews should be facing a huge problem. As a way of getting into this, let's start by examining a preliminary question which scholars seem not quite sure how to answer. What specifically constitutes the "sacrifice" which Christ offers, and where has it taken place? The "event" which the writer constantly focuses on seems not to be Christ's death itself, but his action of entering the heavenly sanctuary and offering his blood to God. This is the redemptive action, the offering of himself. Obviously, the writer sees things this way because his Platonic philosophy requires a parallel to the earthly cult; in the tent on earth, it is the entry into the inner tabernacle and the offering there of the blood of the sacrificed animal which is the determining element of the Day of Atonement rite, not the slaughter outside which produced the blood. Thus the center of gravity in Hebrews is the entry of Christ into the heavenly sanctuary, bringing his own blood as an offering to God. This is what the writer seems to define as the act and location of the "sacrifice."

Such an image has caused more than one commentator discomfort, for it is faintly distasteful, they have noted, to envision Jesus going from Calvary to heaven with his own blood in tow, and anyway what had he done with it during the three days in the tomb? (Remember that Hebrews is canonical and must therefore represent some kind of divine truth.) Montefiore also fusses over the point that Jesus shed very little blood on the cross, apart from the nails to his hands and feet!

Unfortunately for our understanding of things, all the writer ever refers to is this entry of Christ into the heavenly sanctuary. He never refers to Calvary, to Jesus' historical death, as part of the redeeming action. He never itemizes the death as a distinct feature of the sacrifice. (The passing reference to "the cross" in Hebrews 12:2 is not in any context of location, sacrifice, redemption or history.) And yet, the actual "shedding of blood" is a part of things, for Hebrews 9:22 says that without it "there is no forgiveness." So it would seem he regards the death of Jesus (wherever it took place) as part of the heavenly sacrifice, though not part of the most important action inside the sanctuary itself. *Heavenly*, because this sacrifice is "spiritual, eternal and unblemished" (Hebrews 9:14). Earthly sacrifices cleanse earthly copies, but "better sacrifices are required to cleanse heavenly things" (Hebrews 9:23). In the Platonic thinking of the writer such sacrifices, such blood, can only be spiritual and eternal.

And yet, *there* should be his problem. Jesus' blood was neither. He had lived on earth, he had been human in his incarnation, and human blood, the blood of matter, coursed in his veins. It was shed on a hill on earth, material, red and sticky. The sacrifice—or at least an essential part of it, a part which the tradition he supposedly received would certainly have regarded as essential—took place in the earthly realm, in the world of the transient, unreal copy of the heavenly. But such an earthly dimension would shatter his Platonic comparison. It would irreparably contaminate the purity of the earth/heaven, high priest/High Priest contrast on which his whole theology is based. The sacrifice had not been confined to the heavenly realm. It had a foot in both camps, and thus to some extent the writer would be comparing an earthly thing with another earthly thing.

At the very least, *he would have had to address this anomaly*. He would have had to explain why "human" blood shed on earth could at the same time be spiritual and cleanse the heavenly sanctuary (Hebrews 9:23). He would have had to justify why, when every Christian circle around him (presumably) thought of Christ's sacrifice in terms of its occurrence on Calvary, he has ignored such a venue and placed it in heaven. He would have had to qualify his Platonic picture.

Of course, he does not. He shows no sign of being perturbed by any conflict in his theoretical universe. Instead, the picture is uniform because the author has extrapolated earthly figures and activities (the Jewish sacrificial cultus) into a heavenly embodiment which is the perfect archetype of the lower world copy. And he has supported it by a Platonic reading of scripture, which he regards as a picture of the higher world of true realities where Christ operates. There is no historical Jesus, no sacrifice on an earthly Calvary, lurking in the background to disturb this finely drawn duality.

Problematic Solutions

It is astonishing that so few scholars show any awareness of the above conundrum, even as they recognize the spiritual, Platonic nature of Hebrews' thought world. Moffat can say: "For the complete sacrifice has been offered in the realm of the spirit."[23] He remarks on Hebrews 9:14 that the sacrifice of Christ "had been offered in the spirit and—as we might say—in the eternal order of things...it belonged essentially to the higher order of absolute reality."[24] Dods, analyzing the same passage, declares that Christ's ministry has a greater efficacy because it has been "exercised in a more perfect tabernacle and with a truer sacrifice."[25] In other words, they recognize Jesus' sacrifice as an event which in some way takes place in the world of Platonic-type myth, in the higher world of the spirit. Nor is any of this declared to be metaphorical.

A few more recent scholars have played down the Platonic nature of the writer's thought (such as Ellingworth in the *New International Greek Testament*), no doubt sensing the problem it creates. But that a document which inhabits an Alexandrian-style milieu would nevertheless not embody the fundamental principles of Middle Platonism is impossible. Older scholars such as Dods and Moffat had no such doubts.

---

[23] Moffat, *International Critical Commentary, Hebrews*, p. xlii.
[24] Ibid. p. xliii.
[25] Dods, *Expositor's Greek Testament*, p. 332.

Such observations as Moffat's do the Mythicists' work for them. They show that it is possible even for orthodox scholars to recognize the mythical realm and to envision the sacrifice of Christ within it. Of course, there is the inevitable attempt to compromise, to introduce an historical Jesus into the Platonic equation. Here is some of what Moffat has to say:

> The writer breathed the Philonic atmosphere (of Middle Platonism) in which the eternal Now overshadowed the things of space and time, but he knew this sacrifice had taken place on the cross, and his problem was one which never confronted Philo, the problem which we moderns have to face in the question: How can a single historical fact possess a timeless significance?[26]

Well, the writer of Hebrews never gives any indication that "he knew" of such an earthly sacrifice, nor that he faced a problem which Philo did not. Hebrews never asks or addresses Moffat's question, or other "problems" like it. He in fact follows directly on Philo's way of thinking, for Philo also referred to the Logos as High Priest, also envisioned the activities of this High Priest (though they were not sacrificial) as confined to the "intelligible world" of higher realities. The Epistle to the Hebrews inhabits the same conceptual universe, and if the writer had deviated so far from its spirit as to confer all this Platonic thinking on an historical, earthly man, he could not have failed to address such a radical innovation.

Nor does the writer of Hebrews support Buchanan's attempt to get around the epistle's Platonic pattern. Buchanan declares that the relationship between heavenly prototypes and earthly antitypes is "understood in terms of historical sequence and faith that is foreign to Platonism."[27] But the epistle itself shows no such understanding. It is true that in regular Jewish biblical exegesis, prototypes in scripture could be seen as anticipating later antitypes "that were also historical and earthly." But this is clearly not the course followed by this epistle, which focuses all its attention on the work of Christ in the heavenly world. It never bends its Platonic

---

[26] Moffat, *International Critical Commentary, Hebrews*, p. xliii.
[27] Buchanan, *Anchor Bible, Hebrews*, p. xxv.

principles to accommodate an "historical sequence" or an earthly sacrifice. Once again a scholar, under the influence of preconception, has chosen to read into a document ideas which are not presented by the document itself.

Montefiore goes so far as to say that the author intended no thought of a sacrifice in heaven at all.[28] Rather, the ministry of Christ in the heavenly sanctuary was simply one of intercession with God on humanity's behalf. All the talk of entering the sanctuary with his blood and offering it there is, as it were, metaphorical and refers back to Calvary where the actual sacrifice and offering had taken place. In discussing this point, Montefiore writes the word "Calvary" three times in the space of one page,[29] yet he seems not to wonder how the writer could be presenting such a metaphorical meaning and not likewise be forced to refer to the scene of Jesus' death and the fact that it had taken place on earth. He also argues that blood could not be offered in heaven because "heaven is the sphere not of flesh and blood but of ultimate reality." But what is this ultimate reality if not the more perfect forms of the earthly copies? By letting his Gospel preconceptions govern his whole interpretation of the text, by dismissing any concept of spiritual blood—blood which could be carried into a heavenly sanctuary—Montefiore has castrated the epistle's thought and rendered meaningless the whole Platonic structure the author has carefully put together. He has left him comparing an earthly cult with an earthly sacrifice.

That sacrifices could be offered in heaven is also shown by the Testament of Levi, third part of the Testament of the Twelve Patriarchs, a Jewish document (from probably a little earlier time) with certain amendments which scholars label "Christian." In chapter 3, sacrifices are depicted as being offered to God in a heavenly temple by angels of the third heaven. In this multi-layered universe, the third heaven contains an archetypal sanctuary whose copy is the earthly temple. Here the

---

[28] Montefiore, *Epistle to the Hebrews*, p. 133f.
[29] Ibid. p. 134-5.

archangels "offer propitiatory sacrifices to the Lord in behalf of all the sins of ignorance of the righteous ones" (as in the earthly rite on the Day of Atonement). "They present to the Lord a pleasing odor." Such sacrifices are declared to be "bloodless," although sacrifices in heaven involving blood are to be found in later Kabbalistic thinking.

Searching for Historical Events

Can we confidently maintain that for the writer of Hebrews Christ's sacrifice was in no way "a single historical fact," as Moffat puts it; something which had taken place on earth in his own time? Let's look at a few specific things the epistle says.

Just as Paul in Galatians 3 viewed the Law as a temporary measure until the coming of the present time of salvation through faith, the writer of Hebrews does something similar in 9:8-11. He sees the outer tent of the earthly sanctuary as symbolizing the old way, the old type of sacrifice. Throughout history, it has obscured the sight of the inner tent which symbolized the new way which was coming, the priesthood of Christ and his eternal sacrifice. Now this new way has been revealed—through the community's own reading of scripture and its conviction of inspiration. The outer, imperfect tent with its old, imperfect sacrifices has been removed, swept away. This idea, by the way, places the group which produced the epistle within a larger, diverse movement that rejected or aimed at reforming the Temple cult, a significant stream of thought within the wider Judaism of the first century. It is also an argument for placing the writing of the epistle before the destruction of the Temple, when such goals would have become moot.

How does the author describe the present time, when the new way has been revealed? He calls it a "time of reformation," of "amendment" (Hebrews 9:10), not the time of Christ's ministry or sacrifice. The entire epistle is concerned with God's revelation in scripture and the inaugurating of the new covenant. It began with the declaration that in this final age God has spoken to the world through the Son, but this is a Son, as we have seen, who speaks only in the sacred writings. In Hebrews 9:11 the author says that "Christ has come," but is this a reference to his life on Earth? Rather, the context indicates that he is referring to Christ's "entry" into the new tent of his heavenly priesthood, the spiritual sanctuary. (Ellingworth supports this.) He stresses that this tent is "not of this created world," a point which Buchanan seems to have ignored. This Christian writer can speak of Christ's "coming" and yet say not a word about any of his work on earth, only of what he did in heaven. Clearly, such a "coming" of Christ is entirely in terms of his spiritual world activities, as revealed in scripture. In the broader sense, it could also entail the thought of his coming to the believing community through the revelation about him, an idea found in other epistles as well.

In Hebrews 9:15 the author speaks of the death of Christ, making the point that the new covenant, like all testaments, can take effect only after the testator's death. But he does not specify when or where this death occurred. The actual death of Jesus remains a glimmer on the edges of the sacrifice. Its most significant mention comes in Hebrews 2:9, where it characterizes Jesus as a heavenly paradigm: "crowned with glory and honor because he suffered death," and "in tasting death he should stand for us all." This passage is reminiscent of the Christological hymn in Philippians, suggesting an entirely mythical setting.

A resurrection for Christ, as outlined above, rates scarcely a mention, and in any case plays no role in redemption. The idea of a resurrection in the Gospel sense is completely missing in this epistle.

A Sacrifice "Once for All"

In Hebrews 9:24f, the writer speaks again of Christ's entry into the heavenly sanctuary, and here he uses a favorite word, "once" (*hapax, ephapax*), a concept which he applies to Christ's sacrifice (as also in Hebrews 9:12). But what is it that has happened "once"? We need to look at the extended passage, a very revealing one (here slightly altered from the NEB):

²⁴For Christ has entered...heaven itself to appear [the verb *emphainizo*] now before God on our behalf. ²⁵Nor is he there to offer himself again and again, as the high priest enters the sanctuary year by year with blood not his own. ²⁶ªIf this were so, he would have needed to suffer many times since the foundation of the world. ²⁶ᵇBut as it is, he has appeared [the verb *phaneroo*] once for all (*hapax*) at the completion of the ages to abolish sin by his sacrifice.³⁰

The most important thing to realize is that the act of "appearing" throughout these verses relates to one thing: Jesus' sacrifice, which is synonymous with his entry into the heavenly sanctuary to make his offering to God. The "appearing" in verse 26b is not some sudden shift to a general reference to Christ's birth or life on earth, something which is never even touched on when discussing the sacrifice. The "appearing to abolish sin" of this latter verse is in the same category as the "appearing before God" of the earlier verse 24. All of it takes place in heaven.

It is true that those two "appearings" do not use the same verb, but Ellingworth points out that "there is no sharp distinction or contrast in Hebrews between *emphainizo* (verse 24) and *phaneroo* (verse 26b)."³¹ Some scholars³² recognize that the idea of "appearing" in verse 26b is focused specifically on the sacrifice, and this, as we have seen, the author nowhere makes a point of locating on earth.

But what of that unusual feature, the use of the word *hapax* ("once"), which is a deviation from strict Platonic thinking? The author has defined this entry into the heavenly sanctuary, not in the way the later Sallustius regarded the myths of the savior gods, as something which "always is so," not something timeless and constant, but as a spiritual event of a singular nature, something done "once." And he seems to locate this event in the present, "at the completion of the ages."

Why does he do this? Perhaps most importantly, the "once" makes Jesus' ministry superior to the sacrificial cult on earth, in which the high

---

³⁰ Hebrews 9:24-26.
³¹ Ellingworth, *New International Greek Testament, Hebrews*, p. 480.
³² For example: J. Swetnam, *Hebrews*, p. 233.

priest must renew the Day of Atonement sacrifice year after year; Christ, on the other hand, had only to perform it "once for all." The writer's theological needs, to establish the superiority and perfection of the heavenly side of the equation, may well have determined this aspect to his thinking.[33]

He may also have tied the spiritual event of Christ's sacrifice with the present time and regarded it as "once" because it is now and only now that the revelation about Christ and his sacrifice has been made. The event is spoken of as "occurring" at the time of its revelation, at the time when it takes effect. In fact, the choice of the verb *phaneroo*—a "revelation" word—in verse 26b may be influenced by this, reflecting the idea of the present-day manifestation of Christ to the world. This is further indicated by the use of the perfect tense which focuses on present effects rather than on an historical happening.

But we can go further. That the writer does not have any earthly event in mind in this entire passage is indicated by a verse coming shortly after the Hebrews 9:24-26 quoted above. Verse 28a is a virtual restatement of 26b: "So Christ was offered once to remove men's sins…"

This removal or abolition of sin, spotlighted in both 26b and 28a, is tied in the former to the act of sacrifice and in the latter to the act of offering. But these are synonymous, for the act of offering *is* the act of sacrifice. And this act, as we have seen, is always presented as the entry of Christ into the heavenly sanctuary carrying his sacrificial blood. Thus the reference to "appearing" at the completion of the ages (in 26b) is a reference to the *heavenly* event. Nowhere is anything earthly in view.

Other passages, such as Hebrews 7:27 and 10:10, also associate the "once for all" idea with the act of "offering" which is located in the heavenly realm. The epistle consistently portrays a spiritual act taking place in the spiritual world. We can conclude, therefore, that no earthly life or

---

[33] The point of the "once for all" language is to contrast the Son's sacrifice with the *many* repetitions of earthly Levitical sacrifices. And this heavenly sacrifice, set within a realm of Platonic archetypes, must be understood along the lines of an Augustinian "eternal now." (Editor's note.)

event is implied by anything the writer says, and that the Epistle to the Hebrews knows of no historical Jesus.

Standing on Mount Zion

Such a conclusion is clinched by the epistle's climax in chapter 12, a final peroration in which the writer urges steadfastness on his readers and gives a dire warning against apostasy. "Remember where you stand!" he cries (Hebrews 12:18), first calling to their minds the scene of the granting of the old covenant, before the blazing fire of Mount Sinai where a cowering Moses heard the oracular voice of God. When he turns to the scene of the new covenant, where does he place his readers' vision? Are they invited to stand upon the mount of Calvary? Beneath the cross where Jesus of Nazareth hangs? Perhaps in front of the empty tomb? No, where Mt. Sinai symbolized the old covenant, it is Mt. Zion—still a scriptural motif—which for this writer symbolizes the new.

On Mt. Zion, before the heavenly Jerusalem, the scene is one of angels, God the judge of all, and Jesus the mediator of the new covenant. But when the writer enjoins his readers to "see that you do not refuse to hear the voice that speaks" (Hebrews 12:25), we hear no voice of Jesus. Instead it is God himself who speaks, through one of his scriptural prophets. How is it possible, in providing a new-covenant counterpart to the voice of Moses and the divine oracles on Sinai, that a Christian writer would *not* offer the voice of Jesus: the Son of God himself when recently on earth, teaching, enlightening, admonishing, bringing a new Law, even speaking from the cross? In the Gospels, the concept of understanding and heeding the things which Jesus spoke is a major theme. The phrase on Jesus' lips, "He who hears my words," is a recurring motif.

Scholars should *weep* before the total ignorance, the complete disinterest, indeed the sheer disdain which writers like that of Hebrews seem to show toward the voice and persona of Jesus of Nazareth. How likely is it that a Jewish-Christian writer, presumably converted by a response to the figure of this human Jesus into a faith which his whole heritage would have regarded as blasphemous, how likely is it that he would choose to ignore the entire earthly record of this very figure? What personal disposition would lead him to exclude from his presentation all the motifs of his new faith, to draw inspiration and illustration from ancient writings which were only a prophecy of the real thing? Why, for virtually all the first-century Christian letter writers, was it dusty passages from the Prophets and Psalmists which inspired their Christologies, their eloquence, their poetic imagery, and not the vibrant words and images of the recent incarnation of the Son of God which should have been hanging in the very air of their daily lives?

No string of unlikely argumentation such as scholarship regularly indulges in can be judged adequate in the face of the overall stultifying silence on Jesus of Nazareth found in the New Testament epistles, no defense even distantly sufficient for the utter void in the early Christian writings which should be filled by the Gospel Jesus. The argument from silence—a silence as pervasive and as irrational as this one is—must be considered fully vindicated.

Epilogue: A Pair of Smoking Guns

But there are two passages in Hebrews which spell out for us the fact that this writer knows of no Jesus of Nazareth, no Son incarnated to earth. One involves an ancient scriptural prophecy, the other a feature of the comparison between heavenly and earthly activities of the old and new priesthoods.

A First or Second Coming?

The great Day of the Lord in Jewish prophecy and expectation was turned by certain early Christian preaching into the coming of Jesus, the spiritual Christ. (But not all: some epistles, such as James and 1 John, as well as the Didache, retain the idea of the arrival of God himself, with no sense of a Parousia of Christ.)

But it is the Epistle to the Hebrews which contains the most fascinating passage on this subject:

> "For soon, very soon (in the words of Scripture), 'he who is to come [*ho erchomenos*] will come and will not delay'" (Hebrews 10:37, NEB).

This is from the Septuagint version of Habakkuk 2:3. The prophet was referring to God himself, but by the beginning of the Christian period, this was one of many biblical passages that were being reinterpreted as referring to the Messiah. The Greek participle *erchomenos*, which the Septuagint here uses, became a virtual title, used with a masculine article—"*the* Coming One"—and referred to the expected savior figure who would arrive at the End-time. This is clearly how Hebrews is using it.

But stop and think a moment. The writer is affirming his belief that "the Coming One will come, and soon," for so the prophet has promised. Is he referring to the Gospel Jesus and his supposed Second Coming in glory? It is certainly the coming in glory at the End-time that he has in mind, but how can this be a *second* coming, for the writer has made no room for a previous one. If the prophet had prophesied Christ's coming, this would have been earlier fulfilled in his incarnation, when he came to earth as Jesus of Nazareth. This in fact is how Christians later interpreted all those prophetic passages about the Messiah: they referred to Christ's life on earth. But the writer of Hebrews makes no allowance for such a thing. Even if he wishes to apply Habakkuk's words to the Parousia of Jesus instead of the incarnation, he needs at least to make some reference to that earlier coming, if only to avoid confusion. Yet he does not. His silence plainly shows that for him Christ's coming is still to be, that he has no concept of him already having been here. As Hebrews 10:37 expresses itself, the scriptural promise of Christ's arrival has not yet been fulfilled.

But there are those who will protest, pointing to an earlier passage. Here is how the NEB translates Hebrews 9:27-28:

²⁷And as it is the lot of men to die once, and after death comes judgment, ²⁸so Christ was offered once to bear the burden of men's sins, and will appear [literally, he will be seen, or will reveal himself] a second time [*ek deuterou*], sin done away, to bring salvation to those who are watching for him.

Scholars claim that here at least—and they are willing to allow that it is *only* here in the entire corpus of New Testament epistles—a Christian writer clearly refers to the End-time coming of Jesus, the Parousia, as a *second* coming. But is there such a reference even here?

The above analysis of Hebrews 10:37 would suggest there is not. But we can contest it on the basis of 9:27-28 alone. If the "*ek deuterou*" means a second time, the parallel with verse 27 is destroyed. Verse 27 is saying that "first men die, and after that (or 'next') they are judged." There is no sense here of a "second time" for anything; the writer is simply offering us a sequence of events: death, followed by judgment. Does this not imply that verse 28 is offering a sequence as well? "Christ was offered once, and after that (next) he will appear to bring salvation" (Hebrews 9:28).

The idea of appearing "a second time" would be intrusive here. Since the writer is clearly presenting his readers with some kind of parallel between verses 27 and 28 (note also the "once" in both parts), it seems unlikely he would introduce an element which doesn't fit the parallel, especially one he doesn't need. "*Ek deuterou*" can have the alternate meaning of "secondly" or "next in sequence," like the similar word *deuteron*, which appears in this sense in 1 Corinthians 12:28. Just as men's death is followed by judgment, so is Christ's sacrifice followed by his appearance, but with no indication of how long a time between the two. Before the turn of the century, Vaughan translated verse 28 this way: "Christ died once and the next thing before him is the Advent."[34] Thus even in Hebrews it would seem that we have no Second Coming of Christ.

---

[34] Vaughan, quoted in: Dods, *Expositor's Greek Testament*, vol. 4, p. 340.

No Footstep Heard

Finally, there is a startling statement made in Hebrews 8, one which most commentators manage to gloss over or ignore completely. The writer is speaking of Jesus' ministry in the heavenly sanctuary and begins to compare him to the earthly high priest. At verse 4, he says: "Now, if he had been on earth, he would not even have been a priest..." No matter how one tries to detect a feasible qualification to this phrase, there is no denying that the writer seems to be saying that Jesus was never on Earth. The Greek is *"ei men oun en epi ges,"* which is literally: "Now, if accordingly he were on earth..." The verb *en* is the imperfect, which is strictly speaking a past tense, and the NEB (quoted above) chooses to reflect this. But the meaning within the context is probably present, or at least temporally ambiguous, much like the conditional sense in which most other translations render it: "Now if he were on earth (meaning at this time), he would not be a priest."

However, the writer has qualified this statement in no way whatever. He does not say, if he were *now* on earth (instead of earlier), if he returned to earth, if he were still on earth; not even: "While he was on earth, he was not a priest..." The writer says nothing which shows any cognizance of the fact that Jesus *had* been on earth, recently, that it was on earth where an important part of his sacrifice, the shedding of his blood, had occurred. (In contrast to scholars, who regularly feel constrained to point this out.)

The point he is making in this verse is that Jesus on Earth would have nothing to do, since there are already earthly priests performing the duties which the Law prescribes, and they do so "in a sanctuary which is only a copy and shadow of the heavenly" (Hebrews 8:5). Yet how could any writer say that Jesus would have nothing to do on earth when he did, in fact, have so much to do? How could he imply that earth is the scene only of human duties in a human sanctuary when here was where Jesus had performed his sacrifice, shed his blood—on a hill called Calvary outside Jerusalem? Surely no writer could express himself this way without at least a qualification, something which would give a nod to Jesus' recent presence in the physical arena. (Of course, such a life and death on earth, as noted earlier, would have thrown a monkey wrench into his carefully crafted Platonic picture.)

Ellingworth has glimpsed the edge of the abyss, and hastily drawn back. In analyzing this passage, he questions the normal interpretation of the imperfect *en*, and with it the NEB translation (which he admits "is grammatically possible") because it "could be misunderstood as meaning that Jesus had never 'been on earth'."[35] He claims that this "goes against the context"—which is to say the common assumption over the last nineteen centuries that a historical Jesus existed, one who had in fact been on Earth. In the face of the overwhelming evidence which Hebrews alone provides, it is time to question that very assumption, rather than try to reject the natural meaning of an innocent verb.

"Jesus Christ is the same yesterday, today and forever," the author intones in Hebrews 13:8. Could a divine Son, pre-existent in heaven before his incarnation, who was born fully human in Bethlehem in the days of Herod the Great, who grew up and ministered in Galilee, was slain in Jerusalem and rose bodily from the dead to return to heaven—could he be spoken of in this fashion? But of a mythical Christ who operated entirely in the spiritual sphere, in a timeless, Platonic existence, one who had never been to earth and was known only by divine revelation from the pages of scripture, such an affirmation would be perfectly apt.

---

[35] Ellingworth, *New International Greek Testament Commentary, Hebrews*, p. 405.

Chapter 11: The Jewish Myth of Jesus
By Stephan Huller

The simplest explanation is the best explanation. This understanding, first articulated by Claudius Ptolemy, has become a cornerstone of scientific research. Yet there is a fine line between being mindful of simplicity and being simple-minded. Ptolemy himself offers us the simplest of all explanations of how the universe functions, yet his model is ignored by modern astronomy. His model for the cosmos achieved 'simplicity' by trying to explain a limited number of facts. The same is true, I would argue, with regards to those who contend that the best understanding of the gospel is that Jesus was a historical person.

It would certainly make Christianity 'easier to understand' if we just took the gospel to be an ancient biography. But the Gospel of Mark does not give the impression that it was conceived as a *bios*.[1] Rather, in its Alexandrian form certainly, it was used by "those who are being initiated into the great mysteries"—in short, a liturgical text used in a mystery religion.[2] This is the place that 'the gospel' continues to occupy in the oldest traditions of Christianity. The reason this is generally ignored is the fact that the spirit of Protestantism dominates the study of the historical Jesus. It is quite easy—that is to say *simple*—to make yourself sound like a 'serious scholar' by stripping what are seen to be 'the facts' of the narrative away from all the 'spiritual mumbo jumbo.'

---

[1] L. Grollenberg, Unexpected Messiah or How the Bible Can Be Misleading. (London, SCM, 1987), pp. 59, 60.
[2] T. Talley, "Liturgical Time in the Ancient Church: The State of Research." In *Liturgical Time*, p. 45.

Just as it's very hard to take the icing off a finished cake, it's even harder to call what's left *a cake*. There is a point in the process of deconstruction where we lose the original essence of a thing. This is especially true with neo-Protestant attempts to extract 'history' from the mystic core of the gospel narrative. It often feels like scholars aren't even aware that they are cheating. For instance, no one ever seems to mention that the name 'Jesus' doesn't appear *as* a name for the main protagonist in the gospel in our earliest surviving manuscripts. Of course, those who study the historical Jesus want us to believe they are dealing with simple facts—even the actual truth. But the bare facts are that his name is—for all intents and purposes—never written out as Ἰησοῦς (or Iesous) in the earliest Christian manuscripts.[3]

Let's be honest about this one thing. In order for us to have certainty that the main character of the gospel was a historical individual we have to make the mental jump from $\overline{IS}$ or $\overline{IHS}$ or $\overline{IH}$—the actual names which appear in the manuscripts—to 'Jesus.' We've been doing it for centuries. Yet when we look at the process with open eyes, we can no longer avoid seeing that Iesous doesn't appear as his name. We've just ignored, or mentally and unwittingly 'redacted,' what's actually there. What appears in the ancient manuscripts is $\overline{IS}$, $\overline{IHS}$ and $\overline{IH}$. $\overline{IH}$ and $\overline{IHS}$ are utterly meaningless terms. On their own, they are little more than literary gobbledygook. But $\overline{IS}$—that is, IΣ with a super script above it—is by far the most widely-attested name for the Savior. If we stop ourselves from reading 'Iesous' and see $\overline{IS}$ for what it is—i.e., as a well-attested divine appellation—$\overline{IS}$ represents a unique challenge to our assumed name, Jesus.

What is required for us is to stop ourselves and prevent our old habits from bubbling up into our minds. $\overline{IS}$ is all there is. We don't need to play mental gymnastics to read this as 'Jesus' any longer. Justin Martyr, our oldest historical Christian witness, tells us repeatedly that the main

---

[3] P. Comfort, Encountering the Manuscripts: An Introduction to New Testament Paleography and Textual Criticism. (Nashville: Broadman & Holman, 2005), p. 221.

character of the gospel appeared in the Pentateuch as the angel 'Man.'[4] In fact, Justin Martyr explicitly tells us the Savior of the gospel is properly named Man.[5] With this knowledge we can start the process of disembarking from the 'Jesus-train' once and for all. So let's summarize the evidence—(a) by far the most common name for the main character of the gospel in early Christian manuscripts is $\overline{IS}$,[6] (b) $\overline{IS}$ is the standard Greek transcription of the Hebrew word for 'man,' that is *ish*,[7] and as we have started to show, (c) our earliest Christian source tells us the main character's name is 'man.'

The word for man in Hebrew is *ish*, spelled *aleph yod shin*. Yet various Hebrew manuscripts point to the likelihood that at one time *man* and *fire* were spelled the same way—that is, *aleph shin*.[8] On the other hand, the third-century Church Father Origen explicitly spells out the Hebrew word for man—*ish*—with the Greek letters *iota sigma*.[9] The standard Greek translation of the Hebrew Bible—the LXX—spells out various names which begin with this Hebrew word for 'man'—that is $\overline{IS}$.[10] As such, even though historical Jesus people won't want to admit it, the

---

[4] Justin Dialogue 34, 48, 58, 59, 62, 76, 125, 126, 127, 128. Cf. 113, "For I have proved that it was $\overline{IS}$ who appeared to and conversed with Moses, and Abraham, and all the other patriarchs without exception, ministering to the will of the Father; who also, I say, came to be born Man by the Virgin Mary, and I lives for ever."

[5] M. Marcovich, *Notes on Justin Martyr's Apologies*, in Illinois Classical Studies, 17, (1992), p. 324.

[6] Comfort, *Encountering the Manuscripts*, p. 203: "thus in its earliest form it is possible that Jesus' name was written in the contracted form as IS."

[7] Origen, Letter to Africanus, 12.

[8] Ezekiel 8:2 MT has "that appeared like fire" (*'esh* [th784, zh836])...The LXX, however, read *'ish* [th376, zh408], "man" for MT's *'esh*, relying perhaps on references in 1:26 and 40:3. *Ezekiel*, Daniel D Thompson and E. Carpenter; Cornerstone Biblical Commentary; Carol Stream, IL: Tyndale House Publishers, 2010), p. 76. In 1.26 he is described in terms of being a likeness of Adam which has puzzled scholars. See also the play on words in 2 Kings 1.11—15 between Elijah the 'man of God' and who brings the 'fire of God' down from heaven. The section clearly influenced Luke 9:54-55. It should also be remembered that the Babylonian fire god Ishu greatly resembles the preferred Marcionite name for the Savior Esu.

[9] Letter to Africanus 12.q a.

[10] Ishboshet in the Books of Samuel is just one example.

reality is that there is a very persuasive argument that 'Jesus' wasn't the name of the main character of the gospel. His actual name is the nominative form of the most common *nomen sacrum*. We no longer need to play tricks with the manuscripts.

But let's take things one step further. Mothers didn't name their children $\overline{IS}$. Thus he main character of the gospel had a name which couldn't possibly be the identity of a historical individual. Everything depends on us training ourselves to read IESOUS in place of what the manuscripts actually say—$\overline{IS}$. How did we learn to 'fake it'? I strongly suspect that the mental gymnastics here were mandated to avoid the tradition associated with Justin Martyr, Marcion, Valentinus and most of second-century Christianity. Where the name 'Man' was retained so too was the understanding that he was not a mortal man. Those who preserved this name saw him for what he was—a god, even the second god of Israel, mediator between humanity and the higher divinity.[11]

That's why it is so important for us to stop adding letters to the *nomen sacrum* $\overline{IS}$. Jesus wasn't the name of the main character of the gospel. Irenaeus explicitly denies this possibility.[12] He says there are those who read the *nomen sacrum* as Ἰησοῦς and they are wrong. So what are you left with? A faith that a Jewish mother would name her new baby boy 'Man'? Impossible. *Ish* is simply unattested as name for a Hebrew child at any period of Jewish history. But then again, the gospel tells us that it wasn't Mary who named him. He received the *nomen sacrum* by the decree of an angel.[13] What's more, many of those who accepted his Virgin Birth

---

[11] In the description of the angel announcing the birth of Samson the angel is called "man" (*ish*), "man of God" (*ish*)*ha'elohim*), and *mal'akh* ("angel") all in the same chapter (Judges 13).

[12] Irenaeus, *Against Heresies*, 2.23.

[13] Luke 2:21. Origen's commentary on this verse demonstrates the strangeness of this scene. After identifying IS as 'the name above all names,' Origen goes on to note that "[i]t was not fitting that this name should first be given by men or brought into the world by them, but by some more excellent and greater nature." *Homilies on Luke* 14. But the Virgin Birth took place centuries after the Patriarch Joshua ("Jesus") and—more importantly—the tens of thousands of Jews

assumed that 'Man' was a heavenly being who descended into Mary's womb like water passing through a tube.[14] Don't you see? We're getting further and further from the certainty that Christianity had a historical individual named Jesus as its founder.

'Man' was a traditional name given to a class of angels in Judaism. The *ishim*—i.e., Men—occupied the sublunar realm.[15] Indeed one of the strongest identifiable characteristics of the Christian and pre-Christian communities was their desire to live their earthly existence as angels.[16] The Greek name of this community—the Essenes—has been interpreted by at least a few scholars as deriving from the name *Ishim*.[17] We may presume that Christians were originally called *Ishim*—as Epiphanius records[18]— because the separating wall between divine and mortal men had—with the coming of IS—been thrown aside. The Ishim claimed $\overline{IS}$ as their founder or perhaps that they had become like the heavenly *Ishim*. Don't you see? This sort of community would need to have a *heavenly* founder. History and historicism turns out to be antithetical to attaining otherworldly perfection.

---

and Samaritans who bore this Hebrew name. Origen, like Irenaeus before him, is plainly thinking that the *nomen sacrum* is not 'Jesus' but a name which stood on its own for its uniqueness.

[14] Irenaeus, *Against Heresies*, 1.24.2.

[15] Cf Josef Stern, *The Matter and Form of Maimonides' Guide* (Cambridge: Harvard University Press, 2013), p. 23: "In Mishneh Torah 'Foundations of the Law,' iii:7, the *'ishim* are introduced as the intermediate causes that enable prophecy, i.e., in their epistemological role; in iv:6 the *'ishim* function as the divine instrument through which each material entity (*golem*) is given its intelligible form, their cosmological role."

[16] While Josephus only says that the Essenes had esoteric knowledge of the names of the angels (*War* 2.142) the fact that they wore white (2.123) likely meant they understood themselves as angels, as is true among various Christian monastic orders. Note also that the followers of Mark identified themselves not only as *'maskilim'* (the wise) but also as the 'purified' and those 'made white' (Daniel 12).

[17] B. Vellas, "On the etymology of the name Essaioi," *ZAW 81*, (1969), pp. 99f.

[18] Epiphanius, *Panarion* 29:1-7 from a suggestion by Eusebius in *Church History* 2:17. The etymology Epiphanius gives is not a plausible one.

In the second century there was a plurality of Christian sects each with a different understanding of how this heavenly Man came to start a new religious community. Some said that 'Man' passed through Mary's womb; others, the Marcionites, thought 'Man' descended straight from heaven to Judea.[19] Still others, the Valentinians, included 'Man'—that is *Anthropos*—as one of the heavenly powers of their gnosis.[20] To this end, the evidence for a strong second-century tradition that Christianity was founded by an angel named 'Man' is incontestable. The 'Jesus' tradition is nowhere to be found.

Even the Gospel of Mark presents his main character as simply 'a man'—someone with no history, no background—an anonymous person.[21] For the Marcionites he was simply "the Stranger" who "crossed the boundary and descended to us."[22] We are told he is the stranger because "he has no name."[23] This is also the sense behind the traditional Jewish literary method for speaking about the founder of Christianity. He is *oto ish*—'that man.'[24] But if we go back to Justin for a second, the Church Father tells us over and over again to take note of the mysterious 'man'

---

[19] S. Stout, The "Man Christ Jesus": The Humanity of Jesus in the Teaching of the Apostle Paul. (Eugene, OR: Wipf & Stock, 2011), pp. 35f.

[20] F. H. Borsch, *The Son of Man in Myth and History* (Philadelphia: Westminster, 1967), p. 55. This chapter lists at least a dozen early Christian sects who venerated the Savior as Man including the Naasenes: "Man of a greatly exalted Name" (Hippolytus, *Refutation* 5.6.4), Valentinus (ibid. 6.30.3), Mark (ibid 6.11) and many others.

[21] J. Trimmer in his *Four Dimensional Jesus* puts it best: "At the outset Jesus is an unidentified stranger and an unfathomable mystery. As the story progresses, the question on everybody's lips is, 'Who is this?'"

[22] Ephrem, *Prose Refutations*, 46:10–15.

[23] Ephrem, *Hymns Against Heresies*, 41.6. See the discussion in Judith Lieu, *Marcion and the Making of a Heretic*. (New York: Cambridge University Press, 2015), p. 161.

[24] The earliest known example is "They silence that man who says [in leading the Prayer of Eighteen], 'May thy mercy reach [even] the nest of a bird,' or 'May thy name be invoked for the good,' or 'We give thanks, we give thanks.' [These are not sanctioned liturgical formulae, because they have heretical overtones.]...Over the nest of a bird Your mercy extended, but over that man (אותו האיש) Your mercy did not extend." (Y Berachot 5:9)

who appears throughout the Pentateuch, visiting Abraham, wrestling with Jacob, instructing Moses and commanding Joshua. That heavenly man, Justin says, is the founder of the Christian religion.

The existence of a heavenly man '*ish*' goes back to the relatively well known example of Zechariah 6:12. Philo discusses the words "Behold the man (*ish*) whose name is rising" and says that it is a reference to the Logos.[25] Zechariah 6:12 was also a strong 'proof text' for Justin who posits that this angel or god was born into Mary's womb. In one reference Justin tells us that he is called "the Rising" by Zechariah because of the star the Magi followed and also 'Man' owing to the announcement of his name by Gabriel:

> ...and that He became Man by the Virgin...[T]he Virgin Mary received faith and joy, when the angel Gabriel announced the good tidings to her that the Spirit of the Lord would come upon her, and the power of the Highest would overshadow her: wherefore also the Holy Thing begotten of her is the Son of God; and she replied, 'Be it unto me according to thy word.' And by her has He been born, to whom we have proved so many Scriptures refer.[26]

In other words, a version of that heavenly 'man' tradition that was passed on to Philo also made its way to the Virgin Birth tradition of Justin.[27]

Once we come to terms with the widespread acceptance of a 'second god' named $\overline{IS}$ in ancient Jewish and Samaritan cultures, we can finally address some of the outlandish assumptions of Richard Carrier's mythicism. To read Philo as if Alexandrian Judaism venerated a god named 'Jesus' completely misses the mark. Samaritans to this day accept 'Man' as the name of an angel who appears throughout the Pentateuch.[28] Similarly Philo's commentary on Zechariah 6:12 and dozens of other

---

[25] Philo, On the Confusion of Tongues, XIV. 60-63.
[26] Justin, *Dialogue* 100.
[27] D. T. Runia, Philo in Early Christian Literature: A Survey. (Assen 1993), p. 99.
[28] B. Tsedaka, ed. and trans., S. Sullivan, ed., The Israelite Samaritan Version of the Torah: First English Translation Compared with the Masoretic Version, p. 3.

references to '*anthropos*' as a reference to God, all point back to an Oniad tradition originally preserved in Hebrew and which became, in time, remembered only in Greek. Philo knows nothing about a 'heavenly Jesus' only a heavenly $\overline{IS}$.[29]

The same thing can be seen in the allusions to a heavenly man in the writings of Paul. The same Oniad understanding of the angel $\overline{IS}$, especially from the first chapters of Genesis, is at the heart of the antithesis between the earthly man Adam and a heavenly Lord $\overline{IS}$ in 1 Corinthians.[30] The Marcionites are perhaps the best and earliest known exclusive Pauline sect. Not surprisingly, the mystical significance of the term *anthropos* resurfaces time and again in Tertullian's writings against the sect. A frequent theme is his rhetorical questioning of the Marcionite acceptance of their Savior as 'Man' while denying his humanness.[31] At other times Tertullian puzzles over the Marcionite understanding of Christ as 'Son of Man' implying—he says—that 'Man' was the name of Christ's Father.[32] In either case, a simple solution—accepting that the Marcionites

---

[29] A. J. M. Wedderburn, "Philo's 'heavenly man," *NTS,* 15 (1973), pp. 301-326.
[30] Ibid.
[31] S. Stout, *Man Jesus Christ*, p. 35f. The orthodox manner of reading the creation myth of Genesis is different from the 'heretics' insofar as the latter always see THREE entities involved in the process—Adam, his Creator and the image and/or likeness he was created from. The orthodox stress that man belongs to the Creator owing to his having been made by this god. The heretics assumed that man belongs to Man because of their resemblance. Indeed the orthodox complain that when Man takes man from his Creator it is an act of plunder. Tertullian also questions the salvation of man by Man – "[i]f the regeneration of man, how can he regenerate, who has never generated?...He therefore seals man, who had never been unsealed in respect of him; washes man, who had never been defiled so far as he was concerned; and into this sacrament of salvation wholly plunges that flesh which is beyond the pale of salvation!" (*Against Marcion* 1.28.3). Yet the salvation process isn't so complicated—Man makes man 'like him' as was done with Moses and then Joshua.
[32] *Against Marcion*, 4.10.5. Interestingly, Tertullian doesn't know—or won't tell the reader—how the Marcionites understood the relationship between Man and Son of Man. He does hint at a common understanding of a heavenly power Man. "One thing alone can help you in your difficulty: boldness on your part...to surname your God as actually the human father of Christ, as Valentinus did with his aeon."

read the *nomen sacrum* $\overline{IS}$ as 'man' as Justin did—effectively blunts Tertullian's bluster.

It is plain that the Marcionites did not take the main protagonist of the gospel—the one 'marked' by the *nomen sacrum* $\overline{IS}$ in the manuscripts—to be the expected Christ of the Jewish scriptures.[33] Given Tertullian's relentless effort to consolidate all divine titles into one almighty ruler of the universe, this understanding is repeatedly condemned. But Jews and Samaritans always understood that the one who is to come is distinct from the divinity. A frequent criticism that Tertullian levels against the sect is that they deny the scriptures. Nevertheless, at other places in his writings the Church Father admits that the Marcionite version of the Pauline writings retained at least some reference to the Jewish writings.[34] Moreover, other sources on the Marcionites revealed that they had developed interpretations of the Pentateuch, Isaiah and Daniel.

Tertullian's reporting on the Marcionites suffers from his own religious fanaticism. Instead of allowing for the possibility that the Marcionites represented a continuation of a Jewish tradition that venerated more than one divine power, he interprets their veneration of another god beside the Creator as proof that they hate the God he presumes to be the ruler of the universe. Because the Marcionites distinguished their beloved divinity Man from the 'Christ' manifest through the Jewish scriptures, Tertullian claimed they denied prophecy. In other words, the evidence seems to suggest that the Marcionites like other of the earliest sects of Christians understood 'Man' and 'Christ' to be separate entities. It is a pity the Church Fathers won't let us hear what these traditions actually had to say. But what evidence is preserved all points to them continuing the Oniad tradition of Philo of Alexandria.[35]

The twin theses of this Oniad tradition—namely that 'Man' was a secret divinity in the Pentateuch, and Joshua was the awaited 'one like

---

[33] Tertullian, *Against Marcion*, 3.2.
[34] Cf the discussion in D.S. Williams, "Reconsidering Marcion's Gospel," *JBL* 108. (1989): pp. 477–496.
[35] Cf Lieu, *Marcion*, p. 78; Tyson, *Marcion and Luke-Acts*, p. 44.

Moses'—ultimately became heretical or obscured thanks to the efforts of men like Tertullian. That Alexandrian Judaism perpetuated the understanding that Man was the god of the gospel is confirmed by the writings of Clement of Alexandria.[36] With respect to the latter exegesis, the ancient Jewish understanding was preserved by a relatively obscure Alexandrian presbyter named Ammonius Sakkas who was the teacher of Clement's successor, Origen.[37] As a respected philosopher, Ammonius' understanding of the scriptures was necessarily shaped by established exegesis.[38] It is the soundness of Ammonius' methodology which will ultimately help us unravel the role that Jesus had in a gospel almost wholly devoted to $\overline{IS}$.

There were—and still are[39]—traditions which venerate, or at least acknowledge, the existence of a heavenly god man named $\overline{IS}$. It is reasonable to presume that there were traditions which identified the founder of Christianity as this angel. These traditions necessarily depended on Alexandrian Judaism. While Philo was the visible 'face' of this tradition, the evidence leads me to conclude that Philo was only a leading member of a tradition of exegesis I identify as Oniad Judaism. When Ptolemy fled Judea with the leading priestly families, they brought with them the earliest traditions for understanding and interpreting the Pentateuch. Alexandrian Judaism not only venerated the angel Man but, as I will show—the earliest understanding of the person of Christ.[40]

The Jews and Samaritans who came over to Egypt with Ptolemy identified the one who was to come as the Patriarch Joshua—or if you will in

---

[36] Cf Runia, Philo in Early Christian Literature, pp. 4f.

[37] Cf Lillia, Clement of Alexandria: A Study in Christian Platonism and Gnosticism (London, 1975), pp. 5f.

[38] It seems impossible to believe that some whom no less an authority than Porphyry declares as having "attained the greatest proficiency in philosophy of any in our day, derived much benefit from his teacher in the knowledge of the sciences" (Eusebius, *Church History* 6.19.5-7) could have maintained anything but a reasonable and rational interpretation of the prophecies of the 'Old Testament.'

[39] Clement of Alexandria, *Instructor* 1.7.

[40] Tsedaka, ed. and trans. by Sullivan ed., *The Israelite Samaritan Version of the-Torah*, p. 3.

Greek—*Jesus*. This pre-existent Alexandrian Jewish interpretation clearly makes its way into Alexandrian Christianity.[41] My book stitches together how these two core Alexandrian exegeses—i.e., the angel $\overline{IS}$ and the Christ Jesus—went on to shape the composition of the gospel, or at least the gospel used in the Christian mystery religion of Alexandria. As much as it would have helped the sales of my book if I sensationally claimed that Jesus never appeared in earliest Christianity, the evidence won't quite let me do that.[42] I think 'Jesus' does finally make an appearance in the original gospel of Alexandria but much later than anyone would have ever suspected.

At the core of the gospel is the understanding that IS comes into the world to fulfill the 'Deuteronomic' prophecy of the one like Moses—that is, to 'raise' the Patriarch Joshua in the final section of the gospel. Let me go through a few of my assumptions. The mystic Gospel of Mark referenced in Clement's *Letter to Theodore* was the Alexandrian mystery gospel.[43] This text allows us to infer the existence of an ahistorical gospel narrative as, by Clement's own description, it is focused on symbolism rather than 'history.'[44] Thus it is not an overstatement to say that the Alexandrian community which venerated this gospel was less interested in having a historical founder than a supernatural foundation. They wanted

---

[41] P. Sigal, *The Emergence of Contemporary Judaism*. (Pittsburgh: Pickwick Press, 1980), vol. 1, p. 311.
[42] For instance, Justin acknowledges the existence of the angel Man from Judaism and his role in the typology of Joshua.
[43] For a background on the discovered text, cf my article (with D. Gullotta), "Quentin Quesnell's Secret Mark Secret," *Vigiliae christianae* 71, (2017), pp. 353-378. On the appropriateness of the title 'mystic gospel' as opposed to 'secret gospel,' cf S. Brown, *Mark's Other Gospel: Rethinking Morton Smith's Controversial Discovery* (Waterloo, Ontario, 2005).
[44] Already in Adele Yarbro Collins, *The Beginning of the Gospel: Probings of Mark in Context* (Minneapolis: Fortress, 1992), p. 27: "Mark focuses on Jesus and his identity not in the interest of establishing his character or essence, but in order to write a particular kind of history...defined as a narration of the course of the eschatological events." Collins' "apocalyptic historical monograph" necessarily becomes weakened to a mere "apocalyptic monographic" when the outlandish claims of mystic Mark are accepted as original to the text.

to be like the angels and so—like the very *Ishim* or 'Essenes' they claimed as their forefathers, they had as their head an angel named 'Man.'[45]

So it was that the controversial scene from the gospel which is the subject of Clement's correspondence—the resurrection of an unnamed youth across the Jordan River—provided them with that metaphysical hope. What the Savior did to this youth changed human history and in fact ultimately stood outside of human history as such. What happens 'across the Jordan' in a sense takes place outside of the natural order of things. It was understood to be an event foretold in the aforementioned 'Deuteronomic' prophecy. What we are witnessing through Mark's storytelling is the resurrection of the Patriarch Joshua—that is, Jesus, the one like Moses—in the person of the unnamed youth. It is of critical importance to see that the youth was not originally named 'Jesus.' Before the 'event' he clearly went by another name. Clement of Alexandria might have understood the youth to have been Philip the disciple, saying that "when the Lord put his passions to death he rose from the grave and lived to Christ."[46]

Whatever the case, the actual gospel does not give us his prehistory because the text isn't interested in history. It is concerned only with the fact that prophecy has been fulfilled. We are meant to know only that after his resurrection 'Jesus' was in the world *as promised*. We can piece together his new identity from the clues that appear in the narrative. Up until that point preserved in mystic Mark, the angel Man was wandering about Judea attempting to demonstrate to the people that he was the god known to their ancestors.[47] This is the first part of the narrative that takes

---

[45] Clement of Alexandria, *Exhortation to the Greeks* 10. 106. 5: "Believe Man, man and God; believe, Man, suffered and adored. Believe, ye slaves, Him who died; believe, all ye of human kind, Him who alone is God of all men."
(πίστευσον, ἄνθρωπε, ἀνθ ρώπῳ καὶ θεῷ· πίστευσον, ἄνθρωπε, τῷ παθόντι καὶ προσκυνουμένῳ, θεῷ ζῶντι πιστεύσατε οἱ δοῦλοι τῷ νεκρῷ· πάντες ἄνθρωποι πιστεύσατε μόνῳ τῷ πάντων ἀνθρώπων θεῷ· πιστεύσατε καὶ μισθὸν λάβετε σωτηρίαν).
[46] Clement, *Stromata*, 3.25.4.
[47] Cf. Tertullian, *Against Marcion*, 3.2.

up about five sixths of the book. It sets up the final act of the gospel—$\overline{IS}$ will raise 'Jesus'—that is, the Patriarch Joshua—in the person of the dead youth.

While I have hitherto only referred to this prophecy as 'Deuteronomic,' I wish to qualify that now. It is only understood to be 'Deuteronomic' owing to deliberate changes which were made to the text of Exodus at the turn of the Common Era.[48] Why Exodus had portions shared with the Book of Deuteronomy excised from the Masoretic text is anyone's guess. The indisputable fact is that it occurred, and it mirrors charges of textual manipulation with respect to the Christian canon in the same period.[49] Thus the mystic gospel of Mark is understood to have been written in a period when the original text of Exodus was presumably widely accessible. The prophecy regarding the one who is to come should now be understood in its original context from the Book of Exodus as explaining why the Oniad tradition in Alexandria identified 'Jesus' as its fulfiller.

Immediately after the giving of the Ten Commandments in the Book of Exodus, God addresses the frightened people, consoling them with the words, "I will raise up for them a prophet like you from among their brethren and will put my words in his mouth. And he shall speak to them all that I command him. And it shall be that the man who will not hear his words which he will speak in my name, I will require it from him."[50]

---

[48] F. Dexinger, "Reflections on the Relationship between Qumran and Samaritan Messianology," *Qumran-Messianism*, ed., J. H. Charlesworth, H. Lichtenberger, and G. S. Oegema, (Tubingen, 1998), pp. 83-99.

[49] Marcionite and Orthodox canons had gospels and apostolic letters with large missing/added portions. But Irenaeus' charge (*Against Heresies* 1.9.3 with a parallel in Tertullian *Prescription Against Heretics* 39.4) that the heretics moved material out of a unified whole is more relevant here. See the discussion in D. Bingham, *Irenaeus' Use of Matthew's Gospel in Adversus Haereses*. Traditio. Exegetica Graeca 7 (Leuven: Peeters, 1998), pp. 17f. The idea is also reinforced in the eastern Christian understanding of the four canonical gospels as 'separated' texts owing to their removal from a unified whole gospel; Cf. W. L. Petersen, *Tatian's Diatessaron: Its Creation, Dissemination, Significance and History in Scholarship*. VC Sup 25. (Leiden: Brill, 1994).

[50] Tsedaka, ed., and trans. by Sullivan, ed., *The Israelite Samaritan Version of the Torah*, p. 234.

The idea is clearly that they should be frightened of him—i.e., God—but that another will come after Moses whom they should heed. If they do not adhere to what he says God will punish them. The lengthy proclamation continues through a variety of other subjects down through to the end of Exodus chapter 23. It is here that a closing section begins with some hints of 'what will happen in the future' which in my mind must have served as the basis for the construction of the gospel narrative.

The closing words of this lengthy speech were clearly understood to foretell the role that $\overline{IS}$ will have setting up 'the one like Moses.' We read:

> See, I am sending an angel ahead of you to guard you along the way and to bring you to the place I have prepared. Pay attention to him and listen to what he says. Do not rebel against him; he will not forgive your rebellion, since my Name is in him.

The echo of what would become the opening words of the Gospel of Mark are not coincidental. The gospel is rooted in this section in Exodus. The warning against not heeding $\overline{IS}$ is clearly understood to be the cause of the destruction of Jerusalem. But it is worth also noting that what follows in Exodus chapter 23 was originally read as 'predicting' the conquest of Canaan by Joshua. The language is unmistakable. The angel $\overline{IS}$ will clear the way for Joshua, the one like Moses.[51]

---

[51] Cf the argument in the last chapters of Justin's *Dialogue*: "And it is plain that this was spoken not of Judah, but of Christ. For all we out of all nations do expect not Judah, but Jesus, who led your fathers out of Egypt. For the prophecy referred even to the advent of Christ: 'Till He come for whom this is laid up, and He shall be the expectation of nations.' Jesus came, therefore, as we have shown at length, and is expected again to appear above the clouds; whose name you profane, and labour hard to get it profaned over all the earth (Dial. 120)...and the name of Jesus laid up in your understandings; saying that this is He who would blot out the memorial of Amalek from under heaven. Now it is clear that the memorial of Amalek remained after the son of Nave (Nun): but He makes it manifest through Jesus, who was crucified, of whom also those symbols were fore-announcements of all that would happen to Him, the demons would be destroyed, and would dread His name, and that all principalities and kingdoms would fear Him; and that they who believe in Him out of all nations would be shown as God-

While this was certainly the normative manner of reading the material—i.e. that it pertained to Joshua the son of Nun. This plainly authoritative reading of Exodus could easily give way to a still future revelation of Joshua redivivus.[52] That the mystic gospel of Mark was one such text is manifestly evident from the narrative cited by Clement. It is based, in my opinion, on the 'final clue' thrown into the original Exodus narrative. Moses goes up to the top of the mountain, first with an assembly of the leading men of Israel, but finally only with Joshua in order to reinforce that he is the one to come:

> Then Moses set out with Joshua his aide, and Moses went up on the mountain of God. He said to the elders, "Wait here for us until we come back to you."...When Moses went up on the mountain, the cloud covered it, and the glory of the LORD settled on Mount Sinai. For six days the cloud covered the mountain, and on the seventh day the LORD called to Moses from within the cloud. To the Israelites the glory of the LORD looked like a consuming fire on top of the mountain. Then Moses entered the cloud as he went on up the mountain.

In no uncertain terms, Joshua stands outside the tent to reinforce that he is 'next in line' to the described 'divinization process.' In other words, this is the final sign in Exodus that Joshua is the 'one like Moses.'

---

fearing and peaceful men... Yet after this you made a calf, and were very zealous in committing fornication with the daughters of strangers, and in serving idols. And again, when the land was given up to you with so great a display of power, that you witnessed the sun stand still in the heavens by the order of that man whose name was Jesus, and not go down for thirty-six hours, as well as all the other miracles which were wrought for you as time served; and of these it seems good to me now to speak of another, for it conduces to your hereby knowing Jesus, whom we also know to have been Christ the Son of God, who was crucified, and rose again, and ascended to heaven, and will come again to judge all men, even up to Adam himself." (ibid., 131, 132).

[52] R. Pummer, Early Christian Authors on Samaritans & Samaritanism: Texts, Translations & Commentary, TSAJ 92. (Tübingen: Mohr Siebeck, 2002), p. 26.

Marvin Meyer points out quite convincingly that the scene in mystic Mark is developed from this very narrative in Exodus.[53] The youth waits for 'six days' and then is finally initiated on the seventh day. This is not coincidental because the resurrected youth is now Joshua redivivus. As such the mystic gospel of Mark provides us with the exact point in which 'Jesus' was originally introduced into the narrative. Not at the beginning of the gospel. Not with the baptism by John which plainly absent in heretical gospels such as that employed by the Marcionite. 'Jesus' is only introduced five sixths of the way through the original narrative because of the 'one like Moses' prophesy originally found in the Book of Exodus.

By now my readers have heard me make several references to the fraction 'five sixths.' The reason I keep hearkening back to this bizarre statistic is that it happens to have been the number established by the Hexateuchal model for the arrangement of the gospel according to the brilliant Anglican scholar Austin Farrer.[54] While Farrer is best known for his arguments against Q—i.e. the hypothetical source or 'quelle' for various sayings found only in Matthew and Luke—Farrer also speculated about the structure of the Gospel of Matthew, arguing that it was arranged in sections which conformed to the Hexateuch—i.e., the first six books of the Bible. Thus, according to the parallel arrangement of mystic Mark, the resurrection of the youth happens to conform to the 'Joshua section' of Farrer's study of Matthew. I think this is deeply significant.

According to Farrer's model, the resurrection narrative of the mystic gospel of Mark occupies the very starting point of the 'Joshua' section of this Hexateuchal model. While Farrer had absolutely no knowledge of this letter of Clement when he devised his scheme, there are clearly a number of clues in the Letter *to Theodore* which strengthen Farrer's presumptions about Matthew—albeit making mystic Mark something of a

---

[53] Marvin Meyer, *Secret Gospels: Essays on Thomas and the Secret Gospel of Mark*. (Harrisburg, Pa.: Trinity Press International, 2003), p. 124.
[54] A. Farrer, "On Dispensing with Q," in *Studies in the Gospels: Essays in Memory of R. H. Lightfoot*, Dennis E. Nineham, ed. (Oxford: Basil Blackwell, 1955), pp. 55-88.

proto-Matthew. Indeed, understanding mystic Mark as proto-Matthew might have already taken place in the writings of Ammonius. Aside from a lost text which demonstrated 'Jesus' was the one like Moses, Ammonius was most famous for his canons for a 'harmony of the gospels.'[55] This latter work placed parallel passages of the last three Gospels alongside the text of Matthew, effectively demonstrating that the latter was the source for the former.

This arrangement made at the turn of the second century had an important influence on both Origen and Eusebius in their reconstructions of the relations between the gospels. However, it should be noted that Ammonius isn't remembered only for an arrangement (or 'canon') for understanding how the four gospels *could* 'run together' as one continuous narrative, but for also having in his possession an actual 'gospel harmony.'[56] In other words, Ammonius was associated with a text which arranged the stories from Matthew through John in one continuous narrative. Could this 'super gospel' have been none other than the Alexandrian mystic gospel mentioned in the letter to Theodore? I strongly suspect so. Moreover, I think we get a glimpse of this super gospel in what is now—under Eusebius's handiwork—identified as a 'Commentary on Matthew.' I assume that it was—in its original form—a commentary on his master's super gospel.[57]

In any event, there are clear signs and features that the mystic gospel of Alexandria had features which resembled known gospel harmonies

---

[55] Eusebius, "*Ad Carpianus Ammonius the Alexandrian*, having employed much industry and effort (as was proper), has left us the fourfold Gospel, placing the corresponding passages of the other evangelists beside the Gospel of Matthew so that the continuous thread of the other three is necessarily broken, preventing a consecutive reading." Trans. Timothy D. Barnes in *Constantine and Eusebius* (Cambridge: Harvard University Press, 1981), p. 121.
[56] Petersen, *Diatessaron*, pp. 34f.
[57] Cf my forthcoming article on this, but also T. S. Memes, *The Christian Treasury: A Selection of Standard Treatises on Subjects of Doctrinal and Practical Christianity*, p. 32. It would be nothing short of incredible if Origen did not use his master's tables during the composition of the *Commentary*. I strongly suspect the dependence went beyond that.

used, e.g., by the school of Justin Martyr.[58] It is not that difficult to imagine that Christianity—in the period before the last generation of the second century—was wholly dominated by the fulfillment of the Joshua redivivus paradigm. Then Ammonius becomes a critical figure for our understanding of the transmission of the Alexandrian tradition. For Ammonius helps provide circumstantial evidence that the gospel used by Alexandrian Christians resembled Matthew with the Hexateuchal structure identified by Farrer and others.

As already noted, Ammonius was a respected Platonic instructor who was born a Christian and ultimately became an apostate—that is, he lapsed back into pagan philosophy. We know that he wrote a work entitled "The Agreement between Moses and Jesus," which was incorporated into Book Three of Eusebius' *Demonstration of the Gospel*.[59] The core argument in that text is suspiciously similar to the traditional Oniad interpretation of Deuteronomy 18:15—namely, 'Jesus' (that is, Joshua) was the awaited one like Moses. As with Eusebius' handling of Ammonius' canon, he expands the philosopher's original argument. But Ammonius himself would have certainly read Deuteronomy as if it pertained to Jesus son of Nave. We should think that such erudition would effectively prevent the wildly fanciful 'prophetic proofs' developed by less intelligent Church Fathers.[60]

---

[58] Petersen, *Diatessaron*, p. 35.
[59] Cf. J. E. Bruns, "The Agreement of Moses and Jesus in the *Demonstratio Evangelica* of Eusebius," *VC* 31. (1977), pp. 117–125.
[60] An example from the existing text of Eusebius: "We must consider thoroughly why this was said. Moses was the first leader of the Jewish race. He found them attached to the deceitful polytheism of Egypt, and was the first to turn them from it, by enacting the severest punishment for idolatry. He was the first also to publish the theology of the one God, bidding them worship only the Creator and Maker of all things. He was the first to draw up for the same hearers a scheme of religious life and is acknowledged to have been the first and only lawgiver of their religious polity. But Jesus Christ too, like Moses, only on a grander stage, was the first to originate the teaching according to holiness for the other nations, and first accomplished the route of the idolatry that embraced (b) the whole world. He was the first to introduce to all men the knowledge and religion of the one

Where exactly would this leave his gospel and its relation to Jesus the one like Moses? Let's start with the working hypothesis that the unnamed youth initiated into the 'mystery of the kingdom of heaven' becomes Joshua redivivus. Mysteries of kingship necessarily invoke the original king of Israel.[61] I won't enumerate all the arguments that appear in my book which identify the 'Joshua' theme of the passage in question. But I can at least summarize them as follows. First, *context*, the initiation taking place where the Patriarch Joshua crossed into the Promised Land; second, *language*, because mystic Mark speaks of one of the two men in the narrative 'arising' in an apparent allusion back to the Joshua prophecy, and, third, *symbolism*, when the raised man crosses the Jordan like Joshua at the beginning of the Jewish year during a Jubilee which accounts for the 'redemptive' language elsewhere in this section.

There's another way of looking at this. Justin identifies the final appearance of $\overline{IS}$ in the Hexateuch as that before Joshua immediately preceding the destruction of Jericho.[62] The scene itself must have been originally understood as the fulfillment of the two prophecies from Exodus—viz. "I will send my angel" (i.e., $\overline{IS}$) and "I will raise one like Moses" (i.e., Joshua). But I strongly suspect the gospel was developed to provide another fulfillment narrative. Now $\overline{IS}$ raises Joshua redivivus on the other side of the Jordan in the person of the resurrected youth. The raising of Joshua—i.e., the bringing back of the paradigmatic king of Israel—is to destroy Jerusalem for the sin of the Jewish people for not recognizing IS.

Almighty God. And He is proved to be the first Author and Lawgiver of a new life and of a system adapted to the holy" (*Demonstratio* 3.2.90, 91). The words apply more logically to the 'historical' Joshua than the Jesus of the gospel.

[61] Cf. Ian Wilson, *Kingship and Memory in Ancient Judah*. (New York: Oxford University Press, 2017), p. 71: "As Knauf notes, in Samaritan tradition, Joshua becomes the first king of Israel when he succeeds Moses as the people's leader. In the *Samaritan Chronicle* (a.k.a. "Samaritan Book of Joshua" [Sam Josh]: a text from the medieval period) God, via Moses, 'invest[s] him with kingly authority' (Sam Josh 2), and throughout the book Joshua is called 'the king.'" Thus 'the mystery of the kingdom of God' from a Samaritan perspective is at once quite compatible with mysteries of Joshua—even Joshua redivivus.

[62] Justin, *Dialogue*, 34, 61, 62.

Ammonius' student Origen already sees Jesus' entry into Jerusalem as a gospel parallel with Joshua's destruction of Jericho.[63] But our hypothesis would take this one step further. The early Christians read Exodus as if it foretold the events surrounding the end of the Jewish religion of sacrifices. The choice of Joshua redivivus as the one chosen to bring this to an end, might seem odd at first. But this begins to make sense when we take note of a hitherto unrecognized disconnect between the Pentateuch and the Book of Joshua. In the former, Moses established a priesthood to offer perpetual sacrifices (*olat tamid*) on the altar of the desert tabernacle. But the Book of Joshua makes clear that once Israel leaves the wilderness and crosses the Jordan, the *olat tamid* disappear. This apparently did not escape the notice of the author of the mystic gospel.

Joshua's first act as it were is the destruction of Ai. Notice at once that accompanying the catastrophe is a crucifixion—"[Joshua] impaled the body of the king of Ai on a pole and left it there until evening. At sunset, Joshua ordered them to take the body from the pole and throw it down at the entrance of the city gate" (Joshua 8:9). Ammonius' student Origen clearly understands that 'a mystery' was contained in the crucifixion of the king of Ai. It foreshadowed the 'double crucifixion' of the gospel—viz. where at once "the Son of God was indeed visibly crucified in the flesh, but invisibly on that cross the Devil 'with his principalities and authorities was affixed.'"[64] Once again, the Book of Joshua is a seminal influence over the Passion narrative of the gospel.

And then there is the whole idea of the Patriarchs being able to 'reincarnate' in future ages. The Jewish doctrine of *gilgul* or metempsychosis is as old as the Book of Job. But the specific understanding that prophets could come back is embraced again by Origen. There is a strong sign that Christian metempsychosis was rooted in Platonism. The Carpocratians, the only ancient sect specifically linked with the mystic gospel, were especially attached to this doctrine.[65] I demonstrate in my book that the very

---

[63] Origen, Homilies on Joshua, 10.2.
[64] Origen, Homilies on Joshua, 8. 3.
[65] Irenaeus, *Against Heresies*, 1.25.4.

phrase which prompts Clement's dispatch of a letter to Theodore—'naked by naked'—is taken from a famous discussion of reincarnation in the contemporary Platonic philosopher Maximus of Tyre.[66] There can be no doubt, then, that the Christian Platonism of the Alexandrian Church could have supported a belief in Joshua redivivus.

Origen makes this clear in his examination of the gospel passage which tells of Herod's suspicion that John the Baptist is the resurrected Elijah:

John was not Elijah in actuality, as those who hold the doctrine of transmigration say, alleging that the soul of Elijah came in John. For he does not say "in the soul of Elijah"—because it was not a transmigration—but he says "in the spirit and power of Elijah." For there was spirit and power upon Elijah, that is, a spiritual gift as it happened to each one of the prophets.[67]

In other words, it stands to reason that, if one prophet was 'brought back' into the world in the person of John, that Joshua could have been brought back in the youth of the mystery gospel. Origen clearly hints at that when he speaks of a "spirit" associated with each of the prophets.

Therefore we necessarily conclude that Ammonius could well have accepted that Joshua—that is, Jesus—came into the gospel narrative through metempsychosis. Joshua was the one divinely appointed king of Israel. He could rightly be interpreted to be the paradigmatic 'Christ' of Israel based on the expectations set forth in the Pentateuch. The evidence suggests that in Alexandria at least the ancient expectation for Joshua redivivus was sublimated into a mystery rite in which individuals were baptized to become living reincarnations of Joshua. As such, given that the gospel was written as a mystery religion text, Christianity could well have had a historical origin without having a historical founder named Jesus.

Philo's absolute silence regarding the person of Joshua is also very intriguing. Could the Alexandrian Jewish community have already expected a Joshua redivivus appearance? The messianic pretender Theudas who

---

[66] Maximus of Tyre, *Discourses*, 30.
[67] Origen, Commentary on Matthew, 13.1.

would part the river Jordan seems to confirm such an expectation in the Jewish community at large.[68] Theudas was a Joshua, but he was 'Joshua' in the sense of being a living tabernacle for the spirit of Joshua son of Nun. The manner in which Theudas' followers understood 'Jesus' to have reappeared in the world precludes 'Jesus' from being a historical person. The same thing is true when we turn to examine the gospel. I don't think mystery texts should be employed to help reconstruct history. The gospel tells us a lot about Alexandrian Jews but very little about their Jesus—*other than that he never actually lived in the Common Era.*

---

[68] Josephus, *Antiquities of the Jews*, 20, 97-99.

Chapter 12: Jesus: Pre-Existent and Non-Existent
By Robert M. Price

Theophany and the Sacred King

Christian doctrine, following the Gospel of John, holds that Jesus Christ existed in heaven with God as the Word, a cosmic principle of creation and proportion, as described by Heraclitus, the Stoics, and Philo of Alexandria. Then he entered human history as Jesus of Nazareth. In a strange way, though there actually was no "historical Jesus" (at least in my considered opinion), he did indeed possess a long pre-history. I want to sketch the broad outline of that history here.

In my view, both Jesus Mythicists and Jesus Historicists have neglected an important aspect of Israelite religion/mythology, namely the Royal Ideology of the Sacred King.[1] In a sense, this myth is older not only than the New Testament but also even than the Old. Several passing references to it remain as suggestive vestiges of the myth in this and that Old Testament passage, but the implied story was purged by the

---

[1] Ivan Engnell, *Studies in Divine Kingship in the Ancient Near East*. (Uppsala: Almqvist & Wiksells Boktryckeri, 1943); Sigmund Mowinckel, trans. by D.R. Ap-Thomas, *The Psalms in Israel's Worship*. (Nashville: Abingdon, 1962); Aage Bentzen, *King and Messiah*. Lutterworth Studies in Church and State. (London: Lutterworth Press, 1955); Geo Widengren, "Early Hebrew Myths and their Interpretation" in S.H. Hooke, ed., *Myth, Ritual and Kingship: Essays on the Theory and Practice of Kingship in the Ancient Near East and in Israel*. (New York: Oxford University Press, 1958).

Deuteronomic School in their thoroughgoing retooling of Israelite religion.[2] In ancient Near Eastern monarchies, the divine mandate of the king was renewed annually at the New Year Festival. In full view of the crowd, the king would submit to being slapped and ear-tweaked by the high priest. The priest even knocked the crown off the king's head. Why? The end of the year marked the exhaustion of vegetation, and this signified the ebbing of divine favor because of the sins of the people during the year just past. The symbolic suffering of the humiliated king denoted his role as the representative of his nation and his atonement for their sins. He would also engage in a mock battle with men in a dragon costume. He would first pretend defeat, then rise up victorious. Regaining his crown, he would then mount the temple steps, enter in and, behind closed doors, ascend into heaven (of which all temples were microcosms),[3] where he would be vouchsafed a glimpse of the heavenly Tablets of Destiny, preparing him to meet the challenges of the coming year.[4]

As below, so above (cf. Matt. 16:19): the king was miming the primordial victory whereby the young warrior god (Yahweh, Baal, Marduk, and, farther afield, Indra, Zeus, and Odin) had engaged the Chaos Dragons (Leviathan, Rahab, Lotan, Mot, Yamm, etc.) in combat (Ps. 74:14; Isa. 2:1; Job 26:12-13; Ps. 89:10; Isa. 51:9) only to be first slain, then devoured, and finally resurrected, often by the help of his consort. He slew the monster from the inside out, whereupon the other gods hailed him as their new king. Then he fashioned the world from the remains of the monsters. As Yahweh had become king of gods, so had the king renewed his role as Yahweh's counterpart on earth.

---

[2] Margaret Barker, The Older Testament: The Survival of Themes from the Ancient Royal Cult in Sectarian Judaism and Early Christianity. (Sheffield: Phoenix Press, 2005), e.g., pp. 96-97, 145, 191-192.
[3] Mircea Eliade, *The Sacred and the Profane: The Nature of Religion*. Trans. Willard Trask. (New York: Harcourt, Brace & World, 1959), pp. 40-43, 58-62; Margaret Barker, The Gate of Heaven: The History and Symbolism of the Temple in Jerusalem (London: SPCK Press, 1991), pp. 63-64, 74.
[4] Geo Widengren, *The Ascension of the Apostle and the Heavenly Book*. King and Saviour III Uppsala Universitets Arskrift 1950:7. (Uppsala: A.B. Lundequistska Bokhandeln, 1957), pp. 20-21.

This myth long survived the end of the Israelite and Jewish (and other) monarchies, the kingship ritual morphing into purely agricultural rites in which the death and resurrection of a savior deity (Attis, Adonis, Osiris, Tammuz, etc.) guaranteed renewed fertility. Subsequently, in the Hellenistic age, these agricultural rituals evolved into cults of mystical initiation and spiritual rebirth. Geo Widengren drew a direct line between Babylonian creation myths and much later Manichean redeemer myths.[5]

Mythicists (and other critical New Testament scholars who do not go quite so far) suggest that the Christian savior Jesus began as one of these deities (or was at least remodeled in their likeness by Christian converts from competing Mystery Religions who brought some of their familiar beliefs with them).[6] Given the many striking similarities, it seems hard to deny that Jesus either began as a dying-and-rising Mystery cult savior or became one. For instance, Jesus' "words of institution" at the Last Supper, though offered to gospel readers as a reinterpretation of the Passover, makes absolutely no sense that way. Jewish blood drinking, even metaphorically? Instead, with its explanation of sacramental bread as the body of the Savior and of the wine as his blood, we are very obviously dealing with fertility sacraments like those of the equivalent deities Dionysus and Osiris.

But these similarities may not stem synchronically from contemporary Mystery Religions. They may just as well go back much further. As Widengren argues, the ancient, pre-Deuteronomic Israelite cult of Yahweh must already have featured the death and resurrection of a savior God, Yahweh himself. He was already like Marduk and Aleyan Baal

---

[5] Geo Widengren, *Mesopotamian Elements in Manichaeism (King and Saviour II)*. Studies in Manichaean, Mandaean, and Syrian-Gnostic Religion. Uppsala Universitets Arskrift, 1946:3. (Uppsala: A.B. Lundequistska Bokhandeln, 1946).

[6] Richard Reitzenstein, trans. by John E. Steely, *Hellenistic Mystery-Religions: Their Basic Ideas and Significance*, Pittsburgh Theological Monograph Series 15. (Pittsburgh: Pickwick Press, 1978), p. 149; Wilhelm Bousset, *Kyrios Christos: A History of the Belief in Christ from the Beginnings of Christianity to Irenaeus*, Trans. John E. Steely. (New York: Abingdon Press, 1970), Section III, "The Gentile Christian Primitive Community," pp. 119-152.

before he was like Attis or Mithras. Widengren[7] points to the ritual acclamation "Yahweh lives!" (Psalm 18:46) as an exact parallel to the joyful proclamation, "Aleyan Baal lives!" and the announcement by the priests of Attis at his resurrection feast, "Rejoice, ye of the Mystery! For your god is saved! And we, too, shall be saved from ills!"

As is well-known, "Jesus" or "Yeshua" means "Yahweh Saves," a perfect name for one believed to have come to earth as the avatar of Yahweh on a saving mission. And, according to Margaret Barker,[8] that is what early Jewish Christians believed Jesus to be. Yahweh had many times appeared as a theophany to Israelites in the past (Genesis 16:7-14; 18:16-21; 21:17; Joshua 5:13-15; Judges 6:11-24; 13:2-20), and there was nothing to say he hadn't done so again in recent history. As per Deuteronomy 32:8-9, Yahweh was the divine Son of El Elyon, as Baal was El's son and Marduk was Ea's. This was the Father of whom Jesus speaks in the gospels. Barker reminds us that Jesus is never called "the Son of the Lord," i.e., of Yahweh, but only "the Son of God," i.e., El. And if Jesus was supposed to be the theophanic avatar of Yahweh, his death and resurrection were already part of the myth package centuries before Christianity began.

The old Sacred King mythos continued in popular Jewish Messianism: like the ancient kings, Jesus was the Christ ("Anointed," Psalm 2:1), the Son (Psalm 2:7), the atoning sin-bearer (Isaiah 53:4-6), the victor over the Infernal Powers, and the Risen One. We have long heard that Christian Christology did not reflect the Messiah-concept of "normative Judaism," which is why few Jews ever acknowledged Jesus as their Messiah. The Jewish Messiah was not believed to be divine or to die and rise, much less to atone for sin. Where did Christians get these ideas? Why, from the still-pervasive myth of the Sacred King. Deuteronomic and, later, Rabbinic Judaism had dropped these features and redefined the expected Messiah as a merely human heir to David who should restore Jewish sovereignty. The more modest Messiah concept was of a piece with the

---

[7] Widengren, "Early Hebrew Myths and their Interpretation," p. 191.
[8] Margaret Barker, *The Great Angel: A Study of Israel's Second God*. (Louisville: Westminster/John Knox Press, 1992), pp. 192 ff.

Deuteronomic repudiation of the old Jewish polytheism and the later Rabbinic suppression of the recurring mystical doctrine of "two powers in heaven."[9]

But old doctrines die hard, and when they do, they tend to rise from the dead. When supposedly critical New Testament scholars tell us that no one would have invented a belief in a crucified Messiah because it was unprecedented in Judaism, they are captive to the Rabbinic apologetics which seek to pretend that Orthodoxy goes all the way back to Moses.

No News Is Good News

A cardinal tenet of Mythicism is that writers who might have been expected to mention Jesus do not. A strange silence, given the spectacular splash Jesus is said by the four evangelists to have made. Imagine, if you will, the editor of The Galilee Gazette sifting through various articles submitted by his staff reporters. "Hmmm... not a lot of room left in the issue! Here's something: 'Man raises the dead and walks on water.' Tempting, but I'd better use this piece on the Capernaum Flower Show instead."

Christian apologists and mainstream scholars would like to think we do have one ancient mention of Jesus as an historical individual, namely, the Testimonium Flavianum, a highly disputed paragraph in Josephus' Antiquities of the Jews. Even to its defenders it is an embarrassment that Josephus (if indeed it is really he) forthrightly says of Jesus, "He was the Christ." William Whiston, eighteenth-century translator of Josephus' works, understood the implication: Josephus must have been a Christian! Because if he wasn't, he'd never have said this! Especially since he was famously on record saying that Vespasian was the Christ!

Whiston was half right: whoever wrote the Testimonium was indeed a Christian; he just wasn't Josephus. Most likely the author was Eusebius,

---

[9] Alan F. Siegel, *Two Powers in Heaven: Early Rabbinic Reports about Christianity and Gnosticism*, Studies in Judaism in Late Antiquity. (Leiden: E.J. Brill, 1977), vol. 25.

the fourth-century church historian, who was the first to "quote" it—because he interpolated it into Josephus' book. Ken Olson[10] has demonstrated that Eusebius fabricated a passage designed quite specifically to vindicate his Christology against the opinions of pagan critics to whom he was replying. It fits too well; it is "tendentious." He wanted to give the impression that the "truth" about Jesus was confirmed by even a non-Christian source.

Paul J. Hopper[11] has put the Testimonium under the microscope, showing how the structure of the sentences, in which Pontius Pilate is merely mentioned in subordinate clauses, in modifying phrases, and in the passive voice, is completely at variance with that of the adjacent paragraphs in which Pilate is the primary subject. These two pieces of research, I think, are the final nails in the apologetics coffin containing the Testimonium.

But conservatives just cannot let the passage go. It has become fashionable to suggest that the basis of the passage is genuinely Josephan, though it has been subject to Christian interpolations: in short, all the bits that mark the author as a Christian believer, the ones that disqualify the passage in the eyes of critics. How does it escape them that they are just laundering a bad piece of "evidence" to make it fit their project? The more modest remnant of the Testimonium fits the demythologized "historical Jesus" whittled by critical scholars.

Let us suppose their modest, bowdlerized version is as authentic as they say. They would have simply traded a bad problem for one that is much worse, for now the question must be asked: how could this unspectacular historical figure have merited the attention of an historian—or of the early Christians? It would be like saying we have stripped away myths, legends, and inflated reports to reveal a "historical Superman," and he was

---

[10] Ken Olson, "A Eusebian Reading of the Testimonium Flavianum," in Aaron Johnson and Jeremy Shott, eds., *Eusebius of Caesarea: Tradition and Innovations* (CHS Research Bulletin, vol. 1.0.11). http://chs.harvard.edu/CHS/article/display/5871.
[11] Paul J. Hopper, "A Narrative Anomaly in Josephus: Jewish Antiquities xviii, 63." Available at: https://www.academia.edu/9494231/A_Narrative_Anomaly_in_Josephus.

only Clark Kent! These half-critics, half-apologists are proud to have disarmed the Mythicist argument that first-century silence about Jesus was only to be expected given that he was really pretty typical for the times. But they have destroyed the village in order to save it! Either a real miracle-working Jesus would have received ancient attention but didn't, hence there was no real historical Jesus; or a modest Jesus who was "human, all too human" shouldn't have received notice but somehow got it anyway!

It is a most amusing irony: in seeking to rehabilitate the Testimonium Flavianum by cutting out inconvenient pieces of it, its defenders are engaged in the same sort of falsification practiced by Eusebius (or whomever) when he slipped the whole counterfeit passage into the text of Josephus which he viewed as inadequate for its silence about Jesus!

Disconnecting the Christ

A related matter concerns Jesus' connection (or lack thereof) to the events and figures of his day. Some of the wondrous events in the life of Jesus in the gospels (e.g., annunciation, miraculous conception, deliverance from evil forces seeking to kill him in the crib, child prodigy stories) are also to be found in the stories of Cyrus the Great, Caesar Augustus, Plato, and Alexander the Great, and these men were certainly real historical individuals. Might not Jesus, too, have been a real figure of history? If the others accumulated barnacles of legend on their historical hulls, why not Jesus? The difference turns out to be significant. These others are widely attested as having been integral to world-historical events. To remove them would leave gaping, unfillable holes in the historical fabric. But Jesus is in no way tied securely to the events or figures of the lifetime the gospels assign him.

Was Jesus not persecuted by Herod the Great? Not if the whole story was copied from Josephus' Nativity of Moses. Was he not swept up in the empire-wide census of Quirinius? No, for Roman records know of none such. Did he not stand trial before Herod Antipas? No, because that episode in Luke is plainly copied from Mark's trial of Jesus before Pilate.

Then how about Pilate? Didn't Jesus encounter him at least? No, because the scene is drastically out of character for the historical Pontius Pilate, whose anti-Jewish atrocities are well described by both Josephus and Philo. It is flat-out impossible for Pilate to have lifted a finger to save Jesus, much less for him to have caved before the intimidations of a crowd of nameless rabble in the streets. And to release a convicted anti-Roman insurrectionist instead? Nonsense. Was not Jesus subjected to a kangaroo court hearing before Caiaphas and the Sanhedrin? Again, simply out of the question. Mark seems not to have realized that the chief priests of the Jews would never have scheduled such a meeting on Passover Eve.

Scripture's Christ

Perhaps the most powerful reason to classify Jesus with Mithras and Krishna as a complete fiction is that virtually every gospel episode is more naturally accounted for as a Christian reworking of older material, most drawn from the Old Testament, though some from Homer and even Josephus. Many scholars have put forth cogent arguments for the secondary, purely literary origin of various gospel narratives, though few seem to see the implication. The Annunciation of Jesus' upcoming birth swarms with elements of the biblical stories of the prophetic calls of Moses, Isaiah, Gideon, and Jeremiah, as well as theophany stories in which the Angel of the Lord blesses a hitherto-barren mother to be.[12] Matthew's Nativity story is rather too close to Josephus' retelling of the Exodus Moses Nativity, substituting Herod the Great for Pharaoh, while Luke's bears more than a little resemblance to the Moses Nativity from the Biblical Antiquities of Pseudo-Philo.[13] Young Jesus demonstrates his dialectical superiority to the scribes even as Josephus (says he) did (Life of Josephus, section 2). He

---

[12] Gerhard Lohfink, trans. by Daniel Coogan, "The Annunciation of the Birth of Jesus," *The Bible: Now I Get it! A Form Criticism Handbook*. (Garden City: Doubleday, 1979), Part III, Chapter 8, pp. 114-126.

[13] Robert M. Price, *The Christ Myth Theory and its Problems*. (Cranford: American Atheist Press, 2011), pp. 154, 169.

is transfigured into solar brilliance atop a mountain, just like Moses. Like Elisha, Jesus multiplies a small amount of food to feed a great number. He strides across the waves even as Hermes did in the Iliad.[14] Asleep in a boat, then awakened by disciples who fear the crashing waves, he stills the storm like Jonah did.[15] The Triumphal Entry and Cleansing of the Temple appear to be derived from Josephus' account of the entry of Simon bar Gioras into the Temple during the Roman siege, greeted by olive-branch-braving crowds.[16]

Jesus' interrogation before the Roman procurator looks like it is based on the questioning (and flogging) of the Jerusalem prophet Jesus Ananias before the procurator Albinus, as we read in Josephus' Wars of the Jews (6.5.3).[17] His crucifixion in Mark's version is a padded rewrite of Psalm 22, to which Matthew adds material from the Wisdom of Solomon.[18] The story of Jesus' cross-mates expiring but not rising probably comes from Josephus' recollection of his petitioning Titus to take three of his friends down from their crosses, after which two die anyway, but the third survives.[19] Matthew mines Zechariah for details such as the betrayal price of 30 silver coins.[20] Much of his Empty Tomb story is composed from bits and pieces mined from the Book of Daniel.[21] Luke's story of Jesus and his disciples on the Emmaus Road is startlingly parallel to a well-known story of Asclepius revealing himself to a couple on the road home and healing the wife who had been disappointed of a miracle back in the god's Epidauros shrine.[22] One hardly need say that the Ascension matches quite

---

[14] Dennis R. MacDonald, "Hydropatetics," *The Homeric Epics and the Gospel of Mark*. (New Haven: Yale University Press, 2000), Chapter 19, pp. 148-153.
[15] Randel Helms, *Gospel Fictions*. (Buffalo: Prometheus Books, 1989), pp. 78-80.
[16] Josephus, *Wars of the Jews*, Books 4-7.
[17] Theodore J. Weeden, The Two Jesuses, Forum New Series 6, 2, Fall 2003.
[18] Price, *Christ Myth Theory*, pp. 147-148.
[19] Life of Josephus, Section 76.
[20] Price, *Christ Myth Theory*, p. 134.
[21] Ibid. pp. 158-159.
[22] Epidauros Stele 2.25. Emma J. Edelstein and Ludwig Edelstein (ed. and trans.), *Asclepius: Collection and Interpretation of the Testimonies*. (Baltimore: Johns

closely that of Moses according to both Philo and Josephus.[23] On and on it goes. There is a good deal more.

Zero Sum

Perhaps the silliest argument offered in refutation of Christ Mythicism is the claim that no such myth could have gathered from the mists and coagulated given the short time span available. This is, it will be recognized, a slight variant of the old standby that the period between Jesus' death and the composition of the gospels would have been insufficient for legends, exaggerations, and fabricated sayings to have clustered about the historical Jesus.[24] That claim turns out to be mistaken,[25] but at least it was coherent. But the extension of it to cover Mythicism is simply absurd. The chronological bottom drops out. If Jesus never existed in the first place, where is the starting point from which to measure the evolution of the Jesus myth? Can there be a more perfectly circular argument? "Jesus must really have existed since not enough time had passed since his earthly life for the myth to have formed."

Why Do You Seek the Historical Among the Myths?

I have reviewed the most important considerations that have led me to favor the Christ Myth hypothesis. No certainty on the question is

---

Hopkins University Press, 1998), p. 234; Also available in Mary R. Lefkowitz and Maureen B. Fant, eds., *Women's Life in Greece and Rome: A Source Book in Translation*. (Baltimore: Johns Hopkins University Press, 1982), p. 122.
[23] Price, *Christ Myth Theory*, pp. 235-237.
[24] John Warwick Montgomery, *History and Christianity*. (Downers Grove: Inter-Varsity Press, 1974), p. 37; F.F. Bruce, *The New Testament Documents: Are They Reliable?*. (Grand Rapids: Eerdmans, 1962), pp. 13-14, 30, 45-46.
[25] Bart D. Ehrman, "Eyewitness Testimonies and our Surviving Gospels"; "Distorted Memories and the Death of Jesus," *Jesus Before Christianity: How the Earliest Christians Remembered, Changed, and Invented their Stories of the Savior*. (New York: HarperOne, 2016), Chapter 3; Chapter 4, pp. 87-130; 131-177.

possible. All historical judgments must be held as provisional, tentative, always potentially open to replacement by some hypothesis that better accounts for the evidence. Or new evidence may be discovered, or newly recognized as evidence. In the present state of the evidence, it seems to me that the burden of proof rests with those who seem so sure of a historical Jesus of Nazareth. Equally, it seems to me, from reading many, many works of apologetics for over four decades, and from publicly debating many apologists, that they defend their Jesus as ineffectually as the disciples did in Gethsemane, wielding the paper swords of special pleading and question begging. They pretend to be objective scholars but are in fact spin doctors for an institution in which they have far too much invested to ever seriously reconsider the issues.

Chapter 13: Mark's Gospel: A Performed Play in Rome

by Danila Oder

This chapter summarizes, then builds on my 2019 book, *The Two Gospels of Mark: Performance and Text*, available at www.thetwogospelsofmark.com.

Executive Summary of the Book

The author known to history as "Mark" was a playwright of Judean ethnicity in Rome. He wrote a play whose protagonist was Jesus, a heavenly being and the Son of YHWH.

At the beginning of the play, Jesus descends from the heavens to the earth on a mission to die. Satan, the antagonist, attempts to divert him from his mission. (The Temptation scene in Matthew 4:1–11 may well be Mark's original scene.) Satan continues to interfere with Jesus' 'career' on earth, mainly via the Satanic spirits. At the end of the play, Jesus dies, then returns to the heavens.

Jesus' 'career' is largely composed of dramatized scenarios that are inherent in or emulate Scripture (LXX plus).

Mark's audience/congregation already knew these scenarios. Their pleasure at recognizing Mark's emulations compensated for the static dramatic quality of some scenes of the play.

The play was performed in a Greek-style, two-level theater in Rome in 90–95 CE.

The play's subject—the earthly career of YHWH's Son—was sectarian and therefore not of interest to the general public. The performance was private. The audience was Mark's congregation and their slaves and guests.

During the scene set in Bethany, the Jesus actor is anointed by a woman. He avers that she will have eternal fame, "wherever the good news is proclaimed in the whole world, what she has done will be told in remembrance of her" (Mark 14:9 NRSV[1]). Yet in the world of the play, no character has even been *praised* by Jesus. The audience expects the promise to the woman to have dramatic consequences within the play. But the woman does not even return to the stage! The promise, however, makes sense if it applies within the world of the *audience*. I suggest that the Jesus actor spoke the promise to the congregation's female patron. *She* played the role of the anointing woman, and came up to the stage for this scene.

The patron was Flavia Domitilla, niece of the emperor Domitian. Flavia is independently documented as a follower of Judean ways. She donated catacombs that were initially decorated with Judean motifs, then with Christian ones—the earliest Christian catacombs in Rome. We can infer that she belonged to a congregation with a Judean identity that evolved into a Christian identity.

Mark wrote a playscript for the performance. The script has not survived. Mark also wrote a condensed, literary text that preserved the performance. A modern analogue is a novel based on a filmed screenplay. This condensed, literary text is the direct ancestor of the Gospel of Mark we have now.

Mark polished this literary text, and retained dialogue that pointed to his sources in Scripture. This suggests that for at least the near future, Mark expected his congregation to be Scripturally knowledgeable.

Flavia's patronage is sufficient to explain the original pro-Gentile elements of GMark.

---

[1] All biblical quotations in this chapter are from the NRSV.

Flavia's patronage has implications for the social status of the congregation going forward.

Every 'chapter' of GMark has been edited, and scenes have been deleted, added, and reordered. However, the assumption that Mark wrote a stageable play still allows for a great deal of reconstruction of the action of the play. I present all my proposals for the action of the play in an appendix.

Discovery of the Gospel of Mark as a Play

My research on GMark began with the question: Why was Christianity the last successful version of Judaism, apart from Pharisaism (the ancestor of all modern sects of Judaism)? I did not believe that Jews in antiquity were so impressed by a human Jesus of Nazareth that within a few decades of his death they gave him divine status.[2] More likely, they thought of "Jesus" as a mythical or heavenly figure. So I assumed mythicism from the start. I have read widely, including the leading modern mythicist scholars, and have found no reason to change this assumption. In my book and this chapter, I take mythicism for granted.

I decided to trace the origin of the Jesus story. I went back to the source, the Gospel of Mark. I read it aloud, like readers in antiquity.

I noticed that GMark had many features of a playscript: The Jesus character is onstage in almost every scene: he must be the protagonist. A Chorus ("multitudes") is usually present. Characters and locations are never described, only named. And the text includes many physical actions that are obviously stage directions (e.g., "And when [Jesus] had stepped out of the boat, immediately a man out of the tombs with an unclean spirit met him" Mark 5:2).

---

[2] Yes, I realize that my assumption was not correct: in the first century CE, there were a number of Judean sects and some included a divine intermediary they understood as "Wisdom," "Logos," or "Jesus."

Although GMark is playlike, it does not have enough dialogue for a performed play. It omits some of the dialogue that was spoken in performance (for example, the healed demoniac "went away and began to proclaim in the Decapolis how much Jesus had done for him" Mark 5:20. And "For many gave false testimony against him, and their testimony did not agree" Mark 14:56.). GMark is not the script of a performed play.

I inferred that GMark was one step removed from a play. GMark preserves some of the audience's experience of the play because it provides stage directions that enable the reader to imagine much of the stage action. Mark also added a number of literary features. For example, he narratized the action that the audience saw onstage. He added names of people and places that had not been mentioned during the performance. He structured some (and possibly originally all) scenes as chiasms. Because of this literary polish, I call the (original of the) received text of GMark the "polished text."

I tried to retrieve Mark's performed play. What did the text have to say? I had some experience with plays: I had worked as an actor, taken a playwriting class, and studied a classic textbook (*Playwriting* by Bernard Grebanier).[3]

I took the physical point of view of a director or stage manager. I concerned myself with the movements of the actors. From this point of view, the text deconstructed consistently into performable, stageable scenes.

Focusing only on the physical reconstruction of the play, I did not enquire into the sources of Mark's scenarios. I did not try to determine Mark's religious beliefs or the sources of his concept of "Jesus." I did not try to reconstruct dialogue that was omitted or described in the text. I recognize that all of these things are important. They affected how the actors enacted the play and how the audience understood the play. But they are irrelevant for a first pass at the staging of the play.

---

[3] Bernard Grebanier, *Playwriting: How to Write for the Theater.* (1961; repr., New York: Barnes & Noble, 1979).

I found that the play used a limited number of locations. The orchestra served first as the Jordan River, then the Sea of Galilee. After the boat returned from Bethsaida, the orchestra was redefined as the Way to Jerusalem. The permanent set included a mountain, a rock tomb that opened, and a garden. A second level was required: the Last Supper was held there in an "upper room."

The play was sectarian, and therefore performed privately for Mark's congregation. At first I assumed it was staged in a dining room or courtyard. But these spaces could not provide an "upper room." I reluctantly concluded that a two-level theater was required.

I found that, though rare at the time, private theaters did exist. The emperor Domitian had one on his country estate. Flavia Domitilla was Domitian's niece. If anyone had access to a private theater in Rome, she did. She alternatively could have had a wooden theater constructed for the occasion. My theory that Flavia was the patron and was honored during the scene in Bethany solved the unrelated problem of finding an upper room for the Last Supper.

Demonstrations that Mark's Text Preserves the Performance of a Play

Many theatrical effects were revealed when I imagined the performance behind the text. Here are five examples:

1. At the Temple Incident, the tables of the money changers and dove sellers are overturned. In consequence, coins fell into the orchestra and doves flew away. The coins, I suggest, were real; they functioned as gifts for the audience (gifts were common at public performances), especially for children in the front row who would have scrambled to retrieve them (Flavia had two young sons). The doves were probably attached to strings

and caught by the audience. This was a miniaturized version of a known theatrical effect.[4]
2. The stilling-of-the-storm scene. Let us imagine the staging: Jesus, asleep on a cushion, and disciples are in the boat, crossing the orchestra. The wind rises and the disciples "bail water." They awaken Jesus. The boat arrives at the other side of the stage (Gerasa). Jesus exorcises the demon spirits, which then occupy some pigs. From the mountain there, pigs throw themselves into the "sea" and are drowned. The only stageable translation of "pigs" is "Roman soldiers" (as some exegetes have proposed). Therefore, these actors acrobatically throw themselves, i.e., dive, from the mountain onstage into the orchestra. I suggest that they landed on the cushion. The Jesus actor had thrown it overboard while he bailed water during the storm!
3. Jesus prays alone in a deserted place (Mark 1:35). Only the audience hears his lines; the Chorus and disciples have not yet entered. A standard, formal prayer from the world of the audience has no theatrical value because it does not advance the action. Instead, I propose that in this speech, *Jesus reviews his plans to fulfill his mission on earth.* This speech allows the audience to overhear Jesus' "master plan" for his behavior going forward. (The audience is now better informed than any of the human characters in the play!) This is also the time for Jesus to justify his itinerary in Galilee, if he does so at all.

---

[4] In Alexandria, at the Ptolemaiea festival procession "[spectators] caught the pigeons, ring-doves, and turtle-doves which flew forth from a cart and were equipped with nooses tied to their feet so that they could be easily caught by the spectators." Jens Koehler, "Pompai. Untersuchungen zur hellenistischen Festkultur," (Ph.D. diss., Frankfurt: Peter Lang, 1996): 150, cited in Angelos Chaniotis, "Theatricality Beyond the Theater. Staging Public Life in the Hellenistic World," *Pallas* 47 (1997): 247. Available at: http://www.jstor.org/stable/43685038.

4. An effect is set up during the Transfiguration scene. On the mountain and hidden behind a cloud, the Jesus actor swaps his ordinary, Cynic-teacher clothes for clothes of shining white. He is still wearing his white clothes when he is mocked and beaten. After he is stripped, the soldiers gamble for them. Now bloody and tossed on the floor, they movingly testify to the audience how far Jesus has fallen.
5. In Gentile Gerasa, Jesus heals the naked, possessed demoniac. (This is a comic role.) The demoniac dons clothes, then exits as he proclaims how much Jesus has done for him. For at least a few moments, this actor monopolizes the audience's attention. This attention to an isolated secondary character is unique in the original play.[5] Therefore, I suggest that the demoniac was played by a guest-star comic actor, someone worth attention on his own. I also suggest that Mark gives this actor a *second* appearance: at the arrest, he (again comically) plays the young follower who interferes, then is declothed and flees naked. Note that the actor has been elegantly restored to his initial nakedness.

I hope that these examples demonstrate that rich theatrical experiences are inherent in the text if it is understood as a preserved staged play. In the book, I analyze the entire text in this way.

GMark as Performance

My proposal that GMark preserves a performed play has precedents. Other scholars have proposed that part or all of GMark was performed.

---

[5] I believe that editors wrote the received Herod banquet scene—in which Jesus is absent—and the Syro-Phoenician woman scene—which ends with Jesus absent and the woman's discovery of her healed daughter.

One group of contemporary scholars called performance critics argues that Mark's entire text was read dramatically.[6] I agree that such readings have some entertainment value. However, the text was not written for that purpose. A single observation proves the point. Events occur too quickly to make an impression on the listener, for example, the trial (Mark 14:53–65) lasts less than two minutes when read dramatically. And, as noted above, the text explicitly states that dialogue is missing. If Mark had wanted his *polished text* to be read aloud, he would have lengthened the trial for dramatic impact on the listeners.

A similar proposal is that Mark wrote a "closet drama." This term refers to a *play* intended to be read aloud.[7] The existence of a genre of closet drama has been proposed based on the authentic extant dramas of Seneca the Younger. The performability of those dramas is debated. But even if there was a recognized genre of closet drama in Mark's Rome, Mark's play does not belong to it. Mark's language and literary style are different from Seneca's, and Mark's play was fully stageable.

A third group of scholars holds that the Passion (or, rarely, the entire received text of GMark) is a transcript or other secondary version of a performed play. J. M. Robertson's views are closest to mine. Robertson

---

[6] For example, see Whitney Shiner, *Proclaiming the Gospel: First-Century Performance of Mark*. (Harrisburg, PA: Trinity Press International, 2003). Dramatic readings are available on video, e.g., "Whitney Shiner Performs Mark 7:1-30," July 19, 2011. Available at: https://www.youtube.com/watch?v=kBxwqKozFpk.

[7] Ernest W. Burch has proposed that the Gospel was a closet drama, "Tragic Action in the Second Gospel: A Study in the Narrative of Mark," *Journal of Religion*. (July 1931), 11(3), p. 346. Available at: http://www.jstor.org/stable/1196612. Gilbert Bilezikian says that Mark "adapt[ed] some of the formal features of tragedy to meet the exigencies of his own story" about Jesus of Nazareth, *The Liberated Gospel: A Comparison of the Gospel of Mark and Greek Tragedy*. (1977; repr., Eugene, Oregon: Wipf & Stock, 2010), p. 29. But Bilezikian thinks that the Gospel was written for oral delivery, p. 119. Stephen H. Smith writes in "A Divine Tragedy: Some Observations on the Dramatic Structure of Mark's Gospel," *Novum Testamentum*. (July 1995): 37(3), pp. 209–31. Available at: http://www.jstor.org/stable/1561221; "Mark's Gospel is *not* a play, and was never written for performance by actors," p. 222. Instead, "he intended it to be presented to a specific audience in the manner of a closet drama," p. 229.

asserts that the received text of GMark consists of two parts: a performed tragedy (the Passion) that was transcribed, and a narrative. He states that some of the scenes prior to the Passion may have been presented dramatically, but leaves the matter there.[8]

Building on Robertson and Alfred Loisy, Livio C. Stecchini and Jan Sammer propose that the Passion was a performed tragedy. They usefully detail many stagings of the performance. However, they implausibly propose that Mark and Luke saw a performance, Matthew worked from Mark's narrative, and John wrote his own narrative from a copy of the script.[9]

Independent scholar Michael Turton suggests that the *entire* GMark was a staged play. Unfortunately, he does not pursue this line of analysis.[10]

I believe that the Passion *was* originally a separate, conventionally structured tragedy. I think it likely that Mark had already written it—that is why he had it available to repurpose for the Jesus play. The tragedy's plot concerned a charismatic individual who challenged the authority of the current community leaders (a possible model was the Trial and Death of Socrates, which must have been dramatized frequently).

I believe that Mark revised and incorporated his earlier play into a longer, *stageable and staged* play. It is a single dramatic work, united by the plot. The plot begins in Mark 1, when Jesus appears on the stage, sent to earth by his Father on a mission to die. Satan, the antagonist, appears,

---

[8] J. M. Robertson, *Pagan Christs: Studies in Comparative Hierology*, 2nd ed. (London: Watts, 1911). Compression, 197. Main argument, 197–201. The Passion "is an addition to a previously existing document," p. 201. Pre-Passion scenes in the gospel story may have been presented dramatically, pp. 203–204.

[9] Livio C. Stecchini and Jan Sammer, introduction to *The Gospel According to Seneca* (N.p.: Monica Stecchini, Steven Stecchini, and Jan Sammer, 1996) (formerly online).

[10] Michael Turton, "Chapter 9: Excursus, Was Mark Meant to be Performed?" *Michael A. Turton's Historical Commentary on the Gospel of Mark*, last modified December 31, 2004, http://www.michaelturton.com/Mark/GMark09.html#9X. Turton insightfully comments, "the writer's vague geography and lack of geographical description and detail may reflect the expectation that those items would be presented visually."

and throughout the play tests Jesus' commitment to his mission (think of how often "Satan" and "unclean/demonic spirits" are mentioned in GMark). The plot ends in Mark 16, when Jesus, having completed his mission, ascends to the heavens.

The Genre of GMark

If Mark's play was not a tragedy or comedy, where did it fit into the contemporary dramatic spectrum?

I assign Mark's full play to the dramatic genre of mime. Mime conventions differed significantly from the conventions of tragedy and comedy. Mime was more of an attitude than a format. It originated in earthy folk performance. The style of mime performances was informal and comic, with the freedom to be vulgar and countercultural. The mime style had trickled upwards from street performances to dinner-party entertainment (e.g., the variety show at Trimalchio's dinner) to staged plays.

Mime *plays* had been presented in Rome at the annual spring festival, the *Floralia*, since 173 BCE. "From that time the sponsored plays must have been subject to rehearsal for approval before purchase; thus they will have assimilated towards the regular structure of comedies and their dialogue will have abandoned improvisation for a formal script."[11] In Mark's time, "According to the telling evidence provided by Plutarch—a widely travelled man—in Rome there were performed mimes with 'multiple actors' and 'dramatic plots.'"[12]

Mark's play had many characteristics of mime:

---

[11] R. Elaine Fantham, "Mime: The Missing Link in Roman Literary History," *Classical World*. (January–February 1989), 82(3), p. 155. Available at: https://doi.org/10.2307/4350348.

[12] Stavros Tsitsiridis, "Greek Mime in the Roman Empire (P. Oxy. 413: *Charition* and *Moicheutria*)," *Logeion* (2011), vol. 1, p. 184. Available at: https://www.logeion.upatras.gr/node/145. This article is well-worth reading.

- A nontraditional dramatic structure: here, a journey story (epic) attached to a mini-tragedy, both integrated by an overall plot;
- A foolish second actor: Peter;
- Nudity: a naked young man flees during the arrest scene;
- No masks;
- Female actors: the twelve-year-old girl, the women who had accompanied Jesus in Galilee, etc.;
- A raucous mêlée at the end: the arrest scene that ends the pre-Passion section of the play. The full play, I believe, also ended with a raucous mêlée: an ascension scene during which some of the actors onstage fled offstage. (The current empty-tomb scene, in which the ascension is *reported*, was written by an editor.)

When I assign Mark's play to the genre of mime, I do not mean to imply that Mark's play was a farce, or that the dialogue was vulgar or jokey—or improvised. But—prior to the Passion—it is often humorous. Perhaps more than is obvious. The core disciples often misunderstand Jesus, though from ignorance about his identity rather than stupidity.[13] Whitney Shiner, a scholar who gave dramatic readings of GMark, noted, "Once the audience has decided that the disciples are comic, the other scenes of misunderstanding tend to be perceived that way as well."[14] The

---

[13] It is a mistake to think that Mark intended the audience to think that the core disciples were dim, or that Mark intended to insult any real men who had borne these names. The core disciples are not dim or foolish; they are *ignorant*. They know less than the audience. The core disciples were not yet onstage when the Voice of God announced Jesus's identity to the audience. Nor were they onstage at the (original) Temptation, or when Jesus prayed alone (1:35) and allowed the audience to overhear his plans for his mission on earth. Given the prestige of his patron, it is reasonable to think that Mark expected readers of the polished text to think of his text as preserving a staged play.

[14] Shiner, *Proclaiming the Gospel*, pp. 96–97. He adds, "It is easy to play the disciples for comic effect from Chapter 4 through the recognition scene in Chapter 8," p. 96.

Gerasene demoniac is comic. The possessed characters whom Jesus heals may behave comically. Satan and the Pharisees might be comic. Even the Chorus might be comic at times.

I also note that mime was a living theatrical genre at the time, the successor to the now-antiquated genre of comedy.[15] In fact, if my theory is correct, the only complete mime play to survive from antiquity is preserved in GMark.

The Inductive Method

Yes, all of this is speculative. That does not mean my conclusions are wrong. My conclusions should be judged by how well they make sense of the data. Here, the data are the received text of GMark.

My method is inductive. I look at data and propose a situation that could have caused them to occur. For example, GMark combines stageability and unstageability. I propose that this observation is explained by "Mark wrote a performed play that he revised into a secondary text." I call that statement a "provisional fact." I then use that provisional fact in my reconstruction of the situation. I assume it is valid until I find something that cannot be made compatible with it, either internally, or from my study of the texts and scholarship of first- and second-century proto-Christianity.

I built up my overall theory using provisional facts as cantilevers. My overall theory consists of cantilevers extended on cantilevers. Sometimes I have been wrong and had to discard a cantilever. But sometimes I have extended a cantilever and found that it met a cantilever that originated

---

[15] Eric Csapo adds, "If mime was the successor to comedy, pantomime was the natural successor to tragedy." Eric Csapo and William J. Slater, eds., *The Context of Ancient Drama*. (Ann Arbor: University of Michigan Press, 1995), p. 372. Csapo notes there is "literary and textual evidence for performances of mime or pantomime which continue on both the public and private stage until at least the sixth century AD." *Actors and Icons of the Ancient Theater*. (Chichester, UK: Wiley-Blackwell, 2014), p. 154.

from a different direction. I believe that the scenario that I present in the book is internally consistent.

Still, induction only provides a plausible explanation for the data that exist. Other explanations remain possible. And it is possible I am right on some points and wrong on others.

Insights into Mark's Congregation

I propose that Mark's play was performed, and the congregation's patron was Flavia Domitilla. What does this situation imply about the congregation?

The pope from 88–99 is traditionally designated as "Clement." Flavia Domitilla's husband was named "Titus Flavius Clemens." "Clement" derives from "Clemens." I infer that the home of the popes descends from Flavia's congregation.[16]

I suggest that the play was performed only once. A second performance, with an ordinary actress in the role of the anointing woman, would have diluted the honor given to Flavia at the first performance and suggested that she had been only play-acting. A single performance of a commissioned play, on the other hand, would have displayed Flavia's wealth and ability to command labor, while also providing her congregation with an exquisite "night to remember."

The play was an entertainment. It might have been presented at Passover as part of the holiday celebration, but it was not part of a religious ritual. Nor were religious rituals performed during the play: audience involvement was too risky, because it might derail the play's dramatic

---

[16] Either the later orthodox church retroactively acknowledged the prominence of Flavia and Clemens in the congregation when it gave the congregational leader during their membership the papal name "Clement," or "Clement" was the real name of a congregational leader at the time, perhaps one of Clemens's freedmen. I note that my theory is supported by the fact that the orthodox theologian known as Clement of Alexandria (died c. 215) chose the full name "Titus Flavius Clemens."

momentum. Nor was the play's purpose evangelical. Only a Scripturally educated audience could appreciate Mark's many references to Scripture, e.g., the emulation of Elijah's calling of Elisha in Jesus's calling of the fishermen.

When Mark chose to preserve the play as a text, he was operating in a very different intellectual context. I do think that Mark saw his text as a candidate for Scripture. Mark had a reasonable expectation that his work, which testified to Flavia's patronage, would survive for the foreseeable future. Flavia's patronage meant that the congregation would survive as an institution for the foreseeable future. So Mark, I think, felt that it was worthwhile for him to create a complex and resonant work that could be used as Scripture in the same way Scripture had served him.

In the polished text, Mark retained dialogue that pointed to his sources in Scripture. I infer that he expected to have Scripturally educated readers.

Mark's congregation identified as Judeans, not Samaritans. The polished text references the Judean-focused LXX books of Kings, Psalms, and Isaiah; and the play portrays Jesus as the high priest in the heavenly analogue of the Jerusalem Temple.[17]

In the play Jesus has disciples named "Peter," "James," and "John." I think it is likely that these names refer to early Jesus-movement leaders who were known to Mark's audience; otherwise, three arbitrary names would have weakened the play ("Why did Mark use *these* three names?").

The play emphasizes Jesus' openness to Gentile followers. To review some of the contributing theatrical elements: Jesus heals Gentiles. He opposes the Pharisees' purity rules that prevented Judeans from dining with

---

[17] "Mark 1-6 contains a programmatic statement of Jesus' claim to a high priestly identity as the 'holy one of God' (1.24), with a high priestly contagious holiness (1.40-45; 5.25-34; 5.35-43), freedom to forgive sins (2.1-12) and the embodiment of divine presence in a Galilean cornfield (2.23-28). As true high priest he makes divine presence 'draw near' to God's people (1.15), where before they had to 'draw near' to the Jerusalem temple." Crispin H. T. Fletcher-Louis, "Jesus as the High Priestly Messiah", pt. 2, *Journal for the Study of the Historical Jesus*. (2007) 5(1), p. 63, doi:10.1177/1476869006074936.

Gentiles. He performs the (one) feeding miracle in the play in Gentile Bethsaida. And his last loyal follower (the naked young man at the arrest scene) is a Gentile. (He must be uncircumcised, otherwise his naked flight from the stage has no dramatic effect—he is just an ordinary member of the Galilean/Judean multitudes.) This pro-Gentile slant can be explained as flattery of the patron.

I cannot rule out the possibility that Mark knew the original (pre-Marcion) Letters of Paul. But the pro-Gentile slant of GMark is sufficiently explained by Flavia's patronage.

The doctrine in GMark is not a map of the congregation's doctrine as it would have been expressed in a sermon or official letter. It was skewed pro-Gentile by Flavia's presence and benefaction. I repeat, *the doctrine in GMark is not a map of the congregation's doctrine as it would have been expressed in a sermon or official letter.* The doctrine expressed in the play needed only to be acceptable to the congregation in a one-time entertainment that honored the Gentile patron.

Because Jesus was the protagonist of the play, he was onstage in almost every scene. We cannot infer that "Jesus" had an equally central role in the doctrine and regular worship of the congregation. We should not infer that their religion was "all Jesus, all the time."

GMark has been edited. It is fair to assume that the editors were primarily interested in shaping the doctrine presented. An editor can easily alter dialogue and leave no trace on the action of the play. That is why we cannot treat the received text of GMark as representing Mark's doctrine. I *can* say that doctrine that is expressed in the play's *action* is much more difficult to alter and very likely original. For example, Jesus is portrayed as the heavenly high priest. Also, the fact that Jesus 'fulfills' many scenarios from Scripture implies that the congregation's Jesus figure had been developed by exegesis of Scripture.

The congregation consisted of people whom the patron would be comfortable with socially: well-to-do, respectable, and Hellenized, Judean-born and Gentile-born. However, the congregation undoubtedly also included slaves and freedmen. It must have been routine for congregations/synagogues to have deacons for members of various classes and levels of literacy, e.g., the "widows and orphans" in the Shepherd of Hermas 1.2.4.

The wealth and Judean identity of Mark's congregation in Flavia's time is consistent with the wealth and Judean-scripture–based identity of the headquarters congregation of orthodoxy in the second century. This is another reason to think that Mark's congregation became the home of the popes.

Flavia and Clemens were respectively exiled and killed by the emperor Domitian in 95 CE. Probably their associates were also killed. (These events, I believe, are referenced in 1 Clement 1:1 as the "sudden and repeated calamities and reverses which are befalling us." Such was the 'persecution' by Domitian.) The Roman congregation's historic relationship with Flavia and Clemens explains why the congregation preserved GMark into the second century but did not circulate it.

Implications of My Work for the History of Christianity

Now I go beyond the book and speculate on the world after Mark. How does my theory contribute to the history of second-century Christianity?

Flavia's patronage provides a date for GMark: before Flavia's exile in 95 CE. (I do not date GMark by the content of the Olivet Discourse, because the lines that refer to flight and disaster (Mark 13:14–19) are not original.)[18]

Still, GMark was, in a way, a reaction to the Jewish War. I think that a play about "Jesus" could not have been written before the War. The

---

[18] In the book, I propose a reconstruction of the Olivet Discourse. I follow the rule of playwriting that *"any given speech must convey only one important dramatic idea and/or only one ruling emotion"* (italics in original). Grebanier, *Playwriting*, 256. The received text of the Olivet Discourse does not conform to that rule. I infer that it has been padded.

War's destruction left Diaspora Judeans on their own, to carry forward their cultural and national identity without the Temple, which depended on the Judean peasants and their agricultural pilgrimages. Mark's congregation, like the Pharisees and their scribes/rabbis, already had a functional alternative concept for Judean cultural and national identity.

This congregation is the direct ancestor of the second-century orthodox church in Rome that insisted that "Jesus" was the son of YHWH and had been predicted in Judean Scripture. The persistence of this point of view in the second century implies to me that the Roman congregation continued to be a meeting place for rich Judeans who wanted to retain their heritage, even as they interpreted the Law symbolically and dined with Gentiles. Probably enriched by refugees after 135, this congregation remained in an intermediate position in the Judean cultural universe between those philosophers/Gnostics who were not grounded in Scripture; and the Pharisaic scribes/rabbis, who immersed themselves in it. Eventually, though, the Roman congregation that had initially understood Jesus as the heavenly high priest bowed to necessity and authorized the belief that the Jesus of the harmonized Gospel story had been in some way a man on earth.

What the ordinary Roman congregants believed in the second century, however, is another question. Given that the congregation was using catacombs donated by Flavia, the memory of Flavia and Clemens' benefaction must have lasted for many decades if not centuries. How could the congregation forget that Flavia had produced a "night to remember," and the author had left a physical record of the play in the congregational archives?

My characterization of the Roman congregation gives us new insight into the political struggle within second-century orthodox Christianity. The second-century Roman congregation is no longer an indistinct overlay of possibilities drawn from 1 Clement, Romans, the Shepherd of Hermas, Papias, Acts, a possible visit by Marcion, the inferred life-history of Irenaeus, etc. Instead, it is an institution with a distinct history and personality. I believe that it brought that history and personality to its negotiations with the orthodox Asian group—probably headquartered in Ephesus—whose members considered "the anointed one" to be the Davidic messiah, wrote GLuke/Acts, sent Polycarp to Rome, created the first canon list, and fought to co-opt and/or refute local Marcionites, Paul-followers, Samaritans, Gnostics, and Jewish-Christians.

The Asian group produced many more texts, and had a much larger membership. Yet the headquarters of the orthodox church ended up in Rome. Its ultimate victory, I think, was largely due to the wealth, prestige, and connections that the congregation had acquired from Flavia Domitilla's patronage. Subsequently, people of Judean heritage in Rome, unless they prioritized intellectual speculation/gnosis, would have wanted to belong to that congregation *for social reasons* if they possibly could. For socially ambitious Judeans, the Roman congregation was and remained the only game in town. (The Judeans dominated the congregation long enough to ensure that its valuing of Scripture had become congregational policy by the time that Gentiles had became a significant minority, or the majority.) The congregation's internal ecumenism complemented the Asians' external ecumenism.

The two centers therefore could make common cause on creating a church. Which they did: with its own history, canon, internal rules for organization, and so on. It just so happened that Mark's text was available, once it became necessary to provide a biography for a human Jesus of Nazareth. I suspect that the Roman congregation, and its leaders, knew perfectly well that this figure was a fabrication, and continued in that belief for some decades if not centuries. But they allowed the creation of Jesus of Nazareth as an accommodation for the less educated—and for those eastern Judeans who were interested in Jesus only if he were defined as the Davidic messiah. And probably they insisted that GMark be included in the canon, even though most of GMark had been incorporated into GMatthew. GMark was the *Roman* gospel: proof that Rome had had the Jesus story first.

Chapter 14: Is There a Man Behind the Curtain? A Response to Bart Ehrman.

By Robert M. Price

I guess you might say I think not only that there is no great and powerful Oz, but that there's not even a man behind the curtain. Bart Ehrman, on the other hand, agrees Oz is an illusion, but if you pull back the curtain, you'll find the anti-climactic Professor Marvel.

First, is Christ Mythicism some kind of novelty, dreamed up by skeptics living far enough after the events to be able to get away with it? Bart and many others think so.

"The idea that Jesus did not exist is a modern notion. It has no ancient precedents."

"Even the enemies of the Jesus movement thought [that Jesus had existed]; among their many slurs against the religion, his nonexistence is never one of them."[1]

I'm not so sure of that. Justin Martyr ascribes to his dialogue partner Trypho (perhaps to be identified with the historical Rabbi Tarfon) the allegation, "You have received a futile rumour, and have created some sort of Christ for yourselves."[2] We always hear apologists explain this away as if it meant "you Christians have nominated your own Christ/Messiah," or "you Christians pretend your Jesus was the Christ." But that's rather

---

[1] Bart D. Ehrman, *Did Jesus Exist? The Historical Argument for Jesus of Nazareth*, (New York: HarperOne/HarperCollins, 2012), p. 96, 171-172.
[2] Hanson, R. P. C., ed. and trans., *Selections from Justin Martyr's Dialogue with Trypho, a Jew*, World Christian Books, No. 49, Third Series. (New York: Association Press, 1964), p. 23.

different. Would the rabbi have said the partisans of Simon bar Kochba had "created" their "own messiah"? I don't think so. It seems less contrived to take Trypho as charging that the Christian Savior was a figment of pious imagination.[3]

Celsus, the second-century critic of Christianity, says, "It is clear to me that the writings of the Christians are a lie, and that your fables have not been well enough constructed to conceal this monstrous fiction."[4]

And then there's 2 Peter 1:16-18: "We did not follow cleverly devised myths when we told you of the power and coming of our Lord Jesus Christ." Some allege that "we," ostensibly "Simeon Peter" and his colleagues, were devising myths about the *coming* of Jesus. That sounds to me like an accusation that the apostles fabricated the whole business.

I picture the emergence of Jesus Christ like that moment when, in the process of evolution, enough small mutations accumulate to cross the taxonomical line to amount to a new species. Old myths mutated and morphed over a long time. But Bart attacks the "committee invention" model, and I think that is a straw man, though one created by Mythicists themselves.

And I believe that I detect here a fault line running beneath his whole argument. At least eleven times in *Did Jesus Exist?* Bart says we can trace traditions of Jesus back to within a very few years of Jesus' supposed crucifixion. For Bart, Mythicism assumes that schemers invented Jesus at the same point in history when the gospels have Jesus appear. But if there *was* no historical Jesus, as we wild-eyed, tinfoil hat-wearing Mythicists suggest, the bottom falls out of the whole thing. There is no way to determine when the timeline began, no way to say what or when is "early." To say, for instance, "In nearly all our sources Peter was Jesus' most intimate companion and confidant for his entire public ministry after his baptism,"

---

[3] Yes, thereafter Trypho speaks as if there was a real Jesus, but this is surely "for the sake of argument."
[4] Origen, trans. By Henry Chadwick, *Contra Celsum*. (Cambridge: Cambridge University Press, 1965), p. 62. Chadwick italicized the portions of Celsus' text quoted by Origen, but I have instead placed them in quotation marks.

seems to presuppose the factual character of the narrative, which is just the point at issue.

Bart well expresses, then deconstructs, a common Mythicist objection to Jesus' historical existence. How could contemporary observers have ignored a man who performed miracle after miracle to great public acclaim? But Bart replies that contemporary writers would probably not have taken much notice of any historically plausible Jesus, an itinerant sage and faith healer, one who did not miraculously multiply food, turn water into wine, walk on water, raise the rotting dead, banish storms at sea, and so forth. Isn't this like asking whether the historical Superman really had superhuman powers "beyond those of mortal men"? Should we decide that there was indeed a historical Superman but that he was merely Clark Kent?

> You can shape a tradition about Jesus any way you want so that it looks highly legendary. But that has no bearing on the question of whether beneath the legendary shaping lies the core of the historical event.[5]

Let's try to imagine what these hypothetical pre-legendary originals might have looked like:

> They came to the other side of the sea, to the country of the Gerasenes. And a great herd of swine was grazing on the hillside. But immediately some wild dogs began to bark, and the swine took fright and stampeded down the steep hillside, and they were drowned in the sea. (The original story behind Mark 5:1-13?)

---

[5] Ehrman, *Did Jesus Exist?*, p. 190. In our debate on October 21, 2016, Bart denied that he meant to suggest that individual stories about Jesus grew in the telling, but rather that on the whole the Jesus figure generated stories that were legendary to the core. But this seems to represent a change of opinion compared with the passage from Did Jesus Exist? I have quoted here, where the evolution/embellishment of particular stories is in view. Also see Bart D. Ehrman, *How Jesus Became God: The Exaltation of a Jewish Preacher from Galilee*. (New York: HarperOne/HarperCollins, 2014), p. 13: "Scholars have had to...determine which stories, and which parts of stories, are historically accurate...and which represent later embellishments..."

And when Jesus had crossed again in the boat to the other side, a great crowd gathered about him; and he was beside the sea. Then came one of the rulers of the synagogue, Jairus by name; and seeing him, he fell at his feet, and besought him, saying, "My little daughter is at the point of death. Come and lay your hands on her, so that she may be made well, and live." While he was still speaking, there came from the ruler's house some who said, "Your daughter is dead. Why trouble the Teacher any further?" And Jesus said to him, "Poor man! You have my sympathies. Now who's up for lunch?" (The historical core of Mark 5:21-23, 35?)

As he went ashore he saw a great throng, and he had compassion on them, because they were like sheep without a shepherd; and he began to teach them many things. And when it grew late, his disciples came to him and said, "This is a lonely place, and the hour is now late; send them away to go into the country and the surrounding villages and buy themselves something to eat." And he answered them, "You have said it." And he dispersed the crowd. And they all ate and were satisfied. (The historical core of Mark 6:32-44?)

Immediately he dismissed the crowd and he made his disciples get into the boat to go to the other side, to Bethsaida. And he got into the boat with them. And when evening came, the boat was out on the sea. (The original version of Mark 6:45-51?)

On the third day there was a marriage at Cana in Galilee, and the mother of Jesus was there; Jesus also was invited to the marriage, with his disciples. When her wine gave out, the mother of Jesus said to him, "Have they no more wine?" Now six stone jars were standing there, each holding twenty or thirty gallons of wine. Jesus said to them, "Now draw some out, and take it to the steward of the feast." So they took it. When the steward of the feast tasted the wine, he called the bridegroom and said to him, "Every man serves the good wine first; and when men have drunk freely, then the poor wine; but you have kept the good wine until now." (The historical core of John 2:1-11?)

What's left? Who would have even remembered these unremarkable incidents if they in fact happened? *And why would it have occurred to anyone to embellish them?* In terms of evolution, these tepid anecdotes would have had no survival value. To treat such gospel episodes the way Bart suggests is to trim away the element that would have caused the story to be passed on in the first place. It sounds like the old time Protestant Rationalism ridiculed by D.F. Strauss.[6] Boiling the spectacular down to the mundane, just to provide a toehold on historical reality. This is a modern version of ancient Euhemerism: the attempt to salvage the myths of gods and demigods by positing they were mythologized versions of ancient celebrities. Osiris was a king, Ares a mighty warrior, Asclepius a doctor, Hercules a weight-lifter, Apollo the owner of a tanning salon.

Could the Christian religion have begun with the modest historical figure Bart and his colleagues have whittled from the oak of the gospels' Jesus Christ? There was no such historical figure. Jesus possesses the grandeur of the mythical demigods because that's what he was. *That's* why no contemporary historian mentions him.

Testimonium Flimsianus

Did Jesus come in for mention by ancient historians? Bart regards the well-known statements of Pliny the Younger and Cornelius Tacitus about "Christos" and/or "Chrestus" as textually authentic (as they may well be). But, as he readily admits, these writers quite likely learned what they said about "Christ" (not "Jesus") from Christians. Here are multiple attestations—of hearsay. The weakness and scantiness of these "attestations" only accentuate the paucity of the supposed non-Christian documentation of a historical Jesus.

And then we have to ask, why are the gospels' witness to Jesus any better founded? Bart says that "stories about Jesus circulated widely

---

[6] D. F. Strauss, trans. By George Eliot (Mary Ann Evans), *The Life of Jesus Critically Examined*. Lives of Jesus Series. (Philadelphia: Fortress Press, 1972).

throughout the major urban areas of the Mediterranean from a very early time. [Our] written sources...are based on oral traditions."[7]

In other words, hearsay, just like Pliny and Tacitus. Thomas Arnold famously said the resurrection of Jesus was "the best-attested fact in history." But, as R.G. Collingwood observed, "its being well attested only proves that a lot of people believed it, not that it happened."[8]

Did Josephus mention Jesus? Bart says, "The majority of scholars of early Judaism, and experts on Josephus, think...that one or more Christian scribes 'touched up' the passage a bit. If one takes out the obviously Christian comments, the passage may have been rather innocuous."[9] Nothing like "He was the messiah." No resurrection appearances. Bart ventures that, "The pared-down version of Josephus..., contains very little that could have been used by the early Christian writers to defend Jesus and his followers from attacks by pagan intellectuals."[10] His point is that the unspectacular version cannot have begun as a wholesale Christian interpolation, so it must be genuine to Josephus, right? But my question would be: Why would *Josephus* mention such a nonentity? Who does *The Daily Planet* report on, Superman or Clark Kent? No, the scaled-down version of the passage, omitting "he was the Christ" and the resurrection appearances, makes as little sense as the authentic words of Josephus as they do as a Christian interpolation.

Paul J. Hopper, an authority on the linguistics of Classical literature, has, in my opinion, decisively refuted the "scaled-down non-interpolation" theory. He compares the *Testimonium*'s treatment of Pilate with the adjacent Pilate episodes in the context and concludes that the *Testimonium* is after all a Christian interpolation intended to rehabilitate the

---

[7] Ehrman, *Did Jesus Exist?*, p. 86.
[8] R. G. Collingwood, *The Idea of History*. (New York: Oxford University Press, 1946), pp. 135-136.
[9] Ehrman, *Did Jesus Exist?*, pp. 60-61.
[10] Ehrman, *Did Jesus Exist?*, p. 62.

image of Jesus and to shift the blame for his death from Pilate to the Jews.[11] In the authentic Pilate stories, the Procurator initiates actions against the Jews, but in the *Testimonium* he is manipulated by the Jewish leaders. Jesus is no more of a protagonist; everything said of him occurs by way of allusion and at arm's length, in summary fashion, all aimed at vindicating the Christian movement in the writer's day: despite all this, the faith goes on! "And up until this very day the tribe of Christians, named after him, has not died out."[12]

The *Testimonium* first appears in Eusebius' *Demonstration of the Gospel*. Our copies of Josephus are centuries later than that, and many scholars have suggested it was Eusebius' writing, falsely ascribed to Josephus, that crept into our later copies. Ken Olson shows how, whereas the *Testimonium* passage sticks out like a sore thumb in the text of the *Antiquities* where scribes inserted it, thinking they were restoring an accidental scribal omission, the passage fits its Eusebian context so well that, well, you'd think it was made for the purpose. And it was. The particular things said about Jesus in the *Testimonium* all address specific pagan criticisms of Christian beliefs about Jesus current in Eusebius' own day and which he is discussing in the context.

Bart dismisses Mythicist suggestions that this or that "historical Jesus-leaning" passage in Paul's epistles is a subsequent interpolation: "Here we find, again, textual studies driven by convenience: if a passage contradicts your views, simply claim that it was not written by the author."[13] But aren't "consensus" scholars doing the same darn thing with the

---

[11] Paul J. Hopper, "A Narrative Anomaly in Josephus: Jewish Antiquities xviii, 63," p. 157. Available at: https://www.academia.edu/9494231/A_Narrative_Anomaly_in_Josephus. See D.M. Murdock's valuable commentary on this important article in her "Josephus's Testimonium Flavianum Examined Linguistically: Greek Analysis Demonstrates the Passage a Forgery In Toto." Available at: https://www.academia.edu/10463098/Josephus_s_Testimonium_Flavianum_Examined_Linguistically_Greek_Analysis_Demonstrates_the_Passage_a_Forgery_In_Toto.
[12] Ehrman, *Did Jesus Exist?*, pp. 60-61.
[13] Ibid. p. 253.

Testimonium Flavianum? They dearly want Josephus to have mentioned Jesus, but the passage as it stands, they admit, cannot have been the work of a non-Christian Jew like Josephus. It's a bad text for their purposes, so they redact it, as Matthew redacted Mark, in order to make it suitable for their use. Just exercise the line-item veto: remove the offending passages. *Now* we can use it as evidence to establish a historical Jesus. No you can't.

Bridge to Nowhere?

Most Jesus scholars believe one can build a bridge from the canonical gospels over to the historical Jesus. Suppose the gospels themselves are based on prior gospels? That helps. But if we run out of planks, maybe we can close the rest of the distance by tossing sturdy ropes of oral tradition over to the other side.

Bart enumerates the pre-gospel gospels, the hypothetical sources used by Matthew and Luke: Mark, Q, M, and L. Matthew and Luke each used both Q and Mark.[14] Where Matthew presents material not found in Mark or Q, he got it from "M." In the same way, stories and sayings unique to Luke must have been borrowed from "L." And for all we know, Mark, M, and L, like Q, may be compilations of earlier oral or written sources. But Walter Schmithals demonstrates to my satisfaction that all the uniquely Lukan parables are either drawn from general Hellenistic Judaism or composed by Luke himself to serve his special interests in persecution, prayer, possessions, etc. Schmithals also argues that all the uniquely Matthean parables are his own creations. He notes, too, that, if Luke and Matthew were really drawing on streams of oral tradition, it seems remarkable that we should find no overlaps, i.e., non-verbatim parallels, between the so-called M and L.

But, in his gospel's preface, doesn't Luke refer to numerous predecessors? Yes, but I think Luke is trying to do what Bart is trying to do, to

---

[14] Ehrman, *Did Jesus Exist?*, p. 81.

provide a (possibly fictive) paper trail back to Jesus. The fabricators of Islamic *hadith* (ostensible traditions of the Prophet Muhammad and his teaching) always supplied an attestation chain (*isnad*) for their fabrications. "I heard this from Abdul Alhazred, who heard it from Ras al Ghul, who heard it from Abu-bekr, who heard it from the Prophet, peace be upon him." Luke is supplying an *isnad*. It is part and parcel of Luke's apologetic motif of eyewitness apostolic guarantors.

There is a fine point in the apologetical exploitation of Source Criticism that we shouldn't skip over. Q is a helpful theoretical model for organizing the data of the gospels. Others slice the pie in different ways. Q, M, and L are theoretical, purely hypothetical, not like known but lost documents like the Gospel according to the Hebrews.

Bart also appeals to the Gospels of Thomas and Peter and the so-called Egerton Gospel as independent witnesses to a recent (and therefore historical) Jesus. But many think these texts are heavily dependent on the canonical gospels. Something that is itself a matter of intense debate can hardly be taken for granted as a building block for one's case.

Risky Patristics

Papias was a bishop of Hierapolis in Asia Minor, a city forming a triad with the biblical Colossae and Laodicea. Around 125 CE he wrote a work, now lost except for several quotations by church fathers, called *An Exposition of the Oracles of our Lord*. But it is very difficult to grant any credibility to a man who says he heard from the hearers of the holy apostles that Judas Iscariot had swollen up to the size of a parade balloon, unable to squeeze between two street corners, and urinated live maggots—before he exploded like Mr. Creosote in *Monty Python's The Meaning of Life*! I don't mean to suggest that Bart is willing to accept such nonsense; he doesn't. But the astonishing thing is that, even in the face of it, he still accepts Papias as an important source. Again, to appeal to such a worthless source only underlines the paucity of the evidence. Did he get *this* "tradition" from associates of the apostles? If he says he did, then his claim to apostolic hobnobbing must be considered just as fanciful.

Is Ignatius of Antioch an independent witness to the life of Jesus? No, for he quotes a piece of unmistakable Matthean redaction: Jesus was "baptized by John that all righteousness might be fulfilled by him." Does 1 Peter 2:21-24 preserve valuable tradition for a historical Jesus? First Peter 2:21-24 is not anyone's historical recollection but rather an allusion to Isaiah 53.

Paul's Jesus

What do the Pauline Epistles tell us about Jesus? Bart says, "He never mentions Pontius Pilate or the Romans, but he may have had no need to do so. His readers knew full well what he was talking about....If they were already fully informed about Jesus, then there was no need for Paul to remind them that Jesus walked on water, raised Jairus' daughter from the dead, and was executed in Jerusalem."[15] But suppose his readers *were* familiar with these stories: Bart believes such stories are pure legends. If the Corinthians or the Thessalonians "knew" about these miracles, that doesn't mean they knew anything about a *historical* Jesus.

What is at issue in the question of Paul not mentioning Pilate or the Sanhedrin as the culprits in Jesus' death? Paul never describes the crucifixion as a mundane execution at the hands of earthly governing authorities (though of course nothing he says rules out that possibility). What he does say is that Jesus was done to death by "the rulers (*archons*) of this cosmos" (1 Corinthians 2:8), "the Principalities and Powers" (Colossians 1:16; 2:14-15). Mythicists infer that the author of these epistles was writing at a time when Christians believed in a celestial Man of Light who had not appeared on the earth to teach and heal and die on a Roman cross, but who had been ambushed and slain by the demonic entities

---

[15] Ehrman, *Did Jesus Exist?*, pp. 124-125.

(fallen angels, archons, elemental spirits) inhabiting the lower heavens. As we read in various surviving Gnostic texts, this death would have occurred in the primordial past. His slayers harvested the sparks of his Light-body and used them to seed the inert mud-pie creations of the Demiurge, imparting life and motion to them, beginning with Adam. Thus the death of the Primal Light-Man turned out to be a life-giving sacrifice, much like that of the Vedic Purusha.

Eventually the Revealer was sent forth from the divine world of light to regather the divine photons, redeeming them from imprisonment in this world of "solid flesh." The Gnostics, naturally, considered themselves to be the elite light-bearers who had heeded the call of the Revealer, manifest among men in the form of Gnostic apostles. At some point some of these Gnostics "historicized" their salvation myth, envisioning the sacrificial death of the Man of Light as taking place down here in the sub-lunar world. At first, the coming of this Christ was understood as what we would call a hologram, an illusion of physical presence among mortal men and women. The enlightened could discern the purely spiritual character of the Savior, while those mired in mundane consciousness took him for a man of flesh. Eventually this unenlightened, genuinely incarnational Christology became normative. The Pauline literature would represent a pre-historicized period of Gnostic Christian belief, or a faction which retained the earlier version when others had adopted a historicized Christology/Soteriology. This is the model that makes most sense to me.

Paul "refers on several occasions to Jesus' teachings."[16] What? Where? Of course, Bart is referring to *two* passages from 1 Corinthians. "To the married I give charge, not I but the Lord, that the wife should not separate from her husband…and that the husband should not divorce his wife" (1 Corinthians 7:10-11). Are we so sure Paul is quoting a saying of the historical Jesus, and not passing on a command vouchsafed him by the ascended Christ? I think the latter is more likely. We can't be sure Paul does *not* mean he has a historical Jesus quote on hand, but if this notion of

---

[16] Ehrman, *Did Jesus Exist?*, p. 130.

Paul passing on private oracles is even a plausible suggestion it is not fair simply to assert he is quoting Jesus. The same applies to 1 Corinthians 11:23-26, where Paul quotes the Words of Institution of the eucharist. Conservative apologists contend that the words, "I received from the Lord what I also delivered to you," imply that Paul is repeating an account given him by his apostolic predecessors, an account of Jesus' Last Supper. The "received, delivered" language is familiar from Rabbinic tradition. But, especially in Paul, it can just as easily mean the opposite. "I would have you know, brethren, that the gospel that was preached by me is not according to man. For I did not receive it *from* man, nor was I taught it, but it came through a revelation of Jesus Christ" (Galatians 1:11-12). Note the similarity to "I received from the Lord" in 1 Corinthians 11:23. Why doesn't it denote in 1 Corinthians what it most certainly does in Galatians?

We may also compare the situation of the gospels and the Pauline Epistles to that of the Synoptics versus John. As Maurice Casey notes, it is obvious that the unique and powerful sayings/discourses attributed to Jesus in John's gospel cannot be authentic sayings of a historical Jesus because no such materials (e.g., the numerous "I am" declarations) appear in the Synoptics. Is it reasonable to argue that Jesus really said such things but that *none* of it had reached the ears of the Synoptists? Of course not. As all critical scholars admit, these sayings did not yet exist, hence were not circulating in the period when Q, Mark, and Matthew (throw in M and L if you want) were being written. They arose within the sectarian Community of the Beloved Disciple later on. Shouldn't we understand the absence of Jesus material (sayings and stories) from the Pauline literature in the same way? It simply did not yet exist, or we should be seeing some of it in the epistles.

Mythicist Mischief?

Is it possible that any texts in the Pauline epistles that imply belief in a recent historical Jesus might be secondary scribal insertions? Bart does not suffer interpolation theories gladly. "It is only the mythicists, who have a vested interest in claiming that Paul did not know of a historical Jesus, who insist that these passages were not originally in Paul's writings. One always needs to consider the source."[17] The trouble is: these suggestions were *not made by Mythicists*. William O. Walker, Jr., discusses a whole raft of proposed early interpolations, not one of them the proposal of a Mythicist. Each suggestion comes with its own reasoning. A. D. Howell Smith, in his *Jesus Not a Myth*, showed how Galatians 1:18-19 might have been interpolated.

> Unless the allusion is interpolated, Paul had an interview with a brother of Jesus, who was one of the three "pillars" of the Church of Jerusalem (Gal. i, 19). There is a critical case of some slight cogency against the authenticity of Gal. i, 18, 19, which was absent from Marcion's *Apostolicon*; the word "again" in Gal. ii, 1, which presupposes the earlier passage, seems to have been interpolated as it is absent from Irenaeus's full and accurate citation of this section of the Epistle to the Galatians in his treatise against Heretics.[18]

J. C. O'Neill, in *The Recovery of Paul's Letter to the Galatians*, contended that Galatians 1:4-5 "originally comprised a short creedal affirmation in poetic form," added by a scribe.[19] Jean Magne, in *From Christianity to Gnosis and From Gnosis to Christianity*, argues that 1 Corinthians

---

[17] Ehrman, *Did Jesus Exist?*, p. 133.
[18] A. D. Howell Smith, *Jesus Not a Myth*. (London: Watts, 1942), p.76.
[19] J. C. O'Neill, in *The Recovery of Paul's Letter to the Galatians*. (London: S.P.C.K., 1972), p.27.

11:23-26 is an interpolation intended "to authorize certain innovations to the Eucharistic service."[20]

I have made a case that 1 Corinthians 15:3-11 was interpolated into its present context, but then I don't count, since I'm a crazy Mythicist. But little did I suspect that others, not Mythicists, had beat me to the punch. Winsome Munro "suspects" 1 Corinthians 15:1-11 of belonging to a subsequent, post-Pauline stratum of the epistle,[21] while J. C. O'Neill also deems it most probable that "1 Cor. 15.1-11 is a later creedal summary not written by Paul." R. Joseph Hoffmann speaks of "the interpolative character of 1 Cor 15.5-8."[22] Not one of these scholars was/is a Mythicist.

The Scandal of the Cross

Was there no Jewish precedent for a suffering messiah? Bart says that "today many Christians appear to think that this is what the messiah was supposed to be, God the savior come to earth. But this is not and never was a Jewish view."[23] "Since no one would have made up the idea of a crucified messiah, Jesus must really have existed, must really have raised messianic expectations, and must really have been crucified. No Jew would have invented him."[24] But maybe they wouldn't have *had* to make up a suffering messiah mytheme.

---

[20] J. Magne, trans. by A. F. W. Armstrong, *From Christianity to Gnosis and From Gnosis to Christianity: An Itinerary through the Texts to and from the Tree of Paradise*, Brown Judaic Studies 286. (Atlanta: Scholars Press, 1993), p. 33.
[21] Winsome Munro, *Authority in Paul and Peter, The Identification of a Pastoral Stratum in the Pauline Corpus and 1 Peter*, Society for New Testament Studies Monograph Series 45. (New York: Cambridge University Press, 1983), p. 204.
[22] Joseph R. Hoffmann, *Marcion: On the Restitution of Christianity: An Essay on the Development of Radical Paulinist Theology in the Second Century*, AAR Academy Series 46. (Chico: Scholars Press, 1984), p. 131.
[23] Ehrman, *Did Jesus Exist?*, p. 159.
[24] Ibid. p. 164.

Ancient Israel borrowed the institution of the monarchy from the surrounding nations, replacing an earlier, much looser tribal confederation. With it came an ideology exalting the king's authority to that of a god on earth. The king was Yahweh's vicar, his son and anointed, i.e., Messiah. The king annually renewed his divine mandate to rule, and with it the very vigor of the cosmos and the fertility of the land, by ritually re-enacting the myth of how Yahweh became king of the gods.

The gods were frightened by the menace of the Chaos Dragon(s), seven-headed Leviathan, Nehushtan, Rahab, Behemoth, Yamm and/or Tiamat. The young god Yahweh volunteered to destroy the dragons if the gods would make him king. He did destroy the monsters, being slain, then resurrected, in the process, like Baal, Marduk, Tammuz, and the rest. Then he took the throne alongside El Elyon. From the carcasses of the dragons he created the world. The ancient Near-Eastern kings would act out the death and resurrection of their gods, ritually assuming the burden of the fertility of the land and the sins of the people. Sometimes this entailed a mock death or else a mere ritual humiliation, redeeming his people in a ritual atonement in which he himself had played the role of scapegoat. Isaiah 52:13-15; 53:1-12 seems to reflect the Hebrew version of the same liturgy.

Margaret Barker demonstrates how monotheism was a Deuteronomic novelty imposed with incomplete success onto Israelite faith just before the Exile, and that the suppressed, newly "heretical," traditions continued alongside the newly-minted monotheistic orthodoxy right on through the New Testament period, furnishing the categories, ready-made, for New Testament Christology.[25] In the meantime, the old traditions had taken the forms of Apocalypticism, incipient Gnosticism, Merkabah Mysticism, and Philonic Logos speculation. Even the later "redeemed redeemer" theology of the Gnostics seems to stem from the pre-Deuteronomic royal ideology.

---

[25] Margaret Barker, *The Great Angel: A Study of Israel's Second God.* (Louisville: Westminster/John Knox Press, 1992).

One often reads that the Christology of the New Testament goes far beyond the modest Jewish messianic expectation. Contemporary Jews expected a mortal warrior-king like David, righteous and godly, to be sure, but neither a divine being nor a resurrected sin-bearer. Here it looks as though the role and character of the sacred king has been cut down to size, its original divine elements trimmed away, so as to safeguard a newly regnant monotheism. They did not want the Messiah to be regarded as a second God alongside Yahweh. But Christian belief about Jesus as Messiah so closely parallels the outlines of the ancient sacred king mythos that we have to suspect it represents the popular, "underground" survival of the old royal ideology, beyond the grasp of officially sanctioned messianic theology. As such, the New Testament view of the Messiah may actually be closer to the Old Testament prototype than the later "official" Jewish one. What Bart says about the absence of "Christian" elements from the messianic job description applies only to the truncated version bequeathed by the Deuteronomic revisionists. And that wasn't the only messianic game in town.

Anxiety of Influence

To me one of the most powerful arguments for Mythicism is that virtually every gospel story can plausibly be understood as a rewrite of this or that Old Testament tale. Bart is not willing to go nearly that far. He writes:

> Some of the followers of Jesus believed he was the spokesperson of God like Moses of old, and so they told stories about him to make the connections with Moses obvious. Many other followers considered him to be a prophet of God and the Son of God. And so they naturally talked about him in the ways they talked about other Hebrew prophets, such as Elijah and Elisha and Jeremiah.[26]

---

[26] Ehrman, *Did Jesus Exist?*, p. 200.

What Bart envisions is reminiscent of Strauss' dictum that early believers in Jesus' messiahship simply reapplied Old Testament stories to him on the widespread expectation that anything Moses and Elijah did the Messiah would do better. Only Bart wants to have it both ways: the stories are borrowed but they also happened. Take away the Old Testament "color" and what have you got left? Beyond this, I have to wonder how much sense it makes to discount the Old Testament elements of a gospel story as mere window dressing. Is there going to be anything much left in the window?

Chapter 15: A Rejoinder to James McGrath's Case for Jesus

By Neil Godfrey

I have selected three arguments James McGrath has used to make the case for the historicity of Jesus to address in this chapter. There are many other points he has made, usually by way of rejoinder to this or that statement found in an internet discussion or other blog comment, and I have addressed most of those remarks on my Vridar blog over the years. But here I focus on McGrath's positive arguments for Jesus' historicity.

1. The "Crucified Davidic Messiah" Argument

We begin with James McGrath's outline of his "crucified Davidic messiah" argument. He set out his argument as early as 2008[1] and most recently summed it up in an online discussion[2] and a blog post[3]:

> ...I was asked if I am "sure" Jesus existed as a historical figure, and if so why. I tried to give a short answer as follows:
> "Sure" is relative. I'm as confident as one can be for a figure in the ancient world who did not mint coins or erect edifices on which he placed inscriptions about himself.

---

[1] James McGrath, *Did Jesus Exist?*. (2008).
[2] McGrath, 2019. "Comment #4376995121." A Popular Blunder: Bringing Something Into Existence with an "If." (blog). Available at: https://www.patheos.com/blogs/crossexamined/2019/03/a-popular-blunder-bringing-something-into-existence-with-an-if-christian-hypothetical-god-fallacy/#comment-4376995121.
[3] McGrath, 2019. Mythicism and the Bacterial Flagellum. Religion Prof: The Blog of James F. McGrath (blog). Available at: https://www.patheos.com/blogs/religionprof/2019/04/mythicism-and-the-bacterial-flagellum.html.

The shortest argument (which, like a short argument for anything, may not seem persuasive unless it is expanded on) is this:
– the anointed one descended from David referred to the king and the restoration of that line to the throne
– being executed by the Romans before establishing one's throne disqualified one's claim to be the one to restore the Davidic dynasty to the throne
Therefore
– it is less likely that early Christians invented from scratch a crucified anointed one and went around trying to persuade their fellow Jews to accept him, than that there was a figure that they believed to be this messiah who was then executed, and they managed to maintain that belief despite the cognitive dissonance resulting from this counter-evidence.

McGrath makes it clear that these few words are only a short form of the argument, but fortunately he has had opportunity in a lengthy discussion to expand on it. To underscore aspects of this argument, McGrath elsewhere stated:

Paul was trying to persuade his contemporaries that a crucified man was nonetheless the restorer of the Davidic kingship…[4]
The Davidic anointed one was the awaited king that it was hoped would restore his dynasty to the throne and usher in a golden age of one sort or another. Being crucified pretty much disqualified you from being the person in question. Is it probable that a group that was concocting a message about the long-awaited king, which they planned to proclaim to others in order to persuade them to believe, would also

---

[4] McGrath, 2019. "Comment #4382989018." A Popular Blunder: Bringing Something Into Existence with an "If." (blog). Available at: https://www.patheos.com/blogs/crossexamined/2019/03/a-popular-blunder-bringing-something-into-existence-with-an-if-christian-hypothetical-god-fallacy/#comment-4382989018.

invent that this individual was executed and thus at least apparently a failure and a thoroughly implausible candidate for the role?...[5]

In response to your last question, it is unlikely that if someone is inventing a Davidic Messiah that they plan to ask people to believe in, they will invent a failed one...[6]

You hadn't seemed to yet have grasped my extremely basic point about the unlikelihood of a group having invented a crucified Davidic messiah as the focus of a belief they wanted to convert their fellow Jews to...[7]

Cognitive dissonance, indeed! A crucified failure as the conquering Davidic messiah? That would surely be a miracle if Christianity started from *that* foundation. Yet the argument fails for two reasons.

The first problem was pointed out by Earl Doherty in an online exchange when McGrath raised the same argument in 2011:

> There is a subtle piece of question-begging going on here. The latter alternative is only more likely if indeed such a man existed. One cannot assume he did so, or adopt as an axiom that the Gospels represent the story of a real man, and then on that basis declare the latter alternative is more likely. The question is: does the evidence in the record as a whole indicate that such a man did live and that the Gospels are meant to be history? Mythicism makes the case that both answers are "No." One cannot appeal to the Gospels as history to prove that the

---

[5] McGrath, 2019. "Comment #4383133310." A Popular Blunder: Bringing Something Into Existence with an "If." (blog). Available at: https://www.patheos.com/blogs/crossexamined/2019/03/a-popular-blunder-bringing-something-into-existence-with-an-if-christian-hypothetical-god-fallacy/#comment-4383133310.

[6] Ibid. "Comment #4383168537." Available at: https://www.patheos.com/blogs/crossexamined/2019/03/a-popular-blunder-bringing-something-into-existence-with-an-if-christian-hypothetical-god-fallacy/#comment-4383168537.

[7] Ibid. "Comment #4386048729." Available at: https://www.patheos.com/blogs/crossexamined/2019/03/a-popular-blunder-bringing-something-into-existence-with-an-if-christian-hypothetical-god-fallacy/#comment-4386048729.

Gospels and their central character are histories. A historical Jesus is not to be found anywhere else until the Gospels become disseminated and *interpreted* as history.[8]

One might add that, even if a historical Jesus had been crucified, then one would have needed witnesses to a literal miracle of a real resurrection, and for those witnesses to have been able to perform real miracles as we read in Acts, for Christianity to have gained traction. Perhaps it is more plausible that initial belief came about much the same way as it does for most believers today: hearing the story and believing it. And the appeal of that story is *not* that it declares a crucified failure to have been the messiah but rather announces a victory over death. Rather than disqualifying the messiah, the earliest message we have is that it qualified him.

McGrath's entire argument rests on a blinkered reading of our evidence. Let's set aside the question-begging assumptions and consider the evidence of both Paul's letters and the gospels. We will see that Jesus is consistently presented as the Davidic Messiah who has conquered all enemies, including death itself. Cognitive dissonance is only a possibility if followers were trying to convince their neighbours that a dead man was their saviour.

The mythicist argument is entirely coherent with the earliest evidence and preaching by and among those who were never eyewitnesses of a historical crucifixion.

Paul says in Romans 1:3 that Jesus was "having come of the seed of David according to the flesh/γενομένου ἐκ σπέρματος Δαυεὶδ κατὰ σάρκα." Let's set aside all the known oddities associated with that passage

---

[8] Earl Doherty, 2011. "Earl Doherty's Concluding Responses to James McGrath's Menu of Answers for Mythicists." Vridar (blog). Available at: https://vridar.org/2011/04/26/earl-dohertys-concluding-responses-to-james-mcgraths-menu-of-answers-for-mythicists/.

and just accept that Paul was saying that Jesus was born as the heir to David.[9]

In 1 Corinthians 15, Paul applies Davidic Psalms 110 and 8 to the crucified and resurrected Jesus. In Psalm 110 (NIV), David sings:

> The Lord says to my lord: "Sit at my right hand until I make your enemies a footstool for your feet."
> The Lord will extend your mighty scepter from Zion, saying, "Rule in the midst of your enemies!"

Paul quotes Psalm 8, where David writes, "[T]hou hast put all things under his feet," applying that passage to the Davidic Messiah's rule.

Paul makes it clear that Jesus has fulfilled that Davidic hope by orders of magnitude. Thus 1 Corinthians 15:17-26:

> And if Christ has not been raised, your faith is futile...But Christ has indeed been raised from the dead...when He comes...Then the end will come, when he hands over the kingdom to God the Father after he has destroyed all dominion, authority and power. For he must reign until he has put all his enemies under his feet. The last enemy to be destroyed is death.

Paul did not pick up on the "cognitive dissonance" that McGrath assumes must have troubled the first apostles at least for a moment. What was being preached was that Jesus, through death and resurrection, had become the ultimate fulfilment of the all-powerful and cosmos-ruling Davidic Messiah. Admittedly it might have been difficult to persuade many people that the crucified Jesus was the messiah, but Paul was never a witness to Jesus and was able to persuade others of his belief in Jesus' victory over death nonetheless.

---

[9] Among scholars who have questioned the authenticity of these opening verses of Romans are Alfred Loisy, J. C. O'Neill, Hermann Detering. Links to their respective views and a broader discussion of the authenticity of the passage are online. Available at: https://vridar.org/2015/02/17/jesus-the-seed-of-david-one-more-case-for-interpolation/.

When we come to the gospels, we find that the crucifixion is portrayed in a thoroughly Davidic context, again suggesting that there was no "cognitive dissonance" in the idea of a David figure facing death. The evangelists partly modelled Jesus on the David who was first and foremost a pious exemplar who suffered. David was renowned as the psalmist who suffered despite his piety. Though God's anointed (= messiah), he cried out to God as one forsaken and persecuted (Psalm 18, 142). In Psalm 22 he cried out in pious agony, "My God, My God, why have you forsaken me?" His persecution is a badge of his honour, not shame, in the eyes of all who look to him as a model of piety. He is betrayed by his closest followers and ascends the Mount of Olives to pray in his darkest hour. If early Christians ever thought to apply the Davidic motifs to Jesus they surely did so with remarkable precision. David may have ruled a temporal kingdom, but Jesus demonstrated his power over the invisible rulers of the entire world. Even though ruler over the princes of this world, he was still betrayed, deserted and denied by his closest followers. Like David, he ascended the Mount of Olives to pray in his darkest hour. He suffered the injustice that the righteous have always proverbially suffered, even crying out with David, *My God, my God, why have you forsaken me?* But as in the Psalms, God delivered David from the depths of hell to exalt and vindicate him before his enemies, so did God deliver and exalt Jesus.

That was the positive and victorious message preached by Paul and he needed no first-hand historical witness of a crucified body to believe it. The same story is narrated by the author of Acts in the context of a dramatic Pentecost miracle and hundreds of visitors to Jerusalem believing the same entirely on the basis of "fulfilled scripture" and with no need to witness a crucified Jesus. As we read in the first sermon in Acts 2:

> [29]"Fellow Israelites, I can tell you confidently that the patriarch David died and was buried, and his tomb is here to this day. [30]But he was a prophet and knew that God had promised him on oath that he would place one of his descendants on his throne. [31]Seeing what was to come, he spoke of the resurrection of the Messiah, that he was not

abandoned to the realm of the dead, nor did his body see decay. ³²God has raised this Jesus to life, and we are all witnesses of it. ³³Exalted to the right hand of God, he has received from the Father the promised Holy Spirit and has poured out what you now see and hear. ³⁴For David did not ascend to heaven…"Therefore let all Israel be assured of this: God has made this Jesus, whom you crucified, both Lord and Messiah."

That's an appealing story, one best told as an event that began quite some time earlier and that assures hearers that the Davidic Messiah is ruling from heaven with everything, even the future and death itself, under control. What is appealing and persuasive is the story as we read it: apostles witnessing the risen Jesus and accounts of preaching backed up by miracles. But whether the story is grounded in "history" is another question.

Conclusion

So did the first disciples struggle with cognitive dissonance over the embarrassment of seeing their hoped-for messiah crucified? Did they somehow manage to convert enough followers to start a new religion by preaching that a dead failure was the Christ?

Certainly, "—being executed by the Romans before establishing one's throne disqualified one's claim to be the one to restore the Davidic dynasty to the throne"[10] would disqualify a historical messianic claimant. But the mythicist argument asserts that such a problem only exists on the assumption of the story being historical. That's not what Paul or the first Christians appear to have believed for a moment. They believed that it was through crucifixion and resurrection that Jesus conquered the powers of death and would come to finish the task by conquering his human

---

[10] McGrath, 2019. Mythicism and the Bacterial Flagellum. Religion Prof: The Blog of James F. McGrath (blog). Available at: https://www.patheos.com/blogs/religionprof/2019/04/mythicism-and-the-bacterial-flagellum.html.

opponents in the final judgement. Crucifixion qualified Jesus and this was proven by his resurrection.

Now, back to the question of historicity.

No one argues that the story was "invented from scratch." The evidence points to a story coming together as a result of emerging Second Temple era interpretations of Jewish scriptures (e.g. the evolution of a suffering servant and son of man messianic figure from Isaiah to Daniel to Enoch). The first believer we have on record boasts that his belief came about entirely through visions and revelation in Scripture and from that foundation he made converts. Only decades later does a "fleshed out" story in our gospels, set in a time and place no longer accessible to most readers, emerge.

That does not prove Jesus was not historical. But it does leave the door to the question somewhat ajar.

2. The "If Jesus Had a Brother" Argument

Another argument for the historicity of Jesus presented by James McGrath is expressed much more simply:

If Jesus Christ had a brother, then Jesus Christ existed.[11]

The argument centres around Galatians 1:19 where Paul writes:

I saw none of the other apostles—only James, the Lord's brother.

Sometimes one encounters the argument that "Lord's brother" denotes a special cultic title whose meaning is now lost to us, but McGrath understandably finds such arguments more speculative than what he takes as the "obvious meaning":

Here's the crux of it: If Paul knew that all Christians were Jesus' brothers, then isn't the most likely meaning, when Paul singles out someone as "the brother of the Lord," that that person was "the brother of Jesus" in a biological sense, since that would be the only obvious

---

[11] McGrath, 2018. "Mythicist Math." Religion Prof: The Blog of James F. McGrath. (blog). Available at: http://www.patheos.com/blogs/religionprof/2018/07/mythicist-math.html. McGrath is ironically quoting Richard Carrier here.

meaning that could single out someone as "brother of the Lord" from among all the Christians who were "brothers of the Lord"?[12]

More comprehensively, McGrath explains in his blogpost, *James the Lord's Brother*:[13]

Paul refers to "James the Lord's brother" and to "the Lord's brothers." We have no evidence for the use of the phrase "the Lord's brother(s)" as denoting anything other than biological brothers of Jesus.

Even if we were to allow (despite the lack of evidence) that the phrase in the plural could denote Christians, since Paul is writing of meetings with Christian leaders, there is no way that he could have been using it in that sense in Galatians, since it would not have served to distinguish this James from others.

Other sources refer to Jesus having a brother named James. Some attribute to him a leadership role in the early Church in Jerusalem parallel to what Paul indicates in his letters, and some also look back to him as having opposed Paul, again in agreement with Paul's own letters.

If Jesus had a brother then obviously Jesus existed. The flaw in the argument enters when we confuse "We know Jesus had a brother because Paul met him" in an absolute, factual sense with a closer look at the evidence itself. The evidence cited for Paul having met Jesus' brother is in a letter that has weathered many heated theological debates in its early years so that today:

a. It is believed by a significant number of scholars to contain glosses [interpolations];

---

[12] McGrath, 2012. "Mythicism and James the Brother of the Lord (A Reply to Richard Carrier)." Religion Prof: The Blog of James F. McGrath (blog). Available at: https://www.patheos.com/blogs/religionprof/2012/03/mythicism-and-james-the-brother-of-the-lord-a-reply-to-richard-carrier.html.

[13] McGrath, 2013. "James the Lord's Brother." Religion Prof: The Blog of James F. McGrath (blog). Available at: https://www.patheos.com/blogs/religionprof/2013/11/james-the-lords-brother.html.

b. And found to contain a statement about the brother of Jesus that is curiously not testified in other early sources despite strong reasons to expect to see it in early debates about Christ's humanity.

Despite the unlikelihood that the letter as it is read today is an exact rendering of what Paul first wrote, James McGrath expresses complete trust in "a single verse" to establish the argument for the historicity of Jesus:

> [A]ll we need for the case for the historicity of Jesus to be solid is some evidence that weighs strongly in favor of his historicity. And we have it, and so in theory, mythicism should simply vanish....[14]

That is not how research works, though. An odd piece of data can mean that our entire hypothesis is wrong, granted, but it can also mean that there is something we do not understand about the one misfit. To quote one prominent historian, Geoffrey R. Elton:

> Historical research does not consist, as beginners in particular often suppose, in the pursuit of some particular evidence that will answer a particular question.[15]

If that's what historical research is not, Elton goes on to explain what it is:

> ...it consists of an exhaustive, and exhausting, review of everything that may conceivably be germane to a given investigation. Properly observed, this principle provides a manifest and efficient safeguard against the dangers of personal selection of evidence.[16]

---

[14] McGrath, 2018. "Jesus Mythicism: Two Truths and a Lie." Religion Prof: The Blog of James F. McGrath (blog). Available at: http://www.patheos.com/blogs/religionprof/2018/07/jesus-mythicism-two-truths-and-a-lie.html.

[15] Scot McKnight noted with respect to G. R. Elton, "most historical Jesus scholars are fundamentally Eltonion": Scot McKnight, *Jesus and His Death: Historiography, the Historical Jesus, and Atonement Theory*. (Waco, Tex: Baylor University Press, 2005), p. 16.

[16] G. R. Elton, *The Practice of History*. (Sydney: Collins, 1969), p. 88.

Let's take the passage as it is in Galatians 1:19 and apply some Eltonian investigation to it. We start with the staunchly anti-mythicist scholar, R. Joseph Hoffmann, reflecting on the passage through other data "conceivably germane to the investigation":

> The early Christians were renowned for their use of familial terms to describe their fellowship, a fact which led to their rituals being castigated as incestuous by pagan onlookers. In short, the use of the term "brother" to refer to James is honorific (religious) rather than genetic. Paul nowhere refers to other "Jameses"—no biological brother, no "James the Just" or "the righteous" or "the younger." Those characters are created by necessity and fleshed out in the future, by gospel writers, and perhaps echo late first and early second century confusion over misremembered details of the historical period that Paul represents, more or less contemporaneously. In the light of Paul's complete disregard for the "historical" Jesus, moreover, it is unimaginable that he would assert a biological relationship between James and "the Lord."[17]

Let's look even more "exhaustively" at the available evidence and see how it might modify our view of the Galatians passage.[18]

In Acts there is a James who is a leader at the Jerusalem Council (Acts 15) but if he were the brother of Jesus the author curiously failed to point that out.

In the New Testament's Letter of James the author (someone pretending to be James) did not think to make "his" authority clear by stating that he was the brother of the Lord.

---

[17] Joseph R. Hoffmann, 2009. "The Jesus Tomb Debacle: RIP." The New Oxonian, (blog). Available at: https://rjosephhoffmann.wordpress.com/2009/05/15/the-jesus-tomb-debacle-rip/.

[18] Some of the points listed here are based on a case presented by Tim Widowfield and another by Earl Doherty: Tim Widowfield, "The Function of 'Brother of the Lord' in Galatians 1:19." Vridar, (blog). Available at: https://vridar.org/2016/01/16/the-function-of-brother-of-the-lord-in-galatians-119/ and Earl Doherty, *Jesus: Neither God nor Man: The Case for a Mythical Jesus*, (Ottawa: Age of Reason Publications, 2009).

In the Letter of Jude we see that the author chose to identify himself as the brother of James but with no mention of Jesus—surely an odd thing if they were indeed brothers of Jesus.

In 1 Corinthians we find another mention of James but there Paul sees no need to identify him as "the brother of the Lord" or as some other James.

In Galatians Paul elsewhere expresses a strong dislike for James. He calls him a "so-called pillar" and complains that he sent spies to undermine his freedom to eat with gentiles in Antioch. In this context it may seem a little unnatural that he would identify this James so positively as "brother of the Lord". Surely another less exalted sobriquet could have been found.

Very early in the third century, Tertullian wrote a lengthy diatribe against the teachings of Marcion. One of those teachings was that Jesus was not a literal human as we are but only took on the appearance of a human. Though Tertullian made many references to Marcion's copy of Paul's letter to the Galatians, and though he regularly castigated Marcion for chopping out verses he did not like as interpolations, Tertullian makes no mention at all of Paul ever having acknowledged that James was the brother of Jesus. It is as though that passage did not exist in either Marcion's or Tertullian's copy of the epistle.[19]

Another author, A. D. Howell Smith, arguing against the Christ Myth proponents of his day, noted a further indication that Galatians 1:18-19 was unknown to anyone, "orthodox" or "heretic," until the third century:

> There is a critical case of some slight cogency against the authenticity of Gal. i, 18, 19, which was absent from Marcion's *Apostolicon*; the word "again" in Gal. ii, 1, which presupposes the earlier passage, seems to have been interpolated as it is absent from Irenaeus's full and

---

[19] Accordingly, Jason D. BeDuhn in The First New Testament: Marcion's Scriptural Canon, states that Galatians 1:18-24 "is unattested," p. 262.

accurate citation of this section of the Epistle to the Galatians in his treatise against Heretics.[20]

Several scholars[21] have concluded that within a few verses of our James passage there is evidence of interpolation or marginal glosses having been inserted to clarify the identity of Cephas, another one of the three pillars of the Jerusalem church. It is surely odd that Paul would have referred to the same person by two different names, Cephas and Peter, in the same sentence. It is reasonable to conclude that a marginal explanatory gloss, Peter, has found its way into the main body of the letter.

In later writings (Eusebius: *Church History* Book 2) we learn that there were confused and incompatible traditions about the identity of James and the three main leaders of the early church. Some said that Peter, James and John (Peter given prominence by being named first, followed by the sons of Zebedee) humbly gave up the leadership of the church to James the Lord's brother; another tradition held that the resurrected Jesus first appeared to James the Just, Peter and John.

As for the only other indication in the gospels that Jesus had a brother named James we find historical Jesus scholar Paula Fredriksen's raising doubts: Jacob (= James), Joseph and Judah are three of the most prominent of Israelite patriarchs, and Simeon, too, is strongly associated in this status with Judah.

---

[20] A. D. Howell Smith, *Jesus Not a Myth*. (Watts, 1942).

[21] Other scholars who have argued for Peter being textual emendations or gloss to Galatians: W. C. van Manen (1887), Adalbert Merx (1902), P.-L. Couchoud (1926), Henri Delafosse (1927), Ernst Barnikol (1929-31), David Werner (1950-51), Karl Holl (1964), J. C. O'Neill (1972), Hans-Martin Schenke (1975), William O. Walker, Jr. (2003). For bibliographic details see: Hans Dieter Betz, Galatians: A Commentary on Paul's Letter to the Churches in Galatia. (Philadelphia: Fortress Press, 1979), and William O. Walker, "Galatians 2:7b-8 as a Non-Pauline Interpolation." *The Catholic Biblical Quarterly*. (2003), 65(4), pp. 568–87.

It's a little like naming a string of Olsons Washington, Jefferson, Hamilton, Franklin: the names themselves convey a close identification with the nation's foundational past.[22]

And I have not yet factored in that other strange church tradition in which we read that James was such an unusual character that the whole of heaven and earth was created just for him!

Jesus said to them, "Wherever you are, you are to go to James the righteous, for whose sake heaven and earth came into being."[23]

There really is something odd about James.

Conclusion

Putting all of the above together, it is surely a reasonable hypothesis that an early reader or scribe who was aware of competing traditions has added what he believed to be a clarifying note, "brother of the Lord," beside the name James in Galatians 1:19. This hypothesis would account for several oddities associated with the passage including the fact that it appears to have been unknown, despite its potential usefulness in debates with heretics, until the time of Origen in the third century.

3. The "Evidence for Things Said and Done" Argument

The third argument by James McGrath for the historicity of Jesus that I address asserts that all the scholarly work identifying in the gospels what Jesus probably said and did makes the existence of Jesus the only "probable" conclusion anyone can reasonably draw:

> I've long been perplexed by the frequent complaint from mythicists (i.e. those who claim that Jesus was a purely invented figure, not even based on a real historical human individual) that those working on the historical Jesus simply assume as a presupposition that Jesus existed, rather than addressing the question directly.

---

[22] Paula Fredriksen *Jesus of Nazareth, King of the Jews: A Jewish Life and the Emergence of Christianity*, (New York: Knopf, 1999), p. 240.

[23] Thomas O. Lambdin, trans. by *Gospel of Thomas*, Saying 12.

I think such individuals are looking for a demonstration by historians, in the introductory part of their book about Jesus, "proving" he existed, before going on to discuss anything he may have said or done. That this is what is meant seems clear because one may cite a saying or incident that is generally considered authentic, only to be met with the retort, "But how do you know he even existed?"

Such objections reflect a serious misunderstanding of the historical enterprise. I think it is safe to say that there is *no* historical figure from the past that we know existed apart from evidence for actual things he or she said or did. We know George Washington existed because he wrote documents, because he served as President of the United States, because he slept here or there. There is no such thing as proof of a historical person's existence in the abstract or at a theoretical level. There is simply evidence of activity, of speech, of things said or done, of interaction with others.

And so when historians engage in the tedious but ultimately rewarding process of sifting through the relatively early texts that mention Jesus, and painstakingly assess the arguments for the authenticity of a saying or incident, they are not "treating the existence of Jesus as a presupposition." They are providing the only sorts of evidence we can hope to have from a figure who wrote no books or letters, ruled no nations, and did none of the other things that could leave us more tangible forms evidence.[24]

The way scholars assess what are the most likely historical acts and sayings of Jesus is circular as even several of those scholars have conceded. E. P. Sanders, author of several books on Jesus, is clear:

> There is, as is usual in dealing with historical questions, no opening which does not involve one in a circle of interpretation, that is, which does not depend on points which in turn require us to understand others....One must be careful to enter the circle at the right point,

---

[24] McGrath, 2010. "Mythicist Misunderstanding." Exploring Our Matrix, (blog). Available at: http://www.patheos.com/blogs/exploringourmatrix/2010/02/mythicist-misunderstanding.html.

that is, to choose the best starting place....We start by determining the evidence which is most secure.[25]

We will see that Sanders' suggestion that the circularity problem is "usual" with historical questions is not true outside the field of historical Jesus studies. But how does Sanders decide what evidence is "most secure" and get around this problem? He relies upon the assumption that early Christians would not have made up a story that their messiah, Jesus, was baptized by John and certainly they would not have made up the idea that he was crucified. Those are just two examples but the rest of his "most secure" points likewise rest on what is termed "criteria of authenticity". An event is thought to have been most likely historical if, for example, early followers of Jesus would have been too embarrassed to have invented it. This reasoning is clearly circular. It begins with the assumption that our earliest narratives really were addressing "embarrassing" events related to Jesus. Yet Paul, our earliest witness, says he "boasted" in the cross of Christ (Galatians 6:14)! No embarrassment there. We really don't know what would have been embarrassing to our first Christians. No wonder the criteria of authenticity have come under criticism by scholars.[26]

Another well-known historical Jesus scholar who acknowledges the circularity of his method is Dale C. Allison:

> I can think of no line of reasoning that is not, in the end, strictly circular. Nonetheless, there remain some observations that, though they do not firmly establish anything, remain suggestive...[27]

Suggestive seems a tad subjective for a serious researcher. One of these "suggestive" observations is that "it is more than a safe bet that Jesus was

---

[25] E. P. Sanders, *Jesus and Judaism*. (Philadelphia: Fortress Press, 1985), p. 10.
[26] Two extended criticisms of the criteria of authenticity by mainstream biblical scholars are Theissen, Gerd, and Dagmar Winter, *The Quest for the Plausible Jesus: The Question of Criteria*. (Louisville, Ky: Westminster John Knox Press, 2002); Chris Keith, *Jesus, Criteria, and the Demise of Authenticity*. (T&T Clark, 2012).
[27] Dale C. Allison, Jr., *Constructing Jesus: Memory, Imagination, and History*, Reprint edition. (Grand Rapids, Michigan: Baker Academic, 2013), p. 23.

a teacher and, beyond that, an itinerant one"—exactly as the gospel story says he is! To use this as an argument for the historicity of Jesus is entirely circular. We cannot begin with the assumption that the gospels are documenting oral traditions that originated with the very persons and events they are writing about.

If in doubt, just consider the many stories we have of all sorts of figures. No historian wastes time applying the criteria of authenticity or memory theory to the accounts of Heracles, Paris and Helen of Troy, Theseus of the Minotaur fame, even though we have their deeds and sayings narrated at length in works by an ancient historian (Herodotus) and biographer (Plutarch). Further, McGrath's example of George Washington undermines his argument. Historians don't rely upon historical narratives alone to know that Washington existed. George Washington's existence is supported by independent strands of evidence, both material and written. Hence historians are able to test what they read in narratives about Washington against external controls, other independent evidence such as primary sources like diaries and contemporary documents discussing Washington. Without such independent means of testing our sources it is impossible to know if they have a historical figure behind them or not.

4. Comparing Historical Jesus Studies with Ancient History Generally

And that leads us to the final point I want to make about the claims of James McGrath in favour of the historicity of Jesus: the great divide between historians of the ancient world as distinct from biblical scholars, including historical Jesus scholars. I begin with some words of a highly renowned historian of the ancient world, Moses I. Finley, in a discussion he undertook with a leading biblical scholar in his day, Maurice Goguel. Finley has been one of the most influential ancient historians, so much so that a professor of ancient history at Cambridge University recently wrote of his legacy:

His books and articles were not merely reprinted in his lifetime, but have been re-issued in a whole range of formats since his death. No living ancient historian—and only Arnaldo Momigliano among the dead—can match his place in the citation indices.[28]

Maurice Goguel argued for the authenticity of a particular saying of Jesus in the Gospel of Mark. Goguel wrote before the term "criteria of authenticity" was in vogue but his justification followed those same principles. Finley pointed out the problem that a nonbiblical historian like himself confronts with the argument (with my added emphasis):

> One simple example will suffice. When asked by the Pharisees for 'a sign from Heaven', Jesus replied, 'There shall be no sign given unto this generation' (Mark viii, 11-12). Goguel comments:
>
> This saying is certainly authentic, for it could not have been created by primitive Christianity which attached a great importance to the miracles of Jesus...This leads us to think that Jesus did not want to work marvels, that is to say, acts of pure display.
>
> It follows that stories like those of Jesus walking on water are 'extremely doubtful'. His healing, on the other hand, may be accepted, and, in conformity with the beliefs prevailing at the time, 'it is true that these healings were regarded as miracles both by Jesus himself and by those who were the recipients of his bounty.'
>
> This application of the 'psychological method' is neat, plausible, commonsensical. But is the answer right? Not only in this one example but in the thousands upon thousands of details in the story upon which Goguel or any other historian must make up his mind? I do not know what decisive tests of verifiability could possibly be applied. The myth-making process has a kind of logic of its own, but it is not the logic of Aristotle or of Bertrand Russell. Therefore it does not follow that it always avoids inconsistency: it is capable of retaining and even inventing sayings and events which, in what we call strict logic,

---

[28] Robin Osborne, "The Impact of Moses Finley." *British Academy Review*, no. 29. (January 2017), pp. 24–27.

undermine its most cherished beliefs. The difficulties are of course most acute at the beginning, with the life of Jesus. One influential modern school, which goes under the name of 'form-criticism', has even abandoned history at this stage completely. 'In my opinion,' wrote Rudolph Bultmann, 'we can sum up what can be known of the life and personality of Jesus as simply nothing.'[29]

Finley is not a lone voice. Another prominent historian, Donald Akenson, writes in a study of the Bible (again with my emphasis):

> [I]t is appropriate to discuss the questions of when specific [New Testament] texts were written, how the early versions were stacked together, and what their dates of origin may be, and how these matters of dating relate to early Christianity and to the questions of the "historical Jesus." In that discussion…I shall suggest that, from the viewpoint of a professional historian, there is a good deal in the methods and assumptions of most present-day biblical scholars that makes one not just a touch uneasy, but downright queasy. Try as I might, I cannot come even as close to believing in the soundness of their enterprise as King Agrippa did to believing in Pauline Christianity: "Almost thou persuadest me …"[30]

When it comes to our written sources of ancient history, a classicist like Finley acknowledges limits of that some historical Jesus scholars seem to think they have the tools to breach:

> It is in the end not very surprising that university students of history, with some knowledge of the sources for, say, Tudor England or Louis XIV's France, find ancient history a 'funny kind of history'. The unavoidable reliance on the poems of Horace for Augustan ideology, or in the same way on the Eumenides of Aeschylus for the critical moment in Athenian history when the step was taken towards what we

---

[29] M. I. Finley, *Aspects of Antiquity: Discoveries and Controversies*. (Harmondsworth, Middlesex, England: Penguin, 1972), p. 178.
[30] Donald Harman Akenson, *Surpassing Wonder: The Invention of the Bible and the Talmuds*, New edition. (Chicago: University of Chicago Press, 2001), p. 214.

know as Periclean democracy, helps explain the appellative 'funny'. But the oddities are much more far-reaching, extending to the historians themselves in antiquity, in particular to two of their most pervasive characteristics, namely, the extensive direct quotation from speeches and the paucity of reference to (let alone quotation from) actual documents, public or private.[31]

Finley underscores the difficulty of knowing about the ancient past yet further than some modern readers would like:

> Unfortunately, the two longest ancient accounts of Roman Republican history, the area in which the problems are currently the most acute and the most widely discussed, the histories of Livy and of Dionysius of Halicarnassus, were composed about 500 years (in very round numbers) later than the traditional date for the founding of the Republic, 200 years from the defeat of Hannibal. Try as we may, we cannot trace any of their written sources back beyond about 300 BC, and mostly not further than to the age of Marius and Sulla. Yet the early centuries of the Republic and the still earlier centuries that preceded it are narrated in detail in Livy and Dionysius of Halicarnassus. Where did they find their information? No matter how many older statements we can either document or posit—irrespective of possible reliability—we eventually reach a void. But ancient writers, like historians ever since, could not tolerate a void, and they filled it in one way or another, ultimately by pure invention.
>
> The ability of the ancients to invent and their capacity to believe are persistently underestimated.[32]

Finley addresses a series of other examples of what we find lacking in our ancient sources. He adds:

---

[31] Finley, *Ancient History: Evidence and Models*. (ACLS History E-Book Project, 1999), pp. 12-13.
[32] Finley, *Ancient History: Evidence and Models*. (ACLS History E-Book Projects, 1999), p. 9.

Otherwise, the lack of primary sources for long stretches of time and for most regions of the Mediterranean creates a block not only for a narrative but also for the analysis of institutions.[33]

By "primary sources" he means sources that can be established as contemporary with the events being investigated.

What that means for the historian of ancient times is that many questions they would like to answer are lost forever. Finley himself established his reputation in ancient history by studying what could be ascertained from the available evidence, such as social customs and values of a particular era and how "economics" worked back then, not the details of what heroic figures known only from narratives without independent controls said or did.

What of figures like Socrates who lacks any monuments or coinage to give us "hard evidence" of their existence? Historians can be reasonably confident of Socrates' existence because they have writings by his pupils (Plato, Xenophon) as well as comments from a contemporary critic (Aristophanes) ridiculing him. Comparable evidence for Jesus would be verifiably genuine letters from Peter and another by a rabbi discussing in detail their personal debates with Jesus.

What of other ancient figures about whom myths and miracles were told by historians? The emperor Hadrian liked to identify with Hercules; Alexander the Great with Achilles and Dionysus. Could not we have the same happening with Jesus? Mythical accretions do not mean a person did not exist, after all. The difference is that with figures like Hadrian and Alexander historians have other independent sources to testify of their existence and they can see where history ends and myth begins: even the ancient sources themselves make the distinction clear. With Jesus, however, there are no sources independent of Christianity itself. And at this point we call upon one of the most recognisable names in biblical scholarship, Albert Schweitzer.

---

[33] Finley, *Ancient History: Evidence and Models*, p. 12.

[S]trictly speaking absolutely nothing can be proved by evidence from the past, but can only be shown to be more or less probable. Moreover, in the case of Jesus, the theoretical reservations are even greater because all the reports about him go back to the one source of tradition, early Christianity itself, and there are no data available in Jewish or Gentile secular history which could be used as controls.[34]

Schweitzer, of course, believed in a historical Jesus. Yet he had the intellectual integrity to acknowledge the fragility of the case according to normal historical methods.

A pioneering book by Philip R. Davies in 1992, *In Search of Ancient Israel*, brought to wide attention the methodological problems of basing the research into ancient or "biblical" Israel on the Old Testament writings. Davies saw clearly the circularity of that method. Scholars assumed that the texts they used for finding real history were written by authors with the primary purpose of recording genuine history. The texts they used sometimes claimed to have been written at precise times and places and they described precise details about events. Where books were clearly written long after the events they narrated it was assumed that those events had been passed on either orally or through other records through generations. Davies pointed out how all of those features—specific settings, detailed narration—are also marks of fictional types of works. We may just as easily assume the authors fabricated the stories. So what is a historian to do? Turn first to primary evidence, archaeological remains, known to be from the time being studied. Only then turn to the much later texts and see how best to explain what we read in them.[35] We may not have archaeological finds to help us with the question of Christian origins but we do have a wealth of Jewish and other Greco-Roman literature of the

---

[34] Albert Schweitzer, *The Quest of the Historical Jesus*. (Minneapolis, MN: Fortress Press, 2001), p. 402.
[35] Philip R. Davies, *In Search of "Ancient Israel."* (Sheffield, England: Sheffield Academic Press, 1992).

period to help us understand the background to changing religious beliefs and literary expressions of them.

In 2012, Davies applied his thinking to the question of Christian origins and historical Jesus studies in an article on *Bible and Interpretation*: I don't think, however, that in another 20 years there will be a consensus that Jesus did not exist, or even possibly didn't exist, but a recognition that his existence is not entirely certain would nudge Jesus scholarship towards academic respectability.[36]

---

[36] Davies, "Did Jesus Exist?" The Bible and Interpretation. (2012). Available at: http://www.bibleinterp.com/opeds/dav368029.shtml.

Chapter 16: "Everything Is Wrong with This" The Legacy of Maurice Casey

By Timothy A. Widowfield

Introduction

What shall we make of the legacy of the late British New Testament scholar Philip Maurice Casey? In the rarified air of the academy, the good that men do lives after them; the evil is oft interred with their bones. Consequently, reading Casey's obituaries from 2014 reveals his indisputable achievements, but practically none of his less-than-exemplary behavior.

We learn, for example, that Maurice Casey wrote several books dealing with the hypothetical reconstruction of the Aramaic antecedents to the canonical Gospels. These works aligned well with his training and interests. Later, he tackled the much broader and more difficult task of writing a biography of Jesus. This project, which culminated in the book, *Jesus of Nazareth*,[1] led him far beyond his abilities as a trained theologian[2] with a knack for ancient languages. Modern biblical scholars frequently dip their toes in the waters of history, sociology, and linguistics, with mixed results.[3] More often than not, they underestimate the vastness of the

---

[1] Maurice Casey, Jesus of Nazareth: An Independent Historian's Account of His Life and Teaching. (London; New York: T&T Clark, 2010).

[2] Casey earned a BA in Theology and a PhD in Divinity, both from the University of Durham. See University of Durham Gazette, Vol. XXII, (1978), p. 66.

[3] See, for example, the current fad of scholars citing "memory theory" when they clearly have barely skimmed the surface.

subjects, as well as overestimating their own abilities to gain the necessary comprehension to speak effectively on those matters.

Casey never lacked confidence in his own mental prowess. On that point few would disagree. We may, perhaps, speculate that the unshakable certitude in his own correctness drove him to his strident rejection of the idea that the historical Jesus never existed. Whatever his motivations, Casey stood as one of the few modern self-proclaimed historical Jesus experts who attempted to write a book-length repudiation of mythicism and mythicists. Unfortunately, his animus toward the idea frequently spilled over onto the people who propounded the idea or even—as in my case—onto those who believe that the problem, owing to the state of the evidence, defies solution.

In the interest of full disclosure, I must admit that I, surprisingly, found myself on the receiving end of Casey's wrath. I earned nearly three pages of vitriol in his final work, *Jesus: Evidence and Argument or Mythicist Myths?*,[4] in which he called me Blogger Widowfield, a label I choose to accept as a term of endearment. He spent the first two paragraphs mocking my childhood experiences in a fundamentalist Protestant sect, The Church of the Nazarene, countering it with his personal experience with the only Nazarene he had ever met. Regrettably, Casey fell seriously ill and perished before I could ask him whether he thought anecdotes were data.

While *Mythicist Myths* may be the first and only work by a prominent scholar in which my name will ever appear, I cannot recommend it. Casey's powers were fading, and for whatever reasons, he could not seem to separate his disgust for the idea of mythicism from the human sources of those ideas. For example, he wrote:

> The two most important points are that Mark and Matthew should be dated long before the fall of Jerusalem in 70 CE, that Mark is full of Semitisms which indicate his use of Aramaic sources, and both

---

[4] Maurice Casey, *Jesus: Evidence and Argument or Mythicist Myths?*. (London: Bloomsbury, 2014), pp. 35-37.

Matthew and Luke include some such passages too. Mythicists ignore both points: they do not learn Aramaic, so that they cannot see the evidence of the use of Aramaic sources, and they do not read the major works of secondary literature.[5]

Leaving aside Casey's eccentric beliefs in the early dating of Mark and Matthew, I must note here that all the mythicists (and historical Jesus agnostics) I know have spent a great deal of time reading secondary literature. On his second point, as I will further explain below, my issue is not with the *appearance* of Aramaic or Semitisms in the Gospels. I concede fully on the point of their existence. We should further concede Casey's expertise in ancient languages, especially Aramaic. What Casey refused to acknowledge was this: The appearance of an Aramaic phrase does not necessarily prove the existence of an Aramaic source, nor can it prove that that source, should it exist, came from the lips of Jesus. Casey never took seriously the possibility that an author could *compose* an Aramaic phrase or a Semitism or that an author could have deliberately composed in a style of Greek which imitated that of the Septuagint.

I claim no special expertise in the Bible, history, linguistics, sociology, biology, or anthropology. On the contrary, I am fully aware of the fact that with every day that passes, humanity creates a mountain of information. Every day I wake up significantly more ignorant than the day before. As Harry Truman put it, "The only thing new in the world is the history you don't know."

I would not and could not engage with Maurice Casey on, say, the correct translation of a passage in the Book of Daniel or on the best Aramaic reconstruction of a verse in the Gospel of Mark. However, I do challenge his basic logic, his characterization of the evidence, and his use of knowledge outside his expertise. We will see the following sorts of errors:

Presenting plausible events as probable events.

Offering conjecture as fact.

---

[5] Casey, *Mythicist Myths*, p. 244.

Not recognizing the difference between a literary conclusion and a historical conclusion.
Blurring the line between narrative logic and historical fact.
Confusing depth of knowledge with breadth of knowledge.
Behaving as though expertise in one subject confers expertise in all subjects
Failing to resist the temptation of confirmation bias.

Let us now examine a few of the mistaken ideas Casey propounded. I wish not to denounce the dearly departed, but to examine his work from a different (i.e., outside the guild), more critical perspective. Casey committed many errors, but he was not alone, and his impact lives on today in the works of his students.

Linguistic Expertise

Maurice Casey touted himself as the world's preeminent Aramaic scholar. He used that expertise in order (so he believed) to look behind the Greek of the canonical gospels and see the original Aramaic lurking underneath. However, despite his command of Koine Greek, Biblical Hebrew, and multiple dialects of Aramaic, he committed several linguistic blunders. For clarity of presentation, I have divided this section into historical and applied linguistics.

Historical Linguistics

The field of historical linguistics examines the ways in which human languages evolve over time. Hence, practitioners expand their focus beyond languages themselves to include factors such as history, comparative culture, and sociology.

Language Stability, Aramaic Idioms, and Transmission

Casey insisted that Aramaic was stable over many centuries, which allowed him to infer a linguistic reference point for the utterances of Jesus. All living languages change over time and over geographic areas. Divergence in pronunciation, dialect, vocabulary, syntax, morphology, etc., are always occurring. The only truly stable language is a dead language. Yet Casey maintained that the Aramaic of first-century Palestine differed little from the Aramaic spoken centuries later in other parts of the Ancient Near East.[6]

Why this insistence? Because we have next to nothing in the way of written *Galilean* Aramaic, especially from the first century CE. Casey needed a stable foundation for the supposed boundaries (vocabulary, syntax, etc.) of the Aramaic used by Jesus and his followers. He created that stable reference point by arguing from authority via bald assertion.

> In the first place, Aramaic words extant in earlier documents were certainly in existence before the time of Jesus, and the Aramaic language was spread in a relatively stereotyped and official form. The probability of words extant in old sources still being extant is therefore high. For similar reasons, we should not hestitate [sic] to use later sources with care.[7]

Casey took Joseph Fitzmyer to task for his conservative take on the use of later (i.e. third- or fourth-century CE) Aramaic as a basis for first-century translations or reconstructions. He bemoaned:

> ...Fitzmyer's attempt to exclude Late Aramaic from work on the substratum of the teaching of Jesus. There is still too little Aramaic extant from the Second Temple period for this to be satisfactory.[8]

---

[6] Maurice Casey, *An Aramaic Approach to Q: Sources for the Gospels of Matthew and Luke*. (Cambridge, New York: Cambridge University Press, 2002), p. 58.
[7] Casey, An Aramaic Approach to Q, p. 56.
[8] Maurice Casey, *Aramaic Sources of Mark's Gospel*. (Cambridge, New York: Cambridge University Press, 2004), p. 53.

Fitzmyer tried to bring greater controls and fewer flights of fancy in his essays on Aramaic,[9] preferring to rely on definite occurrences from contemporaneous sources. In his rebuttal to Geza Vermes' essay from the very first issue of *Journal for the Study of the New Testament*,[10] Fitzmyer reiterated his belief that the term, "the Son of Man," in the canonical Gospels is a titular expression. Vermes had argued that in at least some cases one could properly translate בר נש [bar nash(a)] as a circumlocution for the first-person pronoun.

Casey noted this argument in *The Solution to the "Son of Man" Problem*, characterizing it as "Fitzmyer's original reaction to Vermes' interpretation of the idiomatic use of בר נש as a simple substitute for 'I', a very large change from the otherwise-known usage of this term…"[11] From Casey's comment, the unsuspecting reader might mistakenly think that Fitzmyer had issues solely with ὁ υἱὸς τοῦ ἀνθρώπου being translated as a circumlocution for a first-person reference. Here is what Fitzmyer actually wrote:

> But I am not too sure that one can adopt the solution that Vermes finally suggests for the understanding of the New Testament phrase *ho huios tou anthrōpou*: that one should simply render it as 'man' (when it is used generically) or as 'that man' (when it is used as a self-reference), as does *Nueva Biblia Española*. The strangeness of the arthrous phrase in the Greek of the New Testament argues against that; it is precisely this strange form that shows that it is being used by the evangelists as a title. This has to be understood of level III of the gospel

---

[9] See, for example, Joseph A. Fitzmyer, "The New Testament Title 'Son of Man' Philologically," *A Wandering Aramean: Collected Aramaic Essays*. (Missoula: Scholars Press, 1979), pp. 143ff.
[10] Geza Vermes, "The 'Son of Man' Debate," *Journal for the Study of the New Testament*. (1978), vol. 1, pp. 19-32.
[11] Casey, *The Solution to the Son of Man Problem*. (London: T & T Clark International, 2009), p. 47.

tradition,[12] the meaning that the phrase assumes under the pen of the evangelists.[13]

Whether that titular term ever found currency in Aramaic either by Jesus or his followers is, according to Fitzmyer, "quite another question."[14] But in any case, he rejected both the translation of "I" *and* "a man," because the oddness of "*the* Son of *the* Man" stands out starkly as something other than a clumsy literal translation. To him, it must have had special meaning to the evangelists.

Nonetheless, we lack sufficient evidence to determine at which historical level the title entered the tradition. He writes:

> As it now appears in the Gospels, the arthrous form must be understood as a title for Jesus. Whether it stems from an Aramaic phrase that he himself used, either of himself or of someone else [e.g., the eschatological judge of the world], may be and will continue to be debated, because it is a question to which in the long run only a speculative answer can be given.[15]

Fitzmyer's acknowledgment of the limits of scholarship stands in contrast to Casey's unwarranted certainty. Casey asserted that the evangelists rendered every occurrence of the Aramaic plural as ἄνθρωποι, and every occurrence of the singular (at least when it referred to Jesus) as ὁ υἱὸς τοῦ ἀνθρώπου:

> This was an excellent strategy at three different levels. First of all, it is a literal translation, fully in accordance with literal translations which were normal in the culture of the translators. Secondly. it retained the

---

[12] Fitzmyer is referring to the supposed three levels or stages of gospel tradition. The sayings and deeds of the historical Jesus comprise the first level. In the second stage, tradents preserved those deeds and sayings in memory and passed them on orally. Finally, in the third level, evangelists committed the traditions to the written page.
[13] Joseph A. Fitzmyer, "Another View of the 'Son of Man' Debate," *Journal for the Study of the New Testament*. (1979), vol. 4, p. 65.
[14] Fitzmyer, "Another View of the 'Son of Man' Debate," p. 65.
[15] Fitzmyer, *A Wandering Aramean*, p. 154.

most important level of meaning of all the original sayings, the primary reference to Jesus himself. Thirdly, it created a major Christological title, and thereby satisfied the need of the target culture to express the centrality of Jesus.[16]

Casey believed he had solved the Son of Man problem, but in order to do it, he had to convert assumptions into evidence and transform speculation into fact. He also believed he had decisively proved that all the occurrences of "son of man" in the books of Enoch meant nothing other than an ordinary term for "man." Accordingly, he all but mocked his predecessors for thinking otherwise. For example, he chastised Andreas Gottlieb Hoffmann for his translation of the Similitudes of Enoch.

[Hoffmann] began the angel's response, 'Dieses [sic] ist der Menschensohn, dem Gerechtigkeit ist…' (46.3). The capitalization is doubly natural in German, a language in which the capitalization of proper nouns is universal. Nonetheless the combination of capitalization with the comma gives the impression that Menschensohn is a title, an impression which Hoffmann carried through in translation and discussion alike.[17]

Casey appears to have misunderstood the archaic spelling of "*Dies*" (which often appeared with the scharfes S)[18], writing "*Dieses*" instead—a peccadillo we can easily forgive. However, his comments about capitalization and commas leave me baffled. He should have known that Germans capitalize *all* nouns, not just proper nouns. Moreover, anyone with at least a beginner's grasp of the language knows that in German one always marks subordinate clauses with commas. Yet Casey, a scholar of languages, chose to view conventional capitalization and required commas as

---

[16] Casey, "Son of Man" Problem, p. 317.
[17] Casey, "Son of Man" Problem, p. 92.
[18] The text of Hoffman's translation actually used the old long S (Dieſs), which had largely disappeared in English by the end of the 18th century, but persisted in German into the next century. See: Andreas G. Hoffmann, *Das Buch Henoch*. (Jena: Croecherschen Buchhandlung, 1883), p. 347.

some covert plot to elevate an Aramaic idiom into a Christian honorific title.

We could almost allow this bizarre, wrongheaded, ad hoc argument to pass without further comment, but the master linguist repeated himself when quoting from Adolf Dillmann's translation of the Similitudes. He wrote:

> "Here again, the combination of capitalization with the comma reinforces the impression that *Menschensohn* is a title, an impression which Dillmann does not seem to have seriously questioned."[19]

Before moving on, we must marvel at Casey's singular purpose and tenacity, which allowed him to argue that the Ethiopic translators had worked directly from the Aramaic originals, since, as he said:

> There is no evidence that there ever was a Greek version of the *Similitudes of Enoch*. This notion seems to have got into scholarship because there really are Greek versions of some other parts of *1 Enoch*.[20]

Recall that Casey spent most of his career reconstructing Aramaic versions of gospel traditions, recreating documents he claimed *must have* existed (but which no person has ever seen or even claimed to have seen). But here he argued that no Greek intermediate translation of the *Similitudes* existed, chiefly because we lack tangible evidence. On the other hand, several modern Enoch scholars have concluded that a Greek intermediate translation from either a Hebrew or Aramaic *Vorlage* probably did exist.[21]

Let me be clear: like Fitzmyer, I tend to think that the Gospel writers in most instances viewed "the Son of Man" as a unique title, probably Messianic in nature, which pertained exclusively to Jesus. But I claim no special expertise here. More relevant to our examination of Casey is the

---

[19] Casey, "Son of Man" Problem, p. 92.
[20] Casey, "Son of Man" Problem, p. 93.
[21] Olegs Andrejevs, "The Background of the Term 'Son of Man' in Light of Recent Research," *The Expository Times*, vol. 130(11), p. 480.

fact that even now, well into the twenty-first century, we still find absolutely no consensus regarding the Son of Man problem. Scholars of similar expertise and stature continue to argue forcefully on all sides. Did the character of Jesus in Mark's Gospel mean (1) "*I* (this man) am lord of the Sabbath," (2) "*Man* (humankind) is lord of the Sabbath," (3) "*The Son of Man* (the eschatological judge who sits on a throne of glory) is lord of the Sabbath," or (4) some complex theological admixture of the three? We have no definitive answer.

Similarly, controversy still exists over whether Mark invented the titular interpretation of the Son of Man independently, borrowed it from the Enochic tradition, or inherited it from the existing tradition stream. We lack adequate evidence to say for certain. Yet from this incomplete and contradictory body of evidence, Casey claimed to have produced probable conclusions, if not actual historical truth.

Latinisms, Septuagintal Greek, and Wax Tablets

Wherever an oddity in Greek appeared in the gospels, Casey tended to see proof of an Aramaic source. Mark 2:23 offers a prime example. In this verse, Mark uses the rather unusual "making a path." While common in English and in Latin, we rarely find this idiomatic expression in Greek. For Casey, this proved Mark used a written Aramaic source.[22]

Casey soberly asserted that not only did Mark use an Aramaic document, but that he misread that document, which is understandable since "Mark will have had a text written on something like a wax tablet or a sheet of papyrus, and these could be difficult to read."[23] It would appear he attributed Mark's odd use of Greek to a mixture of hard-to-read source material, bad eyesight, and the fact that he was "a translator who was again

---

[22] Casey, Aramaic Sources of Mark's Gospel, p. 86.
[23] Casey, *Jesus of Nazareth*, p. 65.

suffering from interference."[24] (We will take up the subject of linguistic interference in more detail below.)

We might be tempted to accept Casey's argument as definitive, given his expertise and undeniable zeal, were it not for the fact that the Septuagint used the same turn of phrase.

…ὁδὸν ποιεῖσθαι [hodon poieisthai] (to make one's way) may correspond to ὁδευεῖν [hodeuein], but this is not the same as ὁδὸν ποιεῖν [hodon poiein] (to construct a road). Thus, using this criterion, the middle would be expected in Mark 2:23, but in fact the active occurs. "And his disciples began to make their way (ὁδὸν ποιεῖν [hodon poiein]) while plucking the heads of grain" (Mark 2:23).

Yet, this assumption that the classical distinction is lost may be challenged. A possible explanation is that the disciples began to make a way, i.e., to open a path, by plucking the ears of corn. But this cannot be maintained as an inviolable rule, for the LXX clearly uses ὁδὸν ποιεῖν [hodon poiein] in the sense of *to make one's way, to journey.* "Then the man departed from the city, from Bethlehem of Judah, to dwell wherever he might find a place, and he came to the hill district of Ephraim to the house of Micah *as he made his journey* (τοῦ ποιῆσαι τὴν ὁδὸν αὐτοῦ [tou poiēsai tēn hodon autou])" (Judges 17:8).[25]

We know for certain that Mark had access to the Septuagint, or at least something very much like it. See, for example, Mark 7:6-7, in which Jesus quotes from Isaiah 29:13. Hence, we have no need to postulate a lost Aramaic source when we can more easily imagine Mark following a Septuagintal pattern. Upon review and more careful scrutiny, Casey's theory of transmission melts like a wax tablet exposed to the sun.

Nevertheless, he imagined elaborate historical situations based on his wax-tablet theory, scenarios poignantly reminiscent of Percival Lowell's

---

[24] Casey, *Jesus of Nazareth*, p. 64.
[25] Georg J. Cline, "The Significance of the Middle Voice in the NT," Grace Theological Seminary. (1983).

Martian canals, which spawned whimsical speculation about an advanced but dying race of hapless Red Planet denizens.

As a tax collector, the apostle Matthew would be very experienced in writing information accurately and legibly on wax tablets. It is entirely natural that one of the Twelve, who was a tax collector, selected himself to write down material about Jesus during the historic ministry.[26]

Casey seemed unable to distinguish between speculation and fact, frequently promoting the former to the latter without sufficient explanation. And while he called himself "an independent historian," he was, in fact, neither. He depended heavily on the narrative of the gospels to weave his biography of Jesus. By *depended*, I mean that he naively believed the stories "must have" reflected real events that were diligently recorded by truthful eyewitnesses. He built upon those supposed eyewitnesses' accounts, while guessing the underlying conditions of, as well as inventing motivations for, the characters in the stories. He then promoted these hunches to facts. For Casey, things that probably happened *must have* happened. Nor is it always clear whether Casey's "must-haves" are at the narrative level or the historical level, or whether he knew the difference. I offer some examples below, with added bold emphasis.

> At the time his name was understood to mean 'YHWH saves' or the like, with the name of God at the beginning, so effectively 'God saves'. Joseph, Miriam and Jesus **must have** been aware of this understanding of his name, and it is reflected at Mt. 1.21, where an angel of the Lord tells Joseph that Mary will bear a son 'and you will call his name Jesus, for he will save his people from their sins'.[27]
>
> Mary Magdalene **must have** been very distressed for such an extreme exorcism to have been carried out, and that experience would have made her dependent on Jesus. The same must to some extent have been true of the other women whom he healed.[28]

---

[26] Casey, *Jesus of Nazareth*, p. 87.
[27] Casey, *Jesus of Nazareth*, p. 143.
[28] Casey, *Jesus of Nazareth*, p. 193.

Jesus **must have** had the ability to perceive when people were able to come out of illness situations and be restored to normal life.[29]

This [Mark 2:3-5] shows that the five men had a very strong investment in the success of the healing event. They **must have** been absolutely determined to get the paralytic healed, and he **must have** been ready to be healed.[30]

The long version at Mark 10.2-9 is however unique. This version, founded on vigorous interpretation of the Torah from a prophetic perspective, **must be** authentic teaching of Jesus, as it fits into his innovative ministry, and its origins cannot otherwise be explained. It recounts an incident when a question was put to him by people who **must have** known that he had unusual teaching to give on this subject.[31]

Jesus' words [Mark 14:18-20] also lead us to a very important conclusion: Jesus **must have** known that Judah of Kerioth would betray him.[32]

We are not reading the words of a Christian apologist here, but of an amateur historian who viewed the synoptic gospels as largely trustworthy, despite the lack of requisite external corroboration. As a substitute for external controls, he sought out internal cohesion and various elements of supposed contact with his Aramaic reconstructions. Having thus constructed a plausible historical model, he then felt safe in labeling this or that saying, deed, or event as *authentic*, because it "fit."

Casey was committing an error even competent historians have fallen into. He promoted a model of a thing as if it were the actual thing. David Hackett Fischer called this practice *the fallacy of hypostatized proof*.[33] In it, the historian mistakes his theory of X for X itself, rejecting any other

---

[29] Casey, *Jesus of Nazareth*, p. 266.
[30] Casey, *Jesus of Nazareth*, p. 259.
[31] Casey, *Jesus of Nazareth*, pp. 295-296.
[32] Casey, *Jesus of Nazareth*, p. 432.
[33] David Hackett Fischer, *Historians' Fallacies: Toward a Logic of Historical Thought*. (New York: Harper & Row, 1970), pp. 55-56.

interpretation as false, since it does not fit with the accepted theory. Casey would insist that a saying fit "perfectly" with his model of the historical Jesus, assert that it looked like a translation from Aramaic, and claim that early Christians would have no reason to make it up. Conversely, if a saying did not fit his criteria, to him it must be inauthentic. As far as I am aware, Casey never realized, or at least never publicly acknowledged, the circularity of his arguments.

Confusing Depth of Knowledge with Breadth of Knowledge

We know quite a bit about the Qumran community thanks to the Dead Sea Scrolls. The DSS have given us tremendous insights into their theology, community rules, rites, and language. However, depth does not equal breadth. We may have learned, for example, that the concept of two messiahs existed in Qumran. However, we cannot say for certain that this concept was widespread or even known outside of this separatist community. It is obviously a live option, but we would be wrong to treat it as common across other sects of Judaism.

Similarly, we have learned a great deal about the degree to which Hebrew had penetrated the Qumran authors' usage of Aramaic. From that knowledge Casey concluded, "We must therefore accept that what we had previously thought of as Hebraisms may be evidence of written sources in Aramaic."[34] That statement may be true, but it does not follow that Hebraisms *must be* or even that they *probably are* evidence of written sources.

As we have seen, Casey went even further. He asserted that written sources not only proved the antiquity of the sources (i.e., necessarily pre-dating Mark's Gospel), but also indicated the authenticity of those reconstructed hypothetical sources. We could read, he argued, the actual words of Jesus himself in some verses of Mark, once he (Casey) had reconstructed them. As supposed proof, he said his reconstructions "fit" with

---

[34] Casey, Aramaic Sources of Mark's Gospel, p. 86.

the life of the historical Jesus. Often they would fit "perfectly." He also would claim that the later Church would have had no reason to invent these authentic, historical, eyewitness items—a claim he offered without substantiation.

Aramaic as a Criterion of Authenticity

Casey, like many scholars before and since, employed literary arguments to establish historical facts. We can accept the fact that if Casey could establish a saying as having an Aramaic source, then it is *ipso facto* older than the Gospel in which it appears. However, it is a mistake to equate the antiquity of a saying with its authenticity (i.e., with respect to the historicity of Jesus). In the following passage, Casey claims to know more than it is possible to know with respect to the pronunciation of Aramaic in Galilee, and he also mistakes antiquity for authenticity:

> The first two words, *Talitha koum*, are Aramaic for 'little girl, get up', so Mark has correctly translated them into Greek for his Greek-speaking audiences, adding the explicitative[35] comment 'I tell you', as translators sometimes do. Moreover, I have followed the reading of the oldest and best manuscripts. The majority of manuscripts read the technically correct written feminine form *koumi*, but there is good reason to believe that the feminine ending '*i*' was not pronounced. It follows that *Talitha koum* is *exactly* what Jesus said."[36]

Here, Casey has extracted a historical rabbit from a linguistic hat. Note that the author himself italicized "exactly" with breathless excitement, and he does so again later in the same paragraph:

---

[35] Casey is referring to the concept of explicitation, in which a translator feels compelled to make explicit in the target what was implicit in the source. See Elisabet Titik Murtisari, "Explicitation in Translation Studies: The journey of an elusive concept," *Translating and Interpreting*. (2016), vol. 8, no. 2, pp. 64-81.
[36] Casey, *Jesus of Nazareth*, p. 109.

> [T]here should be no doubt that the whole of this healing narrative is literally true, and that it is dependent ultimately on an eyewitness account by one of the inner circle of three of the Twelve, who were present throughout, and who accordingly *heard and transmitted exactly* what Jesus said.[37]

This is not a slippery slope, but rather a cliff. We have slid from "good reason" to believe Mark has transliterated into Greek the correct pronunciation of Galilean Aramaic and plummeted to the declaration that Jesus and the Twelve must therefore have existed *and* that these apostolic "eyewitnesses" remembered and recorded an actual discrete event. Plausible evidence can only lead to plausible conclusions. Yet somehow Casey transformed possible evidence into verified conclusions.

Applied Linguistics

The field of applied linguistics examines the ways in which humans use, learn, transmit, and translate languages. Related fields of study include psychology, brain physiology, anthropology, philosophy, and sociology.

Linguistic Interference

Casey had a superficial understanding of linguistic interference, which he employed as one of his ad hoc arguments to explain Mark's Greek. He wrote:

> A correct understanding of interference is essential if we are to understand our Gospel translators, and consequently essential if we are to have any confidence in our Aramaic reconstructions.[38]

---

[37] Casey, *Jesus of Nazareth*, p. 109.
[38] Casey, Aramaic Approach to Q, p. 55.

Unfortunately, Casey failed to provide a clear definition of interference, and a full examination of his work demonstrates that he tended to use it in a haphazard manner. In one case, we read that Mark did not understand his Aramaic sources, while in another that he foolishly translated an Aramaic expression literally into Greek. In each case, whenever it served his purpose, and for whatever reason, Casey would point to "interference" as the convenient cause that explained everything and proved his point.

How shall we define interference? When rendering a source text (ST) into a translation text (TT), a translator must choose from a variety of possible paths and outcomes through a kind of decision tree. Interference occurs when the source language (SL) or target language (TL) unduly influences the translator as he or she creates the TT.[39] These influences may manifest themselves phonologically, lexically, grammatically, syntactically, etc. But these effects happen not only when translating text or speech, but also when composing speech or written texts in the target language.

A growing number of linguists prefer to describe the overall process as linguistic transfer. When one's first language "interferes" with the production of natural-sounding L2 utterances, we call it negative transfer. What, then, is positive transfer? Consider that speed at which English speakers can learn the French language as compared to Korean or Mandarin. While they may find the pronunciation difficult to hear and to produce, the fact that their primary language shares many important underlying structures with French gives them an enormous head start. Moreover, the vast number of cognates helps the English speaker acquire vocabulary relatively quickly.

By consistently using the term "suffer" when referring to interference, Casey revealed his outmoded and limited understanding of the phenomenon. Here are but a few examples (bold emphasis mine):

---

[39] Hadumod Bussmann, et al., Routledge Dictionary of Language and Linguistics, *Routledge Reference*. (London; New York: Routledge, 1996), p. 581.

He was **suffering** from interference, the influence of one of his languages on another. All bilinguals **suffer** from interference, especially when they are translating, because the word which causes the interference is in the text which they are translating.[40]

We have seen that at Mark 1:41, Mark has Jesus be angry (orgistheis). This is inappropriate, and it happened because Mark was translating the Aramaic regaz and **suffering** from interference.[41]

Whereas bilinguals **suffer** from interference anyway, translators **suffer** from it much more strongly, because the text which they are translating always reinforces the interference.[42]

[Charles Cutler] Torrey did not fully understand the translator, who was not only rendering word for word, but also **suffering** from interference.[43]

This last citation warrants some commentary. On multiple occasions, Casey referred to Alexandr Švejcer's 1989 article, "Literal Translation as a Product of Interference"[44] as a main source for understanding interference. Yet here we see him apparently making a dubious distinction between word-for-word translation and literal translation. According to Švejcer, bilinguals frequently create substandard translations because they do not recognize the fact that a word in their L1 source does not have the same semantic range as a word in the target (L2) language. Casey should have said, if he took Švejcer seriously, that the translator was exhibiting signs of interference, which caused him inappropriately to render an overly literal translation. Such mistakes often occur when translators apply syntactic equivalents at the expense of semantic sense.

In the case of idiomatic expressions, translating the ST based on word-for-word translation will all but guarantee a nonsensical TT. In other

---

[40] Casey, *Jesus of Nazareth*, p. 63.
[41] Casey, *Jesus of Nazareth*, pp. 74-75.
[42] Casey, Aramaic Sources of Mark's Gospel, p. 95.
[43] Casey, Aramaic Sources of Mark's Gospel, p. 23.
[44] Alexandr Švejcer, "Literal Translation as a Product of Interference," in H. Schmidt (ed.), *Interferenz in der Translation* (Übersetzungswissenschaftliche Beiträge 12. Leipzig, 1989), pp. 39-44.

cases, a literal translation will produce text that is technically correct, but something a native speaker would never say. Švejcer cites an example in which an English author literally translated a sentence beginning with "*It was*" using the Russian "*Ehto byl*" rather than the normal "*Imenno.*"[45] He explains:

> Typically, a literal translation, based on interference, favors equivalence at the lower levels at the expense of the higher ones. In the above example, syntactic equivalence 'upstages' semantic and pragmatic equivalence.[46]

Casey asserted Mark used the term son of man, because he was "suffering" from interference, which led him to a literal translation of the Aramaic ST. He said interference is "especially important for understanding the production of the translation ὁ υἱὸς τοῦ ἀνθρώπου.[47] Notice that this hypothesis implies Mark mistakenly applied a literal translation because he did not know "son of man" is an idiom with no equivalent in normal Koine Greek. But Casey wanted it both ways: He claimed the supposed Aramaic translators actually *did* recognize the idiomatic phrase when it occurred in the plural, and always translated it as "men" (ἄνθρωποι), a process we have already discussed above. Further, he said the synoptic evangelists only translated the singular Aramaic phrase literally when it referred to Jesus:

> This was a wonderful creative outburst, not some sort of mistake. It selected in the target language the most important reference of the original idiom, the reference to Jesus himself. Any other decision would have been a failure, because the reference to Jesus himself would have been lost, and that would not have been in accordance with the needs of the earliest Christians.[48]

---

[45] As an erstwhile Russian translator, I can confirm this and other similar translation "traps."
[46] Švejcer, "Literal Translation as a Product of Interference," p. 42.
[47] Casey, Aramaic Sources of Mark's Gospel, p. 55.
[48] Casey, *Son of Man Problem*, p. 272.

If what Casey wrote here is correct, then the translators of Q and Mark's sources could not have been suffering from interference. On the contrary, according to Casey's model, they knew they were dealing with an idiomatic phrase. Moreover, they understood the meaning of the phrase at the syntactic and the semantic levels, as demonstrated by the correct (presumed) translations in cases not referring to Jesus. He continues:

> Bilingual translators suffering from interference could continue to see both original levels of meaning in their translation, because the articles could both be interpreted generically, as the second one always must be.[49]

We should endeavor to extend all due deference to the late scholar, but the preceding sentence is unintelligible babble. One simply cannot argue that Mark suffered from interference while simultaneously arguing that he fully grasped the literal meaning of the words as well as the semantic equivalents in Greek. Either he stumbled into a literal translation because of interference, or he knew exactly what he was doing. Both cannot be true.

Casey at times invoked something he called the "double level of interference," which he never actually explained or defined. For example, he discussed an article by Anneli Aejmelaeus[50] that deals with the Hebrew *ki* and the Greek *hoti*. He wrote that:

> ...Aejmelaeus showed that it is often used incorrectly by the standards of monoglot Greek speakers precisely because it is so often used correctly. This set up too close an association between the two words in the minds of translators who were suffering the double level of interference which is inevitable when translators translate texts.[51]

---

[49] Casey, *Son of Man Problem*, p. 272.
[50] A. Aejmelaeus, "OTI causale in Septuagintal Greek," *On the Trail of the Septuagint Translators: Collected Essays*, Revised and Expanded Edition. (Peeters, 1993), pp. 11-30.
[51] Casey, Aramaic Sources of Mark's Gospel, p. 56.

Here, Casey was describing a commonplace form of interference. At times, a word in L1 seems to have an exact fit with a word in L2, but the L1 word has a different semantic range. A common example is the English word "letter," which, when referring to a piece of correspondence, matches up well with the word "brief" in German. However, when referring to a letter of the alphabet, using "brief" would make no sense. An English speaker who uses the German word over and over may "set up too close an association" and mistakenly assume the words "letter" and "brief" have identical meanings over the entire range.

Aejmelaeus points out that the LXX translators often employed the Greek conjunction *hoti* for *ki* in "*that*" clauses as well as "*because*" clauses (the *hoti causale*). While not always incorrect or out of the ordinary, the Septuagintal usage went far beyond the norm, reaching "dimensions not exemplified in contemporary or earlier genuine Greek usage, both with regard to frequency and range of use."[52]

So far, we can accept what Casey proposed, albeit without his idiosyncratic "double interference." The LXX translators did expand the usage of a Greek word, apparently as a result of negative L1 transfer. What he neglected to tell us, however, is that Aejmelaeus discussed the improper use of *hoti* not only in translation *but also in composition*. We must pay special attention here, because it gets to the heart of the matter. Aejmelaeus' article focuses on Luke and Paul as NT authors who used a causal ὅτι (hoti) not just in their quotations from the OT, but in their narrative prose as well.

Now we come to the crucial question: *How can we tell whether Mark was translating or composing?* In the case of the Septuagint, we know the Greek authors were translating a Hebrew text. In the case of Paul's letters, we can safely assume the authors [Paul and/or pseudo-Paul] are composing in Greek. Since writers can produce the same linguistic errors in either case, their mere presence in a text is not proof of either translation or composition.

---

[52] Aejmelaeus, "OTI causale in Septuagintal Greek," p. 11.

A significant problem with Casey's methodology was his tendency to try to convert descriptive tools into predictive tools. Linguists, especially the trained professionals who investigate the art and science of translation, can point to STs and their TTs and opine on this or that process to explain translators' choices. Casey assumed large parts of the canonical Gospels existed first as Aramaic texts. He further assumed that the authors were translators. (Why, we may ask, do scholars assume that evangelists worked alone?) He believed Mark was not merely competent in Greek, but that he was "bilingual."

But the evidence we have cannot establish any of these assumptions as facts. At best, we can accept them as possibilities, among a large range of other more likely, less ornate possibilities.

Social Sciences: Cultural Context

The practice of studying the New Testament from the perspective of social context began to gain wide recognition in the 1980s. Cultural anthropology provided the basis for much of this work, with scholars such as Bruce Malina and John Elliott leading the way. While necessary and often quite helpful, this social-scientific method is not immune from abuse. Too often, scholars have used it in a superficial and ad hoc manner, explaining away contradictions and problems within the New Testament.

High-Context vs. Low-Context Cultures

In his last work, Casey wrote the following:
> There are several things wrong with this [i.e., noticing that Paul doesn't talk about Jesus]. One is that the social context of many scholars, especially Americans, is a low context society, in which a lot of both important and mundane information needs to be constantly repeated. This is one major reason why some scholars grossly misinterpret what Paul does not say, and imagine that it reflects what neither

he nor his converts believed. The term 'low context' society was introduced into scholarship by the anthropologist E. T. Hall.[53] Hall was concerned to discuss the modern world, and the application of some of his insights to the ancient world requires great care, but his discussion of modern American society can be applied directly to mythicists without much trouble or risk of distortion.[54]

Casey and the other historical Jesus apologists who employ Edward T. Hall's models for social interaction in the service of explaining away the enigma of the epistles rely on two things: (1) the majority of their readers will never read Hall or study the phenomena he described and (2) those same readers are receptive to any rescue effort that props up their current beliefs. For Casey, of course, there was the added joy of using knowledge as a cudgel against anyone who disagreed with him. As we will see, the reality is far more complex than Casey presented it.

What can we say about Casey's assertion that Paul's communities were high context (sub)cultures and that his letters are examples of a situational dialect arising from a situational frame? We should approach this question seriously. To do the topic justice, we need to examine the features of high and low cultures, as well as the sources of those features.

Oral vs. Written Language

Before we even look at cultural contexts, we must point out that Paul's letters are written forms of communication. I am stating the obvious, but it has important consequences when discussing high-context (HC) and low-context (LC) societies. People in HC societies rely a great deal on what is "not said." Some of these unsaid, nonverbal cues rely on shared, implicit knowledge, while other cues include body language, body position, hand gestures, facial expressions, vocal inflections, tone, etc. The very fact that Paul used written communication already proves that he

---

[53] See esp., Edward T. Hall, *Beyond Culture*. (New York: Anchor Books, 1977).
[54] Casey, *Mythicist Myths*, p. 46.

thought certain things needed to be spelled out explicitly. Hence, anyone wishing to explain away Paul's silence in terms of cultural context starts off at a disadvantage.

Closed vs. Open Societies

The typical high-context society is monocultural and closed. The more open and multicultural the society, the greater the need for explicit language with less reliance on context. Paul may have created sub-cultures (i.e., his churches), but they were, as far as we can tell, (1) *new*, albeit with supposedly old traditions (the OT), (2) *multicultural*, and (3) *open*. If the majority of his church members were Gentiles, then—even if they were former God-fearers—Old Testament traditions, while old for Paul, were new to them. They were new branches grafted into the old tree. Paul's letters indicate that his churches attracted rich and poor, free and slave, male and female. The mixture of people from different classes, levels of education, backgrounds, and so on, would militate against high context.

Internalized vs. Externalized Rules

High-context societies have lots of unwritten rules. These rules are not simply a list of dos and don'ts that people memorize; they are embedded cultural norms. HC societies need not say aloud or commit to paper what everyone already knows. Christianity grew out of an ancient, well-established, rather closed religious culture. However, the Hebrew religion had a long history of explicit, externalized rules. They celebrated the law, a written set of instructions, and they explicitly argued about exactly what those rules meant.

One can argue that the law was internalized in Second Temple Judaism and in early Rabbinic Judaism, but it was first and foremost the word of God—*explicitly written, earnestly read, and hotly debated*. What about Paul? Paul had no problem stating explicit rules and coming up with his own logic for following them. Knowledge within Paul's churches was explicitly stated to ensure correct compliance, repeated for effect, written for posterity, shared among his churches, logically arranged for better understanding, and copied for preservation.

Power Distance

The research indicates that Paul would have been quite direct and explicit with his congregations, because of the *high power distance index*.[55] Paul was their leader. He was their father in faith. Paul was writing to instruct and often to correct his readers. In this situation, Paul would not be coy, indirect, or implicit. And finally, Paul, at least as he comes across in the epistles attributed to him, did not shy away from telling people exactly what he thought.

A high power distance removes the cultural-context norms. (Bosses are very direct and explicit with employees, for example.) Since Paul considered himself to be a teacher of the gospel sent into the world by God, he felt perfectly justified in berating the congregations at Corinth and Galatia. At the same time, given the fact that the churches preserved and shared these letters, the congregations accepted the teacher-pupil, father-child relationship. We can scarcely overstate the importance of this acceptance. Geert Hofstede wrote:

> Power distance can therefore be defined as the extent to which *the less powerful members of institutions and organizations within a country expect and accept that power is distributed unequally*....Power distance is thus described based on the value system of the less powerful members. The way power is distributed is usually explained from the

---

[55] For examples, see: Geert Hofstede, Cultures and Organizations: Comparing Values, Behaviors, Institutions, and Organizations Across Nations. (Thousand Oaks: Sage Publications, 2005), pp. 79ff.

behavior of the more powerful members, the leaders rather than those led.[56]

Power distance affects not only the tone, but also the explicitness of communication. Dr. David Livermore of the Cultural Intelligence Center put it this way:

> Peers in a high power distance culture would typically be quite indirect in the communication with each other, as an expression of their high-context orientation. However, a boss is likely to be very direct with a subordinate in a high-context culture and high power distance. Or a parent is likely to be very direct with a child. So in this case, status and authority trump being indirect. That is to say, power distance trumps where a culture is on context.[57]

Hence, the current studies on cultural behavior indicate Paul would have spoken and written plainly as befitted his relationship to his audience. Casey believed mythicists, historical Jesus agnostics, and even some respected scholars misinterpreted Paul's silence because we apply our HC sensibilities to a low-context culture, expecting him to repeat mundane information. In truth, Paul repeated himself quite a bit. He always let his readers know that he was an apostle. He said he was at least as good as the other apostles. On the one hand, he called Jesus both "Christ" and "Lord" on multiple occasions, but on the other, he never referred to him as Jesus of *Nazareth* or as the Son of Man. He never referred to other apostles as "disciples" or to Jesus as their "teacher." He may have attributed a policy or rule as coming from "the Lord," but he never quoted the earthly Jesus. We need not hypothesize here why Paul should have omitted these things found abundantly in the gospels; we need only remark that he did not use them, and that cultural context cannot explain it away.

---

[56] Geert Hofstede and Michael Minkov. Cultures and Organizations: *Software of the Mind: Intercultural Cooperation and Its Importance for Survival*. (2010), p. 61.
[57] David Livermore, "Lecture 8, Communication: Direct versus Indirect," *Customs of the World: Using Cultural Intelligence to Adapt, Wherever You Are*. (The Great Courses, 2013).

Current research that shows different situations have a profound effect on a person's directness of communication. Considered within the framework of situational social dynamics and high power distance, Paul's writings look like what they are: *explicit, low-context communications from a strong leader to his subordinates*. He explains what he wants the readers to do or not to do. He reinforces the exhortation with a philosophical argument or perhaps a midrash on the OT. Finally, he caps it off with a quotation from the Tanakh, as the authoritative last word. Paul must have had a reason for not quoting Jesus, but that reason cannot have anything to do with his membership in high-context society.

Conclusion

I chose one of Casey's favorite sweeping judgments—"*Everything is wrong with this*"[58,59,60,61]—as the title for this paper, because it demonstrates both his self-assuredness and his lack of patience with those he deemed less intelligent or obstinately ignorant. He was not afraid to speak his mind, but he also crossed the line quite often, even among his peers and used his supposed superior knowledge as a cudgel.

In fact, we could have spent many pages enumerating the ill-tempered words Casey used to describe those who did not meet his rigorous standards. At the time of his death, of course, those memories evaporated in the hallowed halls of academia. There, only the good survives. And so let it be here as well. Let us leave the unpleasant spite and unbridled arrogance interred with his bones.

For in truth, if we harped on such sleights it would distract us from the real purpose of this paper: namely, to show the many possible errors to which a mixture of self-confidence and unawareness of basic logical

---

[58] Casey, *Aramaic Sources of Mark's* Gospel, p. 144.
[59] Casey, *Mythicist Myths*, p. 128.
[60] Casey, *Jesus of Nazareth*, p. 39.
[61] Casey, An Aramaic Approach to Q, p. 27.

errors can lead. I would call your attention to perhaps the most common error in NT studies: confirmation bias. Our minds are wired to seek data that proves our arguments, which helps explain why Casey and many other scholars have discovered concepts like high-context culture, but have not followed through with due diligence.

If they had, they would have discovered that modern scholars have called Hall's framework into question, and for good reason. It turns out that despite widespread approval from armchair sociologists, business gurus, and human resource directors, we lack the sort of research that would definitively show Hall was correct. A closer examination shows that he often relied on intuition and anecdotal evidence. In his writings, he neither described nor mentioned his methodology. Peter Cardon writes:

> Although he provided few indications about how he collected data, several of his comments suggest that he did so primarily through qualitative interviews and observation. He did not mention using methods for qualitative data collection that would be considered rigorous by today's standards, such as identifying alternative explanations (identifying best fit), negative case analysis, triangulation, review by inquiry participants, expert audit review, theory triangulation, sampling techniques, bias acknowledgment and credibility of researcher (researcher as instrument), coding schemes, analysis framework, or audit trail.[62]

Despite the nonexistence of research corroboration, which should have thrown up red flags all around, people have tended to quote from Hall's works as if they contained hard, scientific facts. Cardon further points out that in cases where the researcher is the instrument for collecting and analyzing data, we need to exercise care so that personal biases do not color the results. Unfortunately, we have ample evidence of Hall's deep biases:

---

[62] Peter Cardon, "A Critique of Hall's Contexting Model: A Meta-Analysis of Literature on Intercultural Business and Technical Communication," *Journal of Business and Technical Communication*. (October 2008), vol. 22, no. 4, p. 402.

In early works in which he developed contexting theory, however, Hall did not indicate motivations or biases. But close examination of *Beyond Culture* indicates that Hall (1976) generally characterized HC cultures in more favorable terms than he did LC cultures. Throughout his work, he strongly criticized LC U.S. institutional behavior in government, businesses, courts, and schools, which each represents the interests of the powerful at the expense of common people. He criticized many of the American tendencies directly tied to LC culture, including engaging only in linear thinking, looking at ideas not events, not taking the time to get to know people, ignoring important parts of context such as relationships, producing bad art, creating bureaucracy, relying on modern management methods, depending on management consultants, using government funds inefficiently and unfairly, conducting inaccurate research in social and biological sciences, manipulating the legal systems to benefit the powerful, having less personal work relations, behaving with ethnocentrism, and scapegoating to protect the powerful.

To be fair, I probably share many of Hall's criticisms. U.S. culture *does*, I think, tend to be too rigid and linear. But I hope I would recognize those biases, remembering continually to check myself and to test my conclusions. Casey, on the contrary, apparently blinded by his own intellect, never seemed to recognize his own biases and how they affected his judgment. I suspect he latched onto Hall's writings (presuming he more than skimmed *Beyond Culture* for serviceable quotes), because of his own antipathy toward the United States. He often used "American" as a derogatory adjective. *American* fundamentalism and *American* atheism were hugely problematic to him. In *Jesus of Nazareth*, he referred to the Jesus Seminar as the *American* Jesus Seminar 23 times.

Where some might color in broad strokes, Casey used a paint roller. Commenting on Hall's belief that America sits on the lower end of the context scale, Casey wrote: "This is blindingly obvious, and partly explains why Americans and their followers imagine that ancient sources should have given far more information about Jesus than they do."

Despite the obvious disadvantage of being born in the United States, Hall found a fan in Maurice Casey.

The passing of Casey did not herald the end of confirmation bias. It lives on in biblical scholarship with dabblers reading and opining on such subjects as oral tradition and memory theory. In the most embarrassing cases, scholars have engaged in quote-fishing—dropping a hook here and there looking for some validation of their preconceived ideas. And while I wish we could rely on scholarly peer review to correct these errors, it has become quite clear that it has failed to do its job.

As I wrote near the start of this paper, I profess to have no special skills, other than a bachelor's degree in history from an *American* university. I do not call myself a historian, because I have no advanced degrees in history, nor have I ever earned a paycheck as a historian. But as an amateur who loves the art of history and appreciates those who seek after the truth, I do not accept the idea that scholars with advanced degrees in theology and divinity should call themselves historians. Their deep, certified knowledge of the Bible does not automatically translate into other fields of knowledge—not history, not anthropology, and certainly not sociology.

In the absence of controls within the guild, it falls to us amateurs to call attention to these issues, even if we incur the wrath of respectable scholars like the late, great Maurice Casey.

Biographies A to Z

Joseph Atwill is the author of *The Roman Origin of Christianity* and *Caesar's Messiah*.

Bill Darlison M.A., B.A. (Hons.), holds degrees in literature and religion, and before his retirement in 2010 he was the senior minister of the Dublin Unitarian Church. He has studied Hebrew, Greek, Latin, Irish, Aramaic, French, and Italian. In the early seventies, he studied for the Roman Catholic priesthood in Rome, but left before ordination. He joined the Unitarians in 1988, becoming a minister in 1994. In 2013-14 he was President of the Unitarian General Assembly of Great Britain and Ireland. He is the author of several books, including *The Gospel and the Zodiac: The Secret Truth about Jesus*, which argues the Gospel of Mark is structured on the signs of the zodiac.

Derreck Bennett is an independent student of Christian origins and biblical criticism, having devoted fifteen years of study to the topic. His work has been published in *The Journal of Higher Criticism,* and he is the author of *Addictus: A Nonbeliever's Path to Recovery*, in which is his story of conquering addiction without belief in God or the supernatural.

Earl Doherty is the author of *The Jesus Puzzle* (1999), *Challenging the Verdict* (2001), and the magisterial book, *Jesus: Neither God Nor Man* (2009). Doherty argues that Paul thought of Jesus as a spiritual being executed in a spiritual realm.

P.C. Emery is a pseudonym for a person who has been working extensively on tracking and recording the history of the Christ Myth Theory

(CMT) throughout time, interviewing current figures, and working on tracking the origins of various modern theories of the CMT from their earliest predecessors to the present forms, reading through works in English, German, Dutch, and Russian to do this. Despite being a self-described "staunch historicist," Emery is far from wishing to dismiss the CMT out of hand, and views it as one of the most important developments in New Testament scholarship. Emery hopes to preserve the memory of this debate, give a new voice to women and racial minorities in it, and to bring to people's awareness the rich developments it provided New Testament scholarship as a whole.

David Fitzgerald is an author, public speaker, and historical researcher who has been actively investigating the Historical Jesus question for over twenty years. He has a degree in history and was an associate member of CSER (the former Committee for the Scientific Examination of Religion). David's book on Jesus Mythicism is the three volume set *Jesus: Mything in Action* (the follow-up book to his NAILED: *Ten Christian Myths that Show Jesus Never Existed at All*) and the newest addition to his ongoing series, *The Complete Heretic's Guide to Western Religion*.

Neil Godfrey, B.A., B.Ed.St. (post grad), Grad Dip Library and Information Science, recently retired, is the owner of the Vridar blog that has attracted praise from academics for its scholarly posts (including detailed book reviews) in biblical and historical studies. Before retirement, Neil was a librarian responsible for managing the digital preservation and open access of academic publications, research datasets, and specialist cultural collections at university libraries in Australia and at the National Library of Singapore. He also has a background in modern and ancient history at the University of Queensland.

Michael Hoffman is the founder of egodeath.com, a site dedicated to research on the origin of religion in visionary and mystical experiences induced by entheogens, or hallucinogens. Hoffman is the leading proponent of John M. Allegro's understanding of "Jesus" as an ancient allegory for the Amanita Muscaria mushroom.

Stephan Huller is the author of *The Real Messiah: The Throne of St. Mark and the True Origins of Christianity*. It explodes the myth that Jesus was the long-prophesied Messiah of the Jewish nation. He argues that Jesus never claimed that role but thought of himself as herald to the true Messiah: Marcus Julius Agrippa, the last King of the Jews and Jesus' contemporary. It was he who truly founded what became known as Christianity, and wanted to build a faith to which anyone could aspire. Though Marcus Agrippa was initially successful, with the passing of time those in charge of the new faith capitulated to the whims of successive Roman Emperors and centered their religion on Jesus instead.

John W. Loftus earned MA, MDiv, and ThM degrees in philosophy of religion and is the editor of several anthologies: *The Christian Delusion, The End of Christianity, Christianity is Not Great, Christianity in the Light of Science*, and *The Case against Miracles*.

Michael Lockwood was born in British India. He earned degrees from Oberlin College, B.A. (English), Boston University, M.A. (philosophy), and Madras University, Ph.D. (philosophy) and taught philosophy for thirty-two years (1966-1998), in South India at Madras Christian College, Tambaram. He has published the books, *Buddhism's Relation to Christianity* (Madras 2010); *Mythicism* (Madras 2013); and *The Unknown Buddha of Christianity* (Tambaram 2019), and was an editor contributor for Indology.

Danila Oder is an independent scholar. She received a BA in history from the University of Chicago and studied at Spertus College of Judaica. She has studied playwriting and worked as an actor. In 2019, she published

The Two Gospels of Mark: Performance and *Text*, www.thetwogospelsofmark.com.

R. G. Price is the author of the book, *Deciphering the Gospels Proves Jesus Never Existed* (2018), with a foreword written by Robert M. Price. For the book, he used his expertise in systematic data analysis to go through the Gospel called Mark line by line, searching for related passages in the Old Testament and Pauline letters using various translations, including the Septuagint (the ancient Greek translation of the Hebrew Scriptures), something that could only be done recently thanks to computers and the internet. Price also wrote a chapter for *The Case against Miracles*, edited by John Loftus.

Robert M. Price is a member of the Jesus Seminar and author of several books including *Deconstructing Jesus* (2000) and *The Incredible Shrinking Son of Man: How Reliable is the Gospel Tradition?* (2003). He's also co-editor of *The Empty Tomb: Jesus Beyond the Grave* (2005), *The Paperback Apocalypse: How the Christian Church Was Left Behind* (2007), *Inerrant the Wind: The Evangelical Crisis of Biblical Authority* (2009), and a few chapters in anthologies edited by John Loftus.

Barbara G. Walker is a researcher, lecturer, and author of 24 books and numerous articles on comparative religion, history, and mythology. She has two essay collections: Man Made God and Belief and Unbelief. Her Woman's Encyclopedia of Myths and Secrets has been in print since 1983 and was named Book of the Year by the London Times. Its companion volume is The Woman's Dictionary of Symbols and Sacred Objects. She received the Humanist Heroine of the Year award from the American Humanist Association, the Women Making Her story award from New Jersey NOW, and the Olympia Brown award from the Unitarian Universalist Association. She is listed in that prestigious 1200-page compendium of notable freethinkers, Who's Who in Hell?

Tim Widowfield currently helps maintain Vridar (https://vridar.org), a history-oriented biblioblog created by Neil Godfrey, where he has contributed a few hundred posts over the past eight years. Tim holds a bachelor of arts in history from the University of Maryland, as well as a master of science in logistics from the Air Force Institute of Technology. As an adult, he has spent most of his free time privately studying history, linguistics, and the Bible.

www.ingramcontent.com/pod-product-compliance
Lightning Source LLC
Chambersburg PA
CBHW032146080426
42735CB00008B/597